INNOCENCE IS NOT ENOUGH

INNOCENCE IS NOT ENOUGH

*The Life and Death of
Herbert Norman*

ROGER BOWEN

DOUGLAS & McINTYRE
VANCOUVER/TORONTO

Douglas & McInytre Ltd., 1615 Venables Street,
Vancouver, British Columbia V5L 2H1

Canadian Cataloguing in Publication Data

Bowen, Roger W., 1947–
  Innocence is not enough : the life and death of
Herbert Norman

ISBN 0-88894-493-4

1. Norman, E. Herbert, 1909–1957.   2. Diplomats –
Canada – Biography.   3. Canada – Foreign relations –
1945–   . I. Title.

FC611.N67B69 1986   327.2'092'4   C86-094375-5
F1034.3.N67B69 1986

Design by Michael Solomon
Typeset by Q Composition
Printed and bound in Canada by
Imprimerie Gagné Ltée.

CONTENTS

To my daughters, Jessica and Anna,
both Canadian-born, who, I trust,
understand the meaning of freedom

"The Death of a Public Servant:
In Memoriam, Herbert Norman"
by Carolyn Kizer

This is a day when good men die from windows,
Leap from a sill of one of the world's eyes
Into the blind and the deaf-and-dumb of time;
Or by ways desperate or ludicrous
Use one of the World's machines for God's,
As George used his gun by the swimming pool
And was found in the flamingo-colored water,
Or John, drowned in a London crater,

Saw a drowned world there before he plunged:
A baby-carriage frame, a plumber's elbow,
Memorials to his dying as he died;
Now you, in Cairo; though I do not know
How that young, dedicated intellect
Was forced away at last from its long service,
Only that Parliament says you were "killed by slander."
Wounds to your name were mortal to your mind.

Dead friends, who were the servants of this world!
Once there was a place for gentle heroes.
Now they are madmen who, scuttling down corridors,
Eluding guards, climb lavatory walls
And squeeze through air-vents to their liberation,
Where the sensitive concrete receives them
From the word's vast, abstract hate;
So they are smashed to sleep.

Or they, found wandering naked in the woods—
Numbed from the buffets of an autumn storm,
Soaked blissfully in its impersonal furies—
Are wrapped and rescued after a long dark night,
Are bustled into hospitals and baths
While the press explains away their abberations:
"Needed a rest . . . and took no holidays . . ."
But even so, they have managed to catch their death.

I mark the fourth of April on this page,
When the sun came up and glittered on the windows
As you fell away from daylight into heaven:
The much of Cairo, and a world silenced forever.
A poet, to whom no-one cruel or imposing listens,
Disdained by senates, whispers to your dust:
Though you escape from words, whom words pursued,
Take these to your shade: of rage, of grief, of love.

The New Republic, 22 April 1957

ACKNOWLEDGMENTS

Biographers compose the portrait of their subject with all the arrogance of an artist but without the artist's trained eye, precise lines, and sense of certainty of what the final product will look like. Biographers can at best offer an impressionistic portrait of their subject, a gross representation of what he/she looks like in our mind's eye. But unlike the portrait artist, the biographer "paints" only what he knows, and what he knows is what others have told him, including, sometimes, the subject himself. This makes us awfully dependent on the vision, knowledge, and wisdom of others, which may, when all is said and done, be woefully incomplete. Realizing this, the biographer is forced to interpret what others share in ways that necessarily dilute the purity of their reflections.

How we choose to interpret what others tell us is what is euphemistically rendered as "artistic license," which in turn may be little more than the imposition of the biographer's ego onto the subject's *real* life. How, then, to untangle biography from autobiography? Is it even possible? Once we acknowledge that biographers only write the biographies of people who interest them, a fact hardly separable from the writer's self, self-perception, and, in ways barely identifiable, identification with his subject, how are we to distinguish between the life realities of the subject and those of the biographer?

No easy answer presents itself. I have tried to distance myself emotionally from Herbert Norman by relying on the vision that others have of him. His family members, friends, colleagues, and enemies can and do speak for themselves: let *them* tell what kind of man he was. This I have tried to do. But I know, and hereby confess, that self-injunctions are the easiest to violate. Why? The answer returns us to the arrogance of the biographer.

None of Herbert Norman's family members, friends, colleagues, and enemies know *everything* about him that I know. Their portraits of the man are even more partial than mine, more impressionistic, less well-defined. Perforce, the imagery of the "mosaic" presents itself. Their separate pieces needed piecing together; this I tried to do, in good faith to the individual fragments that I was given. Assembling them in a structured, orderly, and complete whole was not easy nor was it free of "artistic license." In short, Herbert Norman now makes sense to *me,* but it is extremely unlikely that those good people who gave me their fragmentary visions of the man will recognize in all its dimensions the picture that I have painted. If they see caricature rather than portraiture, I beg understanding.

To say this is at once to acknowledge the incompleteness of any biography. An individual's life is simply too precious to misrepresent, to everyone who cares, to anyone who cares. So, too, is an individual life too complex to capture fully. What did Herbert Norman do, let alone think, on, say, Christmas Day 1940? I do not know, but neither can those who remember him best recall. How did he really feel on that day in 1952 when his mother died? I have cited the letter he wrote to his brother on the day after his mother's death, and have tried to suggest the terrible impact this had, but neither the letter nor my suggestion can have the sort of validity that we would like. Perhaps it is natural to feel humbled before the many existential facts of his life that cannot be completely explained.

But if that is so, I can feel more confident in the task of smashing the two sorts of distortions that have thus far characterized portrayals of his life and death. The one is of Norman the Marxist ideologue or the Soviet dupe or spy. The other is of Norman the idealized Canadian victim/martyr to the forces of American reaction. Both are static pictures that deny the mutability of human character, that see the human image frozen in time, the picture as permanent. The reality which I have tried to portray is that of a man whose ideas and loyalties changed over time, as perceptions, conditions, and circumstances changed. In so doing, I have tried to suggest that those who were intellectually or ideologically incapable of allowing for "growth" were guilty of what Hannah Arendt has called the "banality of evil." Evil, in this case history, was the simple, commonplace product of a narrowness of vision that could not comprehend, because it did not care enough to see that time and circumstance change us all. Concretely, Herbert Norman in the mid-Fifties was not the man he was in the mid-Thirties; but America's fear of communism, unfortunately, did not change in those twenty years, except to become more fearful. Herbert's life and death exemplify this simple truth.

This much, I hope, will be granted by the many good souls who have helped me to write his life story. Here I acknowledge their assistance, but for all the reasons mentioned, absolve them of any witting contribution to the story of his life and death that I have offered.

Herbert Norman's widow, Irene, gave me permission to use the American Freedom of Information law to gain access to all his records; she likewise helped me to crack the RCMP's prohibition against "foreigners" using comparable legislation, but more important, she gave me her confidence. If I were childless, this book would have been dedicated to her.

The Rev. Howard Norman, Herbert's older brother, shared with me thirty years of private correspondence between him and his younger brother; he also gave me his friendship and his affection. He is a singular individual, a man of immense integrity and goodwill, whose courage and tolerance are of heroic proportions. His life story should be written.

Without Irene's and Howard's help, this book *would* not have been written, but it *could* not have been written without the help of a great many other people. The list is not exhaustive, but the names and organizations are mentioned in the spirit of sincere gratitude, although not in every case as an expression of agreement with their opinions: Lorie Tarshis, Arthur Kilgour, John Holmes, Victor Kiernan, Edwin Reischauer, Tsuru Shigeto, Arthur Menzies, Ralph Collins, Geoffrey Pearson, Cyril Powles, Lorne Berlet, Dacre Cole, Robert Bryce, King Gordon, Halim Doss, Cherry Hughes, Sen. George Mitchell, Michael Straight, Margaret Norman, Okubo Genji, Charles Taylor, Robert Lamphere, Gordon Robertson, Guy Lott, the Maine Civil Liberties Union, Chapman Pincher, John Stockwell, the Colby College Social Science Research Committee, Sandy Maisel, the American Philosophical Society, the Association for Asian Studies, Robert Morris, Charles Woodsworth, Ken Woodsworth, William Holland, Paul Bowlby, Harry Ferns, Margot Heinemann, Mounir Abdel Malik, David Martin, Omar Foda, Christopher Cornford, Gwen Norman, Eleanor Hadley, William Reuben, Sid Freifeld, George Glazebrook, John Dower, General E. L. M. Burns, Leonora Park, Norma Nadeau, Phillip Jaffe, T. A. Bisson, John Emmerson, Ed Petty, Jack Brayley, Jon Weiss, Doug Whyte, Donaldson Armstrong, Robert Lamphere, J. J. McCardle, Ralph Collins, Seymour Janow, Verne Newton, Eleanor Hadley, Norman London, John Howes, as well as many other good people who wish to remain anonymous.

Lisa Rydin and Elizabeth Rhoads both served as very capable research assistants, employable due to the generosity of my College, in the latter stages of completing the book. Patricia Kick, with predictable good cheer, helped enter last-minute corrections into our college computer. Betty Corson has been invaluable in both selling and editing the book. Finally, for reasons I do not understand, my family has endured endless dinner monologues that dealt with the meaning of suicide. I can not sufficiently thank them all for their emotional support and for their tolerance.

Roger Bowen
Waterville, Maine
June, 1986

INTRODUCTION

Norman was born September 1, 1909, at Karuizawa, Japan. XXXXXXXXXXXXXXXXXXXXXXXXXXXXXXXXXXXXXXXX. He attended the University of Tokyo *[sic]*, University of Cambridge *[sic]*, England, and received an A.M. degree in 1937 and a Ph.D. degree in 1940 at Harvard University. His student work at Harvard was sponsored by the Rockefeller Foundation. After receiving his Ph.D. degree, Norman presented a thesis on "Japan's Emergence as a Modern State." This thesis was published by the Institute of Pacific Relations, 129 East 52nd Street, New York City. Norman acknowledged in his thesis the assistance which had been given to him by Shigeto Tsuru. Tsuru, a Japanese, returned to Japan in May or June 1942. At the time of his departure, he left at his apartment at Cambridge, Massachusetts, numerous books and literature of a Communist nature. The material left by Tsuru was examined XXXXXXXXXXXXX on November 8, 1942. The day following the examination, Norman contacted the Bureau agents and attempted to secure from them the property of Tsuru. Norman identified himself as the Third Secretary of External Affairs, Ottawa, Canada. He mentioned that he had been the Foreign Language Officer at the Canadian Legation in Tokyo, Japan, from 1940 through 1942. He returned to America August 25, 1942. In attempting to secure the property of Tsuru, he produced a calling card of Tsuru as evidence of his authority to take possession of the property.

Norman first claimed to be on an official mission for the Canadian Government to obtain the books of Tsuru for the use of the Canadian Government in a special investigation.

He indicated that he held diplomatic immunity. Norman stated that he was on a highly confidential mission and could not divulge the details of the mission. Subsequently Norman amended his statement and indicated that he had a personal interest in Tsuru's possessions and was not actually on a special mission for the Canadian Government, to secure the material.

This lengthy quotation appears in a "secret" Royal Canadian Mounted Police report entitled "RCMP Enquiry into Allegations Against E. Herbert Norman." The report itself is not dated, but the date "September 11, 1950" appears alongside the quotation given above. The quotation is itself embedded in quotes, meaning that the information originated from another source. The source is the Federal Bureau of Investigation which, on 11 September 1950, reported exactly what you read above to the RCMP. The quotation appears in verbatim or abbreviated form in no less than a dozen different documents included in Herbert Norman's approximately eight-hundred page FBI file, File # 100–346993. For the FBI, from the time this report was first filed in November 1942 until the RCMP was given access to it in September 1950, the "Tsuru apartment episode" was *the* most, if not the only, significant fact extant about a certain human being named Egerton Herbert Norman. And as matters worked themselves out in the succeeding years, the "episode" served as the very foundation of the mountain of mistrust and suspicion that came tumbling down on Herbert, causing his death in 1957.[1]

The episode had its origins, if Tsuru is to be believed, quite innocently in the spring of 1936 when Robert Bryce, since the 1950s one of Canada's most influential bureaucrats, introduced Tsuru to Herbert Norman. Norman was studying Japanese history at Harvard, his ideological bent at the time was Marxist, and Tsuru was a well-known radical economist with a strong grounding in Japanese history: the match Bryce made was an obvious one. By March of 1937 the three men expanded their circle to include several others in a "new group . . . for the study of American capitalism from the Marxist point of view," according to Tsuru. One of those in the group was Lorie Tarshis, a Canadian economist who had been a year ahead of Herbert at the University of Toronto earlier in the decade, and had preceded Herbert to study at Cambridge, in England. Tarshis had been the one who, on instructions from Tsuru, had passed on Tsuru's "calling card," the one that Herbert had used with the FBI agents in order to gain access to Tsuru's apartment. Later, in 1946, Tarshis would have his own FBI file, #100–19057, as would Bryce, #100–502122.[2]

Herbert, Tarshis, and probably Bryce knew another Canadian who was then studying at Harvard, Israel Halperin. Halperin was later named by Igor Gouzenko, the Soviet cipher clerk who defected in 1945 in Ottawa. Thus it appears that a web of Canadian intrigue had been spun at Harvard University in the late Thirties. But compared with the fate that professional American communist-chasers determined for Herbert Norman, Bryce, Tarshis, and even Halperin escaped political persecution relatively unscathed. Bryce was named publicly by Senate witch-hunters, but nonetheless rose to the summit of Canadian bureaucracy; Tarshis abandoned American citizenship, which he got in 1942, to return to Canada and university teaching; and Halperin, once exonerated, returned to teaching mathematics at Queen's University. Only Herbert paid dearly for what Tsuru would later describe to the American Senate as "youthful indiscretions."[3]

Why Herbert Norman? Why was his life reduced to an FBI file, an RCMP file, an Army Intelligence file, a CIA file, a Naval Intelligence file, a State Department file, a Senate Judiciary subcommittee file, each of which largely duplicated the content found in the others, which repeated the same uncertain and unsubstantiated "facts," which categorized, labeled, insinuated, alleged, and suspected him of wrongdoing, of disloyalty, of being a "Communist," upper-case "C," as it was back then most always rendered. Why Herbert Norman?

No single answer presents itself in this book. Unidimensional characterization of Herbert Norman is impossible. He was a complex personality; he suffered the normal human maladies of guilt, fear, rebellion, uncertainty, self-doubt, egotism, hypocrisy, selflessness, and self-centeredness that afflict human beings in undecipherable human situations. But in his case, because he was an intellectual who verbalized and recorded his thoughts, *his* human condition seems exaggerated. To be sure, his weaknesses betrayed his pitiful mortality in a more dramatic fashion than happens to most of us, but his strengths built themselves into an intellectually structured immortality that most of us can admire but never enjoy. He left his imprint on his Muse of History, Clio, and we who try to understand the tracks he left behind only barely comprehend the direction in which he was heading.

Direction? We can discern direction in human development, but only after the fact. Temporal and spatial distances lend perspective, they help us to see human tendencies, patterns of behavior, inclinations, proclivities, and growth, but with clarity only well after Clio has dispensed with her human playthings, enjoyed her jokes on them before teaching them the meaning of mortality in one, final, fatal lesson. Until then, yes, Herbert Norman's life seemed to have well-defined direction, composed of a multitude of life's vectors that eventually converge to create the human being we suspect he was.

As the son of a missionary, he learned moral absolutes early in life; like the children of other Canadian missionaries—the Endicotts, Walmseleys, Willmotts, and Woodworths—he grew into a student radical naturally; as the son of a preacher and a teacher, culturally and linguistically isolated from the rural Japanese among whom the Norman family lived, he early in life found a sturdy friendship with books, the tools of the scholar. Books and his Japanese background conjoined to make the transition to Japanologist an easy one. The family's dedication to a career of service to humankind helped Herbert into choosing a secular equivalent for his vocation, the diplomatic service. Son, student, scholar, Japanologist, democrat, and diplomat, the direction that his life course took appears so very reasonable, so appropriate.

But human—some would have it inhumane—intervention, motivated by political concerns and sustained by inhuman destructive fears, took what was so reasonable and appropriate and transmogrified Herbert into a suspect, a "man who might have existed," a communist, a victim, a spy, and a suicide. The unnatural dimensions of his life revealed aspects of his "natural" character that play havoc with the sense of direction that otherwise seemed to define his human growth. The "unnatural" help us to understand the intellectual and ideological changes he experienced; they help to explain, not justify, the lies he told to protect himself, his career, and his "natural" self; and they throw into bold relief the awful fears he knew as he contemplated self-destruction.

Herbert's life story demonstrates that no man is truly the master of his own destiny. It shows, too, that in some times, when other persons, powerful persons, are overtaken by pathological fears of global forces, such as communism, that words once spoken can return to haunt, that other words, uttered in fear, can doggedly pursue and even kill.

CHAPTER 1

SON

*My son, attend unto my wisdom, and bow thine ear to
my understanding: That thou mayest regard discretion
and that thy lips may keep knowledge.*

Proverbs V:1–2

Daniel Norman was already forty-five years old and a veteran of twelve years of missionary work in rural Japan when his last child and second son was born. Daniel and his middle-aged wife, Kate, then thirty-nine, named the boy after Egerton Shore, Secretary of the Methodist Mission Board, and Dr. Herbert Schwartz, the physician attending the birth. Herbert, however, was the name that stuck, hinting that the secular rather than the religious influence would prevail in his life.

Twenty-eight years later, when Herbert Norman was studying for his doctorate at Harvard University, and four years before his father's death, he wrote to his older brother Howard about a letter that he had recently received from their father, "telling of his career and the critical turning point in his life. It was," he claimed, "a most moving document filled with autobiographical material of which I was completely ignorant. I will cherish the letter carefully. I respect his character all the more after reading his life, but I can't accept the view that preaching Christ is the highest endeavor of human life."[1]

At age twenty-eight Herbert could easily reconcile feelings of admiration for his father with a gentlemanly disdain toward his career and, given the inseparability of missionary work from Christian values, many of his values as well. The seeds of Herbert's declaration of intellectual, even moral, independence from his father had been in gestation for at least the

[19]

preceding ten years, having germinated out of an unholy and intimate encounter with death during his bout with tuberculosis when he was only seventeen years old. Seen retrospectively from this time, the process of intellectual and moral separation appears as inexorable as it was natural. At the same time, Herbert's break seems no less grounded in the kind of relationship he had with his father, a relationship authoritatively defined by Daniel's Christian beliefs, motivations, goals, and activities. In rejecting these existential dimensions of his father's, Herbert did what many sons have done in all places and in all times: he denied his father's authority in order to assert his own. Rebellion perforce begins at home.

Daniel Norman was no different from many missionaries at the turn of the century. They went to Japan, China, Africa, and elsewhere under the banner of "evangelization of the world in one generation." Theirs was a great and noble Christian *mission civilisatrice*, an arrogant attempt to impose their received "truth" on, and eradicate the "false beliefs" of, nonbelievers. Today we might call them "cultural imperialists" for their insensitivity to and indifference toward the ancient civilizations they sought to indoctrinate. There is, for instance, little evidence that Daniel Norman had learned anything about Japan's culture, history, or religion prior to going in 1897 as, in his words, "an Ambassador of the Cross."[2] Prior to his posting in Japan, he had not studied the language and even after forty years in the country he was unable to write or read Japanese. Moreover, he was seldom reserved about expressing words of righteous indignation over ancient Japanese beliefs and customs, such as Buddhism, the drinking of *saké*, or prostitution, and there is little evidence that he ever understood the relativity of values intrinsic to Japanese society for maintaining social harmony. For Daniel, there existed only right or wrong, defined by holy scripture, the preaching of which was mandated by God.

Daniel Norman had discovered his "calling" relatively late in life. The ninth of the ten children of English-born William (1815–99) and Jane Coates Norman (1827–89), stocky, blue-eyed Daniel worked on the family farm near Aurora, Ontario, until he was twenty-four years old. Though earlier both his father and older brother William had offered to finance his education, Daniel had persistently demurred until William, who also entered the ministry late in life, suddenly died. William's death seemed to have prompted a "religious experience" in Daniel, who then quickly completed high school before entering Victoria College in Toronto at age twenty-six in 1890; he graduated six years later.

Although single-minded in his desire to complete university as a prerequisite for entering the ministry, his education was not wholly instrumentalist. While he was at Victoria three important experiences combined to give permanent meaning to his life. First, he met Catherine (Kate) Heal, a farmer's daughter from Munro, Ontario, whom he would marry in 1901 and with whom he would share thirty-three years of missionary work in Japan. Second, Daniel left Victoria after two years of study to earn enough to finance the remainder of his education and to test his aptitude to preach the gospel; the experience confirmed his choice of vocations because he returned to university in 1894. Finally, in his last two years he discovered the writings of Karl Marx—an experience he would later share with Herbert, seemingly in order to improve communication between them—and participated in left-wing activities on campus, from Saturday evening "communist meetings" to the "Sunday afternoon socialist club."[3]

Coupled with his rural background, the latter experience with socialist ideas combined to distinguish Daniel from other missionaries who worked in Japan in the early twentieth century. Unlike many others, Daniel, after a three-year stint in the Tokyo area beginning in 1897, eventually chose a rural ministry over the culturally less disrupting urban life that promised the companionship of other foreign missionaries, better (more modern) schools and facilities, and greater access to western niceties. Daniel's rural ministry took him among backward farmers, railroad workers, and xenophobic townspeople, many of whom had had little or no contact with westerners, let alone with an alien religion. In the early years, beginning in 1902, he had only one other western missionary

family with whom he could share his frustrations, his difficulties, his experiences. Virtually alone he had to confront
what he called "the dark powers of idolatry"[4] amidst geo-
graphical isolation and antagonistic, ancient beliefs that had
barely been affected by enlightened "modernization."

Cyril Powles, a Canadian historian of Japan with a rural
missionary background similar to Herbert Norman's, writes
that Daniel's choice of locale for his ministry created "a basic
sense of dependence on the local society," in contrast to urban
missionaries who "grew up with a basic sense of separateness
from the Japanese community." Powles further suggests that
the sense of "dependence" translated into a high degree of
intimacy with local Japanese, a "feeling of acceptance." To
illustrate his point, Powles tells the story of one Japanese
child uttering, "Look out, here comes a foreigner!" to which
his companion protests, "Go on, that's no foreigner. That's
Mr. Norman."[5] The same story is repeated in the *United
Church Observer* obituary of Daniel Norman (15 July 1941)[6]
along with similar comments indicating how fully accepted,
even revered, Daniel Norman was among the local population. Yet there is another side to the story, having more to
do with Daniel Norman's purpose in being in Japan and with
his temperament than with how he actually got along with
certain Japanese.

"His aim," says his obituary, "had always been evange-
listic; he wanted to raise self-supporting and self-propagating
churches, yet the church was only a means to an end. His
ultimate purpose was to evangelize the non-Christian people
in the untouched areas and the untouched classes." In short,
Daniel Norman sought to make converts, mainly among those
who figured in his socialist leanings as members of the lower
classes. Yet his alien race, religion, culture, language, and
even his lifestyle would make this task difficult if not impossible.

Daniel himself was not unaware of the difficulties that lay
before him. With all the precision of a mathematician, and
perhaps the naïveté of a blinkered soldier of the cross, Daniel
calculated the enormity of his task in terms of the ratio of
committed "soldiers" to the unbelieving population of his

district: "Soldiers have an average of over 120,000 to each lead to Christ." According to Gwen Norman, Daniel's daughter-in-law, over an unspecified period the indefatigable Daniel traveled 8,516 miles, "reaching" 4,146 men, but gained only three conversions.[7]

His very purpose of winning converts assured that he would be perceived as a self-regarding moralist who presumed moral superiority. And as an alien his presumed moral superiority set him even further apart from the Japanese. Hence, despite his earnest efforts to master the spoken language, to be kind, friendly, open, charitable, considerate, and humble before his unbelieving constituency; despite his efforts to live a socially irreproachable life and to have his family members do likewise; despite his many good deeds for the local community; and despite his attempts to avoid the appearance of pompous piety, Daniel Norman could not fail to seem the alien dignitary whose very *raison d'être* manifested contempt for the beliefs of the native population who, particularly at this time, were avidly learning the lessons of nationalism and cultural pride being taught by a chauvinistic state.

That Daniel built for himself and his family a huge, even luxurious house; that he employed two Japanese maids; that he was the first person, western or Japanese, in the region to own an automobile; that he abandoned his flock every seventh year for furlough, traveling to Canada or Europe or the Middle East; that he owned a summer home in the resort town of Karuizawa; that his closest friends were the other local whites; that he sent all three of his children to private school outside the region—all these suggested a style of aristocratic living that belied the humble Christian message he taught and tried to sell.

His lifestyle guaranteed his alienation from the Japanese population; his refusal to admit the relativity of values—that the ancient values of the Japanese might be as good as the Christian values he professed—assured his failure to convert many to Christianity. This is the paradox and the contradiction of all missionary work, and although Daniel Norman might have addressed it more humanely than most, alienation from the people whom he sought to win over to Christ was a natural outcome of mission.

The sort of alienation described was mitigated, no doubt, by the efforts of his new bride whom he brought back to Japan after they married in Canada in May of 1901. Kate Norman has been described by her son Howard as a "gentle, reticent lady, . . . sometimes given to worry and anxiety," and strongly devoted to nurturing and teaching her children, as well as anyone else who desired her help. Trained as a teacher at Victoria College, she served as sole mentor to all three of her children until they were old enough to be sent to the Canadian Academy at Kobe, and then when the last child, Herbert, was sent, she followed to serve as matron of the Academy. To the women of Nagano, she taught western cooking, the Bible, and gardening. For a while she voluntarily taught English in the local middle school. Through performing such good works she endeared herself to many Japanese, who apparently saw her as the perfect stereotype of the ideal Japanese wife—humble, helpful, self-effacing, and, above all, gentle. Herbert especially was devoted to her, and by all accounts she was especially devoted to Herbert.[8] And there is no doubt that her presence was bountifully helpful to Daniel Norman, both personally and professionally, though the distinction is artificial: evangelists always bring their work home.

Although Daniel was frequently gone from home, calling on potential converts throughout his district, his presence was always felt by Kate and, after Grace's birth in 1903, Howard's in 1905, and Herbert's in 1909, by the children as well. According to Howard's recollections, the family respected Daniel's injunction to behave in ways appropriate to *his* status and mission. "We held father in too great awe to transgress frequently," recalls Howard, who also remembers that the one time he and Herbert physically fought, their father was "mortified that missionary sons should quarrel violently in public." Father, he says, was "too strict," and though mother was "more easily dealt with than father,"she nonetheless worried about "what people would say." All the children were "exhorted" by both parents "to be good and do right." The children were responsive: "He had," writes Howard, "a powerful temper."⁹

In his recollections of his parents, Howard stresses Daniel's good humor, his kindness, and his growing gentleness as he aged. At the same time Howard eschews one-dimensional eulogizing by discussing his father's faults, the greatest of which, particularly from the children's viewpoint, were his frequent absences from home due to Daniel's indefatigable efforts to proselytize. Howard's own experience—forty-three years in Japan as a missionary—permits him to empathize and forgive. But Howard also reminisces about instances of Daniel's temper, his sarcasm, and his emotional "bile." Howard recalls one instance when Daniel showed himself to be especially insensitive toward a blind Japanese evangelist. When the blind man asked to accompany Daniel and others on a pilgrimage to a famous cave whose floor was carpeted in moss, Daniel is said to have replied, "Why do you want to go? You can't see the moss anyway." And on another occasion, Daniel dressed down a young parishioner for failing to attend church. Howard's wife, Gwen, as daughter-in-law, asserts of Daniel, "He was not noticeably sensitive to the feelings of others." In her own case, she recalls trying to resist his "pressure to do things according to his lights, especially in regard to our children." She concludes, "Dr. Norman had a strong tendency to tell others what to do and how to do it."¹⁰

Kate, on the other hand, was, in Gwen Norman's words, "wise, patient, and kind." "She was the stabilizing factor in the family," by which Gwen means Kate served as the mediator, the conciliator, and the peacemaker.¹¹ Kate radiated sympathy and daily demonstrated her gentleness. Gwen emphasizes her stoic attitude toward Daniel's spinster sister Lucy Norman, a "pain in the neck," says Gwen, during the many years she lived with Daniel and Kate in Nagano before leaving to serve as a matron in the Canadian Academy at Kobe.

The contrast in personality between Daniel and Kate, as pictured thus far, is too great and undoubtedly exaggerated.

Insensitive, absentee father; patient, self-sacrificing mother; seldom in life are such extreme one-dimensional depictions accurate or fair. In fact, Daniel gave of himself, as a person and father and not simply as a missionary to agnostics, convicted prisoners, and indebted peasants, just as he gave freely of his spare time to his family, taking them to the Japan Sea or Lake Nojiri or Karuizawa for summer breaks. Kate, for her part, was overly anxious about public opinion, with what is sometimes called the "Ontario syndrome," and was "given to worry and anxiety," according to Howard, and may have been too indulgent toward her children. Herbert, for instance, was allowed to sleep with his parents long after infancy, and Kate made a custom of "tucking Herbert in," even into his adult years.[12]

For the first ten years of each of her children's lives, Kate served as their teacher as well. She taught her children a western curriculum that included heavy doses of Bible lessons in addition to subject matter that any Canadian youth of that era would have studied. Apparently she emphasized Canadian history and society, for each of the children exhibited strong patriotic sentiment that is not simply attributable to the sort of longing for the motherland common to those living in enforced exile. Howard tells the story of how his sister Grace was once being tormented by a nationalistic American woman missionary who took perverted delight in deriding Canada. The woman's harsh words caused Grace to burst into tears before proudly proclaiming, "Canada's *my* country!" Howard also recalls being taught by his mother that Canada was the "land flowing with milk and honey," an opinion that the other children shared as a result of spending furloughs in modern, materialistic Canada. Canada's positive image in the children's minds, moreover, was reinforced at Christmastime when gifts from relatives in Canada were delivered, or likewise, when clothes ordered from an Eaton's catalogue arrived. In addition, formal schooling at the Canadian Academy served to make Canada second only to Christianity as an object of the children's affection. Britain, the Empire, and the Commonwealth collectively finished a strong third. Proud of his British heritage, during the Boer War Daniel strongly voiced support of England, although by the time of the First World War, he was increasingly adopting the position of the pacifist.[13]

No less important as influences in shaping the children's values, and certainly more immediate, were the doctrinal positions that Daniel and Kate took regarding social issues. Daniel was an outspoken advocate of equality among the sexes, classes, and races. He decried licensed prostitution not simply because of religious principles, but also because the practice demeaned women. He refused membership in one foreign summer community because of a racist exclusionary clause that forbade Japanese to own land. For related reasons he proselytized among working-class people. Reminiscent of George Bernard Shaw's claim of the same period, Daniel justified his progressive stand on such social issues with the observation that "Jesus . . . taught communism."[14]

Certainly in the cases of Howard and Herbert, there is ample evidence to indicate that Daniel's progressive outlook influenced their thinking. Howard flirted with socialism in the late Twenties and early Thirties and today proudly boasts a strongly socialist humanist orientation; Herbert joined the Communist Party in the early Thirties. But well before then, when he was only seventeen years old and still living in Japan, Herbert thought as his father's child when he wrote in support of movements to eradicate "licensed vice," "that wretched system," he called it, or when he expressed sympathy for "poor farmers" who rioted against unfair government policy.[15]

Though it was his father's views, political and moral, that Herbert adopted as a young man, it was his mother's character that had the greatest influence on his own. As mentioned before, following Herbert's birth, Daniel was frequently absent from home. One account had Daniel away from home on an average of two to five days each week[16] After Herbert's brother and sister left for school, in 1913 and 1915, from the time he was six years old until he was eleven, Herbert remained at home alone with his mother who perforce served as his teacher, friend, and playmate. When Herbert finally left for school in Kobe his mother followed him and worked at the school as matron. Besides sharing a great deal of time together, mother and youngest child shared physical and personality characteristics as well. Herbert's blue eyes, blondish hair, the shape of his nose and the set of his eyes closely resembled his mother's, as did his "tender-hearted" character, in the words of one Japanese childhood playmate. It is significant but not surprising that in 1940, a year before his father's death, Herbert chose to dedicate his first book to his mother alone. "Herbert was," writes Howard, "greatly devoted to our mother."[17]

But if Herbert was "his mother's child," he was not necessarily a "mama's boy." Though as a child he derived deep emotional satisfaction from retiring indoors to read, he was no less content to engage in physical activities out of doors with Japanese and western playmates. Called "Teddy" by his playmates until in his teens, Herbert is remembered for long hours spent playing with his dog Sport, his passion for kite-flying, and for the sailing of wooden boats in the rice paddies. And as a teenager Herbert excelled in tennis, basketball, and baseball.

At the Canadian Academy, where he matriculated in 1920, Herbert enjoyed a very "normal" adolescence. He was one of "Three Musketeers" known for playing pranks. One Hallowe'en morning the three boys climbed to the roof of a dormitory, each loaded with pails of water, which they poured down the chimney leading to the bedroom of an unpopular teacher. So overjoyed were they by their easy success that they did the same to the dining-room chimney just as breakfast was about to be served. Several classmates from this era describe him as "fun-loving," "quite witty," or as "idealistic." All recall that he was exceptionally bright. His principal teacher of the period, Miss Leonora Park, remembers him as "complete in gesture and mind, with all good qualities to grace a gentleman."[18]

Herbert's intellectual growth, as prodigious as it was astounding to those around him, was no doubt accelerated as a result of encouragement at home, an innate desire to learn, and a sort of skewed cosmopolitanism that is not at all unusual among "mish kids." Howard remarks that the library at home, filled with a wide variety of books, served the purpose of making rainy days seem shorter, much as television does for today's younger generation. Herbert's favorite was always *Pilgrim's Progress,* which because of a lisp he pronounced "Pilgrim'th Progreth"; Howard recalls that his brother read this book when he was quite young, perhaps even before he was six. But there were also the novels of Dickens, Scott, Hawthorne, Sir Thomas Malory, O. Henry, and a wide variety of history books, as well as monthly magazines from Canada which everyone in the family pored over as soon as they arrived. As teacher, Kate Norman was forever present to urge her children to read, but by all accounts Herbert needed little encouragement.[19]

His intellectual development came from travel as well. Religiously oriented though family travel was—furloughs were God's imposed rest once in every seven years—it nonetheless permitted the family, and Herbert especially, to become more aware of the larger world. Some of his earliest extant writings are letters he wrote to his sister Grace in 1923, when she was in Canada studying and he was a young teenager on a trip he took with Howard and their parents to Europe by way of China, southeast Asia, India, and, the most important part of the trip, the Holy Land in the Middle East.

Herbert began describing their journey for Grace after arrival in Haiphong, Vietnam. "It's governed by Frenchmen. I don't like Haiphong a bit. It's sultry, everybody quarrels, and above all, it's stale, everything is stagnant, nothing doing, no traffic, no nothing." Then from Saigon: "We had to travel 40 miles up a tropical river, on either side was a jungle, full of wild beasts. The deep, sluggish river moving slowly toward the sea is hiding alligators and snakes, and we saw wild water buffalo. At last we sighted Saigon on the left side of the river, with the burning, glaring tropical sun beating down mercilessly on the highroofed buildings of the city, the capital of

French Indochina. As we rounded the last curve, we saw large buildings, high trees, the busy river full of a mixture of junks, sampans and launches in one excited glance."

From Saigon, they went on to Singapore, to visit gardens, roam the city, and witness "a Hindoo or Moslem ceremony. It was lit up by torches, and scary looking priests were conducting the solemn ceremony. Everything looked strange and weird." He ended his letter, "With coconuts full of sweet love, like its delicious contents, I'll give my best to you. Your loving brother, Herbert; P.S. I wish ever so much you were along with us. EHN"[20]

From Singapore, the family traveled to Palestine. They disembarked at Suez, where they stayed several days in nearby Cairo before taking the train for a ten-day stay in the Holy Land. Herbert wrote about the Garden of Gethsemane, the Mount of Olives, and the Tombs of the Kings. He wrote with obvious passion about the spots "where Jesus prayed," the Mount "where Christ was supposed to have ascended," the "home where Jesus lived," and "the place where Jesus performed his miracle of turning water to wine." Then on to the Mount of the Beatitudes "where Jesus preached" and the synagogue "where Jesus taught." Howard writes later that "Jerusalem, Bethlehem, Jericho, Nazareth, and the Sea of Galilee" moved their father "deeply." Herbert, too, it seems. He writes about picking several olive leaves from a tree he found in the "quiet, holy garden" situated next to "The Chapel of Agony" in Gethsemane for inclusion in a letter to Grace, closing with expressions of "oranges full of juicy love."[21]

Herbert's Christian travelogue, written for the benefit of his sister, has all the earmarks of an epistle composed by a pious and literary young man with a passion for living history, eager to share his insights and experiences with others, perhaps eager to show off his knowledge as well, and not at all reluctant to reveal sentiment and emotion. No less telling, these early letters suggest an independence of mind: were it not for Howard's own version of the pilgrimage, one might almost conclude from reading the letters that Herbert took the trip on his own. One senses a growing adolescent self-confidence, an independent soul with his own views, buttressed by his own perceptions. In a separate letter to Grace, written before the family's departure from Japan, Herbert boasted of having been ranked first in his class in the high-school preparatory exams, achieving distinction in the subjects of history, Bible study, and arithmetic.[22] Curiously, thirty-five years later, Herbert would write his very last personal letters from the Land of Moses where in the Canadian Embassy, his own secular "chapel of agony," he would unsuccessfully attempt to contend with the conflict raging between the fruits of independent thinking and the expectations of public authorities.

The remainder of that furlough year was spent in Toronto, where the family lived in a missionary apartment on Humewood Drive. For the first time in several years, the entire family was together again. Grace was in her third year at Victoria College, Howard was beginning his freshman year, and Herbert attended Oakwood Collegiate. Aunt Lucy also lived with them.

The joy of a reunited family, however, was diminished somewhat by their joyless financial straits. Whereas in Japan, by Japanese standards, the Norman family lived a privileged existence, in Toronto they were poor. Howard recalls, with Christian pride, "the example of stoicism and frugality" set by his parents when how they both elected to return home by streetcar instead of taxi after all their teeth were removed in operations for pyorrhea.[23]

Howard by then had won an academic scholarship and had decided to imitate his father by studying for the ministry, and thus could accept, even welcome, financial privation. Grace, soon to return to Japan to teach (and later to marry a missionary there), had likewise learned to accept the financial limitations of the missionary's furlough existence.

But for Herbert, that year in Toronto had to have been a terrible shock. The last time the family had been on furlough in Toronto was 1916–17, when he had been too young to be very aware of relative deprivation. Besides, social rewards had more than compensated for economic privation as his father had at that time been awarded an honorary doctorate from Victoria College in recognition of his missionary work. But in 1923 Herbert must have become conscious of the terrible contradiction between enjoying high social status abroad and suffering material privation at home. Hints that this contradiction affected his consciousness, and probably his later choice of a secular vocation, appear in correspondence written while he was a student at Cambridge in the Thirties.

The following year Herbert returned with his parents to Japan and re-entered the Canadian Academy, where he distinguished himself in academics and athletics. In 1925 he won the oratorical contest by giving a discourse on the French revolutionary Georges Jacques Danton. In his last year, 1926, he served as editor-in-chief of *Red and Grey,* the yearbook, played shortstop on the baseball team and guard on the basketball team, was captain of the tennis team, and distinguished himself in Latin, English, and history. The yearbook predicted that "we can expect much of him in the literary field," as "English is his forte." In a less serious vein, the "class prophecy" noted his "neverfailing supply of jokes and stories" in a roast, only half-ironic in retrospect, predicting that he would earn "the following *nom de guerre:* Hard-headed Herb, the Horrible Hobo, or Long-legged Herb [he was already six feet tall by 1926], the Lanky Loon, or again Spider-Herb, the Crazy-crook" and would appear "on the police record under the heading 'Hardened Criminals, Wanted the World Over'."[24]

But graduation for Herbert was not the undiluted moment of celebration that it is for most seventeen-year-olds. He learned that year that he was in the early stages of tuberculosis and that grade thirteen and university would have to be postponed until the disease was cured, if cure was possible. Herbert felt left behind and was troubled by the knowledge that his delayed rites of passage into adulthood would forever separate him from his more frivolous and carefree peers who went off immediately to college or careers.

In the fall of 1926, instead of going to college, Herbert

went to a TB sanitorium in Karuizawa, the mountain resort town where the Normans owned a summer home, located just an hour by train from the family home in Nagano City. Like Nagano City, Karuizawa was engirdled by high mountains and enveloped by a large pocket of clean air. Herbert's treatment consisted of enforced relaxation, "sun baths and plenty of fresh air, rest, and physical buildup upon milk, eggs, etc." he wrote in early October. "It isn't a disagreeable treatment," he emphasized, yet he complained that the doctor's prescribed regimen disallowed him from sitting up to read because "when I sat up and worked at a table, I wasn't resting properly." His most persistent complaint was that the disability "interferes with my studies". He remarks that "I guess I won't worry over my studies until I'm fully recovered," but his letters make clear that he was as much concerned with the progress of his mind as he was with that of his body.[25]

Sometime in that autumn of 1926 Daniel Norman decided that early the next year Herbert should go to Canada for treatment if his health had not significantly improved in Karuizawa. The X-rays had shown that the tubercule bacilli in his lungs were yet in a "very undeveloped state," but showed no signs of disappearing. Thus, as planned, Herbert and his mother set sail early in 1927 for Canada and on 29 March, a Sunday, the two arrived in Vancouver. From the letter he wrote Howard about their arrival, it is clear that Herbert's sense of humor had not been blunted either by the lengthy cruise or by the TB:

> That Sunday was the most heathenist Sabbath I ever spent. It consisted of a prolonged series of immigration examinations, custom examinations, packing and unpacking; tipping, sweating, counting, and rushing. By some unknown, bygone, so-called law, the bloated, officious, self-important, blatant, thick-lipped, unreasoning son of Japeth (this Japeth's shame) politely called the immigration official informed me (but not politely) that due to the almost criminal fact that I was born in Japan (sniff), I had no claims to the status of a British subject, but was considered an immigrant. Mother, of course,

was exempt from the furious cross-questioning, but I had to wait my turn with the masses to get my medical exam, etc. However, I was comforted by the fact that the aforementioned chicken-headed, two-legged animal, etc. nearly choked himself and also ruined his voice by howling and yelling at this fellow to come forward, that one to shutup, this one to sit down, and that one to be damned, etc., etc. Only this last command was usually made under his putrid breath as officers and doctors were within earshot . . . My examination merely consisted in telling him that I had seen seventeen summers, had any disease they wanted me to have such as measles, German measles, mumps, and all such childish ailments, had never had any operation for appendicitis, yes intended to live in Canada but couldn't say whether I intended to die there, and I also belonged to the white race—I distinctly remembered washing my face that morning. The doctor made several feeble attempts to air his musty wit on the subject of my unusual birthplace and then sent me out.[26]

The human comedy ceased to be amusing during the next twelve months, once he entered the Calgary, Alberta, Sanitorium (CAS) for treatment. Now Herbert became consumed by his own human frailty, almost to the exclusion of any other interest save his studies, but even in this regard his attentions focused on more sombre questions of life and death. Separated from family, friends, and home—his mother resided with friends in the town of Calgary—Herbert confronted for the first time the meaning of mortality.

His views resembled those of young Hans Castorp in Thomas Mann's emotionally ponderous *The Magic Mountain*. "A sanitorium is filled with distorted minds as well as bodies," Herbert wrote despairingly shortly after his arrival, adding with youthful perception, "take away ambition from a man and the chances are nine to ten he will become a cynic." Like Hans Castorp, Herbert discovered that a black atmosphere of doubt about the "point and purpose of the business of living" necessarily plagued the minds of those who had little to do but wait for death. His youth and reservoir of energy assisted him in the fight against succumbing to the effects of the disease, though he nevertheless complained, "Since I've come here, I have descended into a lethargic existence of utter listlessness and inactivity." He matter-of-factly recorded his physical problems—weight loss, headaches, fatigue, and worsening eyesight, aggravated by a tracoma contracted years before in Japan—but the budding intellectual could optimistically anticipate the time "when I can get to the stage where I can sit up at a desk and work several hours a day."[27]

Herbert's mood varied according to how he felt: he lived on an emotional and physical roller coaster that offered neither the assurance that he could disembark nor any guarantee of safe arrival. "On bright days I feel like a million dollars and am enjoying myself here in the sanitorium." Visits to town, one train station away, were emotionally uplifting, as were the letters he received from Howard or Grace in Toronto and from his father in Japan. He could cheerfully write of receiving a positive lung examination from "Daddy" Reid, his doctor, and being permitted to go out for a meal. "You can't imagine what a relief it is to get dressed one day even though it is for an hour, after you've been eating in your kimono in the same building for about nine or ten weeks." And his spirits would rise as well whenever he could muster strength enough to read. He discusses in one letter "reading as much as possible, mixing fiction and drama, essays and history with sociology, anthropology and biology . . . and Plato's *Republic*."[28]

But not all of his activities were of the solitary sort. He also writes of socializing with Mr. Moodie, "the somewhat droll and whimsical Scotsman I play chess with; with Mr. Burke, "an old prospector"; "an Englishman Mr Hardie"; and a Mr. Blewitt with whom Herbert would cooperate on deciphering number codes or completing crossword puzzles. Companions, perhaps even friends, they were also Herbert's unwitting tormentors whenever *they* were given to despair. "Strange (or perhaps naturally)," Herbert wrote, "to say that even amongst society which one would call highly destructive, [the] agnostic atmosphere that is impervious to reason, sentiment, or exhortation . . . acts as a wet sponge on one's beliefs unless he can rise above his own gift (or curse) of thought and doubt." Doubt about his own religious convictions began to plague him: "To tell the truth, in matters spiritual and religious I often feel conscience-stricken." Herbert began to understand the lesson taught by Mann: that the spiritual state of man is often and unmistakenly the product of physical disease. In writing about the "notorious chronic grouchers," he identified the "strong tendency in here to cynicism, and, I believe in some extreme people, atheism which, though not vaunted blatantly, undermines with a subtlety comparable to that of small drops of water wearing away a granite slab."[29]

Even the "god-fearing men" like Moodie, he wrote, were given to periodic visitations of skepticism, but Herbert took heart from their eventual return to "the inherent logic, faith, optimism and, I believe greatest of all, *humility* of *their* natures." Though comforted by their examples, he was equally discomfited by the many "agnostics, athiests, iconoclasts, pantheists" and other non-believers who made up the majority of residents. He focused at length on one individual in particular, a "quiet, stoical old crock . . . called Blackwood."

> Blackwood is a typical English gentleman—thoughtful, courteous, cultured, and much respected . . . but inclined to unload himself on matters spiritual, . . . employing bitter, scathing, stinging yet quiet and controlled raking of the Church of God, of its pontiffs, believers, and Head I have never heard before. Hypocrisy was his main weapon. He was not vicious nor raucous about it but I fear only too sincere and hardened . . . . Since he conforms to no church, the visiting clergymen don't pay any attention to him, although he is too well-mannered to repel them should they talk to him. He does not seem to fear death but on the other hand he seems to look forward to a lethargic, pointless state of nothingness, a haven of nonentity, a Nirvana.

Herbert pitied Blackwood's deteriorating condition, calling him a "living corpse," but admired his ability to be both humane and courageous in the face of certain death. Herbert learned from him, especially the lesson of hypocrisy. Herbert writes, "Although I consider myself a staunch Protestant, I often blush inwardly for my fellow churchmen, not only in here . . . . I have noticed that so-called Protestants take the lead in scoffing at the church, at missions, at Christianity in general. They are the most learned in profanity and the best versed in a never-ending stock of obscenity . . . . What I have noticed is an eye-opener . . . [and] I must admit that I am far from a model. In many ways I am too lax, and things that would have shocked me unutterably a year ago do not even rouse my sensibilities now."[30]

Herbert was getting a different sort of education at age seventeen, of the sort that experiential confrontation with mortality alone can offer: he was learning about life, death, god, and godlessness, and about himself. He still prejudged in favor of life and god—dismissing atheism, for example, as "a supercilious, [sic] arrogant pose or affectation due to an exaggerated rating of one's own power and self-judged superiority to the common flock of spoon-fed babies."[31] Nonetheless, his mind had been opened to the antitheses of life and god. He could no longer be the naive young man who indiscriminately attended to his father's wisdom and gained from his understanding, as in the proverb that opens this chapter.

In spring 1928, Herbert left his Magic Mountain cured in body, but his mind had been changed as a result of an experience that had been neither kind nor gentle. He had encountered hypocrisy, cynicism, sick bodies and minds, apostasy, and a kind but hateful iconoclast who had demonstrated that the dying might hate god yet love man. Too, he had discovered that the number of the faithful was much smaller than he had heretofore imagined: "Out of about 1000 casual acquaintances, I believe one is lucky to find *one really good religious man!*" He left the sanitorium believing himself to be one of these, but within a few short years he would abandon his Christian god for a secular substitute: Karl Marx.

CHAPTER 2

STUDENT

Our political attitudes are determined by our point of entry into politics.

Richard Crossman to Michael Straight

In the space of a mere seven years, between 1927 and 1934, Herbert Norman changed from being a Christian to a Christian-socialist aligned with the CCF, to a Trotskyist, and finally to a Stalinist. His ideological conversions were in part products of the unsettled interwar era, but just as certainly they were results of ethical predispositions shaped by the populist Christian faith of his parents. Once Norman abandoned their faith, he filled the spiritual void with a socialist faith promising heaven on earth, in this life already demonstrated, he believed, by the Soviet Union. He became one of those identified by a Cambridge mentor, James Klugmann (1912–1977), who wrote of young Cambridge socialists: "We tended psychologically to identify what took place in the Soviet Union with the establishment of a communist, faultless, final type of society."[1]

Norman's different conversions, for that is what they were, occurred in quick enough succession that it must be wondered whether they were genuine and complete. Evidence aplenty exists to show that as late as 1937, while he kept track of the Spanish Civil War from the American sidelines at Harvard, he thought of himself as a staunch Stalinist. But in the years that followed, his private thoughts, shared in letters to family members, suggest that he ceased being political, without losing an interest in politics. By 1939, the year he joined the Department of External Affairs and concluded his graduate student career, Norman had rechanneled all political drives

[38]

into his scholarship, which clearly did reflect earlier radical views, and into his official diplomatic responsibilities that perforce transcended burning social issues for a "higher" goal of representing and protecting Canada's national interests.

That his Christian background might predispose him to adopt a populist or socialist view was evident as early as 1926 in his first published essay, an editorial published in the Canadian Academy's yearbook, *Red and Grey.* Norman's essay is a paean to the virtues of "humility and simplicity so often displayed in men and women of deep character." He extols the wisdom of Socrates' observation about the limits of what is humanly knowable and praises Tennyson for understanding that truly "great and good men" possess the "admirable quality of meekness which so puts to shame our bigoted and self-centered whims and ideas." Herbert is here eulogizing the simple rural folk, the unpretentious and meek among whom he had lived long in Japan and to whom his farmer-father had preached a simple Christian message espousing these very same virtues. Yet against this example of pure and simple folk, Herbert also posits the contrary examples of such "remarkable and brilliant men" as "the great Earl of Chatham, the sublime egotism of Napoleon, or the overwhelming conceit of Cicero," in order to show that the famous, though "not necessarily 'good'," best demonstrate the importance of having "trust and reliance in their own ability." Norman urged his classmates to endeavor to emulate both the meek and the mighty.[2]

To be sure, Norman's words seem like standard fare for graduating seniors, yet there is no contrived dissembling here: he writes as a missionary's son, urging his classmates to attain "triumphs" by "working quietly and without bluster or boasting about past victories or whimpering over present difficulties and dangers." He enjoins them "to cultivate both true humility and strong confidence," values intrinsic to the Protestant ethic and central to his own upbringing.[3]

As may be recalled, Norman had taken these self-same values into the Calgary sanitorium with him. There he had praised "humble, god-fearing" Christians such as his friend Moody and denounced the negativism of "supercilious, arrogant" nonbelievers who claimed "self-judged superiority to the common flock. . . ." Then Norman could yet align himself with the "common flock," those to whom his father preached and for whose sake, in Norman's view, his father had to suffer worldly deprivations, to be "stoical" as the son so often phrased his father's situation.

Norman's Christian values informed his earliest expressed, strictly political attitudes as well. While still in the Calgary sanitorium, the seventeen-year-old Herbert wrote of studying the writings of Karl Marx, seemingly in order to respond more intelligently to Howard's increasingly socialist views. In a letter of 11 July 1927, to Howard and their sister Grace, he warns them, "I shall now take off my coat and roll up my sleeves in the cause of State vs. Socialism. From this page [2] to page 14 will be nothing more than an effervescence of surplus talking gas projected upon the aforesaid subject," emphasizing the essay quality of his approach and apologizing in advance for its "doubtless wearisome" effects.

From Norman's opening comments, it is clear that in an earlier letter Howard had advocated a democratic socialist position similar to what, in a few years' time, would be enshrined in the Regina Manifesto but which was already being preached by Social Gospelers like J. S. Woodsworth. Howard was arguing in favor of the state assuming public ownership of social goods (health services, hydroelectricity, natural resources in general, etc.). Norman's response was to call into question his brother's socialist credentials: "I don't consider a person who advocates a few such institutional readjustments of property to be justified in calling him or herself a socialist—at best he would be a very lukewarm type of socialist." Herbert proceeds to lecture his older brother about the true meaning of socialism: "The real socialists in my eyes are the disciples of Karl Marx who hold conferences in various European capitals to discuss the teachings of the erascible old Teuton philosopher."

Herbert faults Howard for his naïveté for trying to be

simultaneously a socialist and a pacifist (a position that would similarly plague Woodsworth later, even to the point of appeasing Hitler's aggression). He points out that Marx "boldly states that Socialism necessitates eternal inter-class warfare in order to evolve his great pet theme, the *leveling* of all classes. Pacifism was decidedly not one of his catchwords." When Marx's theory and "shifty logic" is "simmered down," Herbert argues, "they amount to nothing more than a doctrine of the state." Seventeen-year-old Herbert then employs *ad hominem* arguments to attack Marx's teachings: "[Marx] was a man who, embittered by his exile from the intellectual and elite society of Berlin due to his own uncontrollable and caustic tongue, followed the example of the proverbial Reynard who declared that the grapes were still immature. He aroused the baser and ignoble passions of the lower strata of society by telling them what unstable, selfish snobs the upper classes of their countries were, which was all very true without a doubt, but was his antagonistic spirit any better?!" Marx, in short, was the worst of all sorts, he was "an unchristian spirit." Marx sought "not to alleviate the travail and horrors of peasant and slum life, but smacking his lips in anticipation of the longed-for downfall of the governing classes, advocated a policy of poisonous denunciation in place of sympathy and good deeds, and violence, if need be, instead of patience and reason." Socialism, contrary to what Howard believed, is simply the result of "the petty hatred and intolerance of a megomaniacal [sic] misanthrope." Herbert stood firm atop his Christian ideal of "good" men as humble and meek.

He also faulted Howard for his "Utopian pacifist ideal." "Unworkable," said Herbert, since in the real world "opponents do much more than merely slap our face." What about national defense, asked Herbert, since "as long as human nature remains the same, there will be nations and races galore who will take the first opportunity to despoil countries which are more nobly invested and more desirable than their own." The modern world is Hobbesian, warns Norman, and the white man is its hated Leviathan, in danger of being toppled: "Due to the white man's deplorable militaristic and aggressive policies, the ordinarily peace-loving and spiritual Oriental and Hindu are now thoroughly aroused," and would, if the chance came, "overrun and destroy countries (white) that formerly exploited them."

Herbert draws upon his lifelong experiences in Japan to help make his point about the dangerous effect of what he calls the "white man's imperialistic actions," and in what was perhaps an unconscious jab at Howard's and his father's missionary careers, asserts, "By missions, charity, education, etc., he [the white man] is trying to atone for his former misdeeds." Attempts at atonement, he argues, cannot erase "this obvious fact, that the white man is bitterly and often secretly hated." As an illustration, Herbert cites the "felicitations" from the non-white world to Japan after its victory over "white" Russia (1904–05), shattering "the idol of white invincibility."

He predicted a "crisis of universal importance," one in which the non-whites "would unite" against a divided white world. "Christianity is the only antidote for such a troubled world," he wrote, but recognized that it would "take generations to proselytize such nations as Turkey, Persia, China, India, etc.," and therefore "to adopt socialism [and pacifism] would be nothing short of suicide."

Hence, Herbert faulted Howard's socialist and pacifist position on the grounds of racial *realpolitik*, but he also attacked the doctrine for its idealistic misreading of human nature. "Socialism is jealous of any inequality, but as all men are *not* born equal, there must be superior ability, talent, etc. . . . Socialism has a tendency to drag down to the mob level, not to elevate," and perforce ignores "the Iron Law of Inequality." The only way to elevate humankind, he argues, is through education, "not the fanatical teachings of Socialism." A patronizing, youthful Herbert Norman concludes, "As the astute and scholarly King of Sweden epigrammatically said, 'If a man under thirty had never been a socialist, he had no heart, and if a man over thirty was a socialist he had no head!' I hope this is the case with most of the Modern Socialists."

Content aside, the tone suggests that the younger brother is lecturing, maybe even talking down to the older brother. So certain of the soundness of his reasoning and of his learning, Herbert gave little ground on the substantive points; this is a characteristic of almost all of his correspondence to Howard throughout their lives, yet diplomat and gentleman that he was, Herbert unfailingly buried within his letters one or two comments intended to mollify the effect that his opinionated language would have. In this particular epistle, Herbert equivocates slightly: "Don't imagine that I am in favor of ironfisted capital—either extreme [socialism or capitalism] is dangerous and calamitous to the best interests of the people and nation." And with this apologia of moderation he adds, "By the way Howie, please write as much as you wish on the subject: it does not increase my pulse in the least, if anything it increases my appetite!"[4] After effecting intellectual divorce, Herbert had a way of currying an emotional remarriage.

Between the sanitorium and his matriculation at Victoria, (1929) Herbert spent a year at Albert College where his brother was teaching; for Howard the year was a time of "Christian fellowship" between them. But once he began his studies in Toronto, and his letters indicate this, Herbert temporarily forsook heady political questions for the sake of scholarship; he wanted to "catch up" with his studies, ever mindful that he was two years older than his classmates. He felt he had to take his studies very seriously, having discovered at Albert that he was not free of academic deficiencies. There he had excelled in English composition, Latin and French, but got only average scores in English literature, algebra and Latin composition. At Victoria he financially depended on the Hamilton Fisk Beggar Scholarship in Latin, French, and German in order to continue with his studies as a prospective major in Classics. Thus, he accorded higher priority to academics than to his broader political self-education. A good number of his classmates from this period lend confirmation to Herbert's bookishness. One co-ed, for example, writes, "My recollection is of a quiet, scholarly, good-looking boy bent over his books in the library, apparently oblivious of any light-minded whispering and giggling the rest of us might indulge in." Another contemporary remembers him as "an aloof intellectual," while classmate Pauline McGibbon emphasizes "the quiet life" he led at Victoria. Writer Lois Darroch recalls him "standing alone, not anti-social, not absentminded, but thinking, thinking deeply." And a fellow Classics major underscores his solitary and studious nature, adding, "He did not flaunt his brilliance; there was much humility and gentleness about him."[5]

Another contemporary, just a year ahead of Herbert at Victoria, was Lorie Tarshis, who, like Norman, went on to do graduate work in Cambridge following graduation from Victoria; indeed, Tarshis, openly political and radical while at Victoria, expressed surprise recently when I quoted several of Norman's more radical statements written when he was a student in Toronto. Actually, there is no reason why Tarshis should have known about Herbert's developing radical views since he really only began to express them during his last year in college. By then, it would seem, Herbert had learned how to get high marks, and therefore felt secure enough academically to feel free to engage in politics. And with good reason: his academic transcripts show all "Firsts" in Latin and Greek and comparably high marks in his other subjects, especially history. They also show that his scholarship aid had been renewed each year, that in addition he had won a Lincoln Hutton Scholarship for the best English essay, and in his last year an Edward Wilson Gold Medal.[6]

Norman's conversion from a Christian to a Christian-socialist to a Trotskyist happened quickly, sometime during his last two years in university. Yet his conversions seems to have been largely private affairs that he chose to share only with members of his family. His public image, especially during the last three semesters when he took more time for extracurricular activities, appeared anything but political. Several of his more "newsy" letters to family members confirm his classmates' enduring impressions of Herbert as a bookworm. In his letters he writes of leisure reading, of delving into Latin novels and historical novels, of attending classical music concerts, of reading Blake, of preparing an address to the Historical Club ("That in the Opinion of this Club the League of Nations is an Anachronism"), of assiduously following the Sino-Japanese "trouble" (after the Japanese take-over of Manchuria), and of attending very few parties with friends.

Early in his college career, when he does bother to discuss politics, his thoughts and concerns appear ideologically neutral, personal, and emotional. For example, on the "Sino-Japanese trouble," Herbert anguished because he felt, in his words, "all the loyalty one does to one's native land." Yet, he claimed, "I am afraid that Japan hasn't a foot to stand on. The evidence is overwhelmingly against her." While acknowledging that although Japanese imperialism against China was inexcusable, it is nonetheless possible "to show how she was driven to her present position" by international and internal conditions. But now, "a military clique is running away with her, she is facing bankruptcy, her population is seething with unrest . . . . I can't stomach that Bushido [samurai code] rot—it's an outworn feudal ideal that is being exploited by unscrupulous militarists, who in my opinion are driving the country, desperate in the hope they may be able to precipitate a revolution, to create a fascist regime, ruling the country as in the days of the Shogunate [Tokugawa period, 1600–1868]."[7]

Herbert felt less emotional about events in Canada. One of the few comments he made early in his college career that indicates more than a casual interest concerned the Depression. In referring to the unemployment situation, he assured his parents that it was not as bad as a Japanese friend of theirs claimed, but "things are a proper mess. Bennett [Prime Minister, 1930–35], true to form, has just turned down a splendid trade deal with Russia which would have meant ready cash to thousands of our desperate farmers."[8]

By the spring of the same year, Herbert had changed his focus, indeed, concentrated his political views on Bennett and the Canadian political scene almost to the exclusion of everything else. He writes like a CCF-er, like a Christian socialist, echoing the views of the Toronto Conference of the United Church as explicated two years later (and the views of his father from long ago): "It is our belief that the application of the principles of Jesus would mean an end of the capitalist system."⁹ In an April 1932 letter to his folks in Japan, Herbert approached the topic by referring to two Japanese men who had been praised by his mother in an earlier letter for their high character. Herbert began: "There certainly is a scarcity of such leaders in this benighted land. We have only one man of public affairs at Ottawa to whom we can look with admiration for his strenuous career of honest striving for the weak, and with trust for the integrity of his political life. I mean J. S. Woodsworth. He is of course excoriated by the large majority of the Canadian people, who are so determined, it seems, on a stupid, reactionary, ultra-nationalistic, economic program, that it is useless to offer them anything better than Bennett."⁹

Norman's critique was only that: he had reached that point early in the development of a political consciousness, grounded in empirical reality as much as in a Christian ethic, that permitted social criticism in terms defined both by the situation and by the creed: he could criticize as an outraged citizen *and* as a Christian theologue. He could identify his views with those of the "informed minority"—reflecting a political elitism not dissimilar from the social elitism he had known as a child in Japan—in opposition to the vast majority of uninformed and "stupid" Canadians. Doing this was the first stage in framing an independent political consciousness—independent of his parents' Christianity—but far removed from the second stage of elucidating an alternative value structure that would permit consideration of positive correctives. Woodsworth here was his guide and hero, one who could fill that spiritual leadership role for Herbert easily because he came from the same Christian tradition as Norman's father. Woodsworth, and his CCF cohorts meeting in Calgary that year in their founding convention, gave leadership and direction to young Christians like Herbert who began to recognize that political organization must realize Christian principles *in this life*.

Herbert makes clear that his newfound radical critique had been taught in his classrooms at Victoria, from "professors who have the strength of their convictions," from "men whose words are weighty and well-weighed," from "almost any man in the economics department" "whose opinions I have both heard and read." In accepting, even praising their social-minded views, Norman found it necessary to reject the "wisdom" of anyone "whose mind has been *molded* for them by their great grandparents and has been getting *moldier* ever since." He castigated those who are "so narrow-minded that they could look through a keyhole with both eyes."[10] While it is by no means obvious that he intended these remarks as oblique criticism of his parents' political views, seen retrospectively from just one year later when he wrote as a Trotskyist, they may have in fact represented the first instance of the son rejecting his parents' values in favor of his professors'. It does happen.

What is not debatable is his mounting contempt for the Bennett government, which he clearly regarded as the epitome of reaction. Like many other social democrats/CCF-ers of the time, Norman was especially incensed by Article 98 of the Criminal Code, then being used, in his words, as "a virtual suspension of free speech and of thought, invoked with a vengeance," and resulting in the imprisonment of seven Communist leaders, forced "to reside in Kingston penitentiary with thieves, murderers and stock-brokers, *without the right to read.*" He referred to this law as "a diabolical prohibition which even the most reactionary of other countries do not enforce on political offenders." He quotes a Dr. Scott of the Law Department of McGill University in this regard:"So we Canadians, with Japs, Bulgars, and Yugoslavs, walk along the road to progress and high-mindedness, while such degenerate countries as Great Britain, Germany, Spain, and France err grievously in their lenient attitude toward poor misguided men who have the weakness to take their idealism seriously."[11]

Article 98 and the suppression of Canadian communists' rights of free speech seemed hypocritical to Norman in the face of Canadian condemnation of the Soviet Union. He tells his parents, "No more carping at Russia; whatever they do to the bourgeoisie, we politely reciprocate. . . . We are far more humane: we first starve the lower classes and if they rudely and vocally object, we are so kind as to either 1) shoot them and thus save both the state and themselves the trouble of supporting them, as the U.S. now does; or 2) give them free board and lodge in Kingston [penitentiary]."[12]

Herbert realized that his strong language would shock his parents, for nothing he had written in the years before had prepared them for such strongly worded views, but then neither had he been exposed to a depression and the policies of R. B. Bennett before either. Of course, neither had his parents, and Herbert was sensitive enough to anticipate the effect that his harsh words would have, far removed as they were from Canadian politics and the rising CCF political current. He tries to allay their fears: "You are perhaps fearing that I grow rabid, but as one who still pitifully clings to the evidently outworn ideal of individual freedom of thought and speech for all, I can not help but regard Section 98 as the most serious menace to our liberty since Confederation."[13]

Norman argued, using history as evidence, against any suspension of civil liberties for the mere advocating of "revolution in any way, shape or form." "If logically interpreted," he asserts, then it (Article 98) "would place a censorship against such works as the Bible (too many examples of wicked beings being killed), almost all Greek and Latin literature (the Greeks hated tyrants), . . . and last but not least, the Ontario High School History authorized . . . by the Hon. Howard Ferguson, in which text we read incredibly enough, that Cromwell was not altogether to be blamed in his rather drastic amputation of a part of King Charlie's body which had evidently ceased to function." On that lighter note, Herbert again tries to reassure his mother: "I have visions of my dear mother trying to understand *why* I should unload all this verbiage on your innocent heads. You see, I'm indulging in 'skam-letting,' which, like blood letting, may have its uses. I really feel quite cheerful these days, despite the growing proximity of exams, so entertain no fears for my health, sanity, or *orthodoxy*."[14]

Norman was not publicly outspoken; he shared his increasingly radical views only with his family, and then, as seen, not without re-emphasizing his commitment to religious orthodoxy. According to a contemporary who lived on the floor below in Burwash Residences, Norman was disinclined to join in discussions of any sort, political or otherwise, with his fellow residents who, in this informant's words, "were not taking our respective courses as seriously [as Norman]." In fact, says this same source, though "Herb got along well with his fellow residents . . ." he was not above "expressing contempt of some of their activities and opinions." Herbert stood out as an academic elitist. This same contemporary recalls that "Herb never thought 'dirty jokes' he heard were funny, but I can remember him more than once cackling all the way down the stairs to tell us something he had read in Catullus which was every bit as dirty and no more nor less humorous than the common room jokes which he affected to disdain."[15]

Such are the recollections of William Grant, of the Peterborough law firm of Grant and Carruthers, and a Victoria classmate of Herbert's, who also vividly recalls the circumstances of Norman going public with his politics which happened when he "converted" to Trotskyism. Grant was at the time a member of the League for Social Reconstruction and the Ontario CCF and therefore was in close contact with "the radical left," albeit as a social democrat and anti-communist. Grant recalls: "Herb had not shown any particular interest in politics and certainly hadn't identified himself with any political party or group until the last few weeks of the 1933 academic year. It was toward the end of that year, probably in the month of April, that Herb became intensely interested in a chap named Norman Knight who, if he was not the only one, was the most important Trotskyite among the students living in Burwash Residences. Norman [Knight] loaned Herb the autobiography of Leon Trotsky which Herb read with intense interest and which he discussed with Norman night after night in the corner of our common room. Herb then declared himself to be a Trotskyite though I don't know whether or not he ever applied for or was accepted as a member of that group."[16]

The point of Grant's recollection suggests that Herbert Norman made the transition to Trotskyism from Christian socialism through the mediation of one individual whom Herbert found "interesting," and through the intellectual medium of the Trotsky biography. This pattern would be repeated the following year at Cambridge when he fell in with Stalinists, but the core of Grant's story, the conversion, becomes even clearer in a lengthy letter Herbert wrote to his parents and Howard on 15 May 1933.

In this letter, he opens with an apology for "the long spell of silence" since his last letter (of early April, when he was meeting with Knight), offering as an excuse a claim that he had been "hypnotized by the opiate of study and exams" but says he now is well prepared to "enter the lists of friendly controversy—if treated with moderation, tolerance and humor—[about] . . . the two very weighty and convincing replies from Father and Howie" to "my [earlier] little excursion into historical criticism precipitated by the ferment of Marxism as interpreted by Trotsky."

Herbert begins by conceding to "Howie" a point about all humans, Russians included (here Herbert alludes to Howard's sarcasm), quite naturally "becoming drunk with [power]," of being incapable "of exercising power impartially." But he attacks his father's point about Trotsky's biased rendering of history. Norman, the future historian, argues, " *What history that maintains to be impartial is of any use at all?* . . . Of course Trotsky writes and interprets. If there were such a thing as an impartial History, it would be chronological lists of events—a bare, fruitless catalogue. It is the duty of a Historian to interpret this skeleton or scaffold which disappears in the completed building, or at least not trouble the reader with the wearisome list of mere events."

Norman makes his argument with a lengthy listing of the

world's great historians—Thucydides, Pliny, Cicero, Tacitus, Gibbon, Taine, etc— showing the bias in each case, before asserting that Trotsky is no different. Bias can be found in every case, he says, but the burden is on "you the reader to discover the historian's philosophy and to use it as a key or clue" to interpret history as a "stream of cause and effect." He explains the Marxian notion of cause and effect in terms of the Hegelian dialectic and makes the simple point that socialism is the effect of capitalism. Revolution, he says, is the necessary means to "induce the historically bankrupt classes [capitalists]" to admit "that their share in the historical process is now superfluous" and to give way to the succeeding class (proletariat). He quotes Trotsky on this point and cites the Bolshevik revolution as proof that revolution can happen only "when the overwhelming majority of the people" lend their support; *ergo,* all revolution is "essentially democratic," not to mention sanctified by *the* Historical Process.

Herbert concedes to his brother "the present pitiful situation of the peasantry in Russia," and opines that under Stalin "the growing bureaucracy will forget the *end* of revolution, which is Man, for the means, which is toil and discipline, often entailing cruel deprivation and sacrifice." But that is Stalin's doing, not Trotsky's. Trotsky "is a humanist in the original sense of the word—I could quote him a hundred times to prove it." A "fanatic," as his father alleges, yes, says Herbert, but adds, "if any man is true to his ideals, he is a fanatic, but then so is every saint of the church a fanatic; every man loyal to his conscience is a fanatic. . . . Trotsky is a fanatic in that sense, and was driven out of Russia rather than surrender what he believed to be his Historic role."

Norman's paean to Trotsky is based not only on what Trotsky represents but also on what he struggles against, namely, fascism. "Socialism is receiving set-backs on every hand. It is highly possible if for lack of brilliant leaders like Lenin and Trotsky, . . . that under the banner of fascism we will return to medieval peonage—each man kept strictly in his class . . . with big business ruling supreme, supported by Hitler, a military dictatorship. That is the choice as I see it:

Socialism even by Revolution if necessary, if not so much the better, or a retrogression to the Dark Ages in which civilization may wallow indefinitely."

The choice was relevant to Canada, Norman argued as a Trotskyist, since "capitalism is now pure stupidity." "Democracy as we know it is surely passing, . . . capitalism is in its decay and can no longer use the mask of democracy, [hence] it is gradually dropping the pretense. Dictatorships in the U.S. (enlightened more or less under Roosevelt), reactionary under the Bennetts and the Fascists—such is the trend, no place left for true democracy."

Capitalism, or rather its failure in the Great Depression, was prompting Herbert to ask questions that had to be regarded as sacrilege in his father's and brother's eyes, though they undoubtedly understood and appreciated the humanist impulse that lay underneath Herbert's radical phraseology. He asked, "In the light of human misery, does it pay to be born?" His political lament continues: "When men suffer in a state like capitalism today, which has passed its usefulness, their suffering is stupid, like the blind and senseless butchery of a flock of sheep. It is pitiful. Under a socialist state like Russia (before it drifts into bureaucracy, or before they lose sight of the *end,* that the State is for Man, not man for the state), then man will still suffer, but his suffering will be in the realm of the *tragic* live suffering of a creature who is proudly conscious of his destiny and possibilities."

Norman *believed* that socialist revolution alone could show man "the sign on the road to self-realization," but he *knew* that "the prospects here in Canada are bleak. To speak for revolution like Russia is madness—it will drive the timid, wavering liberals into conservatism and together they will crush out radicalism of left wingers by the crude methods in vogue in Italy and Germany." In trying to convince his father and brother, he cited Reinhold Niebuhr's recent (1932) book, *Moral Man and Immoral Society,* as an example of "a soul with an incandescent Christianity" who had come to the same conclusion about the necessity of revolution for putting an end to the worst abuses of "the acquisitive society in power

[that] fights to preserve its privileges." But he emphasized that Niebuhr's analysis concerned the U.S. and not Canada. In Canada "these are questions that, . . . if treated frankly in public, land you in jail under Section 98."

But, as usual, he felt compelled to reassure his mother: "In spite of my earnest attempt at defending Trotsky and the Russian Revolution, mother, you have no need to fear that your son may be run to earth under Section 98. . . ." It was, after all, exam time, and pragmatic, overworked Herbert confessed that "I am feeling very washed out and anything but revolutionary." He complained of insomnia, that the "exams got my goat," and that he worried about trying to stay out of financial debt. Also, as always, he asked after his mother's health.

Norman's entrée into radical politics was obviously incomplete and superficial. His adoption of Trotskyism appears almost whimsical, the product of a personal attraction to its chief, if not only, representative at the college, and of an emotional and intellectual affinity with the humanist aspects of the "doctrine." Perhaps, too, he was drawn to the doctrine because the professing of it set him even further apart from his peers, for whom he openly showed contempt, and served to reinforce his self-perception as being one of the intellectual elite (who, albeit, had high praise for "humility"). Certainly his childhood upbringing lent itself to a self-image of superiority, and no less certainly his success in academics—attributable to being older than his classmates, more widely read, and probably innately brighter—contributed to the intellectual alienation he experienced.

Evidence for Norman's conscious standing apart from his peers goes beyond their observations. In a letter written in early 1932, he pontificates for his parents' amusement on "modern music", especially jazz. "Some jazz, if played consistently, is tolerable." But, speaking of his housemates in Burwash, "they have such classics as 'I want to be bad' (bad ba-a-a-a-a-a- stringed in nasal-ululations) sung by a boop-a-doop girl, whoever she is." 'I'm crying because I'm in someone else's arms' I think is the theme." Those interested in jazz, he labels "boys," and complains of being reproached by them "or commiserated for lacking in contemporary taste in music," whenever he is so bold as to recommend a "change in the variety of pieces sung, played, droned, intoned, bellowed, sobbed, groaned, hissed, scraped, scratched, blared, blatted, belched, and tintinabulated." Proud of his vocabulary, and no less proud to be "above" the ordinary cut of admirers of mass culture, Norman intones, "Progress! Civilization! One's voice cracks with sarcasm."[17]

He saw himself as different from the others, and he wanted to be seen as being different. The best example of this point concerns his courtship of Irene Clark, whom he married in 1935. In his last year at Victoria University Herbert stood six feet tall and weighed an athletic 150 pounds; Irene was no more than five feet four and a petite 110 pounds. She was described by her future in-laws in terms identical to their description of Herbert's mother: "shy, retiring, and very private." She remains so today. The one and only view of their courtship that Irene Norman will give today is of this large, blondish, athletic Classics major, who, as it happened, thought of himself as a Trotskyist, wooing his shy beloved by reading romantic Latin and Greek verse, sometimes in the original, while they sat together alone on a campus bench.[18]

While there exists absolutely no reason to expect that in his private life Herbert should have conformed to a sort of Thirties bohemianism, that is, to behave in a manner consistent with his radical political views, there is reason to suspect that his elitist behavior, not to mention his social standoffishness and his almost apolitical devotion to scholarly activities for most of his college career (1929–33), worked against genuine conversion first to Christian socialism, *à la* the CCF, and then to Trotskyism. There is, in short, something of the political dilettante about his convictions at that time, dabbling first in one doctrine before cavalierly throwing himself into another.

Given the "strength" of his professed convictions as expressed in letters to family members, it seems especially odd that Norman did not participate to a greater extent, either intellectually or publicly, in the great social and political debate then sweeping Canadian politics in the form of Woodsworth versus Bennett. As Herbert himself indicates, Victoria College, Woodsworth's alma mater and center of Methodist socialist-democratic activity in Upper Canada, if not all of Canada, was in the forefront of radical organizing, to wit, the founding of the League of Social Reconstruction (LSR) in 1932 by several of Norman's professors, including F. R. Scott and E. A. Havelock. In them and their work, with the *Canadian Forum* serving as an unofficial political organ, Fabianism became the preferred doctrine during Norman's time at Victoria, yet in his letters very few references are made to these political currents or their representatives. Norman's hero of 1932, Woodsworth, even became honorary president of the LSR, though Herbert did not bother to report this news to his parents.

One must, therefore, conclude that as late as the spring of 1933, Herbert was an "armchair radical," one whose basic philosophy was humanist, which in the midst of the chaos of capitalism, the Great Depression, caused him to look for alternative political paradigms, ones that might offer social and economic salvation to the disinherited. First social democracy, then Trotskyism appealed to him, but chiefly only in intellectual and emotional terms: his priorities still rested in academic achievement which remained ongoing and potentially fulfilling after he learned that he had been awarded a Kylie Scholarship for study at Trinity College, Cambridge University, Cambridge, England, beginning the fall after graduation. *Deus ex machina*, the opportunity to study in Cambridge meant a prolongation of his first love—learning—and a postponement of any decision concerning a future vocation. Not surprisingly, the issue of finding work, of choosing a vocation, had never been broached in any family correspondence; the family seemed to have reached a tacit understanding that his future work would be a continuation of his past achievements in academics.[19] He remained the consummate student, the budding intellectual. And he could do no better than Cambridge, "beautiful peaceful Cambridge, one of the most favored environments in the world for intellectuals," writes Margot Heinemann, Cambridge communist and lover of John Cornford, Herbert's future mentor in the ways and means of Stalinism.[20]

The young Canadian arrived in Cambridge on 2 October 1933, and a week later he wrote to his family that he "was mightily impressed by my first view of Trinity College, the spacious Great Court, the cloisters opening out of Nevile's Court, and the view across the lawn and gardens from the New Court." How could he fail but to be impressed; Cambridge *does* nearly rhyme with privilege in the dazzled minds of anyone who has seen Trinity and neighboring King's and St. John's colleges. After Victoria, certainly one of the loveliest of campuses in North America, only a place like Trinity could impress. Trinity is closer in appearance to a medieval cathedral, with its vast, open courts, its manicured lawns, its imposing portals of rounded arches built of fine stone, its towering beech trees that pompously line the pebbled pathways, its quiet River Cam that winds gently through the spacious grounds, the open courtyards posted with "No Entry" signs directed at nonmembers, its Wren Library of unequalled architectural refinement, the Clock Tower, the Great Gate with its four-story towers on either side, restrictive and monolithic, austere monuments advertising that only the brightest might enter. The school of Newton, Macaulay, and Thackeray, Trinity College reminded its students that though the topography is mostly flat, in the words of F. L. Lucas, much of it lies intellectually at the glacial altitudes of the higher brow.[21]

Norman had "arrived." He was thrilled by Trinity's radical intellectual climate: "Trinity seems to be a very cosmopolitan place and has a reputation for radicalism not confined to students only. One of the History dons has only one portrait in his room, that of Lenin!" Deeply impressed by such open displays of radicalism, and no less deeply impressionable, his brief "conversion" to Trotskyism notwithstanding, Norman seemed to feel that he had entered into his element, that he had become part of a larger political society that not only could accommodate a superior intellect of the sort he boasted, but would even welcome and embrace it. At Cambridge he felt ideological affinity with the growing body of radical leftist students who openly organized in support of the Soviet Union and in opposition to Nazi Germany. Indeed, within two weeks of arriving in Cambridge, as he began meeting a number of Cambridge Stalinists, Norman divorced himself from what he now called "infantile Canadian Marxism." He wrote to family members in Japan that he had to come to believe "that many of the young students who claimed to be Marxists, especially in Toronto, not only knew nothing about what was at stake, but did immense harm to the cause they were supposed to be backing by giving Marxism a slant which is totally unjustified."[22]

However, a simple rejection of the old as a necessary precondition to adopting the new, in this instance Stalinism, was not sufficient for complete acceptance by those Stalinists who defined and led the communist movement at Cambridge. By class, nationality, ideology, and experience, Norman remained an outsider, a poor 'scholarship boy' from Canada, the son of a missionary, with the tainted status of "Affiliated Student" and "Dominion and Colonial Exhibitioner." Moreover, he was not permitted, nor could he afford, to live in college but was instead boarded in a second-floor flat in a modest duplex bungalow located a good mile from the center of the college. From his isolated flat at 17 Kimberly Road (which he shared with another Canadian during his first year), Herbert had to walk or bicycle through Midsummer Common, and up Jesus Lane to Bridge Street before reaching campus. His roommate was an advanced research student in the Sciences, a Queen's University graduate, who had little in common with Herbert.[23]

Norman's letters indicate that he had more in common with his landlord, Mr. Bell, who admitted to his tenant that he was a communist. Herbert notes in admiration of Bell, "I perceive he is extremely unlikely to be deceived by press, radio or other bourgeois propaganda, is a deep sympathizer with Russia and hates Ramsay MacDonald [Prime Minister of National Coalition Government, 1931–35] as only a communist can." Also in Bell's favor, "He is a funny chap, English to the core, with English outlook, a strong family man, fond of wife and child." He cites landlord Bell authoritatively as a reliable social commentator regarding the "strange phenomenon" of churchmen "holding communist or left-wing socialist views." Norman was clearly amazed that ordinary working people, like Bell, could join with clergymen in an open embrace of communism: "It is certainly an agreeable surprise to find men in positions of little or no influence who will not associate themselves with reactionaries."[24]

For Norman, being an outsider at Victoria University had been no psychological burden because the choice had been a conscious one, made in respect of his superior intellect and studious habits, and probably as well because of his age and more philosophical bent. At Cambridge, however, he could hardly claim superior intellect—his exam scores demonstrated this [25]—nor could he claim to possess greater wisdom or philosophical insight than his new-found "comrades" who, he quickly learned, had been pondering the issues posed by Marxism, social inequality, fascism, and so on with a greater degree of urgency for a much longer time, simply by virtue of first-hand exposure to these lingering effects of Europe's contentious past. Herbert, for instance, in his first letter home, on 9 October 1933, remarks on how impressed he was on meeting two "very lively chaps who have [just] spent the summer in [Nazi] Germany; they are Left-wing socialists so they became quite friendly."

As the latter quote suggests, the Canadian student's entrée into Cambridge society was made possible by claiming ideological affinity. He overcame the factors that separated him from the more urbane and cosmopolitan sophisticates of Cambridge by identifying with their radical political views. Ideology served as his social bridge. He wrote, "It seems if one has read Strachey's *Coming Struggle for Power* and speaks highly of it, then you are granted a sesame into their company."[26] Herbert sought inclusion into their society, tried hard to demonstrate his worthiness, and was rewarded by *partial* induction.

That Norman's admittance into left-wing Cambridge society was restricted is demonstrated by his letters and by testimony of those fully admitted. In an early letter home, he mentions that Lorie Tarshis, the former Victoria student one year senior to him and a devoted Keynesian who dabbled in Marxist studies, had introduced him "around" to a number of leftists.[27] One person whom Herbert met through Tarshis was the New Zealander E. C. B. Maclaurin, who operated a small left-wing bookstore in Cambridge and who was later killed in Spain fighting against the Fascists. Another he met early on was a fellow in the College in Mathematics named Ursell whom Norman admired for his refusal to sit at High Table with conservative dons.

These introductions to communists came at Norman's urgings. Tarshis himself was not intimately involved with many left-wingers and, in fact, was surprised at Norman's "Marxist leanings," regarding him as "a classical scholar whose interest ended with the fourth century B.C." Because his politics were Keynesian and Labourite, Tarshis claims, he usually "was frozen out of conversations" between communists. But Tarshis does recall a friendship between Maclaurin and Canadian Robert Bryce,[28] and it was likely through Bryce or Maclaurin that Norman was introduced to "the inner group" of Cambridge communists.

Who were they? T. E. B. Howarth in *Cambridge Between Two Wars* identifies the principal characters in the inner group as Guy Burgess, John Cornford, Victor Klugmann, Donald Maclean, Victor Kiernan, Eric Hobsbawm, and several others, most of whom were active as members of the Cambridge University Socialist Club and who shared intellectual, as opposed to emotional, conversions to communism. Of these mentioned, Tarshis recalls that Norman became especially friendly with John Cornford, son of the famous Cambridge University Plato scholar, F .M. Cornford. Norman also became friendly with Victor Kiernan, as Kiernan himself relates.[29] Likely it was through Kiernan that Norman met many of the others mentioned above, although not one of their names, with the exception of Cornford and Maclaurin, is mentioned in Herbert's private correspondence.

Among this inner group, of course, Burgess and Maclean later became (in)famous for spying for the Soviet Union, along with Kim Philby, who left Cambridge the spring before Norman's arrival, and Anthony Blunt who had come up in 1926. Blunt stayed on after graduation as first a graduate student and then as a teaching fellow; he was on a sabbatical leave during Norman's first year at Cambridge. Burgess had matriculated in 1932 and Maclean the year before. Blunt and Burgess, along with Michael Straight, an American who went up in 1934, also belonged to that elitist Cambridge group known as the Apostles (neither Maclean nor Philby belonged) which, *after* Norman's departure from Cambridge in the spring of 1935, served, in the words of H.R. Trevor-Roper, as "the envelope for an even more secret [more secret than the Apostles] cell: the crypto-communist recruiters of Russian spies."[30]

Within the inner group, there were of course several who were recruited by the Soviets. Burgess recruited Blunt in late 1935, and Blunt recruited Straight in early 1937. Elitist Apostles tended to recruit their own kind. Klugmann and Kiernan, on the other hand, had no desire to be Apostolic, preferring instead to work in the open, frequently among the working classes in the case of Klugmann, and "Third World" nationals in the case of Kiernan. Public-minded political organizers rather than secretive espionage agents, they regarded themselves as products of "the decade of commitment," and, in Klugmann's words, found "their future alongside, and under the leadership of, the working class," whether native or foreign.[31] Cornford was a more flamboyant variant of their "type." Poet and militant, intellectually precocious and prodigiously charismatic, Cornford gave of himself totally to the Cambridge University Socialist Society, and then to the Spanish struggle which cost him his life.

Norman, too, was public about his commitment. A self-described "disciple" of Cornford and a colleague of Kiernan,

Herbert entered the Communist Party, in his own words, under the "tutelage" of Cornford and in a spirit similar to that which led Victor Kiernan to organize colonial peoples.[32] Norman's modest, colonial background, despite the sort of elitist pretensions he showed as an undergraduate in Canada, disqualified him for any serious consideration for membership in the Apostles, and his short, two-year stay at Cambridge minimized his chances of being targeted as a potential mole by the Soviets; as mentioned, Soviet recruitment by proxy did not seriously commence operations until after Norman had left Cambridge. And what was he, after all, between 1933–35, but a Trotskyist in transition, an outsider seeking social and political acceptance, a rough Canadian Marxist attempting ideological refinement, a twenty-four-year-old willing to follow the directions of nineteen-year-old John Cornford?

Tarshis recalls that Norman, during his first year, "seemed to spend a great deal of time in his own rooms (a fairly long walk from the College)." In his second year at Trinity, according to Victor Kiernan, Norman's only Party work consisted of "trying to attract some of the Indians towards the Party," at which he was successful and which Kiernan took over following Herbert's departure. But other than joining in a "hunger march" in 1934, that is *all* that Kiernan recalls Herbert doing.[33] Christopher Cornford, John's brother, and James Cornford, John's son, both with access to John's private correspondence, notes, diaries, etc., say that Herbert Norman is not once mentioned. Similarly, interviews in England with six of Norman's Cambridge contemporaries, all of whom moved in leftist circles in the early Thirties, prompted recollection of Norman in only one case. H. S. Corran, now of Dublin, recalls meeting with the Canadian at a restaurant called the Blue Barn (since razed), which was one of several "rendezvous" for Marxist students to discuss politics, and even then Corran recalls that he regarded Norman as a mere "sympathizer."[34]

Yet if Herbert Norman was not a central figure in the communist movement at Cambridge, he was at least a "peripheral character" as claimed by Chapman Pincher in a recent interview.[35] Norman is similarly remembered by Margot Heinemann, by Cornford intimate Michael Straight, and by Tarshis.

Heinemann recalls "quite clearly meeting Herbert Norman several times during 1934–35, my last year at Cambridge, when I was a member of the Communist Party. I recall him as a slim, spectacled, fair, soft-spoken, intelligent and charming boy and a good friend of John Cornford; and I'm afraid that is absolutely all I do remember." In a more recent interview with Professor Heinemann in Cambridge, she recalled that a likely setting for meeting Norman was the Pem Café, where the Socialist Society held occasional Sunday afternoon teas. Or, she suggested, the college room of James Klugmann, where once or twice a year all the communists in the college would meet. But in any case, her testimony, or lack thereof, seems to validate Norman's peripheral status, even in relationship to his mentor John Cornford.[36]

Michael Straight, the privileged American "Apostle" who was raised in England, later served as the editor of *The New Republic.* Straight knew Norman at Cambridge, though in his autobiography, *After Long Silence,* the Canadian rates just one sentence and then Straight gets the facts wrong. But in correspondence with the author (most of which will be treated later), Straight writes, "I did know Herbert Norman at Trinity, but not well. I have a visual image of him, which may or may not be accurate. I would have known him, I assume, as a member of the Trinity College cell; but then only for a short time. I became a member of that cell in 1935. He left Cambridge, you say, in 1935."[37] Straight's uncertain recollection suggests that their acquaintance was very brief and limited and, indeed, the remainder of Straight's remarks about Norman consists of a series of assumptions about whom the two likely knew in common. But again, since Straight's secret testimony to the FBI in the early 1960s led to the implication of Norman and, most important, Anthony Blunt, I shall return later to a discussion of Straight's opinions.

Lorie Tarshis, of course, did know Herbert well, and testifies that "Herbert went around with communists, but I never heard him say he was one. But on a probability scale of ten, I'd say that Herbert was a nine or ten." Tarshis also remarks that he had seen Norman in the company of John Cornford and shared with him the feeling that Cornford "had a sense of destiny" that attracted followers. Tarshis also believes that Norman's attraction to Cornford meant that his conversion to communism was "a very emotional conversion." No doubt this is partly true, though it is equally likely that motivations behind most "conversions" were mixed. James Klugmann, for example, according to Heinemann, "read his way in" to the Party;[38] Herbert, we have seen, found his readings of Trotsky, Strachey, and others persuasive in clarifying his own ideological leanings, but no doubt in many cases, emotion and reason worked together to effect "conversion."

Such seems to have been the case with Herbert Norman. He wrote to Howard on 21 October 1933, "I am actually experiencing that intellectual rebirth which you so much appreciated in your sojourn here," referring to Howard's experiences in Cambridge several years earlier. In Howard's case, however, "rebirth" was largely mediated by stirring lessons taught in theology classrooms. Herbert, in contrast, gained absolutely no intellectual support, let alone ideological, for his conversion from his conservative tutor, Mr. Kitson-Clark. Norman described him as "a stiff Anglican but quite friendly," as "bumptious, jolly, a bit fussy, very English, . . . and deliberately or unconsciously mixes up Canadian and American universities in a most irritating way, and generally considers all *colonials* and Americans as half-civilized children." More to his liking, though again not ideologically supportive, was his supervisor, Walter Runciman, specialist in Byzantine civilization. Norman described him as "a very queer chap. He is extraordinarily handsome, the sort of man whose face is so delicately chisseled [sic] that you feel he should be a woman. He is extremely effeminate both in tastes and manners." So "painfully shy," Herbert says of Runciman, that "it all gets on my nerves."[39]

It was not, therefore, Norman's instructors and their classes that served as midwife to his "intellectual rebirth," but rather his extracurricular political activities, and the leftists who organized them. Early during his first term he writes of accompanying "two chaps from Toronto whom I knew before coming here to the Cambridge University Socialist Club" in order to listen to author Allan Hutt address the issue of the "Condition of the Working Class in Britain." Norman writes of finding this lecture and the evidence that Hutt cited as convincing, demonstrating that "England's claim to being a fair democratic and balanced polity a bit of a flop." Using Canada's Article 98 as a comparison, Norman cites Hutt's contention that in England "power is passing quietly into the hands of a small capitalist caste whose laws are clearly reactionary and are directed at maintaining power at all costs." He accepts Hutt's contention that English secret police "shadow all known communists or left-wing socialists of prominence."[40]

After-hours events such as these, and the left-wing associations he made as a result, were leading Norman into a more mature understanding of Marx, or so he claimed. He stated that he categorically rejected "bourgeois theorists" for being ideologically blind to the meaning of genuine historical change. "It is [bourgeois] thought, not history, that is unreasonable." Only Marx's thinking, he argued, "realistically" interpreted history. "I am finding," he wrote, "that the study of history reveals more and more wealth and insight when the keen edge of the dialectical tool, such as Marx's, is applied to pry open the mainsprings of man's institutions and psychology." While bourgeois theorists see ideas "as some suprahistorical *deus ex machina*," Marxists correctly see ideas as "facts, e.g., as property relations in historical evolution." Such an idea is grounded in empirical reality and not, as bourgeois theorists would have us believe, "invoked from transcendental skies to shape historical plot." Marxist history is "causal," bourgeois history is illusory; Marxist history is not mechanistic or deterministic because it recognizes change as a product of contradictions; bourgeois history is mechanistic and deterministic because it employs idealistic logic to explain change.[41]

Norman was too much the intellectual to plunge into a Stalinist conversion based simply on emotional attachment to particular people, and he was still too much the son of a missionary to reveal the full depths of his conversion to his parents or even to his brother Howard. Only after John Cornford's death in early 1937, when Herbert was studying at Harvard, would he reveal the depth of his commitment to Stalinism during his Cambridge years. Grief, outrage and the guilt of a survivor joined forces to compel him to tell Howard, and only Howard, that "I was influenced by him [Cornford] more than any of my friends there [at Cambridge] and under his tutelage I entered the party. I not only respected him and his gifts, both intellectual and political, but loved him."[42]

Norman returned to Canada directly after receiving a B.A. in History from Trinity in early summer 1935, and might have then been approached for the first time by the Department of External Affairs to work as a language officer in Japan. Certainly, in 1935, Dr. O. D. Skelton of External first mentioned Norman's name as a potential recruit.[43] Nevertheless, Norman instead chose to serve as a Classics instructor at Upper Canada College while doing graduate studies in history at the University of Toronto. One likely reason for making the choice that he did, a fact made clearer once he began studying at Harvard, was that his reading ability in Japanese language had become more than simply rusty; another was his desire to pursue his inquiries into a Marxist notion of history; but perhaps the most compelling reason was his marriage to Irene Clark on 31 August 1935: with marriage came more serious considerations of a career that might lead to a stable lifestyle. Incidentally, the best man at their wedding was Charles P. Holmes, a close childhood friend from Norman's Canadian Academy days. Like Herbert, Holmes had become, in his friend's words, "an ardent left-wing socialist", a fact that Norman had noted in a letter to his parents written while he was at Cambridge. Not incidentally, according to a later FBI report, by 1950 Charles Holmes had become a member of the Communist Party.[44]

Herbert began graduate studies at Harvard in Japanese Studies in the autumn of 1936. We know a number of interesting details about him at this time because his application for a Rockefeller Foundation fellowship, which he was awarded, was passed on by the president of the Foundation, Dean Rusk (later Secretary of State for Presidents Kennedy and Johnson and a Vietnam "hawk"), through an intermediary to the Senate Subcommittee on Internal Security (SISS) in early 1957, when Herbert Norman was being investigated for the second time for alleged communist loyalties.[45]

Some biographical data about Norman, according to his 11 May 1936 Rockefeller application: he stated his religion as "Christian"; in the section on language competency, he claimed proficiency in French, German, Latin, Greek, and Japanese, though only speaking ability in his childhood language; he said his blood pressure was 120/60, and that he had never suffered any serious childhood ailments, clearly omitting reference to his tuberculosis; he reported astigmatism in both eyes, said he had had an appendectomy in February 1936, stood six feet tall and weighed 150 pounds. His references included Kitson-Clark of Cambridge and Professor Havelock of Victoria.

From the annual reports filed by the Rockefeller Foundation, and again passed on to SISS, we learn that in the first year of his M.A. studies, Norman took courses in both Japanese and Chinese languages, in Chinese history, Chinese historiography, and Japanese history. His professors included Elisseeff, Ware, and Gardner, and based on the strength of their recommendations and "on the strength of his work," he was permitted to write the M.A. exam at the conclusion of his first year. He had earned straight As in his courses. Because his work was of superior quality, he was admitted into the doctoral program the following fall and his fellowship was renewed, thereby making it easier for him to pass up an External Affairs invitation to take the foreign service exam.[46]

Norman did not let graduate studies interfere too much with politics. Although away from the intellectually leftist and heady atmosphere of England, he nevertheless pursued political activities consonant with his Stalinist beliefs. While still in Canada, in 1935–36, he had joined and then served as secretary of a pro-Chinese Communist Party group, Canadian Friends of the Chinese People, and when he came to Harvard he continued his pro-CCP work by writing for the newly formed radical journal, *Amerasia.* He wrote, according to one of the few accurate FBI reports, five articles for *Amerasia* while at Harvard, and he participated in a related, left-wing organization, the League Against War and Fascism.[47] Probably through one or both of these organizations, he met other young radical professors and graduate students who together formed an informal study group dedicated to exploring various contemporary social and political issues from a Marxist point of view. According to his old Victoria and Trinity friend, Lorie Tarshis, who in 1936 was teaching economics at Tufts University, the group included Paul Sweezy, John K. Galbraith, Tsuru Shigeto, and Robert Bryce, besides Norman and Tarshis. (It should be noted that Galbraith does not recall participating and neither does Sweezy, although FBI reports do name Sweezy.)[48]

For evidence of what Norman's private thoughts were during the Harvard years, two sources exist: secret FBI reports written much later and based on interviews with several of Norman's Harvard professors and acquaintances, and his letters to Howard. As might be expected, the latter are the more informative; the former will be touched upon in due course.

Between 1936 and 1938, like the vast majority of intellectuals at this time, Herbert Norman was emotionally consumed by the fundamental issues raised by the Spanish Civil War. He exercised self-restraint on the issue when writing to his parents—"I feel so strongly about it, I will never stop if I get going on it now"—but he clearly opened up when writing to Howard.[49] Several of Herbert's Cambridge friends were fighting against the fascist Franco as part of the International Brigade, so he kept close account of the press reports of the daily fighting. Equally clearly from his notes, while Herbert suffered deep feelings of guilt because he was physically removed and safe from the struggle, yet he felt proud that his former comrades were sacrificing themselves in the fight against fascism. Guilt and pride combined to produce an apotheosis of Stalin and a defense of the political purges going on at this time, justified in Herbert's mind because the Soviet Union was actively assisting the Republican government in its battle against fascism. The Spanish experience, in short, legitimized his allegiance to Stalinism. The clearest example was his letter of 4 February 1937, to Howard.

The letter reports the death "of a very close associate and companion of mine . . . , Maclaurin, of St. John's College, who was killed outside Madrid in the first days of the furious assault on it." Herbert describes Maclaurin as a "brilliant mathematician" [he describes most of his radical friends as "brilliant"] whom he knew "through political meetings etc. in Cambridge and moved leftward together at the same speed and with the same sort of hesitancy and finally reaching the same goal at the same time."

Before continuing, note that Norman's credibility here is open to doubt. First, Maclaurin, who was better known to Kiernan, had been a teacher in York, England, before being fired for participation in "some tipsy frolic." Kiernan also notes that Maclaurin was operating a bookstore in Cambridge when Herbert was a student there; John Cornford's son writes that the bookstore was located near St. John's College, on Rose Crescent. Tarshis, who also knew Maclaurin, confirms his status as a bookstore operator, and, incidentally, as one of those who converted out of emotion, going so far as to marry a working-class woman for reasons of principle.[50] In other words, Herbert's terse description of Maclaurin tends to romanticize the man, perhaps even to the point of misrepresenting who he was, likely for Howard's benefit and perhaps in order to make more credible the grief over Maclaurin's death that he next discusses: "It is difficult and futile for me to describe my feelings when I heard the news. I think both you and I are attuned so closely that you can imagine what I felt—a mixture of shame, pride, and rage—shame at my own safe and easy life; pride in sharing in a political cause and in a love for justice and humanity in common with him and his kind; and rage at the complacency and cunning with which British, American, and French 'democracy' regard German intentions as on par with volunteers in the International Brigade and at the disgusting speed with which Roosevelt and Congress rushed through legislation to prevent hard-pressed and half-equipped Spanish people [from] getting a few pitiful boatloads of secondhand clothes, airplanes, and munitions—all in the name of neutrality."[51]

Shame, pride, and rage: emotions that but a few years earlier Herbert would have scorned, preferring as he once did the value of human reason and dispassionate analysis, even of the sort that permits an intellect of his sort the mild hypocrisy of earning straight As with Rockefeller support whilst privately decrying the "democratic" enemies of "justice and humanity." Yet now the guilt of the survivor and the despair of the helpless onlooker had overtaken him. "I guess," he told his attuned brother, "we Normans are a bit on the sentimental side, but I find myself wondering every once in a while how Maclaurin died, and whether I could have stood the same sort of thing they are facing daily in or near Madrid."[52]

Herbert himself knew the answer to his "wondering" and confessed his feelings of "helplessness" to Howard: "I have thought from time to time very seriously of going to Spain . . . . but I have come to the conclusion that my complete helplessness in things military, etc., would make me of little or no use to the International Brigade." And then he confronts two different facts that in dialectical fashion informed his thinking during the years ahead. First, "I have never discussed [going to Spain] with Irene . . . ." Herbert kept many of his emotional impulses and political attitudes to himself; his spouse, he felt, should be spared the effects of his own insecurities and should be protected from the emotional ravages of politics; Herbert was of the "old school" in nuptial relations: sharing a life together need not involve sharing private thoughts. Similar to the "dialectic of marriage," there was the dialectic of emotion versus reason. In the case of the Spanish Civil War, Herbert confided to his brother: "But the emotional pull to go is very strong and I really am deterred as much by reason of "common sense" and all that means as the above consideration [helplessness in things military] which is something of an emotional compensation salve."[53]

It seems that Herbert coped with the feelings of helplessness and guilt over Spain by coming to the aid of the defenders of Spanish republicans, the Soviets. Now a radically reconstructed Trotskyist, he took to the defense of the Purge Trials then going on in the Soviet Union. He found the Soviet persecution of the Trotskyists justifiable by the "damning evidence" of "plots" to undermine "the building of socialism." Speaking of the Trotskyists, he writes, "It is only too clear that they never for a moment abandoned their bitter hatred of the policy of building socialism [in one country]." Herbert accepts the Stalinist line that the Trotskyists were guilty of "secret sabotage, terrorism, and alliances with the worst foes of socialism—Fascism. The calm insolence of their confessions, the cynicism with which they regarded the trust placed in them by the Soviet Government, was a nauseating spectacle." Further, Herbert attacks western writers who condemned the trials as "medieval witch trials" or instances of "primitive blood sacrifices" as "ridiculous," worthy only of "bourgeois ideologues" who cannot accept the "overwhelming but disgusting truth."[54]

As always, Herbert vented his private thoughts and frustrations to Howard, seeking in the process self-validation by convincing his brother of the correctness of his own ideological beliefs. From the correspondence of this time, it is clear that Howard needed little or no convincing regarding the moral lessons of the Spanish struggle; he confessed to Herbert that were it not for family responsibilities, he, too, would join the Canadian commander of the International Brigade, General Kepler, and fight for democracy and against Fascism. But it is equally clear that Howard disagreed with his brother's assessment of the Purge Trials. Thus Herbert tried to buttress his arguments in support of the purges by sending Howard magazine and newspaper clippings; he even volunteered to give Howard a subscription to the Marxist journal, *New Masses*.[55]

Herbert also shared with Howard information about his acquaintances at Harvard. He wrote about a "Japanese friend here with similar views to mine." No name is mentioned, but the Japanese friend is identified as "the brains behind *Science and Society,* a Marxist quarterly recently started by University men interested in Marxism." The friend was Tsuru Shigeto, who in 1957 would betray Norman in testimony before SISS. But twenty years earlier, Herbert described Tsuru as "one of the most learned and able Marxists I have ever met . . . . He is a paradigm of what a Communist ought to be and ought not to be." Herbert says that "he is a great help to me because we can discuss Japanese politics with complete freedom and understanding and he is amazingly sharp and cutting in his ability to elucidate some involved and murky situation."[56] Indeed, Tsuru more than anyone else provided Herbert with direction and research help in writing his doctoral dissertation, which then became his first book.

In February 1937 the emotional wound caused by Maclaurin's death was reopened when Norman got news of the death of John Cornford. Cornford had been killed the previous December in Spain. "For the past three weeks," he wrote to Howard on 3 March, "I've been trying to shake the gloom that has settled on me after receiving news of the death of the best friend I had in Cambridge, John Cornford. It was a much more severe blow than Maclaurin whom I knew well but not intimately like John. I was influenced by him more than any of my friends there and under his tutelage I entered the party . . . . He was a man of such rare gifts that I firmly believe he would soon have been a guiding personality in the revolutionary movement. But I miss the friend even more than the political educator."

Herbert's reaction to Cornford's death was different from that to Maclaurin's. He indulged in less self-denigrating introspection and instead dwelt more on positive attempts to address survivor guilt. He told Howard that he was setting aside "a small percent" of his Rockefeller stipend each month for the anti-Fascist forces in Spain, and also claimed to "have been collecting for Spain (food, clothes, money, etc.)." He

nonetheless found it necessary to confess, "I feel pretty useless and futile in comparison to those [fighting] in this
conflict."[57]

Herbert worshipped the brave men fighting in Spain; they
were his gods, communism was his theology, defending them
was his mission. He saw their greater glory in a zero-sum
relationship with Howard's god, church, and mission, and
in his lengthy lament of Cornford's death, he made this difference between the two brothers clearer than ever before.
Herbert used a letter from his father (quoted in Chapter 1)
as the strategic medium for conveying his message. After
asserting that he respected his father but could not accept the
notion that "preaching Christ is the highest endeavor of human life," Herbert stretches Howard's credulity when he
adds, "I tried to avoid polemics in my reply [to his father's
autobiographical letter] and rather foolishly enclosed the
obituary of John Cornford and Maclaurin, as evidence that
whatever idealism, etc. Christians possessed has not only
ceased to be their monopoly (which it never was), but that
the real standard-bearer for humanity, for liberty, and for
man's right to develop freely is communism."[58]

Herbert felt the need to choose between Christ and communism, and he had made his choice; but because of his
background he felt obliged to repudiate the Church without
denouncing its well-intentioned representatives. He wrote,
"I feel I should tell you how father's letter affected me and
how strongly I feel about the role of the church as a waster
of healthy human ideals."[59] Communism alone embodied
"healthy human ideals" —humanity, liberty, and the right
to develop freely. The church, the church of his father, of
his brother, of his once flawless hero J. S. Woodsworth, had
wrongly and arrogantly attempted to monopolize human
idealism.

Yet so deeply had he committed himself, he was not content simply to attack his "opponents'" position; he also had
to defend his own. He harked back to a remark Howard had
"made quite a while ago," about a fear that socialism "as
exemplified in the Soviet Union will dry up idealism." Citing

the warnings of Lenin and Stalin, Herbert concedes that socialism in its early stages of development is endangered by a
self-aggrandising bureaucracy and that the "human element,"
man's "hankering for power," can imperil the realization of
socialist goals. But that is all Herbert would concede, as he
proceeds to defend socialism by invoking the recent example
of "Soviet *ius*," Soviet justice as "vindicated" in the Purge
Trials. He argues that the very existence of Trotskyism for
so many years demonstrated the Soviet tolerance of different
"parties," which should not, in his view, be allowed to operate as the "state withers away" into greater democracy.
Democracy need not require plural political parties. "I think,"
he writes, "political parties are only political agents or parliamentary representatives of various classes in society," and
as the Soviet Union "approaches classless society," the existence of differing parties becomes contradictory to
democracy.[60]

Herbert concludes his attack on Christianity and his defense of Soviet democracy with a seemingly emotional *non
sequitur:* "And now cher frère," he asks, "Give Margaret
[Howard's daughter] my love and Irene's too and to Nancy
[Howard's second daughter] for good measure. And the same
to you too. As ever, Herb"

If expressions of love for his brother and his brother's
family seem slightly incongruous coming from this twenty-
eight-year-old Stalinist who had just tried to demolish Howard's very *raison d'être*, the "good news" that Herbert reports
to his brother in the spring of 1937 seems no less out of place.
"My fellowship has been renewed for another year." The
Rockefeller Foundation, the epitome of U.S. capitalism, had
awarded this Harvard communist another year's free ride.[61]
If Herbert was aware of the contradiction, of his moral capitulation, of his self-serving departure from ideological purity, he never said so. And it would seem that Howard was
too much the gentleman to point it out.

No letters to Howard or to anyone else exist to tell us
what Herbert was thinking or doing during his last year at
America's Cambridge (1937–38), although secret SISS reports

make clear that he traveled to New York City at least once to make arrangements to study at Columbia University in order to complete research for his doctoral dissertation while working in association with the Institute of Pacific Relations (IPR).[62] He made other arrangements that year as well. During the summer of 1938, he apparently reinitiated communication with the Department of External Affairs; reference to a letter that Norman wrote to Dr. Hugh Keenleyside on 20 July 1938, from Hamilton, Ontario, exists in External's personnel files.[63] The same file shows that by then Herbert felt that it was unlikely that the Rockefeller Foundation would renew his fellowship for a fourth year. Herbert had concluded that 1938–39 would be his last year as a student, so he made the best of it.

That year spent in New York was both productive and personally pleasant. Howard, his wife Gwen, and their two daughters were on furlough from missionary work in Japan and Howard decided to spend the year at the Union Theological Seminary in New York in an attempt to write a doctoral dissertation about the great Christian reformer, Uchimura Kanzo. Herbert and Irene took a flat near Howard. "We had good fellowship together," Howard recalls, "and more than once he invited me down to meet his friends, [one of whom] was a Chinese scholar and I think a communist."[64] In November Herbert and Irene kept house for Howard and his two daughters while Gwen was delivering their third child, Daniel. Afterward, the two brothers visited frequently.

For his own part, Norman had obtained permission from Harvard to study with Professor Hugh Borton of Columbia, a specialist in Japanese history and language. Besides Borton, he became well acquainted with Asianists on the staff of IPR and with the editor of the New York-based *Amerasia*, Phillip Jaffe.

If later SISS testimony is to be believed, Herbert also became involved in an informal Marxist study group, organized by Moses Finkelstein and led by Professor Karl August Wittfogel of Columbia, a recent immigrant from Germany where he had been a member of the Communist Party. But contrary to Wittfogel's *recorded* testimony (given in August 1951) that he met Norman in this Marxist study group in the *summer* of 1938 on Cape Cod (when Norman was in fact living in Hamilton, Ontario), Wittfogel in a private letter to SISS Research Director Benjamin Mandel, maintains that the official Senate record was mistaken. In that year he claims that he actually met Herbert Norman in Manhattan during the winter of 1937–38, at the very time when Norman was still studying at Harvard.[65] Whether or not Wittfogel misspoke in his public testimony, and maybe even in a private letter to SISS counsel Robert Morris, the important point here is that his testimony had extremely serious negative effects because Wittfogel was the first person to make a public accusation that Norman was a communist. As will be shown later, the accusation caused not only a public uproar in Canada and terrible embarrassment for Herbert, but it also was accepted as fact by the RCMP. Likewise by SISS, even though SISS files also contain a letter, *never made public,* from one member of that Marxist study group, Bill Canning of Babylon, New York, who wrote Mandel on 20 August 1951 that "Herbert Norman did not attend these sessions so far as I can recall."[66]

Although the evidence says otherwise, it is possible that someone in his Cambridge-based Marxist study group had put Norman in touch with a sister organization in New York, and that Herbert, still the Stalinist and political activist, decided to join, either while he was visiting the city during his last year at Harvard, or during the following year when he lived in the city. Whatever the case, the public record, which clearly did damage to Norman's reputation in 1951, was mistaken.

Whatever the extent of his political activity in New York in 1938–39, Norman knew that during his last year of graduate fellowship support he had to complete his doctoral dissertation. The record indicates that in December of 1938, he successfully completed his general exams for the Ph.D. Then on 26 January 1939, he informed Harvard that he had completed his doctoral dissertation, giving it the title, "Establishment of the Modern State in Japan."[67]

Even as he was completing his dissertation, however, which would seemingly put him squarely on the track of an academic life, Norman had not abandoned the idea of a career in diplomatic service that O. D. Skelton had broached several years earlier. Skelton had offered Herbert an appointment in Japan, his birthplace and still the home of his family. Norman perhaps reasoned that a career in academics was something he could always return to later in life, when his activist spirit had mellowed somewhat and his interest in scholarly contemplation had revived. For now, he told Irene, he wanted to help make history rather than simply write it.[68] War had already begun in East Asia, and it seemed only a matter of time before it swept Europe. Perhaps, too, something of the service ethic common to children of missionary backgrounds emboldened him to enter the foreign service. Whatever his reason, his mind was set. On 26 April a letter arrived announcing his appointment as language officer from O. D. Skelton. A short while later, from New York, Norman applied to take the Third Secretary exams for External Affairs, despite having already been appointed by an order in council to become a Japanese language officer. (He reasoned that taking the exams "might strengthen my position in the Department to have the status of Third Secretary as well as Junior Language Officer, just in case our legation in Tokyo were to close down.")[69]

With his career set and his dissertation completed, and anticipating non-renewal of his fellowship, he notified the Rockefeller Foundation on 10 May 1939 that he was resigning his fellowship immediately. He further requested and received permission from External to postpone active duty until his doctoral degree was awarded. He had little to worry about. According to the annual Rockefeller reports secretly passed to SISS, John King Fairbank, one of Norman's dissertation readers, "has spoken highly of it [the dissertation]." (Another Harvard professor who read his thesis, Edwin Reischauer, later told an FBI interviewer that he had found "inaccuracies and errors of thought and interpretation" but added, it "could not be interpreted as an example of intellectual

Marxist thinking.")[70] On the strength of Fairbank's and apparently Hugh Borton's recommendations, IPR decided in late 1939 to publish the thesis as a book, *Japan's Emergence as a Modern State.*

Herbert presented his oral defense of the dissertation before his committee at Harvard in the first week of May 1940. He confided to a friend upon award of the degree, "I have no desire or intention of making regular use of the degree [Ph.D.) or title—not until I am gray-haired and very stoop-shouldered and wise."[71]

Two weeks later, on 18 May 1940, with Ph.D. in hand, a book about to be published, and a guaranteed annual salary of $2,220 from External, the thirty-year-old Norman set sail from Vancouver on the *Empress of Russia* for Japan. On board he sensed his student days had passed after meeting, quite by coincidence, a new colleague, Sir George Sansom, one of the world's leading historians of Japan. Three years later Sir George would write a flattering preface to Herbert's second book.

In the spring of 1940 Herbert must have felt that he was leading a charmed life. This warm and sensitive Stalinist, loving brother, angry atheist, Harvard Ph.D., and published scholar was returning to the country of his birth, where his entire family and in-laws were then living. He could return as a "conquering hero," self-assured, confidant, and full of purpose.

But what purpose? Just three years earlier he had written that communism was the "real standard-bearer for humanity, for liberty, and man's right to develop freely." Yet now, in 1940, he was presumably serving the interests of the Canadian capitalist state. Could he reconcile the contradiction as easily as he reconciled the contradiction of accepting the Rockefeller hand that had for four years fed him? As easily as damning Christianity but loving Christians? As being a radical safely removed from the one great struggle that engaged and killed his party comrades? Could it have been that Herbert Norman in 1940 was an "armchair radical," a left-wing intellectual, a communist without the strength to effect his convictions? He may have been asking himself just those questions as he sailed westward across the Pacific; then again, maybe he avoided posing them because of the intellectual discomfort that he knew the raising of such questions would cause. Time would tell.

But if time could resolve the contradictions between the theory and the practice that informed his life by making Marxist theory irrelevant in the face of the practice of serving his anti-communist government, time was also irrelevant to those rabid anti-communists who, a decade later, would give him the benefit neither of time nor explanation. Time was static for them—once a communist always a communist— and to permit the accused the right of explanation might be mistakenly perceived as presuming innocence.

How could Herbert Norman ever have been innocent? He was, after all, a child of the interwar years, one of those who, in Herman Hesse's words, "belongs to those who have been caught between two ages . . . to those whose fate it is to live the whole riddle of human destiny heightened to the pitch of a personal torture, a personal hell."[72]

CHAPTER 3

SCHOLAR

*Moral interpretations are what we call our 'values' and
these are what our wills impose upon the facts.*
George Grant, *English-Speaking Justice*

D
uring the first half of the 1940s, when the western world battled Japan for pre-eminence in the Pacific and then, with victory, tried to reshape the island Asian nation into a western-style democracy, Herbert Norman was widely regarded as one of the very few genuine Japan specialists in the west. His scholarly writings were widely read and uniformly praised; his counsel and expertise were frequently sought. His 1940 publication, *Japan's Emergence as a Modern State*[1] (hereafter, *Japan's Emergence*), was carefully examined by wartime and postwar Occupation policy makers for the insight it offered into the nature of the enemy's state and for what hints it offered for eventual reform. Similarly, his 1943 monograph, *Soldier and Peasant in Japan: The Origins of Conscription*, was read for reasons mentioned by Sir George Sansom in the Foreword: " . . . if you want to understand a phenomenon like Japanese military power, you had better go back to its origins . . ."[2]

That Norman's expertise was sought in such matters during the Forties was obvious as early as 1942 when first the Americans and then, in 1945, the British tried unsuccessfully to second Norman from his counter-intelligence work for External Affairs into their own anti-Japanese "political warfare" units.[3] In fact, after the war, with the blessing of External, Norman did go to work for the American counter-intelligence service in the Occupation forces of Japan, beginning in September 1945.

Only Professor Hugh Borton of Columbia University, who worked on pre-surrender planning, could boast of credentials and expertise that were as widely solicited as were Norman's during the 1940s. Nevertheless, in most respects it was Norman's decade in the field of Japanese studies. During the Forties he published three books, wrote one monograph (eventually published), seven academic articles and book reviews, numerous unpublished reports, a variety of public speeches, including one given to the prestigious Foreign Policy Association, and gained vast "practical" experience in counter-intelligence service against the Japanese during the war and as an occupationaire after the war, finally culminating in his appointment as head of Canada's Liaison Mission for the years 1946–50. All these accomplishments made Norman singular in the field of Japanese Studies, and probably preeminent.[4]

But what was praiseworthy during and right after the war became first suspicious in the late Forties, and then damnable in the Fifties. Expertise in Asian affairs became even criminal, sometimes treasonable, in the eyes of McCarthyites who sought to attribute a failed foreign policy to the misdeeds, misperceptions, wrong-headed analyses, and seditiously leftist views of the experts. As Herbert's "case" makes clear, the accusations against Asianists went beyond the borders of the nation that gave birth to McCarthy and his 'ism.' Canadian nationality and high-ranking diplomatic status afforded little protection to this Japan specialist. Indeed, Herbert's academic specialization became in itself "evidence" of possible wrongdoing when linked with his many professional associations, personal and institutional, that quite naturally followed from expertise in the field.

Hence, *because* Norman became a scholar of Japanese history, and one of the acknowledged leaders in the field, his reputation suffered assault by anti-intellectuals who eschewed reason in their highly emotional manhunt for left-wing Asianists in the late 1940s and early 1950s. In their pursuit of Norman the Asianist scholar, the McCarthyites, rather than examining his work for its substance, its theses, or its interpretations, glanced at his professional writings for clues about his suspected leftist sentiments, although as often as not, they counted suspicious phrases and politically dubious references and footnotes as evidence of communist culpability. They vetted his work, in short, with a presumption of guilt, with a politically reactionary bias, and a single-minded intention of finding what they were looking for; and they found it, of course.[5] There is no evidence that they actually understood his writings, let alone learned from them. Their reading was uncritical in the academic sense, critical only in the political sense.

In 1939, at the end of his student years, it was Norman's reputation and accomplishments as a scholar that had caught the eye of Canadian officialdom and led to his employment. It was Norman's scholarly insights into Japanese history that made him so valuable as an analyst of Japanese affairs while he worked for External. Today it is his scholarship that has earned him the approbation of "pioneer" in the field of Japanese history by so many in the academic world.[6] Indeed, long after political alliances have shifted in world politics and what once was is no longer, it is Norman's writings that give him immortality: they are his enduring legacy to all thinking people who care about things Japanese. They deserve, therefore, to be understood and treated for what they teach, quite apart from the ideological anti-intellectualism that unfairly politicized them for partisan and reactionary purposes.

Herbert Norman's scholarship needs to be understood initially in terms of the sociology of his knowledge, that is, in terms of how he knew what he claimed to know and the particular context in which he had acquired the knowledge that informs his writings. Of first importance is the basic rule of scholarship that he formulated for himself as early as 1933 when, as a Victoria student, he had defended Trotsky's interpretation of history: "What history that maintains to be impartial is of any use at all?" he rhetorically asked his older brother. "If there were such a thing as an impartial History, it would be chronological lists of events—a bare, fruitless catalogue. It is the duty of the historian to interpret this

skeleton or scaffold which disappears in the completed building, or at least not trouble the reader with the wearisome list
of mere events."[7]

Except for those who believe that the study of history is
simply one of many forms of "value-free" social science,
Herbert's view of what proper history constitutes seems little
more than platitudinous. Interpreting history, for Herbert,
necessarily required of the scholar, who is, after all, a human
being with values, the assigning of values to events, personalities, and change. As a Marxist historian, which he was at
the beginning of his decade of scholarly productivity, this
meant that his studies of Japan would necessarily be concerned with what did and what did not contribute to the
liberation of humans from such exploitative practices as division of labor.[8]

Too, given the timing of his period of scholarly productivity, Herbert would also necessarily be concerned with understanding the roots of Japanese militaristic behavior, if only
in order to defeat it; he would be concerned with comparisons
of Japanese politics with Fascist German and Italian politics;
and he would want to identify those aspects of the Japanese
political, economic and social systems which were amenable
to reform and those which were not and therefore in need of
eradication.

Hence, his scholarly approach would in the first instance
appear profoundly humanistic and, in the second, ideal as the
basis for determining practical policy for reforming Japan
once it was defeated. In fact, fellow Asianists, despite whatever criticism they may have of the quality of his scholarship,
have consistently praised the humanistic quality of his writings, especially his marked concern and sympathy for the
ruled. Similarly, in their radical attempt at democratizing the
post-war system, reformers of Japan during the Occupation
borrowed heavily from his analysis of the prewar Japanese
state.[9] It is probably no exaggeration to say that had Norman
not adopted a Marxist perspective in analyzing Japanese history, his writings would have been significantly less influential than they have, in fact, proven to be.

Yet, again, what can be counted as an asset in one era can be condemned as a liability in another. This can be demonstrated by a brief exegesis of Herbert Norman's writings, which shall be done momentarily, but first a few words about the meaning of the politicization of scholarship in general.

As alleged and as will be demonstrated, Norman lent a particular political perspective to his scholarship, as indeed do all scholars, more or less openly. With sufficient study, any scholarly work can be shown to be laden with political bias and to be anything but objective, value-free, and impartial. Sometimes, to be sure, jargon and obscure terminology can cloak bias, but then that is all it does. Especially guilty of obscuring bias are so-called "liberal" (small-l) scholars who feign objectivity by using such phrases as "on the one hand" and "on the other hand," and then assert that the truth is somewhere in between. By setting up polar opposites, usually nothing more than convenient fictions, they lend credibility to their own "middle-of-the-road" interpretation, which, as often as not, tacitly defends the status quo. The language of their political discourse, moreover, is disquietingly free of such words as "oppression," "class," "contradiction," and so on, using instead such conservative synonyms as "law and order," "income grouping," "disequilibrium," and the like. In short, liberal political analysts rely on different "buzz words," which in North America seem to grate less on the nerves of a status-quo-minded readership.

Once recognized, this difference in political vocabulary and analysis need not bother anyone, so long as all sides in any political debate declare support for academic freedom—the right of scholars to think and publish what they wish. The notion itself is—evidence to the contrary notwithstanding—a liberal one, *à la* John Stuart Mill, who believed that an enlightened citizenry should have the right to be exposed to different views as a necessary precondition to arriving at their own informed views. In this sense, ideas are nothing more than "products" freely "bought" and "sold" in the democratic marketplace; the "consumer" buys what he wants; the citizen determines which ideas are worthwhile. It may be that certain ideas will be resolutely rejected, e.g., communism, but the ideal of academic freedom or free speech nonetheless supports the rights of Marxists to peddle their ideas in the open marketplace. Herbert Norman, as scholar, defended this notion of academic freedom, although as already seen, in his student years he contradictorily defended Stalin's purge trials which prosecuted all non-"true believers."

The less generous and illiberal might choose to deny Norman the right to partake of academic freedom because he himself once chose to repudiate its premises, but then, as implied, they themselves would become guilty of the very "crime" that they attribute, correctly, to Herbert. The same sort would also be guilty of being ahistorical, for as we shall see, Herbert Norman, in word and in deed, came to repudiate that indefensible defense of political censorship.

This departure into the ethics of academic freedom might not be necessary were we living closer in time to the McCarthyite period when academic freedom was more often than not honored in the breach—when, in even stronger but no less accurate terms, America was effecting its own brand of "purge trials" against suspected traitors. The point is that to review Norman's scholarly record without accounting for his own ideological formulations and the ideological vilification of them would mean forgetting that he was pursued *because* of his choice of words, words dictated by a radical and humanist vision of history, one that was Hegelian in its teleology, seeing History as the inexorable and ceaseless efforts of humans striving for ever-greater freedom.

If Norman's scholarship can be understood in terms of the sociology of his knowledge, so, too, can it be understood in terms of the particular kind of intellectual and professional "tools" that he brought to bear.

Prior to going to Harvard for his M.A. and Ph.D. in Japanese (Asian) history, Herbert had been first a student of the Classics at Toronto and then a student of comparative European history at Cambridge. Not surprisingly, therefore, evidence of training in both those fields appears frequently in his later writing in the field of Japanese history. For example, in *Japan's Emergence,* Herbert describes the Japanese peasant as "Janus-head," referring to his contradictory "conservative and radical" behavior in terms of bifurcated class relationships; elsewhere Herbert likened the heavy burden of the peasantry in Japan's modernization to Atlas's burden.

Reflecting his training at Cambridge, Norman utilized comparisons with France and England, and even China, in order to give wider perspective on particular historical episodes in Japan's development, in the process socializing his Eurocentric audience into accepting Japan as part of *world* history. These comparisons also made clear that for Norman the Japanese case of historical development should be treated as one set of data among many and by inference that the Japanese people were no different from human beings of the West. In short, he used cross-cultural comparison to eradicate Kiplingesque and racist notions that the "inscrutable East" was populated by less than human figures.

Another, perhaps more appropriate example of Norman relying (maybe overrelying) on his past training in Classics and comparative European history, is his last monograph, *Ando Shoeki and the Anatomy of Japanese Feudalism* (1949), written while he was serving as head of the Liaison Mission to Occupied Japan.[10] In *Ando,* Herbert endeavors to make his hero understandable to the western reader by invoking a wide range of comparisons between Ando and his ideas on the one hand and many western thinkers on the other. Ando is variously compared with Aristotle's "Magnanimous Man," with Confucius, with Jean Bodin, Montesquieu, Sir Thomas Browne, Critias of Athens, François Quesnay, Epicurus, Gerrard Winstanley, Rousseau, and Sir Thomas More, just to name several of the better known. The range of comparisons seems almost too great, prompting skepticism about the validity of these many comparisons and perhaps slight embarrassment over Norman's apparent pedantry. Yet it is clear to the discerning reader that Herbert's intention was not to impress so much as to clarify, to explain what is universal about Shoeki and his ideas, to give the western reader a familiar intellectual touchstone and in this way minimize the intellectual distance between Occident and Orient.

There is another aspect of Norman's academic training that affected his scholarship in a significant way, and which, in the minds of several of his more severe critics, detracts from its over-all quality. This aspect is his weak Japanese reading ability, a serious liability that is just the reverse side of his strengths in the Classics and comparative history.[11]

Norman, after all, did not begin to study the Japanese language for purposes of acquiring literacy until, at age twenty-seven in 1936, he became a graduate student at Harvard. Before then, like so many missionary children, he quite naturally developed oral fluency in the language without ever learning how to read. Not only was it unnecessary to acquire reading ability as a missionary child, later in university as his interests tended toward western culture and history, he no doubt regarded learning to read Japanese as an extravagance.

His Rockefeller application makes quite clear that his reading ability in Japanese when he entered Harvard was limited to the two *kana* systems *(hiragana* and *katakana)*, the two simple syllabaries used primarily for purposes of pronunciation of the vastly more difficult Chinese characters *(kanji)*. In short, as of 1936, Norman was functionally illiterate in Japanese.

He sought to remedy this weakness by studying both Japanese and Chinese languages at Harvard, and earning A in both. Clearly, he was a capable student of language, yet even allowing for linguistic aptitude, given the difficulty of memorizing Chinese characters, it is impossible to avoid the conclusion that he was inadequately prepared to conduct serious research in Japanese by the time he began writing his dissertation in 1938. Professor Borton of Columbia helped him, and we know that at Harvard his friend Tsuru Shigeto lent considerable research assistance—Norman publicly acknowledged their support, and that of Professor Tsunoda of Columbia in his Preface to *Japan's Emergence*.[12] And it would appear that without their help in translating difficult passages from Japanese, he would have been unable to create the high-quality work that he did.

Further support for this conclusion comes from the in-depth examination of *Japan's Emergence* by Professor George Akita of the University of Hawaii.[13] While Akita's motivations for undertaking his controversial vivisection of *Japan's Emergence* appear all too political, nonetheless several of his many criticisms of Norman's scholarship are objectively on mark. Briefly, he points to some weaknesses: Norman's heavy reliance on English-language materials, his mistranslations, and his misunderstandings of certain passages, probably because of a superficial acquaintance with related Japanese language sources. Akita more than implies that these weaknesses can be attributed to academic dishonesty on Herbert's part, but surely this is too harsh. Norman simply was not yet very proficient in reading complex Japanese and therefore was forced to rely on the help of friends, on extant translations, on his own yet meager abilities to translate, and on the wealth of comparative and classical knowledge that he could bring to bear.

We need not rest on the ideologically biased Akita account to make this point. Also telling is that, after being hired as a language officer in the Canadian Embassy in Tokyo, Herbert himself acknowledged his own weakness in the language by applying to External for permission to take Japanese language classes.[14] Further, after carefully scrutinizing the entire Herbert Norman Japanese language collection of books, housed at the University of British Columbia and consisting of 102 books, many of which are cited in *Japan's Emergence,* it is evident to anyone reasonably proficient in reading Japanese that Herbert's reading abilities were very weak. His marginal notations largely consist of dictionary translations of relatively simple Japanese terms, many of which are included in the basic *Toyo kanji* list of 1,850 elementary Chinese characters usually learned after three years of formal study. By the time he began his dissertation, he had completed just two years of formal study and was working on his third in tutorial form with Professor Borton. Finally, examination of his collection at UBC seems to reveal partial readings of many books, showing that just one or two pages of two- and three-hundred page books have been examined, let alone translated or translated properly.

For reasons other than he suggested, Akita may be partially correct is asserting that "the brilliance of his narrative skill" cannot redeem flaws in his scholarship,[15] but Akita is certainly wrong in overlooking the brilliance of Norman's analysis of the rise of the modern Japanese state, despite its understandable under-reliance on Japanese language sources. Herbert's purpose in writing the book was, in the words of Professor Gary Allinson, "none other than to explain modern Japanese history," and at the time it was published, "the book was a singular achievement."[16] It can be argued that Norman accomplished so much because he knew so little Japanese, making up for this deficiency by relying ever so intelligently on other aspects of his scholarly training and on writing skills equalled by no other Japanologist, save perhaps Sir George Sansom. Hence, though his "academic tools" may have been wanting in one respect, his intellectual tools certainly were not; *Japan's Emergence* remains "an enduring historical work"[17] and a seminal interpretation that made Japan less mysterious and more comparable with the development experiences of western nations.

If there is a single reason for attributing interpretive brilliance to *Japan's Emergence* and to his other early writings, it is Norman's other, yet understated "tool," namely, his Marxist insights. I say "insights" rather than "analyses" because there are strong indications that already, by the late Thirties, he was distancing himself from programmatic Marxist analysis, if only in his scholarship. In *Emergence*, Norman used Marxist terminology without accepting all the premises of Marx, probably because his understanding of Japan's political and social development would not easily yield itself to inflexible Marxist interpretation. In the strict Marxist paradigm of social change, a nation moves inexorably from the feudal to the capitalist stage of development. But Norman's reading of Japan correctly saw a divergence from that paradigm of considerable import. He maintained that the Japanese case demonstrated opposing tendencies in the Meiji Restoration of 1868 when the overthrow of feudalism was effected not by a simple bourgeois class but rather by a merchant-feudal alliance which quickly suppressed "the anti-feudal movement by action from below" as it installed a form of government that he calls "enlightened absolutism."[18] The change from feudalism to capitalism was incomplete, in Norman's view, consequently permitting a great many feudal vestiges to coexist in the new era side by side with developing capitalistic forms of social relations. And not only to coexist, but actually to reinforce government control over the transformation to bourgeois society and even "cushion" the "stress and shock of industrial life."[19] In other words, contrary to what a Marxist ideologue would say, Norman saw positive benefits accruing to the quality of life of the modernizing Japanese from the less than total "political revolution" that allowed the "Spirit of Old Japan" to survive.

Feudal vestiges were manifested in a variety of ways in the "new Japan" of post-1868: in the economy, in peasant behavior and the peasants' forms of agriculture, in the all-important bureaucracy, in the samurai-led military, and in the relationship between the state and the citizenry. Alongside feudal vestiges, the embourgeoisment of modern Japan in the Meiji period (1868–1912) meant commercialization, industrialization and urbanization. The coexistence of feudalism and capitalism led to conflict; e.g., when capitalists struggled to free themselves from "the fetters of feudal economy," though such conflict could in Norman's view produce progressive consequences, as, for example, in the development of the "freedom and popular rights movement" (jiyu minken undo) that attempted to force government to be more responsive to the rights of commercial producers. Yet at the same time he saw correctly that a reactionary and contradictory impulse also resided among these same producers ("Janus-head") which under certain conditions might lend support for an even more authoritarian rule with all aristocratic trappings.[20]

Such empirical observations, validated by careful use of evidence, were extensions of a more fundamental belief, stated early in the book: "The Buddhist doctrine of karma illustrates the tiresome truism that whatever goes before, through the catena of cause and effect, necessarily shapes and conditions that which follows; and so the student is ever pushing back his study of history in search of the *primum mobile*. Yet one need not admit, as would full acceptance of Buddhist doctrine, any ineluctable determinism in the affairs of men and states. The will of man, striking obliquely at the flowing stream of historical development, its channel already partly fixed, can bend its course to this side or that, but can not block it altogether. So it was in Japan; the design lay with the Meiji architects, but the material was largely ready at hand, a legacy of the preceding age."[21]

His "Buddhist doctrine of karma" could easily have been a politically neutral analog for the "Marxist doctrine of historical change" (which his thesis advisors would have had greater trouble accepting!). Regardless, the point is that Norman made allowances for the impact of human will—his individual "architects"—in shaping historical change. Men *can* mold historical clay, which is hardly the view of a historical determinist (which Marx never was, but many Marxists were) or strict materialist.

In other words, even as a young scholar, at most just a year or two removed from passionate political support for Soviet "justice," he wrote as a dispassionate scholar, eschewing any sort of doctrinaire interpretation of political change in Japan. More substantive evidence in *Japan's Emergence* exists to substantiate this claim. For example, in discussing the "breakdown" of Japanese feudalism as background for the Meiji Restoration (1868), Norman largely abandons casual use of such ideologically laden words as "decay," "military caste," and "class" in favor of a humanly sympathetic but historically accurate portrayal of the concrete problems confronting Japan's new leaders; in doing so, he both explains and historically justifies the absolutist posture they adopted after 1868. He notes that "the Japan which the Meiji Gov-

ernment inherited [was] a country torn by revolts, factionalism and civil war. Time was short, resources scanty, and it
is a cause of amazement that its leaders accomplished so much
rather than a cause for blame because they had to leave so
much undone in the way of democratic and liberal reform.
Judged by the standards of a liberal democrat, much was left
undone, but the exigencies of the historical situation, that is
to say, the fact that Japan had to create in one generation
what other nations had spent several centuries to accomplish—meant that Japan had not the time to afford such lux-
uries as liberal institutions." He concludes his apologia for
Meiji absolutism with the startling remark: "The autocratic
or paternalistic way seemed to the Meiji leaders the only
possible method if Japan was not to sink into the ranks of a
colonial country."[22]

In explaining the motivations of the Meiji leadership in this
sympathetic manner, employing the standards of a liberal
democrat, Norman was acknowledging the importance of
scholarly balance. But by no means were the standards he
used for passing historical judgment solely those of the liberal
democrat. Later, in explaining the plight of the peasantry in
the post-feudal period, he describes their situation in a way
that a Marxist or liberal humanist historian might. That is,
he emphasizes the extent to which the peasants and their
production were subject to the whims of capricious market
forces. He writes, "But under the new government the burden of payment shifted from producer to landholder; the
peasants were now freed from the oppressive bondage of
feudalism and at the same time deprived of the 'paternal'
consideration of their lord whose problem it was to see 'that
they neither died nor lived.' In the new society they were
free to choose their own fate; to live or die, to remain on the
land or sell out and go to the city."[23]

Norman's point is that the "tyranny of feudalism" is no
less tyrannical than the tyranny of capitalism, but is simply
a tyranny of a different form. In picturing the plight of the
peasantry largely in materialistic terms, Herbert revealed the
influence of Marx's thinking on his own work. Similarly, in

focusing on the rise of "Japanese liberalism" he shows that the rise of political opposition groups in Japan stemmed from the growth of capitalism. Self-interested landlords led the liberal movement in order to protect against state absolutism the commercial gains they had won since the Restoration. Base determines superstructure, economics determines politics: a perspective he could not have developed without first fundamentally aligning himself with Marx's interpretation of historical change.

But if this is so, how can we believe Japan's leading Marxist historian, Toyama Shigeki, who claims, "But Norman was *not* a Marxist."[24] True, says Toyama, "Norman drew on the fruits of Japanese Marxist historiography" . . . just as "any sensible scholar recognizes the great contribution Marxist historiography made in pioneering the scientific inquiry into modern Japanese history." Yet in the final analysis, Toyama points out, Norman "draws freely and impartially on the research results of various schools: the so-called positivist school, the socio-economic history school, and historical materialism." And Toyama cements his contention by noting, "Quantitatively, non-Marxists [sources] comprise the overwhelming majority of authors cited [in his footnotes]."[25]

Toyama's judgment is impossible to question in this regard. Norman was indeed eclectic in his scholarship, perhaps even indiscriminate in drawing upon the widest variety of interpretations then available. There are reasons for this. His scholarly tools, as observed above, were not yet sharply enough honed to do otherwise. His reading ability in Japanese remained at an intermediate level at the time he wrote and researched *Japan's Emergence;* and he had been reading systematically in the field for only a couple of years before he began writing his first book. What he had to contribute in interpreting modern Japanese history were what his earlier acquired tools would allow—his classical, even poetic training; his near flawless prose style (which will be treated later); his Cambridge studies in comparative history; and a Marxist *bent* that permitted him to ask questions about the relationship between economic and political change that had not yet been posed in any of the English-language works but which were fresh in the mind of his most capable Japanese Marxist economist friend and informal mentor at Harvard, Tsuru Shigeto. In this latter sense, his early scholarship was "made in Japan."

It is difficult to avoid arriving at similar conclusions about his next two major writings. *Soldier and Peasant* (1943) and *Feudal Background of Japanese Politics* (1944–45) were in most every respect elaborations at best or duplications at worst of the ideas and events treated in *Japan's Emergence*. In terms of new and original research, these two wartime publications were half-hearted and politically motivated rehashes of his prewar research.

Soldier and Peasant, a seventy-six page monograph about the origins of conscription in modern Japan, breaks little new ground on the subject but does give important "new" information in English for the first time. In this sense, *Soldier and Peasant* represents a modest advance over *Emergence*. So, too, in another respect, *Soldier and Peasant* is less ambitious in scope and is therefore more scholarly. Yet insofar as its thesis is concerned, *Soldier and Peasant,* like *Emergence,* focuses on the simple comparison of "feudal oppression" and the "autocratic" Meiji government's methods in stifling "the intoxicating air of freedom, following the overthrow of the Bakufu [feudal government]."[26] The plot in this wartime-inspired, unabashed morality play revolved around the use of conscription by the Meiji government as a "counter-revolutionary" device to quell "the growing anti-feudal and democratic revolution which was developing within the country and which was beaten back by the military bureaucracy ruling Japan."[27]

Despite several astute observations and impressive documentation, his thesis suffers from unscholarly assertions, the central one concerning that of a "growing anti-feudal and democratic revolution." While just a few years earlier in *Emergence,* Norman had been satisfied to allow for "historical exigencies" in the rise of autocratic government, in 1943, in the midst of the Second World War, he was less forgiving, not to mention understanding, of the Meiji leaders who had instituted conscription."It [conscription] was introduced without the slightest regard for public opinion and without there being any pressing necessity for it in terms of national defense against any likely aggression."[28] Contrast with this unsympathetic assertion his more thoughtful conclusion of four years before: "The autocratic or paternalistic way seemed to Meiji leaders the only possible method if Japan was not to sink into the ranks of a colonial country."[29]

What accounts for his rather abrupt reversal from his earlier, more balanced and scholarly interpretation has already been alluded to: World War II. *Soldier and Peasant* is, in fact, a snappy piece of wartime propaganda written purposely as a morality play with good versus evil, but written with the flair of an accomplished scholar who was himself intimately involved in counter-intelligence for effecting the defeat of the Japanese. His conclusion to the monograph makes this clear: "The Japanese were unable to secure their own liberty at the fateful hour of the overthrow of feudalism. The time of their liberation will have to be postponed until the forces of the democratic nations can defeat the Japanese army and then, in addition to the primary task of freeing Asia from Japanese conquest, help the Japanese people themselves to secure that liberty and freedom which they have so far been too misguided and weak to accomplish unaided."[30]

As any good patriot of an Allied nation did at that time, Norman criticized the enemy for failing to be democratic (democratic nations, the mythology of the time went, were peace-loving), but in the process sacrificed his scholarly integrity by abandoning basic scholarly principles. Service to his nation and the Allied war effort against the Japanese were accorded higher priority. This is not to say, however, that *Soldier and Peasant* is totally lacking in scholarly value. He did not consistently oversimplify Japanese history for the sake of propaganda. As in *Emergence,* he emphasized the importance of coexisting liberal political and feudal currents, he documented peasant resistance to autocratic authority, and he helped make a point that would later be cited in the postwar democratizing efforts of the Occupation; namely, that while the modern Japanese government was guilty of feudal-militaristic aggression, Japan's people were "unfree" and "unwitting" agents in "riveting the shackles of slavery on other people."[31] Such observations later lent themselves to the arduous work of purging wartime leaders and encouraging *popular* democratic tendencies to develop under Occupation supervision.

No less important to observe about *Soldier and Peasant*, Norman showed himself in this work to have made yet another "conversion" to a different sort of political cause. He wrote the monograph as a civil servant, while a member of External Affairs, a representative of the Canadian government. If, as alleged by some critics, his work was politically instrumentalist—rather than pure scholarship—then his political purpose was to lend greater legitimacy to Canada's and the Allies' battle against fascism, militarism, reaction, and aggression (all words he frequently used in this writing). He was a Whig historian, not at all averse to imposing contemporary values onto historical circumstance, regardless of fit. His values seemed situational, "chameleon-like," to use one of his favorite terms.

This need not be construed as a negative criticism, for many of the values he once attributed to Marxist thinking were compatible with the democratic mission of the Second World War; namely, the liberation of people from the forces of reaction. In some respects, indeed, the Allied effort against fascism and nazism was simply a belated liberal acknowledgment of the nobility of the anti-Franco cause in the Spanish Civil War. Norman had, of course, long been anti-Fascist; then, in 1943, in his External Affairs work and in his writing, he at long last had the opportunity to fight in his own way against the evil that years before had put an end to the lives of his comrades Cornford and Maclaurin.

This interpretation does not rest on a reading of *Soldier and Peasant* alone. His other major wartime writing, *Feudal Background of Japanese Politics* (hereafter, *Feudal*), served a similar political purpose and seemed no less instrumentalist.

The 116 pages of text, single-spaced in the original typescript, introduced very little new material based on original research and reads, with the exception of two parts, very much like *Japan's Emergence redux*. Herbert himself was apologetic about the absence of "the necessary research" to complete his purpose of elaborating on a two-part article published in *Pacific Affairs* in September 1944 that focused on rightist "patriotic" political societies. He quite legitimately cited "exigencies of time" as preventing careful writing, and begged the reader's indulgence for "repetition or platitudinously expressed ideas."[32] Probably for these reasons he never tried to publish the manuscript and resisted attempts by his colleague William Holland to convince him to publish it. In fact, Norman had no special reason to take pride in the work and reason enough to be apologetic to all who had read his *Emergence* years before and could therefore appreciate that *Feudal* was a pale imitation of the earlier masterpiece.[33]

Why then write it at all? Two reasons suggest themselves. First, he yet considered himself a publishing scholar, despite working full time for External Affairs, perhaps even because he worked for External. His position in the war was with "intelligence," and this required careful scholarly analysis of wartime data about the Japanese (as will be shown in the next chapter). His own particular passion was to explain how feudal remnants governed "modern" political behavior and, clearly, he felt that his earlier writings had left much unsaid or insufficiently explained. Too, his scholarly research had uncovered a genuine liberal-democratic tradition in prewar Japan, one that he felt might be emphasized and built upon in the postwar political reconstruction of his birthplace.

The second reason for writing *Feudal* appears, again, politically instrumentalist. In his words, the study might "be of interest to anyone wishing to study the techniques of mass control in Japan and the tactics of the most consistent Japanese expansionists."[34] Derivative of his earlier writing though it may be, it nonetheless might serve to reinforce the lesson of how deeply the roots of Japanese reaction had spread in several hundred years of growth.

Although these appear to have been the primary motivating factors in writing *Feudal,* two other possible explanations exist. First, as with his other two major writings, he wrote *Feudal* for the Institute of Pacific Relations, with which he had enjoyed an uninterrupted affiliation since 1938. Loyalty to the institution and to its leadership, especially to friends like William Holland, and no doubt to its purpose of making Asia better known and understood in the west, may account for accepting this charge. A final reason has to do with what new research he had managed to conduct since joining External. In *Feudal,* Norman shows two new interests: one is historically limited instances of what he calls "mass frenzy" occurring among the commoner population toward the close of the feudal period; the other is evidence of particular liberal activists who challenged autocratic rule in the 1880s. The "mass frenzy" or "mass hysteria" was important because such phenomena had happened elsewhere in the world under similar conditions; in his words, "under any unbearably oppressive social system," prompting the "curbed and repressed" to "blindly" seek some sort of outlet.[35]

His second new interest, or rather an old interest for which he had found newer and more convincing evidence, was liberal activism in the Meiji period. He cited the words and deeds of such democratic reformers as Oi Kentaro and Ueki Emori as evidence of a genuine *democratic* movement, and rendered lengthy translations of their invocations for greater civil liberties. Though these two liberals were ultimately defeated, for Norman their passionate love of democracy helped to demonstrate the competing traditions of reaction and democracy.

Feudal may, therefore, have in part been written in order to give a greater definition to these two more recent research interests. But regardless, as will be made evident in the next chapter, he was able to make practical use of his more recent research after the war as a practising Japanologist whose duty it was to assist in the political reform of Japan. In this capacity he would stress that not all about Japan's past was irredeemable.

Whether either of these latter two reasons is correct, what

is unquestionably certain is that nothing in *Feudal* even slightly suggests an enduring allegiance to a Marxist interpretation of political change. As noted by Professor John Dower, who cites a passage in *Feudal* to buttress an observation about Norman's growing allegiance to "traditional liberalism": "To a certain extent it can be argued that Norman's political premises were in line with the attitude prevalent among most Western spokesmen at the end of World War II." In Dower's opinion, Norman was shying away from attacks on either capitalism or socialism, making the central concern in his writings "the creation of a *genuine* democracy"[36] in the face of obstacles erected by history. Such were the concerns of a typical liberal-democrat; they were Norman's concerns after beginning work for External Affairs, and were voiced by him on numerous occasions, especially after the conclusion of the war when he largely abandoned traditional scholarship in favor of writing essays.

The Japanese term for such convenient ideological conversions is *tenko*, a recantation of earlier held views, in this case, Marxism-Leninism. As might be expected, the Japanese term implies betrayal; it denotes unprincipled self-interest, and suggests that the convert gives in to mere political expediency. Dower observes that some Japanese intellectuals accuse Norman of having done just this, but Dower also explains why such a judgment is unfair. Dower correctly observes that though Norman might have shifted ideologically toward safe and conventionally favored political terrain, he nonetheless remained true to the same sorts of *human* concerns that had always informed his scholarship and political activities.[37] Freedom, democracy, self-government, reason, tolerance, humility—these remained the central principles around which he constructed his academic and diplomatic work, but the context—intellectual, social, political, historical, economic— in which he advocated these values had changed, both for himself and for the world. There is, in short, consistency in his values, but inconsistency in his support of the most appropriate means to implement conditions to effect his values. Norman had always altered his views according to circumstance and he was, after all, an intellectual, sensitive to changes in political currents, forever in search of broader truths, ever anxious to immortalize them in his writings. It may very well have been, though this can not be documented, that after Stalin's ignoble pact with Hitler in 1939, roughly coincidental with the decision to make a career in External Affairs, that Norman's perception of "broader truths" changed and that his career choice simply made easier the transformation of his thinking toward the liberal mode.

It can also be surmised that at this time he chose not to torture himself with the kind of introspection that invariably leads to an awareness of hypocrisy, as he had during the Harvard years when his old Trinity comrades were dying in Spain; that he chose instead to make peace with himself by adopting views in harmony with his circumstances, views in accord with Canada's liberal-democratic and capitalist system. To do otherwise, that is, to remain a Stalinist while in the employ of a capitalist government, would necessitate betrayal of his country and corruption of his soul. Some people, of course, in speculating that Herbert Norman was an espionage agent for the Soviet Union, have suggested just this.

To those who *believe* this—they can not *prove* their suspicions— it might be asked, was Herbert's scholarship, increasingly liberal in tone, analysis, and ethical judgment, simply a clever, duplicitous ruse, however time-consuming and unproductive this ruse was for the "communist conspiracy," and intended solely to provide a better "cover"?

Such a question seems immensely absurd when we look in greater detail at his writings done after the Second World War and after we recall that for someone allegedly interested in preserving a "cover," his scholarly associations with IPR, by then regarded by American right-wingers as a "communist front organization," were egregiously open and public. To his writings first. (His IPR connections will be treated in ensuing chapters.)

In almost every important respect, his next book, *Ando Shoeki* (1949; and hereafter, *Ando),* reveals the quintessential Norman. An intellectual biography of an obscure eighteenth-

century country doctor with a strong anti-authoritarian ideology, *Ando* is most important because it is a biography.
Here Norman tries to reveal in detail and depth the character
of another human being, and to the extent that he is successful, readers of Norman's other writings suddenly become
aware that his humanism has finally found the proper vehicle
for its most heartfelt expression. To be sure, the contrast is
in degree only, not in genuine difference, because as so many
have remarked, Norman's earlier writings are suffused with
humanistic sentiment and concern for the common people.
But with *Ando,* it becomes very clear that the earlier expressions of his humanism lacked refinement, lacked the precision
of painting a face onto his forgotten heroes of democracy,
and lacked character development and exposition. In his earlier works, Norman shows quite clearly that he loved humanity though he seemed to know little about individual
human beings with whose depressing earthly plight he could
intellectually commiserate. In short, in *Emergence* and *Feudal,* we see a scholar empathizing with the "masses," perhaps
because the Marxist orientation yet had hold of his scholarly
perspective. But in *Ando,* we see the liberal humanist, concerned with the *individual* and his ideas, almost to the exclusion of "the people."

Of course, it was not mere coincidence that prompted
Norman to select Ando as his subject. As he explained, he
was attracted to Ando for reasons similar to those which
attracted him to the rebellious "masses" in his earlier writings.
"For some years past I have been curious to learn whether I
could discover any impressive evidence during the centuries
of Japanese feudalism of a philosophy vindicating resistance
to unbridled authority and oppression."[38] Ando was his discovery, and it could not have come at a better time, involved
as he was in the Occupation's attempt to de-feudalize and
democratize Japan. In Norman's eyes Ando served as an object lesson for war-weary, dejected Japanese who wondered
whether democracy in the postwar period had any real roots
in Japanese history and therefore worried whether democracy
might not dissolve once the Democratizers ended their Oc-

cupation. In writing *Ando,* he wanted to give the Japanese a piece of their own history in which they could take pride, and from which they might even derive guidance. The Japanese, for their part, recognized this motivation of Norman's and came to love him for it.

But beyond the politically instrumentalist reason for choosing to study Ando, there is every reason to take Norman at his word, namely, that he wished to find native Japanese, intellectual support for the anti-feudal phenomenon that he had recorded in his other writings and which he felt existed based on his comparative reading of European history. He knew, for example, of the example set by such thinkers as John of Salisbury whose *Policraticus* sanctioned popular resistance to tyranny; he singled out the medieval jurists' notion of *ius resistendum* (lawful resistance); and he carefully documented the anti-authoritarian stance taken by the Levellers and Diggers against aristocratic arrogance and oppression. Reason dictated that similar such figures, "who stood forth to break a lance against despotism,"[39] dared to challenge feudal rule in Japan. His reason and research spit forth *Ando,* but it was Norman's emotional commitment to battling feudal oppression, as much as it was his scholarly faculties, that informed his portrayal of Ando.

In this sense, as John Hall, Yale University expert on Japanese feudalism, puts it, *Ando* is "a fascinating document of self-revelation." Hall elaborates, "In Ando [the man], whose work consists of an extended diatribe against samurai society in favor of a Taoist utopian model, Norman found a kindred spirit."[40] Hall quotes a particular passage from *Ando* which he says "unwittingly provides a self-portrait": "He was a man of passionate intensity, whether in his convictions, or in the pursuit of knowledge, or in his hatred of man's inhumanity to man, or in his love for the humble and industrious peasantry. Consumed by savage indignation at the social injustices of his day, his polemic is violent, his vocabulary sometimes coarse, his argument sweeping."[41]

Similar such "self-portraits" appear throughout *Ando.* For example, "Shoeki was violently addicted to polemic; like an athlete joyously anticipating a contest he revelled in the clash and pull of conflicting ideas. But he was saved from becoming a mere bigot by his intense curiosity, his wide-eyed scrutiny of life and nature and his deep respect for the long-suffering peasantry whose cause he championed."[42] And of Shoeki's writing style, which could describe Herbert's own, "Both by his use of repetition and of pungent phrases which are not weakened by qualification, Shoeki hit upon two of the most effective devices in modern propaganda (a once honest word, in recent years fallen to low estate)."[43] Or, finally by way of elaboration, Norman wrote, "I like to see Shoeki as a simple country doctor . . . ; reserved but yet not cold, neither haughty nor fawning, humane but not condescending, valuing friends but socially not ambitious; stoical in manner but sanguine in outlook; studious of books but more of the living world around him; a man who could look with keen but friendly eyes on Nature and his fellow men, learning from them and so able to teach them. Above all he was a lover of peace and the pursuits of peace; hence, in the proper sense, a *civilized* man."[44]

Such characterizations of Shoeki, and there are a great many throughout the biography, seem to mirror Herbert's own character, and perhaps therefore may be little more than egoistic self-indulgence. Shoeki, therefore, serves two purposes: one, to impart intellectual substance to instances of popular resistance to feudal oppression; and two, to give Norman the opportunity to explain himself. To this latter end, he certainly used in the biography what he said approvingly about Shoeki's style: "use of repetition and pungent phrases which are not weakened by qualification." Sir George Sansom, reviewing the book for *Pacific Affairs* in 1950, described the effect on the reader: "Sometimes, indeed, his comparisons seem far-fetched and sometimes redundant; and his last chapters might have been better for some pruning."[45] It is doubtful that Norman would have disagreed with Sansom's judgment, but it is also doubtful if he would have apologized for redundancy and verbosity. Self-explanation is usually lengthy explanation, exposition of one's character requires flamboyance in prose and verve in its poetic quality. He was capable of all these, and probably, to the extent that all biography is autobiography, was incapable of distancing himself sufficiently from his subject to attain succinctness and genuine objectivity.

But regardless of what faults the book may have, it was praised then by Sansom, arguably the world's greatest Japanologist, as a "volume [that] will be greeted with pleasure by students of Japanese history," and as a "careful, thoughtful and illumined" study, and the author is to be "commended [for] his free use of a comparative method."[46] Thirty years later, America's premier Japanologist, Professor John Hall, is not hesitant to call the book "a scholarly *tour de force.*"[47] And that Norman was able to write the book while serving in the demanding position of Canada's highest-ranking representative to Occupied Japan makes this achievement all the more remarkable.

Yet Norman could not take all the credit for *Ando.* As he himself makes clear in the Introduction to the work, he benefited from the advice and knowledge of a number of Japanese colleagues, chief of whom was Okubo Genji, a translator whom Norman had known through the IPR years before the war and had hired to work as a translator for the Liaison Mission after the war. Okubo, in fact, recalled in an interview in 1977 that for weeks on end, after the conclusion of a normal day's work in the Mission, the two of them would work on the book at night and even into the early morning hours. Norman, he recalled, dictated much of the text from working notes that Okubo had helped compose and, presumably, had translated. It is fair to recall here that the Canadian's literary Japanese remained somewhat underdeveloped, and time constraints then no doubt kept him from attempting much of the translating work himself. Collateral evidence that suggests Norman's reading ability in Japanese was still poor is provided in a letter that Herbert wrote to a leading Japanese historian who had just completed a major book dealing with

Japanese feudalism and the Restoration. In the letter, Norman asks that they meet on a regular basis so that the author might read his new book out loud.[48]

Despite whatever weaknesses in his scholarship that Ando and his other books might reveal, one of their greatest strengths was the positive effect they had on the revival of Japanese scholarship in the postwar period. Edwin Reischauer, former American Ambassador to Japan and Harvard University professor, writes, "In the early postwar years he [Norman] was virtually unique as a deep scholar of modern Japan among the occupation forces. As such, he renewed contacts with the Japanese historians, establishing in this way a valuable link between victor and vanquished. His interest and encouragement helped reinvigorate Japanese historical scholarship. His interpretations, being fundamentally based on Japanese scholarship, gave Japanese friends self-confidence and a realization that among the conquerors were people who understood their fears and hopes about a new Japan."[49] No less did Norman understand their past history of censorship and government repression of intellectuals, and of leftists—one and the same people in many, many instances—making his strong words in favor of resisting tyranny a liberating force at the very moment when the devastating effects of the past were being acutely felt.

Norman's private correspondence confirms Reischauer's claim. It tells of his meeting with Japanese intellectuals and historians, such as Hani Goro, Tsuru Shigeto (his old Harvard friend), Toyama Shigeki, and Maruyama Masao, largely in order to carry on discussions about different interpretations of Japanese history.[50] Too, also coming from his letters, it is clear that Norman served as a medium in introducing these and other Japanese scholars to western Asianists who were participating in the Occupation. Further, he helped to reorganize the Japan branch of the IPR in order to renew scholarly and cultural communication and understanding, and in 1947 he was elected president of the Asiatic Society of Japan (an affiliate of the Royal Asiatic Society), which existed for similar educational and cultural purposes.

As an intellectual force in the immediate postwar period, he seems to have had no equal. The message he had long been preaching—resistance to oppression, compassion and democracy for the common people, the necessity of freedom, and the humanizing effect of history—perhaps never before or since has had such a receptive audience. Even the Japanese Emperor's third son, with General MacArthur's enthusiastic approval, benefited from Norman's democratic interpretation of Japanese history once he began tutoring him in 1946.[51]

He also worked hard to take his message to a wider audience once he was securely ensconced as Head of the Liaison Mission. After 1947 he delivered several speeches to popular and university audiences on the theme of democracy. In Nagano, the town where he grew up, Herbert spoke in mid-June 1947 on the topic, "People Under Feudalism." The point of his address, which he delivered in Japanese, was to explain the impact that hundreds of years of feudal rule had had on "the nature of the Japanese people" and their "patterns of behavior." He wrote, "Life under the onerous despotism of Tokugawa feudalism left deep imprints on the minds and spirits of the Japanese." He generously offered his listeners an excuse for their participation in recent chauvinistic aggression before providing morally uplifting observations about the "inherent humanity and decency of the common people." He reminded them of past good deeds toward foreigners and of their democratic heroes who risked all in order to fight tyranny. He contrasted a tradition of "collective responsibility" with individualism, encouraging the "individual to act according to his conscience." And he concluded by reminding them that Nagano was one of Japan's cradles of democracy in the modern era and that under Occupation reforms, especially that of local autonomy, Nagano could recapture what was best in its past.[52]

In November of the following year, Norman addressed the topic "Persuasion or Force: The Problem of Free Speech in Modern Society," at Keio University. The occasion was the thirtieth anniversary of the founding of the Fukuzawa Research Society, named after the founder of Keio, Fukuzawa

Yukichi, a Meiji-period intellectual and liberal reformer whom Norman favorably compared with Diderot, Alexander Herzen, and Thomas Jefferson.[53]

In this speech he revealed much about his own political beliefs and his conception of the meaning of history. Norman sounds very much like the idealist liberal, who sees historical change as the result of individuals and groups invoking "the battle cry" of freedom and liberty, although he quickly points out that "once they [oppressed groups] themselves have succeeded in gaining political power, [they] have proved as oppressive as the dominant force which was overthrown or compelled to grant concessions." Such, he makes clear, is lamentable but unavoidable, the way of gaining freedom being what it is, "its course tortuous, leading sometimes into a cul-de-sac from which painful detours have to be made." ". . . freedom is not something constant and assured like the air around us. It has to be consciously won and jealously guarded . . . [and] can be lost through negligence or apathy in countries where it has reigned for many years."

He lists many of the great "lovers of liberty," such as Tom Paine, William Cobbett, John Brown, Garibaldi, and Oshio Heihachiro, but reminds his audience that "perhaps more decisive in the campaigns fought on behalf of freedom has been the army of anonymous and less-known humble folk," the lesser names in history.

Equally important in Norman's view, and reminiscent of a remark he had made to his brother Howard years before about Christian arrogance, "The corollary follows that no political party, no religious creed, no social class can claim a monopoly in the service of freedom." Here he is preaching tolerance, a classic liberal value, reminding his elitist and status-conscious audience of university students that the socially high and low, the politically conservative and radical, Christian and Buddhist, faithful and atheist, liberal and socialist, each have intrinsic value and moral purpose and should be encouraged to seek the sort of freedom that is compatible with their needs, circumstances, and moral views.

Norman extends this attitude of tolerance in his more pragmatic urging of "self-government" as the best institutional means of ensuring maximum freedom. He writes, "Now by self-government I do not mean to imply something mystical, abstract, or academic. It is a most reasonable, common-sense, and civilized way of life for any modern society, whether it calls itself republican, a constitutional monarchy, socialist or capitalist, or a mixture of these last two as most societies are today." Whatever the form of government or the socioeconomic system that underlies it, crucial in his view is that the relationship between ruler and ruled rest on an implied social contract; this is the essence of self-government, where "the people look upon government officials as their servants or as their deputies and not as their masters." And to give this message meaning to his Japanese audience, he adds, "It is the very opposite of that old concept, *kanson mimpi* (respect officials, despise people)."

Where people are respected and officials serve in the popular interest, there will be freedom of expression, "the very citadel of a self-governing society," as he called it. Freedom of expression requires that toleration be practised toward all political views, and this means that persuasion, not force, serve as the *modus operandi* in all human relations.

Nowhere did Herbert make a more categorical and unequivocal claim of his belief in liberalism or in the *necessity* of adopting liberal values wholesale. He meant it when he posed the alternatives in such stark terms—"persuade or perish"— and never before had he been so eloquent and persuasive. What is also remarkable is that everything he uttered in this speech is consistent with virtually everything he had written before in scholarly tomes. Before, he had left the liberal door open to the impact of human will, as opposed to materialism and historical necessity, on the course of human affairs. Now he declared that humans must respect human difference, accept human mistakes in the uncertain fight for liberty, and tolerate different approaches to realizing a condition of freedom for themselves. Suddenly his lifelong hatred of feudal oppression takes on world-historical relevance: "The world is tired of war and of force. Not only between classes in a nation but as between nations themselves, force must give way to persuasion and reason if the world is not to retrogress fatally." *Déjà vu;* we recall his condemnation of R. B. Bennett's Article 98, of Franco's fascism, of "iron-fisted capital" ignoring poverty, of Tokugawa rulers exploiting the peasantry, and, by logical extension, now, at long last, of Stalin's ugly purge trials.[54]

These lessons, formalized so forcefully after many years of reflection, were repeated by the Japan scholar often in the remaining years of his life. In late 1949, he traveled to Shizuoka to speak before a "Festival for Democracy" organized by the Occupation authorities. In 1953, in the midst of the Korean War, in a position paper for External Affairs entitled "Japan Since Surrender," he warned of external and internal threats to Japan's democratization policy, citing Soviet and Chinese aggressions as part of a larger picture of "violent change" and the dangers posed within Japan by "the unreformed and unrepentant." And he returned to his favorite themes of freedom, democracy, and the meaning of history in 1956 in a series of essays published in Japan, in Japanese, under the title, *Kurio no kao: Rekishi zuiso shu (The Face of Clio: Random Essays on History).*[55]

Today many of the essays in *Clio,* with the exception of reprints like "Persuasion or Force," read as though they were Norman's swan song to the world of scholarship. They read like "final reflections" on the meaning of history, concluding statements of the sort a man about to retire from academe might make. Little he writes in them is new—readers of his earlier work easily recognize his imprimatur, his elegant prose, his familiar "pungent" phrases, his rhetorical repetitions, and the political refrain intoning against the human and institutional enemies of freedom. Glittering generalities characterize these essays, intentionally, for he used them in part to strike a blow against the growing academic tendency to specialize and thereby to avoid the kinds of unqualified generalizations which he once claimed made the writings of his hero Ando Shoeki so powerful.

Norman's essays need not be cited *ad seriatim* in order to

summarize their purpose, which is to urge readers, and listeners, into civilizing themselves and their era by reading and understanding history, Oriental and Occidental. History, he writes, "is the discipline that makes the whole world kin," and "is for humanity what memory is for the individual." It is not deterministic, "although there are limits to the possible within a given period or situation. Men can be, to a widely varying degree, active and conscious makers of history." But they can not advance the cause of civilization unless they understand history: "It is not too strong to say that no person can be cultivated who has not a feeling for history." Yet, mankind, beware: he warns those who would presume to dictate history or claim to know all of history's secrets that Clio, the Muse of history, "was the most reserved of maiden goddesses; her face is sometimes only partly disclosed," and she will forever upset those, like that "demonic power" Hitler, who try "with dreadful consequences, [to] . . . put back the hands of [her] clock."[56]

With dreadful consequences, there were those who usurped power enough to turn back Clio's hands in an attempt to dictate Herbert Norman's own history, to ignore his liberalism, and to allege that he remained the communist ideologue that he had been as a student. They enjoyed what success, if it can be called that, they did in discrediting Norman precisely because he had elected to make his way in the world as a working Japanologist rather than as an academic Japanologist. Had he written only words of the sort examined in this chapter and stayed away from diplomacy, from the attempt to realize into policy the sort of principles contained in his writings, then Clio's malevolent actors—active and conscious makers of history as they were—would have been kept ignorant of Herbert Norman, just as they were ignorant of every word he uttered before and after he joined External Affairs.

For his persecutors, it was not *what* he said that mattered, but rather *where* he said it. Thirteen pages of Herbert's secret FBI file concern a paper—never found—on "American Imperialism" that he allegedly wrote while at Harvard; else-

where in the file are repeated listings of all his IPR publications
The FBI bibliographies of Norman's writings contain absolutely no annotation.[57] They judged him by his associations,
not by his words.

CHAPTER 4

JAPANOLOGIST

*[The Occupation authorities] showed an increasing sense
of urgency that Japan should be properly integrated into
United States strategy in what used [!] to be known as
the 'cold war' . . .*

Herbert Norman, *1950 Annual Report,
for External Affairs*

Choosing to be a participant in the making of history
rather than a detached, academic observer of its ways
and means exacted an onerous deprivation of the
freedom of this young Canadian shortly after his
return to Japan in May 1940. Japan was already at war in
China when the thirty-year-old Norman arrived, only to
witness the terrible effects of political repression domestically
and military expansion abroad. Westerners were being watched
by the authorities, and consideration of repatriating nones-
sential personnel and families was becoming policy. Within
a year after his return to Japan, with families of embassy
members returning to Canada, Norman and others in the
Canadian Embassy awaited the onslaught of war with Japan.

Pearl Harbor Sunday brought house arrest for the Canadian legation members, and there they remained for the next
seven months while awaiting a prisoner exchange to be effected with Allied governments. "An ideal person to be imprisoned with," said D'Arcy McGreer, the chargé d'affaires
in Tokyo, of Herbert Norman, referring to Herbert's weighty
discourses to legation personnel during the long, tedious days
of imprisonment. As McGreer told Sidney Katz years later,
"In the course of a single night," Norman "might discuss
Persian poetry, the wines used in Italy at the time of Catullus,
the gutty writing of John Aubrey (a little-known literary

figure in seventeenth-century England), and colorful personal sidelights on such writers as Cervantes and Voltaire."[1] Charles Taylor, embellishing this account and presumably drawing upon the testimony of other Canadian internees, adds, "On other occasions he would explore such subjects as how the unicorn got his horn, the mating habits of African tribes or the sewage system of ancient Rome."[2]

Forever the intellectual, delighting in obscure historical anecdotes and, in his friend Maruyama Masao's words, "the lesser names," all trademarks of Norman's personality according to anyone who ever spent an evening with him over cocktails, he was nonetheless the serious Japan specialist who spent the entire decade of the 1940s either working in Japan (1940-42, 1945, 1946-50) or working *on* Japan (1942-45, 1946) for the Department of External Affairs.

This does not mean that he was without career options. In mid–1941 Norman was offered an academic post to teach modern Japanese history at the University of Washington; similar offers came in succeeding years from Yale University and the University of California at Berkeley. Not until the mid-Fifties was he tempted by the University of British Columbia to leave diplomacy for academia, but then as we shall later see, Mike Pearson intervened to dissuade him.

But the focus of this chapter and the next is on Norman's diplomatic work in Japan between August of 1945 and October of 1950, when he was forced to return to Ottawa for a security investigation. The emphasis will be on his work as a *practising* Japanologist and will be treated in Norman's own terms, which make the distinction between an academic Japanologist and a diplomat-Japanologist. Herbert Norman saw himself in the British tradition of Sir George Sansom, as a scholar-diplomat, as one whose scholarly training in the field of Japanese studies was purposely utilized for practical ends.

A second focus, one which is by no means secondary to Norman's life and death, deals with the early beginnings of the American "security" case against him. As alluded to in the last chapter, the "security" file originated, unbeknownst to Herbert, precisely because he put himself into a public rather than a private occupation, because *he did have the influence* to "make events" and affect policy, and because he did enjoy *fame* as a scholar and analyst of Japanese politics. As the epigraph to this chapter suggests, Norman understood the objective goals of American foreign policy in the occupation of Japan, but as the details will show, he was, until too late, abysmally ignorant of the concrete and, for him, tragically individual effects of its Cold War foundation.

Norman had been hired by External Affairs because he was a Japanologist. He had worked throughout the war as a Japanologist in secret counter-intelligence, so it followed quite logically that after the war ended he would continue to work for the Ministry in a similar capacity. He had earned External's and even Prime Minister Mackenzie King's confidence as a result of his wartime duties. Within ten days of repatriation from Japan in August 1942, due to his Japanese language competence, he had been put to work "in highly secret intelligence work in the Examination Unit" in deciphering intercepted Japanese codes.[3] So valuable was his language ability, that the Office of Strategic Services (OSS), the CIA's wartime predecessor, tried to recruit him for work in Washington as a liaison "between Canadian and British Agencies and the Office of Strategic Services."[4] Moreover, his value to External rose all the more once Lester Pearson learned that Owen Lattimore, of the American Office of War Information in San Francisco, had tried to entice Herbert to join its "political warfare" unit. Norman wrote Lattimore, with Pearson's blessing, that his "work in the Examination Unit, building and organizing a Japanese Intelligence Section in collaboration with censorship and Service Intelligence officers" had top priority, but that perhaps future collaboration between his and Lattimore's units might be possible.[5]

The record shows that Herbert was only once released from his secret work in Ottawa, in August 1943, in order to accept Columbia University's invitation to lecture American naval officers being trained for civil administrative work in the occupied territories; no doubt the invitation came personally from Norman's old Columbia mentor, Hugh Borton.[6] When toward the close of the war, in January 1945, Yale University offered the Japanologist a teaching appointment, Mackenzie King intervened, telling Norman's boss Lester Pearson, "We should work to hold our *good* men . . . . make necessary arrangements to that end."[7]

As a result of King's intervention, Norman received a promise of promotion, effective 1 October 1945, before he was assigned to assist in the repatriation of Canadians from Manila, a job he began just ten days after the Japanese surrender in August. He left for Manila on 26 August 1945, with an understanding that he would go on to Tokyo after Manila, "appointed," as the record shows, "under Chungking [Chiang Kai-shek's government] and on loan to Tokyo [the U.S.– Allied Occupation authorities]."[8]

This latter appointment had been recommended by Owen Lattimore in a personal letter to Hugh Keenleyside.[9] Apparently Lattimore had not given up in his attempt to recruit Norman for U.S. counter-intelligence service work and saw the immediate postwar opportunity and the Allied occupation of Japan as the ideal context for making use of Norman's talents. Lattimore had made public his high regard for Herbert in his 1945 book, *Solution in Asia*. "Widely read in Japanese sources, this young Canadian is already the most authoritative contemporary analyst of Japan's economy, society, and government. He is to some extent a disciple, and in a sense the successor, of Sir George Sansom."[10] Lattimore sang the same high words of praise for Norman in his letter to Keenleyside, which were quoted in a memorandum to the U.S. counter-intelligence chief, Brigadier General Eliot Thorpe, in October 1945; Thorpe hired Norman on with a rank equivalent to major in the Counter-Intelligence Corps (CIC).[11]

Lattimore's recommendation of Norman would scarcely deserve more than footnote status were it not for the fact that in 1950 Senator Joseph McCarthy named Lattimore as a communist in one of his famous speeches denouncing the State Department's employees, alleging them to have been responsible for America's "loss" of China, and saying that he would rest his entire case for State's betrayal on the outcome of the Lattimore investigation. It was in the context of this investigation, beginning in March 1950, that Herbert's name was first publicly cited by the U.S. Senate. Though he was not pursued again publicly until August 1951, it was evident by early 1950 that the Senate was prepared to see the Lattimore-Norman link as evidence of pro-communist behavior. Further, this link was seemingly strengthened once the Senate initiated its witch-hunt against the IPR, with which both Norman and Lattimore were associated. That both the IPR and Lattimore were vindicated in a few short years made no difference in the McCarthyites' attitude toward Norman who, unlike Lattimore, never had benefit of a public defense in the United States.

But well before the Lattimore-Norman connection was considered relevant, Norman began working for the American Occupation and as a result became the subject of an FBI and Army Intelligence "security-C" (C for Communist) investigation. Once these two organizations began looking into Norman's past, the State Department, Naval Intelligence, and the CIA joined in the chase as well, and from north of the 49th, the RCMP lent assistance, especially in the wake of the Gouzenko revelations, which had linked Herbert's name to Israel Halperin, one of those named by the Soviet defector. For reasons which will gradually become clear, however, Norman did not become a "clear and present" threat to the national security of the U.S. and Canada until late 1950, when, for a variety of reasons, the Americans and the Canadians compared information for the first time. Until then, Norman had earned nothing but accolades from his superiors, both American and Canadian, for his work in the Occupation. First, we should examine what the Occupation was before looking at Norman's multifaceted role in it.

The Occupation lasted seven years, from almost immediately after the Japanese surrender in mid-August until the close of April 1952, about seven months after Canada and most other Allied nations had signed a peace treaty with Japan in San Francisco. As Occupation expert Kazuo Kawai has made clear, though nominally an Allied Occupation, it was

in fact "Japan's American Interlude."[12] Headed by the brilliant megalomaniac General Douglas MacArthur, whose official title, Supreme Commander of the Allied Powers (SCAP),
captures the near-dictatorial power he enjoyed, the Occupation was, in Kawai's words, a "moral crusade" to demi-
litarize and democratize the Japanese state and society.

In theory, overseeing MacArthur and the formation of
policy was the Far Eastern Commission (FEC), based in
Washington and composed of representatives of the eleven
(later thirteen) principal Allied nations, among which was
Canada. A veto provision, however, was purposely imbedded
into the FEC's machinery that guaranteed so-called big power
control in the form of the Allied Council; but in addition,
there also was a provision that permitted the United States,
and MacArthur, to formulate "urgent unilateral interim directives" without FEC approval. Suffice it to say that in
MacArthur's view, formulating policy was almost always
deemed "urgent": he did not hesitate to take charge and
ignore the FEC. As a result, it appeared to critics and sym-
pathizers alike that the Occupation was, contradictorily, little
more than a military dictatorship existing to create a democracy, albeit directed by a well-meaning and benevolent despot.

Organizationally, MacArthur set up the Occupation's machinery as he would an ordinary military headquarters, with
G-1 in charge of Personnel, G-2 taking charge of Intelligence,
and so on. And like any bureaucracy, military or civilian,
competition for access to the general's ear, rivalry in setting
policy, and personal antagonisms raised to the level of inter-
bureaucratic wrangling, all influenced everyday operations of
the Occupation government. The major figures in the inter-
SCAP bureaucratic struggles were Generals Whitney of G-1
and Willoughby of G-2, respectively MacArthur's "left" and
"right" hand men, literally and figuratively. In brief, Whitney
hired young American Asianists and New Deal lawyers to
help design and implement policy, and Willoughby employed
military intelligence agents to spy on Whitney's men. A relationship fraught with jealousy and mistrust, its effect on
specific individuals was catastrophic and in a most important

sense it foreshadowed the civilian, domestic McCarthyism of the 1950s.

Herbert Norman figured in the Occupation in three different capacities at three different times. During the first phase, devoted to demilitarization, he served in G-2 as a counter-intelligence officer when the civilian section of the branch was headed by General Eliot Thorpe, Willoughby's short-term predecessor. During the first stages of democratization, beginning in early 1946, he served in Washington on the FEC as Ambassador Lester Pearson's official alternate. And finally, when democratization was well under way, by late summer 1946, Norman served as Canada's chief representative in Japan with the title Head of the Liaison Mission, a post he held until mid-October 1950, though after March 1949 with the elevated rank of Envoy Extraordinary and Minister Plenipotentiary. As much as anything, his promotion in rank was in response to MacArthur's suggestion to Mackenzie King that Norman's diplomatic standing be made equal to that of other Allied mission heads.[13]

In short, then, Norman's nearly five years of involvement in and with the Occupation permitted him three different vantage points from which he could assess this monumental American attempt at political and social engineering: from the point of view of a military intelligence functionary, as a participant in the Allied policy-formation process, and as an informal adviser to MacArthur while at the same time serving as a reporter of events to his government and as a representative of its national interests. His Occupation experiences, therefore, were *unique:* no other Occupationaire could boast of such a multifaceted and variegated perspective, and for this reason alone, quite apart from the keen intelligence that his historian's eye lent to his observations, his insights into the Occupation made him extraordinarily valuable to policymakers then and to students of the Occupation today.

But at the same time and for the same reasons, from the point of view of Occupation right-wingers—those who believed, for example, that the resurrection of a Japanese socialist movement, mediated by G-1 personnel who saw

democratic socialism, the labor union movement, land reform, and trust-busting as opportune counterforces to resid-
ual feudal and fascist forces—Herbert's very intimacy with
the Occupation reforms and reformers made him highly suspect. Especially so once they began researching his past political associations, writings, and activities, only to discover
that not only did he make little or no attempt to repudiate
his past but, conversely, seemed to flaunt it by associating
with New Dealers in the Occupation as well as with Japanese
socialists, left-wing academics, and liberal parliamentarians.
As a result of his associations, but unknown to Herbert until
just shortly before his urgent recall to Ottawa, he was the
subject of an on-and-off-again 'security' investigation during
almost all of his five years in Japan (except for his first seven
months of working for Counter-Intelligence, which period
was investigated only after the fact).

In late 1945, his formal position with SCAP (which came
to refer to the Occupation Command as a whole, in addition
to MacArthur himself) was Chief of Research and Analysis
Section, Counter-Intelligence, in G-2. "It is every bit as interesting as it sounds," he wrote to his wife on 26 October
1945, two weeks after assuming the position. "My boss, the
head of CIS, is General [Eliot R.] Thorpe—a frank, blunt,
rough-tongued soldier but so accepts suggestions with so
much ease and affability that sometimes it quite astounds
me."

Norman's duties in late 1945 were largely concerned with
phase one of the Occupation, demilitarization, specifically
submitting background reports on suspected "war criminals"
who were likely candidates for trial and/or purge; assisting
in the release of imprisoned anti-militarists according to orders issued by MacArthur (SCAPIN 93, 4 October 1945); in-
terrogating war resisters and others in order to identify more
precisely the war crimes of the militarists; and composing a
list of, and background information on, political parties and
associations, and societies to be dissolved.[14] Herbert's letters
to his wife show clearly that he loved the work. "You have
no idea how terribly busy I have been the last two weeks,"

he wrote on 26 October, "yet never so excitingly busy in my life . . . . My immediate associates are young officers who are as pleasant and agreeable as can be. It is rather a strange position to be a civilian in charge of a U.S. Army unit. I have a major, one captain, five Lieutenants, and twenty-five enlisted men working in my section and a larger number working very closely in related sections."

In the same letter he reported on "the most exciting experience of my life," which would later be cited, unfairly, as evidence of loyalty to international communism. The "most exciting experience" was "to drive out to a prison twenty miles from Tokyo with another officer [John K. Emmerson] and be the first Allied officials to enter a prison with 16 leading political prisoners, including 2 communists (in prison for 18 and 19 years), 2 Korean Independence leaders [Korea had been a Japanese colony since 1910], anti-Fascist intellectuals (independent), [and] Tenrikyo religious leaders (a sect which does not believe in the divinity of the Emperor). The reception we got was something beyond description. I never enjoyed anything so much as being able to tell them that *according to General MacArthur's orders* they were to be released within a week [by 10 October]. Later we had the opportunity to interview them at greater length and after a few days of liberty they were able to give us political information on current affairs of the utmost interest."

Just six years after the episode, Eugene Dooman would allege in Senate hearings that the courtesies which Norman and Emmerson extended to the releasees lent so much public credibility to communism that the Japanese Communist Party was able to recruit "100,000" new members almost overnight. Dooman himself was not in Japan at that time. In March 1957 Norman's partner in the release, John Emmerson, would, under accusatory and leading questioning, tell a Senate committee that Norman "appeared to agree with the general [socialist] theses" offered by the communists they interrogated.[15]

If Norman had in fact been overly kind in his treatment of the releasees, and if in fact he had expressed general agreement with their socialist analysis of, presumably, the role of specific militarists who were responsible for making war, his "mistakes" were ones which no responsible person would have termed "mistakes" at that time. Central to Occupation goals was the removal of leaders tainted with war responsibility and their replacement with democratic personalities, leftist or otherwise. For the Occupation authorities, partial evidence of democratic potential, or at least of freedom from war guilt, was imprisonment by wartime authorities. War resisters, whether for reasons of religion, politics, ideology, nationality, or vocation, as in the case of prewar labor union leaders, were looked upon as the building blocks of a new generation of democratic leaders who could replace some of the 220,000 wartime leaders purged by the Occupation authorities. That many composing the new democratic leadership which MacArthur sought to resurrect proved to be politically radical was not only known to the Occupation authorities but even encouraged since it was felt that they offered the best hope for the eventual democratizing of Japan. Edwin Reischauer, in speaking of this period, credits "Marxist interpretations" as prevailing among policymakers who justified the unleashing of socialists and the implementation of reform measures, far more radical than acceptable to most Americans, and who believed that prewar Japan was "so thoroughly evil that only drastic measures could correct it." Reischauer adds, in noting SCAP's influence, "MacArthur turned out to be the most radical, one might even say socialistic, leader the United States ever produced, and also one of the most successful."[16]

Norman's own analysis of prewar Japan, as we have seen, was more sophisticated than that which Reischauer attributes to policymakers in the Occupation. For Norman, politics in prewar Japan had represented an ongoing struggle between the forces of reaction, almost always in power, and the forces of liberation, almost always struggling against government oppression. Hence for him the early Occupation policy of removing the worst reactionaries and replacing them with the best democrats made perfect sense. As a counter-intelligence chief, he gloried no less in identifying the "worst" elements for the purge, as he called them, than in freeing the "best."

Lest it seem that Norman was too fervent in resurrecting the left, note that in a letter to his wife, dated 25 September 1945, he defends MacArthur's "slowness to move against the citadel of Japanese reaction [the Emperor]," and makes clear his support for the two-pronged policy of demilitarization and democratization, of which he was only *one* of many functionaries. He writes, "Personally I think it is premature for the allies of Japanese liberal left to attack the Imperial Household — better to demand a purge of the higher bureaucracy, of the parties and of right wing groups (which are still strong), demand minimum reforms in the [Imperial] Household, attack its myths and mystique, [and] demand a rational, scientific history of the Institution (Prof. Suzuki and Takagi, by no means leftists, insist on the need of this last point)." He adds that the Japanese "are not yet ready or politically prepared" to support the "overthrowing of the Emperor" and that therefore the "progressives" would best be served by supporting such modest reforms. He felt quite strongly that the "allied forces should remain neutral in this struggle—but in such a way as somehow to hinder the reactionary elements and let the Japanese do the rest."

Norman had little confidence that the Japanese authorities themselves would carry out the "negative tasks"—"they still seem to lack proper political organization and know-how"— but he had every confidence that, if encouraged, the long-suppressed, incipient democratic forces, imprisoned during the war could *and should* carry out most of the democratic reforms themselves. As a Jeffersonian democrat, he strongly believed that "the only enduring democracy is one of the people's making; one imposed from above would be doomed to fail."

Interestingly, official Occupation policy followed Norman's own prescription for leaving the Imperial institution alone and focused instead on the negative tasks of conducting purges. Herbert himself played a leading role in the identification of the "worst elements" and it would appear, as we shall see, that in almost every instance where he recommended prosecution, his advice was taken, while in the two instances he recommended clemency, it was ignored.

As a leader in counter-intelligence, he spent considerable time composing biographies of suspected war criminals and in submitting recommendations for their prosecution. In November and December he submitted several such indictments, for that is what they proved to be, against "war criminal suspects" to George Atcheson, Jr., a State Department official who in the fall of 1945 served as Political Adviser to General MacArthur. The most important of Norman's reports concerned Prince Konoe, who at that time was Minister without Portfolio in the immediate postwar government of Prime Minister Higashikuni and who was most active in securing influence with MacArthur over the design of the new constitution. Although Konoe lost official status in mid-October as the Higashikuni cabinet was replaced by the Shidehara, as a prewar prime minister and leading oligarch, Konoe's influence remained strong and his attempts to construct a watered-down 'democratic' constitution that would preserve much of the prewar power structure continued unabated.

Norman's analysis of Konoe, submitted to Atcheson, was therefore of vital importance. In a "Top Secret" communiqué from Atcheson to the Secretary of State, dated 17 November, Norman's memorandum on Konoe proves to have been critical. Atcheson notes that Norman's "memorandum comprises, in our opinion, a very able presentation of the political case against Konoye and is of special interest at this time because, we understand, there is considerable reluctance in some quarters to arrest Konoye along with the other major suspects still at large." Atcheson quotes Norman at length in arguing for the prosecution of Konoe as a war criminal, and clearly accepts Norman's judgment that "Konoye set in motion those policies and alliances which could only [have] led to a collision with the Western powers."[17]

While it is true that Konoe's name had been cited as early

as September for inclusion in the War Crimes list, as late as 4 October Konoe had gained an audience with General MacArthur and had spent much of that month jockeying for power within highly placed Occupation circles for the purpose of influencing the content of the new constitution. But, in the words of Dale Hellegers, who has studied this episode in depth, "Konoe's personal doom was not sealed until 5 November, . . . when Herbert Norman . . . submitted to SCAP a devastating critique of Konoe's career." The very next day MacArthur ordered Atcheson to cease all contact with Konoe, and a few days after that Konoe's name appeared in a new list of war criminals. His arrest was ordered on 6 December but he committed suicide before he could be imprisoned.[18]

Norman's successes in removing the "worst elements" from positions in power went beyond Konoe. His memoranda on Kido Koichi, Lord Keeper of the Privy Seal, and Izawa Takio, whom Norman labeled "a Japanese Eminence Grise," were likewise favorably received and acted upon. In both memoranda he revealed his indisputable expertise—cited by Atcheson in his memos to the Secretary of State—but also a morally questionable tendency to rely on *ad hominem* characterizations in discrediting his targets. Konoe, for example, is described in these terms: "He is a weak, vacillating, and, in the last analysis, a contemptible character. Even his hypochrondria is a childish method he exploits to evade unpleasant decisions...."[19] But in the immediate postwar period, "victor's justice" was played out as the fitting outcome in the larger morality play of undifferentiated good disposing of undifferentiated evil; the finer points of law could easily be overlooked. In any event, at least in these three cases, Herbert's judgment was never challenged and as a result his expertise became more widely acknowledged and his credibility more securely established.

Indeed, once the War Crimes Trial preparations got underway, Brigadier Nolan, the Canadian Associate Prosecutor, attempted to convince the Secretary of State for External Affairs to persuade Ambassador to Washington Lester Pear-

son to release Norman from his duties with the FEC to return
to Tokyo for the trials.[20] Similar evidence of his value came
when Herbert left Japan for Ottawa on 1 February 1946,
before reassignment to the FEC in Washington. Norman's
boss, General Thorpe, wrote to Prime Minister King, "I
should like to express to you my personal appreciation of
Dr. Norman's services. His profound knowledge of Japan,
his brilliant intellectual attainments and his willingness to give
of his utmost to our work had made his contribution to the
success of the occupation one of great value. During his tour
of duty with us, Dr. Norman has won the respect and admiration of all who have been associated with him."[21]

For his part, Norman left Japan in February 1946 in an
unusually positive frame of mind about the early successes
of the Occupation and of MacArthur's leadership in particular. In March, he was asked to speak to the Foreign Policy
Association of New York about "Japan in Evolution." At
the outset of his talk he posed the question of whether in
Japanese history "there are any traditions which would make
the present reforms . . . permanent and deep rooted?" He
cited a "tradition of agrarian revolt against social injustice"
as a positive legacy for promoting democratic reform, but
added that the Japanese people, if unaided, were "too immature and politically inexperienced" to "achieve full eman-
cipation." What little reform that had come in the past several
centuries had been "carried out from above," as in the aftermath of the overthrow of the Tokugawa shogunate (1868).
He cited this important event for the sake of comparison,
emphasizing that then, as now (1946), "the original impetus
[for reform] came from above, in the one case from military
bureaucrats and in the present case from the Supreme Commander and the forces of occupation."

Norman then moved from historical observation to undiluted praise: "Fortunately the comparison ends there because the Supreme Commander [MacArthur] and his forces
have followed a course designed to give the Japanese the
maximum opportunity to develop their own democratic institutions whereby the people can participate fully in the

government of their country." Of MacArthur himself, Norman says, "His timing and judgment [regarding reforms] has been superb." Of MacArthur's purge, Herbert calls it "the most important single directive." He referred to MacArthur's order to free political prisoners as "the first important directive."

In his eulogy, the only evidence that suggests Norman had not totally suspended his critical faculties was a reminder of the dangers posed by the reactionary Japanese bureaucracy who "hope by appearing to comply with all the requirements of the Occupation and thus hasten its end, they can in the meantime salvage as much as possible of the old regime." And the more general and philosophical observation, "It is obvious that this process of reform from above can only go so far. Somewhere along the line the Japanese people themselves have to take hold and build up their own democratic regime." These were two reservations that Herbert would repeat frequently and privately in his confidential dispatches to Ottawa following his return to Japan as Head of the Liaison Mission in late 1946, but as of March 1946, his optimism runneth over: "No one is more fully aware of the need for the Japanese people taking hold and performing the task [of democratization] than General MacArthur."[22]

Norman's sanguine assessment and outlook must largely be attributed to his sense of accomplishment in participating in counter-intelligence in the early phase of the Occupation. His recommendations regarding war criminals had been accepted and acted upon; his role in releasing political prisoners—again, on orders from MacArthur's office—had been emotionally liberating; his superiors openly praised his work and contributions; and he had been part of the advance guard in a revolutionary restructuring of the Japanese state, the land of his long years of study, the country of his birth, and the home of his parents. Amazingly, this bookish Canadian, still only in his early thirties, had spoken and American generals had listened. It was a heady experience that at one and the same time lent justification to his personal and ideological impulses and sentiments, and to his choice of professions.

Whoever can giveth can also taketh away: Ottawa needed Norman in early 1946 and so recalled him from Tokyo in order to reassign him to Washington, D.C., where the FEC was based. His new title was Deputy Canadian Representative, but his real duties made him, in effect, Canada's principal representative to the FEC since Ambassador Pearson was otherwise engaged. Norman's tenure with the FEC was brief: he commenced his duties on 9 March and left Washington for Ottawa on 7 June.

During that time, in recognition of his growing responsibilities and his significant contributions, he was promoted to the rank of First Secretary (effective 1 April 1946) and was officially transferred from the Embassy in Chungking.[23]

Though his three-month tenure with the FEC was chronologically short, it was long in impact. Norman was nearly alone among FEC representatives for having enjoyed the "hands-on" experience of working in the Occupation. The others had not, in fact, visited Japan until mid-December 1945, on a fact-finding mission. He had met them first in Tokyo and had returned with them to Washington at the conclusion of their six-week visit. It must therefore be surmised that, despite his youth, many in the FEC deferred to him later, because they perforce would acknowledge his experience and his expertise.

There is some evidence in support of this conjecture. The major issue in which Norman was actively involved while with the FEC was the issue of Japan's proposed new constitution and the related issue of the first general election, due to take place in April. Obviously, for so momentous an event to take place such a short time after defeat was mind-boggling in its implications for democratization. Kazuo Kawai helps to explain what happened: "As was apparent from the outset to almost everyone, the new constitution was drafted in secrecy within General MacArthur's headquarters, sprung upon a distraught Japanese cabinet, and forced through a reluctant Japanese Diet after a few minor changes had been permitted to the Japanese."[24] He might have added that MacArthur totally neglected to consult with his supposedly superior policymaking organ, the FEC.

Norman's part in this was central. He had been named Acting Chairman of the Constitutional Revision Committee, the group within the FEC whose responsibility it was to represent all the Allied nations' views on the future constitution. Quite naturally, this Committee assumed that MacArthur would at the very least consult with it before making any draft public, but on 6 March 1946, the Japanese press printed the completed draft of the new, MacArthur-dictated constitution. For Norman's committee, the central question became whether or not to rebuke MacArthur for exceeding his authority by imposing his own constitution without regard for the wishes of the FEC, not to mention the Japanese people. A "Secret" cipher from Ambassador Pearson to Ottawa puts the Canadian (and Commonwealth) position into proper perspective: "Whatever the facts, publication of the draft in this way has been most unwise and raises in an acute form the question where responsibility for the control of Japan is to be."[25] In other words, MacArthur's dictatorial style on such a major issue finally shocked the FEC into realizing where real power resided.

The related issue was the first general election. MacArthur wanted Japan's first elected Diet (parliament) to rubber-stamp *his* constitution, and even employed the Emperor for endorsing purposes. MacArthur was presenting a *fait accompli* to the FEC, the Diet, and the Japanese people, quite overcome as he was with the missionary's zeal in knowing what is best for others. As Acting Chair of the committee, Herbert Norman had to deal directly with MacArthur's arrogance; simultaneously, he was forced to mediate between committee members who represented wildly varying views, ranging from the Soviet's advocacy of a socialist constitution to the New Zealander's proposal to censure MacArthur for arrogation of power. To his credit, and as clear testimony to his growing powers of diplomacy, Norman skillfully steered the committee toward drafting a message to MacArthur that would remind the General about commonly accepted democratic procedure.[26] The rebuke was mild, and kept private, largely because they all, even his detractors, realized that to go public and censure MacArthur might undermine his credibility and therefore that of the entire Occupation, inseparable as the two were in the Japanese public consciousness by this time.

While the episode must be counted as a defeat for Allied control over Occupation policy, it must also be regarded as a personal and diplomatic "victory" for Norman. Yet at the same time, as influential Japanese leaders today call for revision of the "MacArthur Constitution" for being "un-Japanese," the episode throws into bold relief the caveat about imposing democracy from above which Norman uttered at just this time in his speech before the Foreign Policy Association. He said, "It is not enough even to have the most perfect drafts of constitution and laws promulgated, for only they [the Japanese] themselves can strive to create and implement them."[27] In his own way, he was serving notice to Occupation policymakers, including MacArthur, that he would not remain uncritical forever.

At the same time, Norman was *not* speaking simply for himself. In fact, he was clearly and honestly representing the policy of the Canadian government. This is to be expected, but it is also conveniently forgotten by many of Norman's critics. The point is that he followed the instructions he received from External Affairs without exception, as in the case of the disagreements over the new Japanese constitution. As "Secret" dispatches between Pearson and External make abundantly clear, the Canadian government, as well as other Commonwealth governments *and the Soviet Union,* were angered by MacArthur's unilateral declaration of the new constitution. Pearson makes clear the democratic basis of his criticism of MacArthur, namely, that due process and careful public deliberation and debate must precede the adoption of the fundamental law of the land and that, therefore, in Pearson's words, "the present Diet [elected in April 1946] should not be empowered to pass on the draft constitution."[28] Canada, Pearson, and Norman took seriously the charge given

to the FEC to make policy and MacArthur's supposedly sub-
ordinate duty to implement it. They recognized that to concede to MacArthur in this most fundamental of all reforms
would result in the total emasculation of the FEC and would
deny, again in Pearson's words, "the Japanese people . . . an
opportunity to express their will on that Constitution through
a referendum."[29] Hence, Norman's position was in full agreement with his superiors—democratic, respectful of democratic rights and critical of dictatorial, executive prerogative,
they were simply reminding the American proconsul of the
fundamentals of democracy, even as he dictated democratic
reform.

More should be said about the Canadian government's
expectations of the Occupation and its reforms, if for no other
reason than to set the stage for demonstrating the extent to
which Herbert Norman faithfully represented his government, which in turn will help to explain why a democratic
Canadian representative could run afoul of less democratic
American right-wingers who occupied positions of authority
in the Occupation.

In December 1945, External Affairs Minister St. Laurent
cabled Ambassador Pearson in Washington regarding Canada's policy toward the *zaibatsu,* or "financial cliques," such
as Mitsui, Mitsubishi, Sumitomo, and other behemoths that
had dominated the prewar economy: "We support the principle of breaking up the Zaibatsu. Although under a democratic form of Government they might not constitute a menace,
it seems unlikely that they would make any positive contribution to securing such a Government for Japan. Indeed,
during the formative stage, their retention might well impede
the efforts of progressive and democratic forces."[30] Important
to note, the governments of New Zealand, Australia, *and* the
United States agreed with this policy position. The working
assumption of all these nations, very simply, boiled down to
a deep-seated fear that the concentration of capital was wrong,
potentially unproductive, and lent itself to political manip-
ulation. Advocacy for diffusion of economic power was mir-
rored in Canada's support for diffusion of political power as

well; nothing short of economic and political democracy was Canada's aim, and, needless to say, Herbert shared this goal.

As early as September 1944, in a secret memorandum to Dr. Hugh Keenleyside concerning Canada's postwar Japan policy, he had revealed that he preferred what some later called a "hard peace." For example, he called for the "total disarmament [of Japan], the stripping of its arsenals, the demobilization of its armed forces, and the fitting punishment for its war criminals." He even advocated that the peace treaty "should provide for the prohibiting of the manufacture or use of aeroplanes or naval craft . . . and, most important, *not even a skeleton army should be permitted with a General Staff.*" In short, Norman anticipated by two years the famous Article 9 of the new constitution, which still denies Japan the right or the means to wage war. Given his access to the constitution drafters, especially Charles Kades, who today quite openly admits Herbert's influence on his views, there is reason to believe that Herbert Norman was at least partly responsible for the conception behind the "Peace Constitution."[31]

In the same document, written when he was heading the top-secret counter-intelligence unit in External, Norman called for a cautious deferral of a decision about the ultimate fate of the Imperial institution; for a constitution that would support freedom of speech and thought; for the constitutional recognition of "free trade unions and peasant unions; for thoroughgoing land reform; for the restructuring and demilitarization of Japanese industry; and for support for an extensive purge of wartime leaders and a prohibition against any of them from taking office."[32] In fact, Canadian post-surrender policy was largely defined by this seventeen-page document, meaning that official policy in all its essentials was in effect set by Herbert Norman. Equally important to observe, MacArthur's policies, defined by the U.S. Initial Post-Surrender Policy for Japan, did not differ significantly from Canada's and hence Norman's in virtually every respect, at least through 1947.[33] But beginning in 1947, when MacArthur "reversed course" by retreating on the major issues of trust-

busting and the depurge of wartime leaders, and began supporting the purge of leftists, attacks on the labor unions, and
the imposition of press censorship aimed against left-wing
views, Canadian and American policy parted company, hence
Norman's fundamentally democratic views fell from favor.
His fall from grace occurred midway in his tenure as Canada's
top representative to SCAP.

From his career-long experiences in postwar Japan, first as
SCAP functionary and then as FEC policymaker, Norman was
the natural choice of External to head the diplomatic mission
to represent Canada's interests in occupied Japan. His appointment began with a 2 April 1946 letter from Mike Pearson
to Norman Robertson concerning "the problem of representation in Japan." Robertson replied to Pearson on 16 April,
addressing the relative merits of appointing a civilian liaison
mission versus a military mission, but ruling out "once more
putting a Canadian into SCAP . . . [since] this would seriously
restrict his freedom of action." Robertson decided that preference would be given to a civilian mission, once General
MacArthur gave his permission. Robertson so chose because
he realized that representing Canadian interests "might well
involve negotiations and reports which were to *some degree
critical of* SCAP."[34] Robertson told Pearson to inform the
Americans that Canada wanted an answer to its request for
diplomatic representation by 15 May.

It came before then. Norman learned that he was to be
appointed Head of the Liaison Mission in the second week
of May while he was still in Washington.[35] His "requisition
for appointment" was published on 16 July; it characterized
him as a person with "integrity, tact, keen perception and
good judgment." His rank was upgraded to FSO, Grade 3,
as head of mission, effective 1 August.[36]

As he prepared to leave for Japan, however, he learned that
the Canadian Legation was being occupied by British Commonwealth members of the International Prosecution section
of the War Crimes Trials. With appointment in hand, but
noplace to go, since the British refused to turn over the Legation to its proper owners, Herbert successfully used his

old contacts with SCAP officials to clear the way for reoc-
cupation of the Embassy. He also had to insist that SCAP
reverse an earlier decision forbidding his wife from accompanying him. To set matters straight, Norman and his superiors cabled SCAP to express a willingness to share *their*
legation quarters with Commonwealth representatives but
emphasized that the Canadian Mission must receive space
priority. Canadian plans had the Normans leaving for Japan
in late June or early July. The best laid plans . . . .

Ottawa became frustrated. MacArthur had been slow in
approving the principle of a liaison mission, despite Ottawa's
reckoning that Norman's name would smooth the way for
acceptance. In a memorandum for the Acting Secretary of
State, dated 30 May 1946, we read: "As Mr. Norman is a
distinguished Japanologist and served for a time on General
MacArthur's staff in Tokyo and later as a Canadian delegate
on the Far Eastern Commission during its tour of Japan, it
was felt both that it would be easier to get SCAP's cooperation
if Mr. Norman were named head of the mission, and that he
was the best man we could send. [The document notes that
Norman was approved both by Norman Robertson and by
the Prime Minister]."

It seemed to Ottawa that MacArthur was using the issue
of a housing shortage to delay the establishment of the liaison
mission. Herbert and Irene waited in the wings in Ottawa
for another month before approval came for Herbert alone
to proceed; permission for Mrs. Norman did not come until
late September. Finally, Herbert and his commercial attaché
left on 2 August. They arrived in Tokyo on 14 August. And
there Norman remained for four more years.

In the half year or so that he had been away from Japan,
conditions in the country and within SCAP had changed dramatically. In MacArthur's words, offered to posterity gran-
diloquently on the first anniversary of Japan's surrender, and
just a month after Norman had returned, "A spiritual revolution ensued [since surrender] which almost overnight tore
asunder a theory and practice of life built upon two thousand

years of history and tradition and legend."[37] Even allowing
for MacArthurian inflated rhetoric, the General did seem to
believe that democracy was being imposed from above; that
with a new parliament, constitution, and recycled prewar
'liberal' leaders—all extensions of his predominantly American vision of democracy—Japan was being thoroughly purged
of what he called its "feudalistic overlordship" and its centuries-old tradition of being "the natural warriors of the Pacific." MacArthur asserted that the recent defeat "left a complete
vacuum morally, mentally and physically," and that into this
vacuum "flowed the American democratic way of life."

MacArthur warned, however, that until the "vacuum" was
completely filled by "the great middle course of moderate
democracy," "the clash of ideologies" could imperil his unprecedented attempt to engineer a new polity and society.
Long "regimented under the philosophy of an extreme conservatism," the Japanese "might prove easy prey to those
seeking to impose a doctrine leading again to regimentation,
under the philosophy of an extreme radical left."[38]

MacArthur's words betray the fact that since Herbert's
departure months before, the Cold War had begun to infect
Japan. Not as obvious but nonetheless important, they also
refer to the rising influence of General Charles A. Willoughby, MacArthur's head of Counter-Intelligence and
number-one hunter of communists. Morbidly suspicious of
all so-called "Asian experts," especially those, like Norman,
who had ever been associated with the Institute of Pacific
Relations, Willoughby spent untold hours tracking down suspected left-wingers; Herbert Norman, Japan expert extraordinaire, became one of his chief targets. Within a month of
Norman's return, Willoughby had picked up the scent.[39]

Two facets of Norman's time as Head of the Liaison Mission present themselves, therefore: the first is what he actually
said, wrote, and did in his capacity as Canada's top representative in Japan between late 1946 and late 1950; the other
is what he is alleged to have done as a suspected ideological
foe in the Cold War. Ultimately, in terms of the impact on
his career and life, the suspicions counted more than the

achievements; in the Cold War, public officials, whatever their nationality, were presumed guilty unless (never until) the *accusers* could decide for their innocence. To address the facts first.

Herbert Norman's duties, just as those of any Canadian ambassador, were basic: generally, to look after Canada's national interests, to assist Canadian residents, to report on SCAP and Japanese government policy developments, and to assist Canadian business in reopening trade with Japan. His regular monthly dispatches to Ottawa show quite clearly that he performed all these tasks faithfully, efficiently, and conscientiously. As early as 17 December 1946, with just four months service in Japan behind him, Pearson sent a personal note to Herbert that acknowledged his worth: "I wish you were in the Department to help me, but as that seems impossible, I am glad that you are carrying on in your usual efficient way in Tokyo."

As many of his dispatches to Ottawa indicate, Norman spent much of his time dealing with the mundane: he mentions lending assistance to Quebec nuns, Protestant missionaries, Canadian businessmen; making arrangements for visiting trade delegations. He reports on internecine struggles between G-1 and G-2; on Canadian participation in the War Crimes Trials; on aiding government personnel; on meeting with Japanese business leaders, academics, and bureaucrats; even on attending several labor demonstrations with an eye toward trying to determine the extent of communist influence. All of these he rendered forthrightly. In a 1947 communiqué to Norman, Pearson writes that one of Herbert's dispatches concerning the political situation in Japan is "being given a pretty wide distribution" [within External]. Pearson closes with complimentary remarks about the high quality of Herbert's reporting: "We are fortunate to have in Tokyo a competent observer such as you at this time. Your exposition of Japanese politics makes sense even to the general reader and your resourceful style of writing sustains interest throughout the despatch. I shall look forward to reading more of your despatches."[40]

As his dispatches make clear, Norman also took special care to cultivate friendly relations with MacArthur and members of his staff. On 1 July 1947, he invited General and Mrs. MacArthur and senior SCAP staff members to the Legation for the Dominion Day celebration. (By this time the housing crunch had ended and the Embassy had completely reverted to Canadian control.) MacArthur, by reputation a teetotaller and non-smoker, was reported to have indulged in both of these human vices at the celebration and to have revealed a remarkably paternal attitude toward the much younger man.[41] On another occasion, Norman organized a meeting between MacArthur and a delegation of Canadians—government, military, and business—telling the General that he has "been most anxious that the truly historic accomplishments of the occupation would be understood and appreciated by representative Canadians." Norman also seems to have been not at all reluctant to send MacArthur some of his scholarly writings and copies of his speeches (including the "neo-Marxist" one he gave in Nagano entitled "People Under Feudalism"). In his cover letter for one of these writings, Norman reminds the General about the similarity of their views: "I recall a remark you made during my last interview with you in which you stated that the common people in Japan were by nature kindly and it was only the military caste which were brutal. This speech of mine gives two or three examples from the history of late Japanese feudalism which rather dramatically illustrates this point."[42]

Maintaining a friendly working relationship with MacArthur was, of course, central to Herbert's duties, just as it is for any ambassador to cultivate friendly ties with any head of state. As already observed, in his capacity as functionary for SCAP during the first phase of the Occupation, he was extremely complimentary of MacArthur and the reform measures which the General had executed. A year after his return to Japan as Mission Head, he told the General that "the past year of my stay in Japan, where I have had the privilege of observing the progress of the Occupation at close quarters, has been, without doubt, the most interesting and inspiring in my life." As late as 28 February 1949, Herbert went to some pains to thank MacArthur for having recommended to External Affairs that he be promoted to the rank of Envoy Extraordinary and Minister Plenipotentiary. He said to the General: "I want to write to you in this personal way to express to you my sincere appreciation for the kind interest you have shown in me personally and in my position here as Canadian representative." As before, and again as in this letter, marked "Personal," Norman discussed his scholarly work with the General. MacArthur had recommended to him the week before that he might try writing an article comparing Japan "past and present." Herbert demurred, but told the General about his forthcoming book on Ando Shoeki, into which he would "weave . . . some general considerations which will point to the intellectual freedom now enjoyed in Japan, thanks to those policies which were fashioned and guided by you."[43] Also indicating the growing intimacy of the two men, several letters Norman wrote to the General after this time open with the salutation, "My dear General MacArthur."

The relationship between the two men seems to have been something more than simply cordial. Charles Kades, Deputy Chief of G-1 and one of the architects of Japan's new constitution, recalls that "the first person in GHQ General MacArthur spoke to after the Emperor visited him was Herb Norman, which perhaps is some measure of his closeness to the Commander-in-Chief, and in my opinion Mr. Norman's memoranda and oral advice were very favorably received and influential."[44] Similarly, several of Norman's junior officers in the Mission recall frequent meetings between the two men, oftentimes taking place as a result of MacArthur's request for advice. One of the earliest instances of MacArthur's confidence in Norman came in late September 1946 when Norman was asked to become the private tutor for Prince Mikasa, the third son of the Emperor. Initially, the request for this service came from President Nambara of the Imperial University. Norman cabled Pearson that he viewed "the prospect with mixed feelings," saying that on the one hand the experience would give him "insight into court politics," but on the other hand he had "considerable doubts as to propriety of one in my position." Pearson agreed with the latter position and in a note of 1 October advised St. Laurent against giving Herbert permission. Subsequently, however, MacArthur intervened in favor of accepting the position, presumably for the first reason Herbert cited. St. Laurent overruled Pearson, saying, "it might be difficult for Mr. Norman to refuse this assignment in view of General MacArthur's enthusiastic approval."[45]

On another occasion, this in November 1948, Norman tried but failed (in the short term) to influence MacArthur to commute the sentences of two convicted war criminals, Shigemitsu Mamoru and Togo Shigenori. In a meeting of representatives of all the Allied powers with MacArthur on 22 November, the majority endorsed the findings of the War Crimes Tribunal; Herbert had acquiesced at the meeting, saying he found the judgments against these two men legally fair but that he would not be opposed to the granting of clemency. The following day he wrote MacArthur a "Secret and Personal" letter that shows he had changed his mind. He advised MacArthur to commute their sentences, Shigemitsu's from seven years to two and a half, and Togo's from twenty years to "ten or even five." Herbert emphasized that he did not disagree with the judgment of the Tribunal—he acknowledged the guilt of the two men—but only that commutation as a "political act" might have a "beneficial effect on public opinion." In Shigemitsu's case, he reminded the General that he had already served two and a half years of incarceration while waiting for the trial to conclude, and contended that in Togo's case a lengthy prison sentence for such an elderly man "is rather meaningless." Norman defended his recommendations with the words, "This may not be legal reasoning but I think at least it has in it a quality of common sense and humanity." He further argued, "[commutation] will reveal to the Japanese public in a practical manner that the victorious powers are not motivated by a general and indiscriminate sense of revenge." He made clear that "I feel that I am carrying out my obligations to my government and also following the dictates of my conscience."[46]

Neither in the MacArthur Archives nor in External Affairs records is there a letter from MacArthur answering Herbert's appeal, but curiously, almost exactly two years later MacArthur released Shigemitsu from prison. Herbert's humanitarian appeal had apparently worked.[47] But this speculation is less important than the simple fact that he made the appeal, showing that he felt close enough to MacArthur to attempt to change the imperious General's mind. His plea reveals several other things as well. Like the General, Herbert had once favored a "hard peace", one that would forever destroy Japan's war-making capability, that would vigorously prosecute the "worst elements," that would radically restructure Japan's economy, and so forth. Both men thought such an approach necessary in order to purge Japan of its centuries-old feudal and militaristic tradition. By late 1948, however, Herbert seemed to be showing a change of heart; his long-held humanitarian principles, for several years suspended aloft in the spirit of democratic reconstruction, had returned to him, even to the extent of challenging the Supreme Commander and the consensus of the Allied Powers. He was arguing against "victors' justice," pleading that mercy be shown to the two old and weakened former foreign ministers. Such an argument was far removed from the one he had made in late 1945 against Konoe and others.

No less important, Norman's appeal to the General reveals a growing independence of mind and thinking, a liberal and tolerant disposition toward individuals, and perhaps even a softening of temperament toward defeated Japan. Regardless, what is undeniable is that he took a moral stand that did not rely on any sort of firm ideological foundation, and did so in opposition to the most powerful, and maybe power-hungry, man in Japan. Too, he did so in a defense of men whom just a few years earlier he would have called "Fascists."

Why the change in attitude? In earlier chapters it was shown how ideologically adaptable Herbert was, how his whole series of political conversions were closely related to changing political conditions and circumstance. His own term, "chameleon-like," was earlier used to characterize his conversions, despite professed misgivings about the pejorative connotation of the term. Yet, lest this association take too firm a hold in the reader's mind, let it also be pointed out that whatever his color changes in adapting to changing political environments, there are more basic qualities about him that remain forever the same. As student or scholar or diplomat, Norman's beliefs in human freedom were unchanging, however radically the particular political idiom he employed to profess the value of human freedom might change. During the Occupation, and in his highly responsible position as Canada's chief representative, political context and diplomatic rank determined his political outlook, one which, as discussed earlier when analyzing his work on Ando Shoeki, was as liberal-democratic as was initial Occupation and Canadian policy itself. The truth of this point becomes readily apparent when his political reporting to Ottawa is examined in greater detail.

CHAPTER 5
DEMOCRAT

Once liberty is dead, people must lose their self-respect;
despair, envy, deceit, and malice will grow apace like
weeds in a deserted garden.
Herbert Norman, *"Persuasion or Force" (1948)*

Herbert's most serious thoughts during his last four years in Japan invariably concerned the dangers that Occupation rule and conservative Japanese leadership posed to democratization. In the other-regarding side of his life loomed this passion for democracy and for the people. Indeed, insofar as Norman ever revealed the passionate side of his character, which he was reluctant to do, he did so with a sort of Shelleyan romanticism that extolled the inherent goodness of the people and, from the opposite perspective, the intrinsically evil, power-seeking quality of the state. Very much the liberal democrat by then, in support of his warning about the effects of the loss of liberty, as stated in the epigraph above, Norman could quite comfortably cite classic liberal John Stuart Mill: "A state which dwarfs its men in order that they may be more docile instruments in its hands even for beneficial purposes, will find that with small men no great thing can really be accomplished."

But, as before, Norman's affection for the people was seemingly belied by what others, including Charles Taylor and Sidney Katz, have called Norman's "Epicureanism," an egocentric, potentially self-indulgent philosophy that emphasizes the cultivation of one's own character and the gratification of one's own desires. Testimony from friends and former colleagues, for example, refers again and again to Herbert's eye for beauty, especially feminine beauty. A Japanese academic friend recalls joining a colleague and Norman around 1950 for an evening in a Ginza bar where Norman "was very nice to the girls there." His attitude toward the women, said his friend, "was something more intimate than may be the case with most foreigners who would visit such a place casually." Similarly, early in his stay in Japan he writes privately of visiting a geisha house in the company of several American officers and elsewhere in his correspondence he refers to visits with a Japanese playgirl of some renown.[1]

Herbert enjoyed other diversions during this period as well. Liaison Mission clerk Lorne Berlet fondly recalls the deep affection that Herbert had for his Alsatian named Brandy, how Herbert would run and play with the dog at Meiji Park in Tokyo's center, adding that the relationship between the man and the dog fairly captured "the particular warmth of the man." Years later an Egyptian friend would comment on Herbert's fondness for the two Siamese cats he and his wife kept in Cairo.[2]

But Norman's favorite pastime in Tokyo was tennis. Rumor has it that it was Herbert who in the late Forties commissioned the building of the tennis courts that still today grace the Embassy grounds in Tokyo. His private correspondence of the period repeatedly refers to playing tennis with this or that friend. His brother Howard even recalls once when Herbert arranged a doubles match with the reigning Australian champions.

Partying, playing with pets, and tennis were Tokyo pastimes that Herbert largely enjoyed apart from his wife. Publicly the husband and wife were very separate human beings; Herbert would put in his standard eight-to-ten-hour day before relaxing in the company of male colleagues and friends at a bar or club, or before indulging in a tennis game, or, as his old Occupation friend Eleanor Hadley remembers, joining in informal discussions in the evening with Japanese academics, most of whom were Marxist historians.[3] Mrs. Norman, as friends from the Tokyo period recall, was very much the "homebody," whose public appearances were largely restricted to official entertainment. Shy, dutiful, and always the perfect hostess, Mrs. Norman stood stoically in the shadow which her sometimes self-indulgent husband cast. Herbert's lifestyle and passionate involvement in work left little time for the two as a couple; for this reason as much as anything else the two permanently postponed the decision to have children.[4]

Norman's temperament, his "Epicurean democratic" outlook, was not unrelated to the decision to eschew a middle-class family life. Herbert had long ago decided to forgo the deprivations of his father's missionary existence; he wanted the good life, one replete with opportunities to cultivate the mind through good books and good music and good friends; his career afforded him this, as well as the opportunity to aid the cause of democracy. Mrs. Norman was quite content to serve as an extension of his mighty ego, even to glory in his accomplishments and to be ever ready to provide the private words of encouragement and emotional support that he needed in his measured and intelligent pursuit of self-gratification. She may or may not have seen her role as a series of acts of self-sacrifice, but if she did, then it was because she fundamentally agreed with her husband's more socially productive and politically progressive pursuit of social justice and democracy. It was just this pursuit that informed his dipomatic work in Japan in the late Forties.

Herbert filed quite literally hundreds of pages of dispatches to Ottawa during his four-plus years as Head of the Liaison Mission. His reports were concerned with virtually every facet of the Occupation, from the reforms themselves, to the people who carried out the reforms, to the Japanese public's reception of them, and to larger questions concerning how effective they were in creating a more democratic Japan. Too, he reported on events such as the War Crimes Trials, Japanese elections, and business scandals. Herbert also wrote about more contentious and confidential issues, such as disagreements between the Americans and the Soviets, relations between the different branches of SCAP, and how well or how poorly different Japanese political leaders and parties worked

with the SCAP bureaucracy. And Herbert also shared with
Ottawa a good many insights about the man in charge, General Douglas MacArthur.

All of Norman's's dispatches bore the certain mark of the
scholar-diplomat's knowledge. Time and again they reveal
his wide rage of contacts, including MacArthur himself, the
British Liaison Head, Sir Avary Gascoigne, and individual
SCAP officers with whom he had worked before; and on the
Japanese side, Diet members, civil servants, and journalists.
Because of his wide-ranging contacts and his scholarly ex-
pertise, as noted by Canadian diplomatic expert Michael Fry,
Norman "was consulted, his views were respected, and his
papers were widely circulated . . ." among policy makers in
Ottawa. His dispatches "provided intellectual unity, a foun-
dation on which policy would be constructed." "From the
Canadian perspective," these were "the Norman years."[5]

Fry never quite specifies the elements in Norman's reporting that provided "intellectual unity" to Ottawa's postwar Japan policy, but a fair surmise would be his passionate
interest in the chief goal of the Occupation, namely, democratization. Indeed, if in his multifaceted reporting one
theme above all others can be identified, it is the ways in
which different political developments, events, personalities,
and social contexts contributed to making Japan more democratic. What bias he occasionally betrays in his otherwise
very factual reporting, what judgments he offers, and what
criticism he makes, all are intimately connected with the Occupation's progress in democratizing Japan. In his almost
single-minded devotion to democratization, he exhibits an
unsparing, even harsh, condemnation of all those who stood
in the way of that goal. Neither MacArthur, nor the Japanese
Social Democratic Party, nor the "old guard," nor labor, nor
the press escaped his critical-minded attention when in his
judgment they acted as obstacles to building a democratic
Japan. Similarly, he was equally unsparing in showering praise
on the people and organizations that contributed to the Her-
culean task.

Beginning with one of his first dispatches, reporting events of the month of October 1946, Herbert identifies three problem areas that touch upon the issue of democratization. First, he informs Ottawa that Macmahon Ball, the Commonwealth representative on the Allied Council, had criticized the "confidence and cordiality" that SCAP, and especially MacArthur's political adviser George Atcheson, had invested in the government of Prime Minister Yoshida. Ball felt that the Soviet allegation regarding electoral underrepresentation and vote-buying as reported in the Japanese press was valid, while Atcheson believed that the Soviets were trying "to discredit the whole election." Atcheson "felt that the Council had degenerated into an instrument of criticism of the Japanese Government, and that when a good job had been performed by the Japanese, . . . it was only fair for the Council to encourage them." Norman adds, "among some of the younger United States staff officers there was sympathy with Mr. Ball's stand, perhaps because some of them had had firsthand experience of the disingenuous behavior of the Japanese Government." Herbert's "perhaps" clause suggests that he lent credence to the Soviet and Commonwealth position, no doubt because he, too, was inclined to believe the Japanese press accounts of electoral corruption, but also for a second reason, mentioned elsewhere in his report, and serving here as a second illustration of the problems he perceived with democratization.

In offering an "estimate of [the] strength of the Yoshida Government," Norman observes that "there is very little evidence of its popularity either in the press or with the public at large. It seems to be accepted without enthusiasm as the only possible government under existing circumstances. Aside from what might be called the professional opponents of the Yoshida Government, such as the Communists, and to a lesser extent, the Social Democrats, there are a wide number of critics of its policies in some of the more sober journals." Eschewing an ideological stance, Herbert evenhandedly points out that

... the tenor of these critics ... is not that it is so much conservative, but that it is out of touch with the times; that Japan has lagged behind the rest of the world in the past in the matter, for instance, of developing a sound labour movement, and that the Yoshida Government is not only indifferent but hostile to this development; that its financial policy is leading to inflation; and that its agrarian policy, although committed to reform by the recent bill, is tepid; and that it is shirking its responsibility in regard to the reform of the Zaibatsu system.[6]

In short, it was not so much conservatism that endangered democratization, in Norman's view, but rather the Yoshida government which actually favored reactionary positions that attempted to block major democratic reforms.

In this same report, Norman notes with alarm another piece of evidence suggesting that the forces of reaction remained alive and well. He reports that 3 November had been designated as Constitution Day and set as a holiday to celebrate Japan's new democratic constitution, but that since 3 November is also the birthday of the Meiji Emperor, the conservative Yoshida government had managed to dilute the symbolic significance of the founding of postwar democracy by combining a celebration of modern democracy with the symbol of traditional authoritarianism. He drives his point home in giving a firsthand account of the "mass meeting" held on the Imperial palace grounds "to celebrate the New Constitution":

I mixed with the crowd during this function and was struck by the indifference with which they listened to the speeches from the dais. The only enthusiasm which was shown was when the Emperor and Empress appeared towards the end of the ceremony. On their departure from the dais, on their way to the Palace, the usually restrained crowd rushed the carriage in a cheering mass so that a great number were trampled and injured. The mad rush to get close to the Emperor, and if possible to touch his carriage, had an element of hysteria in it, which in contrast to the apathy attending the speeches and ceremony was sobering, especially when one reflected that this was the Constitution expressly designed to remove not only the mystery, but real power from the hands of the man being so wildly acclaimed.[7]

Though there may be some humor in imagining this tall, fair-headed intellectual and dandy amidst a throng of short, dark-headed masses of Japanese emperor-worshipers, there is no humor in the lesson that Herbert was sending Ottawa: democratization had to contend with ancient old habits of political reaction, manifested in both high and low places in Japanese society. Not that Ottawa was unaware of the problem: as early as October 1945, External Asian specialist Hugh Keenleyside had warned of Yoshida's "very close contacts with the Mitsubishi interests," concluding Yoshida would be disinclined "to take any initiative in limiting the powers of the Zaibatsu." Another worry of Ottawa's was whether the conservative MacArthur might lend assistance to conservative forces in Japan. Keenleyside warned that "it will be very difficult for MacArthur and [Joseph] Grew [former U.S. Ambassador to Japan and advocate of a "soft peace"] to know just where the convenience of supporting the old order should be sacrificed to the necessity of encouraging a growth of economic as well as political democracy."[8]

Ottawa's concerns about the fate of democratization went beyond the problems of traditional party-business alliances and the questionable degree of MacArthur's commitment to democracy. In December 1946, for example, Asian specialist Arthur Menzies sent Norman a newspaper article entitled "Caliber of U.S. Staffs in Japan Held Threat to Democratization," asking him for "corroborative information on this subject," saying it "would be of interest to the Department." As the message in which Menzies's request is lodged makes clear, Norman had written on 21 November that "Despite the over-all fact of friendliness and cooperative attitude of officers in GHQ, because of the tremendous turnover of personnel . . . , there are a great number of green and untrained officers and civilians who, with the best will in the world, cannot cope with the pressing problems with which they are faced." "Seriously understaffed" and "seriously over-burdened" was how he described SCAP.[9]

Just how acute these problems were in terms of their effects on democratization was spelled out in a 26 October 1949 dispatch from Norman that told of a report prepared by Mr. C. E. McGaughey of the Liaison Mission following a tour he made with the U.S. Civil Affairs Group to several northern prefectures where they investigated democratic reform at the local government level. McGaughey characterized the leader of the U.S. group, Cecil Tilton, as a "waspish individual" who "expressed in open and sober conversations his dislike and distrust of the Jews, French, Filipinos, Koreans, Chinese, Institute of Pacific Relations, Far Eastern Commission, and General Marshall." About Tilton's approach to implementing democratic reform in Japanese local government, McGaughey says, "He is interested in the programme of instruction proceeding according to plan. He is not interested in any examination of the results of the programme, and will brook no criticism of it from his subordinates." In his cover letter to McGaughey's report, Norman credits Tilton and his team with demonstrating "lingering traces" of "the old crusading zeal" for democratization, but concludes, "there is not so much zeal as a rather blind and unquestioning faith in all the policies that have emanated from SCAP and a somewhat intolerant impatience with any doubts as to whether there is a discrepancy between the theory and the implementation of occupation policy." Not content, however, to leave Ottawa with the extremely negative impression made by McGaughey's report, Herbert adds, "Even still at this late date members of local Civil Affairs teams can be found who are genuinely interested in their work and also fired by a desire to help the Japanese develop their institutions in a free and equitable manner."[10] Truth for the Japanologist remained the product of dialectical opposites. He also cautioned Ottawa as to the lesson of forming an impression of democratization solely based on "observations in Tokyo." McGaughey's report strongly suggests that democratization in the countryside was lagging far behind the city.

Norman's defense of good Occupationaires, ones for whom the McGaughey indictment is unfair, is just one of many examples of his fairminded approach in judging democratization, which in turn is a simple manifestation of the intellectual's penchant for a multidimensional truth. As early as September 1946, just a month after his arrival, he comments on MacArthur's review of the first year of the Occupation. Norman avers that MacArthur summarized, "with legitimate pride, the accomplishments of the Occupation and the progress Japan has made from its militaristic past." In December the same year, he extols the competence of the Government Section (G-1): "I think it is only fair to state that any impartial observer will readily grant that this Section includes in its roster both men and women with the best talent in GHQ and certainly second to none in their keen interest in their work and their devotion to their duty." And early the next year, in February 1947, he defends SCAP officers against an attack on SCAP's economic policies by Joseph Fromm, correspondent for *U.S. News and World Report*. Fromm accuses SCAP of at best naïveté, at worst incompetence, in its handling of the reparations issue. At the time, SCAP was attempting to ease Japan's reparations schedule in order to encourage growth in the economy. Fromm alleges that the Japanese government "deliberately invited chaos" in the economy in order to secure additional relief and could do so because "the senior officers in this field are not well equipped to grapple with the complex problems of finance or economy." Norman defends SCAP by arguing that "Fromm is going too far" in saying the Japanese government is subverting its own economy; he says that SCAP indeed does understand the overall problem and might even consider intervening in the economy—despite expectations of being accused of undermining "free enterprise"—in order to set matters right. In this instance, Herbert was carefully abiding by Ottawa's preferences. As Michael Fry points out on the issue of reparations, "Canada would, obviously, oppose reparation payments that would hinder the revival of certain export industries and undermine Japan's ability to pay for essential imports." Fry argues convincingly that Canada's liberal dogma "posited the clearest set of positive correlations between economic growth, trade revival and the maintenance of peace." Norman's opposition to Fromm's allegations shows that in defending Ottawa's position on reparations he was perforce defending the Occupation's as well as Canada's "liberal dogma."[11]

Ottawa, as did Norman, reasoned that democratization could progress more quickly if economic growth were not impeded by such artificial constraints as reparation payments. But economic conditions were only one of several problems that retarded the process of democratic growth. Another and perhaps more serious obstacle, not easily surmountable by mere change in policy, was the age-old Japanese pattern of authoritarian rule. At the highest levels of government, Yoshida's conservatives represented this threat, a point that Norman and MacArthur agreed upon, but Herbert also saw that conservative, even reactionary, leaders at the top derived their power from a veritable army of lower-level minions, those whom he labeled "local bosses" in his dispatch discussing events of September-October 1947. He addressed the problem first in discussing police reform.

The reform of the police system followed the same democratic principle that guided the reform of the economic system—decentralization. SCAP's intent was to return police powers to the local governments, to counter the prewar system of tight central control, and to make the police accountable to the electorate at the local level. Norman neither applauds nor criticizes the reform itself, but points out objectively that the reform will confront "the influence of local bosses." He adds, "The reforms would have little meaning if the local bosses were to replace the centralized bureaucracy of prewar days."[12]

In a memorandum of 5 December 1947, Norman elaborates on the problem of local bosses in discussing what was widely termed the "hidden government" of Japan, and does so with the in-depth knowledge that only a Japanologist could possess. He proffers, "It is, of course, not a new discovery to a student of Japanese society that throughout every walk of Japanese life there exist cliques and factions organized in feudal fashion with a leader at the top and blindly loyal henchmen beneath them. The ramifications of these cliques are sometimes even extended far into cabinets and to the upper reaches of bureaucracy. The clique system is popularly known in Japan as *Oyabun-kobun* system *(Oyabun* = Boss; *kobun* = henchman)." Norman then offers a lengthy disquisition on the historical and sociological dimensions of the boss system, applying the concept as it operates in organized crime, labor guilds, the bureaucracy—of which the police are one part—and the political parties. He observes that the boss system is central to the conservative political parties; how it works in uniting "underworld" figures to certain high-ranking members of the Yoshida Cabinet (e.g., Hitotsumatsu Sadakichi, Minister of Communications in the first Yoshida Cabinet and Minister of Welfare in the Katayama Cabinet); and even that the feudalistic boss system operates in the "modern" Japan Communist Party (JCP).

The so-called "boss system" would normally be of mere academic interest were it not for the implications it had for building a Japanese democracy. The boss system's vertical, hierarchical structures worked in a way exactly opposite to that of the horizontal, democratic structure that the Occupation hoped to create. In this regard, Norman observes, "Different sections of General Headquarters were becoming increasingly aware of the resistance to the implementation of their [democratic] directives." And the existence of this centuries-old feudal system takes on added importance once it is pointed out that within the Occupation there were widely varying views on how to interpret its importance and even whether to discuss the problem openly. Norman tells Ottawa that the latter issue is symptomatic of the ideological split between G-1 and G-2. G-1's General Whitney has a "policy of publicizing certain aspects of the 'Hidden Government' of Japan," while the "attitude of [Willoughby's] G-2 is that such publicity does more harm to the reputation of the Occupation and gives foreign opinion the idea that Japan is not completely democratic as it has so often been announced." In short, Willoughby wished to ignore social and historical forces for the sake of a good press, while Whitney wanted to understand and publicize the problem for the sake of democratization.[13]

Clearly, Norman sided with the democratic reformers against the obscurantists. There was no danger in taking sides so long as the reformers had the upper hand in setting policy. But G-1 lost power *vis-à-vis* G-2 once the Cold War began, and it can fairly be said to have been underway by 1947. In that year of growing U.S.-Soviet friction, "loyalty boards" were established in Washington, and in China it began to appear that Mao's communist forces would eventually emerge victorious. As the perception of the communist threat came to be regarded as fact, the Occupation authorities "reversed course" on democratic reform in order to make Japan into a strategic bastion of anti-communism. Practically, "reverse course" meant the depurge of war criminals, the rebuilding of the *zaibatsu,* and the purge of leftists. G-1's loss was G-2's gain, and support for eliminating feudal remnants, let alone for democratic reform, became dangerous. As Michael Fry opines, once the Occupation "reversed course," and Herbert did not, then he "became critical of MacArthur, and ran afoul of a segment of his staff," namely, Willoughby's G-2 which, as shown above, regarded loyalty (manifested by quiescence) as more important than democratization. In this sense, Harold Greer, reporting on the "smearing" of Norman in late summer 1951, is correct when he reported that the untoward publicity about the Canadian representative then stemmed from "Willoughby's . . . vendetta against Dr. Norman."[14]

    This simplifies a much more complex truth. The reasons for Herbert's later trial by smear are different from those suggested by the simple fact that Herbert sided with G-1 or the forces for democratization. This fact explains why Willoughby disliked Herbert, but not why he was recalled by his own government and investigated. How he could have earned Willoughby's ire is relevant, however, in discussing his passion for democratizing Japan.

As a knowledgeable Japanologist, Norman understood what difficulties lay ahead in politically engineering a democratic Japan. Certainly the boss system was one, the incompetence of Occupationaires another. But at a much deeper level was the philosophical but practical problem that he first outlined in March 1946 and repeated in early 1948. When questioning the worth of Japanese apprenticeship in the ways and means of American democracy, he wrote, "Democracy is still being imposed by an authority and the Japanese people understand authority." The contradiction of imposing democracy had obvious and negative consequences: an "apathetic" population, the prolongation of "the completely unrepentant attitude of diehard reactionaries," and a popular complacency toward "feudalistic thinking." The topic of a peace treaty, raised first in 1947, brought to the fore the obvious contradiction: so long as democracy was being imposed, just as traditionally other forms of rule had been imposed on the people, the ruled would remain apathetic or complacent, perhaps even cynical, about the business of rule. For this reason Norman could say of MacArthur's second anniversary address on the signing of the surrender agreement: "General MacArthur emphasized the uniqueness and the success of the Occupation. The ideas. . . were not new and could be criticized for not admitting the slightest possibility that any grounds of criticism of the Occupation existed."[15]

The point to be emphasized is that Norman criticized and praised whenever he thought conditions merited one or the other, basing his judgments forever on the sole criterion—shared by MacArthur and Ottawa—of how well the Occupation was carrying out democratization. The year 1948 was pivotal in this regard, especially as the tempo of reverse course quickened.

Confirmation of this claim comes in Norman's report of his private conversation with George Kennan, author of the "containment theory" and in Japan on a mission for the State Department to assess Occupation policy. According to Norman's "Top Secret" dispatch to Ottawa, the American said, "In Japan, as in other parts of the world, it is time for universal reconsideration of the whole of the postwar settlement in the light of the fact that the period of change and reform following any great war is ending. What was desirable in the Occupation policy in Japan right after the war might not necessarily continue to be so indefinitely." Kennan's message was unambiguous in Norman's mind: democratization had to take a back seat to "economic recovery and social stability" in light of the perceived Soviet-Chinese threat.[16] The words, "reverse course," are not used, but the meaning is clear, especially in light of MacArthur's New Year message, which Norman had reported on just three days earlier. He focused on the "rather unusual attention" that MacArthur gave to the issue of Occupation "control of the Japanese economy," as if MacArthur "was apologizing in advance to interests in the United States who have already shown signs of criticism of *socialist control sponsored by an essentially American Occupation*." Quoting Norman, pressure was being put on MacArthur to create an Allied "economy embodying the principle of private capitalism composed of free competitive enterprise." "Socialist control" had gone on long enough—now was time to unleash the *zaibatsu*, to permit traditional tendencies toward concentration of capital, for the sake of recovery, to redevelop unimpeded.

Part of the hidden agenda in undoing "socialist [Occupation] control" of the economy was America's growing reluctance to subsidize the economic rebirth of its former enemy. But more important was a fact pointed out in a cablegram from the Canadian Ambassador in Washington to External Affairs on 25 March 1948, referring to the so-called "Draper Mission" (Draper was Under-Secretary of the Army) to Japan which signaled official U.S. support for reversing the breakup of the *zaibatsu*. The purpose was "to cut United States relief costs, [and] make Japan a self-supporting ally to resist Russian expansion in the Far East" [quoting, approvingly, a *U.S. News and World Report* analysis]. The cablegram refers openly to a "rapid deterioration in the public relationships of the United States and the U.S.S.R.," to Japan's "importance in the struggle against Russo-Communist aggression,"

and to the "adoption of the late enemy [Japan] as a substitute
for China in the attempt to find a basis for economic stability
in the Far East and as *an advance staging area in preparation
for possible conflict with the U.S.S.R.*" (emphasis mine). The
cablegram concludes that this view of Japan as central to
America's grand design to contain the Soviet Union in the
emerging Cold War "would appear to confirm Mr. Norman's
report from Tokyo of Mr. Kennan's statement regarding the
need for revision of [democratic] policies formulated in the
immediate post-war period."[17] "Revision of [immediate post-
war] policies" refers specifically to a flip-flopping of priorities; the Cold War, then, de-democratized Japan, a radical
policy shift that Herbert could never quite accept.

Symptomatic of the reversing of Occupation policy was its
leaders' behind-the-scenes expressions of relief when by the
close of the year the conservatives under Yoshida had reassumed control of the government. The year had witnessed
three different governments, "a confused scene," reported
Norman, adding that the changes in regimes were "a sordid
and chaotic spectacle of Japanese politics" that eventuated in
"a continuation of the old [prewar and reactionary] Seiyukai
[party]." Premier Katayama, leader of the Socialist Party,
had resigned in February, and was followed by another coalition government headed by Ashida, leader of the Democratic Party. Ashida ruled with Socialist Party support, but
was forced to resign in early October, only to be replaced
by Yoshida's Liberal Party. Norman tells Ottawa that "there
was some opposition in General Headquarters, not shared
by all sections, to Yoshida assuming the premiership for the
second time." The reason behind this opposition was that
"Yoshida was regarded as lazy, dilatory, and what was more
difficult to prove, impervious to proddings from General
Headquarters." He says it was primarily G-1 that opposed
Yoshida because Yoshida disliked General Whitney's reformist proclivities. On the other hand, reflecting the never-
ending animosity between reformist G-1 and reactionary G-
2, Willoughby was delighted with Yoshida's recapture of
power. Herbert says, "It is no secret that Mr. Yoshida and

his friends are highly regarded by General Willoughby, head of G-2, . . . ; their enemies are also Mr. Yoshida's enemies, namely Government Section." Thus, ". . . Mr. Yoshida still had powerful friends in General Headquarters on whom he can rely."[18]

The revival of conservative power under Yoshida has not disappeared; his political descendants continue to rule in 1986. Norman was there at the founding, and understood that the resurgence of conservatism and all that it meant—reconstruction of the *zaibatsu*, the depurging of war criminals, and the purging of socialist elements—depended greatly on the divisions within SCAP, between the rabid anticommunist G-2 and the democratic reformist G-1 which, like Norman, felt that Yoshida's resurrection would permanently stultify democratization.

Norman interviewed Yoshida shortly after the old man, then seventy, reassumed power and reported on the interview on 1 November 1948. On the one hand, he applauds Yoshida for having risked his position in the prewar era by having argued for peace, and compliments the prime minister for being "affable and genial," but on the other hand he characterizes Yoshida as having "the appearance of a genial, easy-going country squire and certainly not an energetic, ambitious politician." Norman adds, importantly, "General MacArthur's characterization of him to me as a placid, old-fashioned type of Japanese, ignorant of politics and economics was borne out by my impressions of him yesterday." He concludes his portrait: "He is in every sense of the word a conservative with little understanding of the position of labour in modern politics, and has no great desire to make the effort to understand it. He is old-fashioned in the best sense of that word, both in his manner and personal tastes, but I fear that in the present age this will not be an asset as a political leader in post-war Japan."[19]

But if Norman found Yoshida out of touch, so did he also find the JCP and the Socialists. He accuses the Communists of "doing their best to fish in these [1948] troubled waters" of rapidly changing governments; he says the Socialists are "riddled with factionalism not only between right and left wing but between personal cliques." The Socialist leader, Katayama, is "indecisive and at times almost inarticulate," and has contributed to the "continual fragmentations of socialist parties which so plagued and weakened Japanese labour organizations in the years before the Manchurian Incident . . ." About all the parties, Herbert concludes his 1948 assessment on a depressing note: "The political parties are in a state of disintegration and slow reintegration. Political principles are recklessly sacrificed . . . The scene is not without its ridiculous touches but the general effect is depressing in the extreme."[20] In the midst of such party disarray, of reverse course and Cold War politics, what suffered, in his view, was democracy.

In Douglas MacArthur, Norman had an unlikely ally in his bleak assessment of the future for democracy in Japan, which might explain why these two great thinkers—so different in personality, background, and experience—could regard one another so highly.

On many of the most pressing issues facing the Occupation, Norman and MacArthur were in agreement. The two men shared a mighty distrust of Yoshida in particular and of Japanese conservatives in general; and both feared that the conservative element was trying to preserve as much of the prewar power structure as possible, especially its financial base, the *zaibatsu*. Moreover, once Washington's policy flip-flopped on the issue of the break-up of the *zaibatsu*, in 1948, it appears that the General began meeting more frequently with Herbert, probably because MacArthur knew that he would be a sympathetic sounding board for the General's complaints about the reverse course being dictated by Washington interlopers like Kennan, Draper, and later Joseph Dodge. In a dispatch dated 18 March 1949, Norman refers to a recent conversation that MacArthur had with the Commonwealth representative regarding the General's fear that "present State Department experts on Japanese affairs [are] anxious to bring back to power the old conservative forces in Japan," adding that "MacArthur in my conversations with him has made similar remarks."

The one conservative who most worried both Norman and MacArthur was Yoshida, especially after his smashing Liberal Party victory on 23 January. For the first time in the postwar era, the conservatives under Yoshida had captured an absolute majority in the Lower House. Norman reported to Ottawa that Yoshida was "basking in his electoral victory" and noted that the press had been warning in the election's aftermath that the conservatives might be prone to "behave too autocratically." Herbert himself dwelt on the character of Yoshida: "In other despatches I have commented on Mr. Yoshida's character as a political leader. To recapitulate here briefly, Mr. Yoshida is very much the old-fashioned Japanese professional diplomat, loyal to his associates and lieutenants, indolent in his work, antediluvian in his economic theory and resentful of the demands of political life such as, for instance, in public relations . . . . Many Japanese refer to him as 'tono-sama' (generic term for a feudal lord . . .)."[21]

General MacArthur publicly applauded "so clear and decisive a mandate for the conservative philosophy of government," but privately he conceded to Norman that despite being "frankly delighted" that there emerged a "clear majority party" and hence promise of political stability, he felt "there is also some danger that Yoshida, through overconfidence, will act too harshly towards labour in general" and said he "intend[ed] to watch against possibly excessive measures in this regard."[22]

Norman clearly appreciated MacArthur's privately expressed views because he agreed with them. In his annual report for 1949, in which he focuses, among other things, on MacArthur's relationship with the Yoshida government, he observed that, "in all fairness to General MacArthur himself, it should be said that he is fully aware of the difficulties inherent in this situation," referring to how Yoshida violated "measures, . . . [that are] quite advanced and democratic on paper [but] . . . *for that very reason*, [are] objectionable to the present majority party with its strongly conservative character." Yet, for the sake of building democracy, according to Herbert, MacArthur "has urged upon his staff the necessity for the policy of non-interference in Japanese Government affairs."[23] MacArthur believed, as did Norman, that the only way to learn democracy was to practise it.

But as both men realized, the situation mocked the belief. Herbert told Ottawa, for example, that when Yoshida wanted a particular piece of legislation passed, he would "tell them [Diet men] bluntly that the Diet had no right to change or otherwise obstruct the passage of a Bill that was virtually an order from SCAP." And "despite [MacArthur's] own expressed wish on this subject [non-interference in Diet matters], we have witnessed the rather confusing spectacle of a Japanese government and GHQ working at cross-purposes, partly because of the essentially different methods by which decisions are reached and carried out by military institutions on the one hand and parliamentary institutions on the other, and partly because of the noticeably antiquated and old-fashioned ideas of the present Yoshida government."[24]

What is important to notice here is not the simple fact, pointed out by Herbert as long before as 1946, that a militarily imposed democracy is no real democracy, but that he credited MacArthur, the enlightened despot in charge of imposing democracy, with not only realizing this anomaly, but also of lamenting its consequences. Referring specifically to Yoshida's undemocratic rule, of his failure to initiate "legislation or implement reforms," Norman concludes, "[this] is not so much the fault of General Headquarters [MacArthur] as of the rather sluggish stand-pat mentality of the Japanese government."[25] Not surprisingly, his generous interpretation accorded with MacArthur's own.

If the election of 1949 was cause for lamenting the new undemocratic conservative leadership, it was also important for raising the spectre of a Japanese Communist Party "victory" in the face of indisputable evidence that Japan's neighboring Chinese Communist Party was about to emerge victorious over the American-favored Nationalists of Chiang

Kai-shek. In the January election that gave Yoshida a majority government, the JCP tripled its popular vote and increased its Diet representation from four to thirty-five members. For Norman's part, he credited the meteoric rise of JCP strength to several factors: first, a negative public reaction to the "widespread [conservative] corruption in the last Diet" that had not touched the JCP; "accordingly [it] gained by comparison some favor"; secondly, factional struggle within the Socialist Party resulted in wide-scale disaffection from its ranks in favor of the communists; thirdly, certain segments of labor defected from the Socialists to the JCP; and fourth, "the Communists worked assiduously throughout the election campaign." Norman elaborates on how the JCP campaigned: "Their propaganda was often reckless and demagogic, e.g., their talk of racial independence (a slogan which thinly disguises their opposition to United States policy). One feature of their propaganda which observers report was shrewdly exploited was the current Communist successes in China, . . . suggesting that it would be wise for the Japanese people to get on the Red bandwagon now before it was too late."[26]

The latter point, whose origin Norman attributes to MacArthur, was repeated in a "Secret" dispatch dealing with his private conversation with the General following the election. Referring to MacArthur, Herbert writes: "He was not seriously concerned over communist gains. They came entirely from fortuitous circumstances which would never again occur. First, and most important, were communist successes in China which came just in time to assist the communist campaign here. Communists in election propaganda had capitalized effectively on communist victories in China. Secondly, was the discrediting of both Social[ists] and Democrats because of corruption and general inefficiency of these parties during the last year by the communists, who are led by able and determined men." He then relates a prediction by MacArthur that, as history would prove, was a self-fulfilling prophecy: "He [MacArthur] insisted that communists have now reached their peak strength and next few years will see a steady decline. He has no intention of making a frontal attack on communists which would drive them underground but will 'watch them like a hawk and if they make a false step will swoop on them.'"[27] The "hawk" did just this once the Korean War began a year and a half later, though not without incurring Norman's disapproval, as we shall see.

The Canadian representative shared MacArthur's initial assessment of the relative *insignificance* of the JCP's electoral success in light of the smashing victory of the conservatives, but it is equally clear that not everyone in SCAP agreed. In early February, Willoughby's G-2 released to the press details of what it *alleged* was incontrovertible evidence revealing the existence of a wartime Soviet spy ring in Japan, the so-called Sorge spy ring that operated from the Thirties until 1941. Though the report had been drafted in December 1947, Norman's dispatch to Ottawa details why its release might have been delayed until just then: "Possibly it was issued so shortly after the recent Japanese elections as a warning to the Japanese against placing trust in communist leadership." And he suggests a possible second reason: "The report may have been in addition an attempt to impress Americans with the need for vigilance against internal espionage."

Yet as Norman points out, if these were the reasons for the report's release, "the method . . . would seem to negate both purposes." His point refers to Major General Willoughby's decision first to take responsibility for the report on 12 February and then to deny responsibility just two weeks later following an announcement in Washington by an Army spokesman who said the release was "a public relations faux pas." Washington observed that the report was badly edited and "was based on unsubstantiated information from [wartime] Japanese police sources." Too, it had wrongly named Miss Agnes Smedley, who immediately launched a lawsuit for libel against MacArthur, compelling Willoughby, with much egg on his face, to waive immunity from legal prosecution in order to protect his boss.[28] Ultimately, Willoughby failed to tie any Americans to the Soviet spy ring—which, of course, was working for the defeat of the wartime Japanese government, as were the other Allies, a fact often overlooked by the McCarthyites.

Norman did not hide his contempt for the report. "It is," he tells Ottawa, "drafted in the flamboyant style more suited to pulp spy novels." He characterizes it "as a sensational story rather than as a factual intelligence report."[29] Canada's Ambassador to Washington agreed. He wrote Ottawa on 19 February: "It has the cloak-and-dagger atmosphere (and something of the approach) of a Grade B movie script, but mostly owing to the fact that it accuses Miss Agnes Smedley, a fairly well-known American writer on Chinese Affairs, of having been a member of the Soviet spy ring in the Far East." The Ambassador opined that the authors of the report "were obviously Li'l Abner fans, and must have been reading the Fearless Fosdick 'Any Face' sequence at the time," alluding to a line in the report that states, "One begins to wonder whom one can trust, what innocent comrade or loyal friend may suddenly be discovered as the enemy. He may have any face."

That mentality, said Ambassador Hume Wrong, "sets a new and dangerous precedent," not only because of the un-supported charges against Miss Smedley, but also because of the basic assumption which underlies the writers' approach: "that the public must be stirred up to catch spies." Just as foreboding in his view was the comparison the authors of the Sorge report made with the royal commission findings on the Gouzenko disclosures. Norman also commented on this fact: "The report refers in many instances to the Canadian case but asserts in the introduction that compared to the Sorge case in Tokyo the Canadian affair was an amateur show . . . probably never in history has there been a ring more bold or more successful."[30] Linking the Gouzenko and Sorge cases, if only by unfavorable comparison and then, of course, to belittle the "amateur" show in Canada, was no doubt an attempt to artificially fashion an immense Soviet espionage fact out of Li'l Abner-style fiction, fueled by a suspicious imagination and driven by a compulsive desire to prove that the enemy "may have any face." Sadly, once Norman was

connected by the FBI and RCMP with one of the people implicated by Gouzenko, Willoughby could easily make a leap
of faith and connect Norman with the Sorge spy ring.

The Willoughby mentality, apparently *not* discouraged by
MacArthur, and encouraged by the communist electoral gains
in Japan and the communist military victories in China, began
to blanket occupied Japan in 1949 with a heavy veil of suspicion and with more concrete anti-communist policies.

There would seem to be a contradiction between Willoughby's reckless pursuit of communists—best represented by the
Sorge *faux pas*—and MacArthur's seemingly more realistic
assessment of the communist "threat," as, for example, his
downplaying of the JCP's electoral "victory" in early 1949.
But the fact of the matter is that MacArthur's thinking about
the communist threat was not static. Norman reports meeting
with MacArthur on 12 June, in the company of Canadian
Lieutenant General Guy Simonds, and documents Mac-
Arthur's changing attitudes: "He did not regard very seriously the repercussions of Chinese communist victories on
the political situation in Japan." Yet he adds, parenthetically,
"This was not General MacArthur's view last January when
he was undoubtedly taken by surprise by the increased communist vote in Japan; at that time he explained it chiefly as
the result of enhanced communist prestige deriving from their
victories in China." But in June 1949, just four months before
the Chinese communists seized power permanently, MacArthur
was convinced that "the same forces which brought about
the downfall of Chiang Kai-shek would inevitably ruin the
[Chinese] Communists also." MacArthur, reported Norman,
cited a shortage of trained personnel, financial problems, and
problematic discipline as the causes of an eventual Chinese
communist defeat. And so far as the CCP's influence on Japan
was concerned, MacArthur pointed to the old racial hatred—
"the Japanese really despise the Chinese"—as a potent divi-
sive force, more relevant in the current situation than "ideologies emanating from either China or Russia" which "were
at a great discount in Japan."[31]

MacArthur's unwarranted optimism regarding the inevitable "ruin" of the communists in China may have made the CCP's victory in October 1949 seem all the more terrifying, and, by extension, the JCP all the more ominous. But in any event, it is quite clear that MacArthur's view about communist power in all of East Asia changed over time. Norman commented on his mercurial mentality in an earlier dispatch, dated 18 March 1949. He begins: "I have commented from time to time on the different moods of General MacArthur. It would be an exaggeration to say he contradicts himself; it would be more accurate to say that on some occasions he emphasized one aspect of a problem and another time another aspect. Some days he is in the mood to blame the die-hard reactionaries in Japan for economic or political difficulties, and on another occasion not so far removed, he will blame labour unions and the communist influence in them."

At the time this memo was written, MacArthur's "mood" was anything but fearful of communism. Norman states that in a recent conversation that the General had with Mr. Patrick Shaw, Head of the Australian Mission, "He [MacArthur] made the same point . . . that he had made on previous occasions with me, namely, that his G-2 had, *so far at least*, failed to secure evidence that the Japanese communists take their orders from Moscow." Herbert, on the other hand, was more realistic than the General; he lends only partial credence to this evaluation by citing Gordon Walker, correspondent with the *Christian Science Monitor*, who had recently interviewed JCP leader, Nozaka Sanzo. Nozaka told Walker that "the Japanese communists were sufficiently strong to dispense with any connection with Russia but that they found it profitable to study closely the methods and theories of the Chinese communists . . . and thus implied that there might be direct links between the Japanese and Chinese communists."[32]

Two important points emerge: first, MacArthur implied that G-2 might eventually prove a link between the JCP and the Soviets but that he was reserving judgment until such time as evidence was found, in contrast to Willoughby, who believed in the existence of the link as intrinsic to an international communist conspiracy, despite the absence of any evidence; and second, Norman was prepared to believe in a link between the JCP and CCP and *was not at all reluctant to tell Ottawa*. A related point, with long-term implications, is the clear suggestion that MacArthur was quite willing to go along with G-2's communist hunt. As a man of many moods, MacArthur would not foreclose on any possibility, nor, as *de facto* head of the Japanese state, could he rationally afford to.

The results of MacArthur's support for Willoughby were evident to Norman in 1949 when one socialist leader, Matsumoto Junichiro, was the first of many leftists to be purged by SCAP. Then, by late June, with a CCP victory imminent, MacArthur's optimism notwithstanding, Norman was citing as authoritative the views of Mr. Hani Goro, socialist Independent in the Upper House of the Diet, who was lamenting a new crackdown on labor as evidence of "a definite return towards the state of affairs under which the Japanese worker laboured in prewar Japan."[33] Just a year later, when G-2 was assisting the conservative government to purge Japanese leftists from government and to censor critical newspapers, Norman was citing unidentified Japanese as saying they felt "they are living back in the thirties."[34]

But if MacArthur was a man of conflicting moods, so, too, was Norman. At the close of 1949, he was, overall, rather generous in his reporting about what he called "this very benevolent military occupation." He was willing to concede that "SCAP [MacArthur] and his staff on some issues may know what is better for the Japanese themselves than their government." But as he had said so many times before, "Yet, by its very nature, democracy presupposes the possibility of making mistakes which can be righted by an aroused public opinion which, in due course, can affect the composition of future governments. Now a brief review of the fate of the post-war government in Japan will show that a parliamentary democracy is scarcely compatible with a military occupation." As evidence he cited the facts about how SCAP had used its power to make and break successive governments.[35]

Norman's concerns about the incompatibility of military occupation and indigenous Japanese democratization did not lessen in this last year in Japan. Indeed, he began to despair about the future of Japanese democracy, especially after the Korean conflict commenced, but indications of his losing hope were present well before. In late April 1950, for instance, he reported on recent developments in the Social Democratic Party. Since it had lost an election in early 1949, Norman noted that the left wing had captured control of the Party, with disastrous results for creating a countervailing force to Yoshida's conservatives. He observed that the opinion polls showed that the Yoshida government was losing support and the Socialists, in a "small triumph for democracy," were more responsive to the needs of "ordinary members." They also showed that communists were discredited due to "the hostility of SCAP and their own toadying to the Moscow line," thereby giving the Social Democrats "a fine opportunity to operate successfully" prior to the upcoming Upper House election. But despite the favorable context for countering conservative rule, Norman wrote that the Socialists had lost their chance to capture power because of "chicanery, opportunism, collusion and ruthless ambition" and because of the "predatory instincts" of the main ideological factions within the Party.[36]

In June, he appraised the significance of the "failure of the Opposition parties to make corruption in the [Yoshida] government one of the issues in the campaign." Herbert identified corruption in semi-governmental business organizations (*Kodan*), the selling of political favors—reaching Yoshida himself—police corruption, and "money politics" as ill-fated signs of the future of Japanese democracy. Worst of all, "the electorate accepted corruption in government as something which could not be cured by party politics and perhaps is regarded as a necessary component as the new order here." He consigned hope to oblivion: "It bodes particularly ill for democratic institutions if the voting public is not aroused by the misuse of public funds [by the Yoshida government] at

a time when the money situation is tight and taxes are relatively high." Popular complacency, in short, was the product
of a military-imposed "democracy."[37]

Shortly after the Upper House election, the Korean War
began and democracy in Japan ceased to be of much concern
to the occupiers. The clearest sign of this was SCAP's purge
in August of 270 journalists who favored neutrality in the
Cold War; SCAP's censorship of what Norman called "out-
standing commercial newspapers" known for their "liberal"
views; and the outright banning of the communist press.
Norman in fact favored selective press censorship in this time
of war, but he also warned that "If the present trend continues, the liberal faction in Japan, which have hitherto been
the staunchest admirers of United States policy, will reluc-
tantly fall away . . ." He added, in his most worrisome note
ever, that constitutional and parliamentary procedure, in this
context, has become "not merely difficult but, rather,
impossible."[38]

If his dispatches written after the Korean War began to
signal his despair for democratization in Japan, they equally
reflect his central role as Canada's representative to Mac-
Arthur's military command structure for waging war in Korea. MacArthur, it will be remembered, served simultaneously
as SCAP in Japan and SCAP in the UN-sponsored Korean War.
Canada was a willing participant in battling communist
aggression by North Korea (and later joined by China) and
was represented in East Asia by Herbert Norman. In fact,
on his recommendation, Ottawa attached its military representative to the UN forces to his Liaison Mission.[39]

Herbert Norman's role in the Korean conflict has only
recently become an important question, following Chapman
Pincher's allegation in his 1984 book, *Too Secret Too Long*,
that Herbert "went far to contribute to Moscow's decision
to give the North Koreans the green light to invade South
Korea in June 1950."[40] In the absence of concrete evidence
to support the allegation, Pincher's claim is unprovable and
therefore must either be believed or disbelieved on grounds
of faith alone. It can be said definitively here, however, that

there exists absolutely no support for the allegation in the existing records of *any* intelligence agencies, either Canadian or American.

But even more important, and quite apart from questions of nonexistent evidence of wrongdoing, the allegation is patently absurd. Two grounds for so saying are important: one, Norman's secret reports to Ottawa about the Korean situation; and two, earlier comments by prominent American officials regarding the strategic importance of Korea. The latter can be addressed first.

As early as 12 January 1950, Dean Acheson, American Secretary of State, in an address to the National Press Club in Washington about Asian policy, "seemingly excluded South Korea from the American defense perimeter in Asia," thereby giving Republican opponents ammunition to charge that he had given "a green light" to the North to attack. Moreover, for months preceding the North Korean invasion of the South, G-2 in Japan under Willoughby and in Korea had been warning of "imminent attack" on the South, pointing to the fact that the Great Powers' division of the country into two artificial states had never been fully accepted by either northern or southern leaders. However one views the origins of the war, it is very clear that the attack which came from the North on 25 June was expected in some very general sense. Moreover, it is also clear that Acheson did not regard South Korea as very important, in part because he felt little loyalty to its dictator, Syngman Rhee.[41]

What Norman reported to Ottawa about MacArthur's views regarding the importance of protecting South Korea from northern aggression meshes with Acheson's view about Rhee. In a 24 May report about a recent interview with the General, he wrote, "In Korea he expected Syngman Rhee and his followers to win the forthcoming elections. After all, the General said, what chance is there for an opposition when 14,000 of them are in prison, without trial and without any expectation of trial? Any opposition to Syngman Rhee is promptly labeled 'Communist' although, as the General stated, it was obviously false in the overwhelming number of cases."[42]

In an earlier communiqué, Norman reported as well what must have been an additional reason for MacArthur's disdain of the dictator, namely, his "trigger-happy attitude," pointing to Rhee's comment to the Tokyo press corps that "he would welcome the outbreak of hostilities with North Korea as he was quite sure that he was strong enough to defeat them." Norman further observed that this attitude of Rhee's "is causing considerable alarm in the State Department."[43]

State Department displeasure derived from its policy of containment, which was exactly contrary to the Army's desired policy of "roll-back". Army could praise Rhee for his "guts," and even welcome the prospect of war, as did the South Korean president. The polar attitudes about dealing with communism were well known in Washington, and Guy Burgess and Kim Philby, Soviet spies there at the time, no doubt obediently reported to Moscow this deep policy division, thereby presumably giving Stalin the confidence to proceed with lending support for the invasion.[44] But if this Washington-based perfidy is in fact true, it nonetheless is far removed from happenings in Tokyo, which, after all, is the place from which Korean policy *was implemented, not initiated*.

Moreover, after the war began, Norman worked in the "front lines" as a purveyor of Ottawa's policies of committing itself to the Korean conflict. On 11 July he cabled Ottawa that he had met with General MacArthur per Ottawa's instructions of 10 July which conveyed Canada's offer of adding three of its own destroyers to MacArthur's UN forces. "He expressed himself as most gratified by the offer," reported Herbert, "and said he deeply appreciated the destroyers, of which very good use could be made."[45] Besides following Ottawa's lead to the letter, Herbert, as mentioned before, went so far as to approve of MacArthur's decision to censor the Japanese communist press: "With a war on in Korea and Japan still under occupation, it is to be expected that the [Japanese] Communist press itself should be controlled; it is, in fact, entirely suppressed now." Moreover, he went beyond what was necessary in supporting censorship when he added,

"Japan is fortunately a long way from the state of drab uniformity which characterizes a Soviet satellite," although, as an unreconstructed democrat, he perforce added, "yet this present step is a move towards the elimination of free expression of opinion·which is the essence and distinguishing feature of a civilized and democratic community."[46]

Thus, with mixed but democratic emotions, Herbert supported censorship in wartime. Another additional measure of his emotional involvement in the war was his acceptance, in a 13 September 1950 communiqué to Ottawa, of MacArthur's optimistic assessment that the war would be ended quickly, that the "boys" would be home by Christmas. Such an intelligence assessment, far from deterring Ottawa from making a full commitment of military forces, must have solidified its support of MacArthur's Korean adventure in favor of its decision to send in 15,000 Canadian soldiers.[47]

By the time Norman sent that dispatch, he was under suspicion for communist loyalties and had just one more month left to represent Ottawa in Tokyo. Indications are that he knew by this time that his days in Japan were numbered, and perhaps this forced upon his consciousness a sense of regret that he had not left earlier when the opportunity of reassignment had presented itself. Discussion of his reassignment had begun in 1949, but he had then made clear his preference for remaining in Japan. In a 12 August dispatch, and in the context of telling about broadening his sources of information and his delight in completing his book *Ando Shoeki,* he wrote: "I do hope that the Department's plans will permit me to continue on for some while as I feel that I am in a position to contribute more usefully with the experience that I have built up over the past three years." Too, on MacArthur's recommendation, his ranking had just been upgraded by Ottawa, likely giving him an enhanced sense of importance.

But in early 1950, when Minister of External Affairs Pearson was in Japan, the subject of reassignment was again broached. Norman wrote to Pearson on 8 February, just shortly after Pearson's departure from Japan, that "I do not

feel that I should press for a longer stay [in Japan]." He
expressed his willingness to go wherever External preferred,
asking only that he be given "a few months [more] to do my
best to tidy up some projects under way" and that he *not* be
posted in Moscow, which was Pearson's preference. Norman
the Japanologist stated that he preferred Ottawa over Moscow, arguing that "with our small staff in Moscow, I do not
think that I could profitably follow much on the Far Eastern
field there, with everything so tight and close as it is." Instead
of Moscow, and if Ottawa was not possible, Herbert requested that China be considered, "if and when we recognize
. . ."[48]

On 22 February a cable from Arnold Heeney informed
Norman that Ottawa had acceded to his wishes, adding that
"after a few more months in Japan, you will be returned to
Ottawa for duty . . . sometime after the middle of May."
But for reasons that are not clear, nothing in the official
correspondence about his reposting appears until 14 July, not
even three weeks *after* the Korean conflict began, when Norman wrote H. O. Moran, Assistant Under-Secretary of State
for External Affairs, about "the question of my return to
Ottawa." He refers to "General MacArthur's expression of
gratification that my return was to be delayed somewhat,"
but reaffirms his desire to return "to Ottawa this fall as
planned." Quite naturally he stresses the importance of keeping abreast of developments in the Korean conflict, but asks
Ottawa to set a definite date for his repatriation: "What I am
concerned with . . . is the fact that I am to be kept here on
a month-to-month basis, depending, in some fashion or the
other, on what should happen in Korea." He says that unless
he hears otherwise, he will return by boat on 27 September.[49]

Norman heard from Ottawa on 18 July. In Moran's words:
"Consequent upon developments in Korea, a decision was
made to postpone indefinitely the transfer of Menzies to Japan
and your posting to the American and Far Eastern division
of the Department in Ottawa." Moran equivocated, however.
He told Norman to keep his return reservation for the 27
September sailing. The see-saw situation continued. As late

as 6 October, Herbert, after having cancelled several departure reservations, stated that he would leave Japan on 9 November. His plans had to be aborted suddenly, however, when on 14 October 1950 he received a cable ordering him to return "immediately." The FBI had informed the RCMP, which in turn had informed External, that Norman had fallen under suspicion of being a communist. His ties with a reputed Japanese communist, Tsuru Shigeto, and with an alleged Canadian spy for the Soviets, Israel Halperin, had been deemed credible enough to warrant immediate investigation. Herbert returned to Ottawa under suspicion.

CHAPTER 6

SUSPECT

One begins to wonder whom one can trust, what inno-
cent comrade or loyal friend may suddenly be discovered
as the enemy. He may have any face.
                              Sorge Spy Ring Report, 1947

While it is true that Herbert Norman's associations and activities were first made into an American security concern in 1942 with the "Tsuru
Affair," as the FBI dubbed the Cambridge episode, the failure on the part of Hoover's men to develop
further derogatory information about him meant that his "file"
eventually would have lapsed into a state of political obscu-
rity. Indeed, the "national security" relevance of the Tsuru
episode would never have been consequential had it not been
for a totally unrelated investigation of Norman, undertaken
for entirely different reasons, by G-2, the counter-intelligence
branch of the American Occupation of Japan, headed by
Major General Charles A. Willoughby. This investigation
began in September 1946, a bare month after Norman had
been returned to Japan as Head of the Canadian Liaison Mission.

He became a target of Willoughby's campaign against so-
called "leftists and fellow-travelers" for two reasons: first,
he played a major role in the release of Japanese political
prisoners in October 1945; and second, he associated closely
with a good many Occupationaires who had or who still
maintained an academic affiliation with the Institute of Pacific
Relations. As with the FBI investigation of the Tsuru Affair,
the G-2 investigation produced "evidence" of alleged leftist
ties that by themselves were less than damning. But once the
FBI and G-2 began comparing notes—as early as May 1950
but no later than August 1950—only to expand the circle of

spy-chasers to include the RCMP by September 1950, Norman became the marked man that he was to remain until his death just seven years later.

The release of Japanese political prisoners—two of whom were communists—proved to be a pivotal event in the attack on his loyalty and in the destruction of his life, especially after the episode was publicized in 1951. Moreover, it definitely proved to impede the upward mobility in America's foreign service of Herbert's friend, and compatriot in the freeing of the political prisoners, John K. Emmerson. How Willoughby chose to interpret their role in this event, therefore, helped in destroying one life and in damaging the careers of two men.

Willoughby provides a one-paragraph explanation of the event in his "autobiography":

> During the first months of the Occupation, the Civil Intelligence Section (CIS) was responsible for effecting the release of those individuals who had been imprisoned, or held under "protection and surveillance," for violation of the multitudinous laws, decrees, and regulations which for so many years had restricted freedom of speech, thought, religion, and assembly of the Japanese people. Actually they [CIS] went overboard in at least *one* case: the release of Japanese Communists *and the members of the Sorge espionage ring*—a fabulous Russian spy organization with important American ramifications which were finally exposed [italics mine].[1]

Let it first be noted that CIS was merely implementing MacArthur's orders, which initially had been dictated by Washington. Second, SCAPIN. 93, the order to release the political prisoners, did not differentiate between communist and non-communist political prisoners—all were to be released. And third, linking the "American ramifications" of the Sorge spy ring with the release of Japanese political prisoners is grossly misleading: the two communists released had been in prison for eighteen years and could not, therefore, have been involved in the wartime Sorge espionage ring. Finally, the two CIS officers who actually implemented the order, Norman and Emmerson, acted on the authority of General Eliot Thorpe, Willoughby's short-term predecessor whom Willoughby believed to be "soft" on communism.

What Willoughby could not have known, but which might be *objectively* relevant to his accusations of infamy in this episode, is that Norman clearly agreed, enthusiastically so, with the intent behind the order. As was mentioned in Chapter Four, shortly after the release of the political prisoners, he wrote to his wife that the event had been "The most exciting experience of my life."

If Herbert delighted in his duty to release these Japanese political prisoners, it was likely because he believed in the reasons behind the SCAP order: the directive was intended to enhance "civil rights" by rectifying, even as Willoughby himself confesses, the violation of same in the prewar period. Norman and Emmerson did not "go overboard," as Willoughby alleges, because they were following orders. In an affidavit on this matter, which he gave in Ottawa on 12 March 1952, in response to a request from John Emmerson who was then being subjected to a State Department "Loyalty Board" hearing, Herbert testified under oath that "John K. Emmerson and I, on the orders of Brigadier-General Thorpe, on 4 October 1945, visited Fuchu Prison, about ten miles northwest of Tokyo, to discover the numbers, status and condition of political prisoners detained there. It is my understanding that this order of General Thorpe's arose in part to implement a memorandum addressed to the Japanese Government on the subject of 'Removal of Restrictions on Political, Civil, and Religious Liberties'." Herbert footnotes the text of this SCAP order correctly.[2] Lest the cynical judge that Herbert was simply covering for Emmerson, let it be noted that Norman was just one of fifty-seven people who filed affidavits in behalf of Emmerson; and that Emmerson was cleared of any wrongdoing, even by the FBI, which secretly investigated him.[3]

SCAP justification for release of political prisoners was the simple one of resurrecting antiwar figures who, in the immediate aftermath of the war, might provide a countervailing

balance to the many pro-war conservatives who still dominated the Japanese political scene and through whom SCAP
was governing Japan. Willoughby clearly never appreciated
this simple strategic device for democratizing Japan. He worked
on the assumption that all communists were in the employ
of Moscow or Beijing, and the related notion that anyone
who assists in the liberation of communists must perforce be
a communist or a fellow-traveler. Obviously Willoughby never
extended this logic to MacArthur himself, despite the fact
that the on-scene order came from SCAP. Willoughby might
be forgiven for overlooking "culpability" since MacArthur
ruled by a double standard, one which invoked the communist threat from abroad while undertaking within Japan
what Edwin Reischauer calls "socialistic" reforms,[4] including
the unleashing of the Japanese Communist Party only to suppress it later once it began to look to Moscow for support.

Willoughby's concerns did not account for such fine distinctions; his was not to reason why, just to suppress leftists,
do or die. The fact that the released political prisoners included Tokuda Kyuichi and Shiga Yoshio, who two years
later wrote a book that gave an account of their release which
named Emmerson and Norman, was enough for Willoughby
to target the two liberators for secret investigation for communist sympathies.

In his enthusiasm for capturing communists, Willoughby
eschewed fact in favor of his fancy of a monolithic communist
conspiracy. One example is his mistaken allegation that Norman was somehow involved in the later repatriation of Yenan-
trained Japanese communist Nosaka Sanzo. In fact, Emmerson *only* was involved in Nosaka's return, having been stationed in Yenan with Mao Tse-tung during the Second World
War, when he got to know Nosaka. But so firmly had Willoughby in his own mind identified Norman with Emmerson
as an agent of international communism—an association
strengthened because of his association with John Service,
who, like Emmerson, was an old "China Hand," having
served in Mao's Yenan, and who was then working in the
Occupation—that he reported to Washington that Service,

Emmerson, *and* Norman "made an abortive attempt to hasten the return to Japan of certain members of the Yenan group."[5]

Neither Norman nor Service had anything to do with Nosaka's repatriation to Japan; in fact, any communication between Nosaka and Emmerson was done with offical sanction, as Emmerson's FBI file shows conclusively. Willoughby was in a position to know this, and indeed may have, but he had come to believe that Norman "exerted tremendous influence [over Emmerson and Service]" and must, therefore, have been involved, despite the absence of proof.[6]

Willoughby's mistaken opinion about Norman's alleged participation in the repatriation of Nosaka is attributable to his cold warriorism that subscribed to guilt by association. The truth about the Nosaka affair is provided by Emmerson in his autobiography, which in turn relies heavily upon secretly collected G-2 evidence that appears in the Emmerson FBI file, i.e., upon evidence that Willoughby had at his disposal but ignored in favor of his own suspicions. The Emmerson file shows that he had initiated communication with SCAP in his attempt to be repatriated. In the process, Nosaka mentioned the names of two American foreign service officers—Emmerson and Service—whom he had known in Yenan, no doubt calculating that by dropping the names of American officers, his return to Japan might be expedited. And so it was, but in Willoughby's eyes, the very fact that Emmerson and Service had once been on working terms with Nosaka in Yenan, despite this having been an official wartime assignment, made them suspect from a "security" point of view. Additionally, Service had been arrested in June 1945 by the FBI on the charge of leaking government documents to several people connected with the IPR and *Amerasia* in violation of the Espionage Act.[7] Along with Service were five others, including Phillip Jaffe, editor of *Amerasia,* journalist Mark Gayn (later a writer for the *Toronto Star),* and Lieutenant Andrew Roth, an officer in Naval Intelligence. In August a grand jury *unanimously* voted against indicting Service; a month later, he was sent to participate in the Occupation as

George Atcheson's executive officer in MacArthur's headquarters.

Service had no part in the ordered release of the Japanese political prisoners, but he was friendly with Emmerson and with Herbert. In many of his letters of late 1945 to his wife (she did not join him in Japan until autumn 1946) Herbert mentions seeing Service, a fact that was not overlooked by G-2. In a 1958 interview with the FBI regarding the lingering question of Emmerson's loyalty, Willoughby linked Norman with a "number of 'old China hands,' including George Atcheson, Jr., later killed in an airplane crash, Thomas Bisson, John K. Emmerson, and John Stewart Service." Willoughby stated that all of them "exhibited pro-communist sympathies." Most important, Herbert Norman "was closely associated with the group" and exerted tremendous influence over them, largely because "Norman had lived in Japan for a number of years, spoke the language and was familiar with the affairs of the country." Most damning for the Canadian, Willoughby claimed to have "reason to suspect that Norman was a communist espionage agent."[8]

Willoughby offered in support of his suspicion an instance when "highly confidential security files of the Tokyo City Police" were obtained by G-2, and subsequently, "through influence with the group [Emmerson, Service, etc.], Norman succeeded in gaining access to the files without [Willoughby's] knowledge." Willoughby adds that the file on Owen Lattimore, another "old China hand and friend of Norman," mysteriously disappeared from these records. Willoughby was careful not to attribute the loss of the Lattimore file to Norman, but the inference of his remark was nonetheless obvious.[9] More about Lattimore in a moment.

Willoughby further cited as evidence of Norman's perfidy the following: "Norman again exerted influence with Service and Emmerson, instigated and was present at a number of interviews conducted by those individuals with a number of Japanese communists prior to their release." Willoughby added that interviewing the political prisoners "was accomplished without [his] authority or knowledge,"[10] though he failed to add that at the time he not only had no authority—General Thorpe then headed the Civil Intelligence Section of G-2—but was not in a position to know that Norman and Emmerson had been *ordered* to interrogate the prisoners prior to effecting their release. Willoughby was also mistaken in alleging that Service took part in the release.

But in Willoughby's mind, Norman was one of those, if not the central figure, in a pro-communist group of Far Eastern experts who had some immeasurable impact on policymaking and implementation during the early stages of the Occupation. Norman's presumed influence over the 'old China hands,' who were legitimately identified with a "hard peace" position, made him an enemy of Willoughby who advocated, along with Eugene Dooman, a "soft peace," one that would give free rein to the right-wing, anti-communist elements who had ruled in prewar Japan. Soft peace advocates, while (ironically) loyal to MacArthur, sided against many of MacArthur's hard peace reforms, whether vigorous prosecution of the prewar right-wing, land reform, trust-busting, etc., all reforms supported by the hard peace advocates, many of whom were old China hands who had seen first-hand the devastating effects of Japanese aggression against China. Despite being an old Japan hand, Herbert sided with hard peace advocates, a position totally in character given his strong anti-imperialist and democratic leanings. This position, as Emmerson, Service, and Lattimore themselves would soon discover, made Norman a target of the Willoughby-Dooman faction. Herbert discovered this sore fact when in September 1951 Dooman resurrected the old charge against him and Emmerson for their role in releasing Japanese political prisoners.

Eugene Dooman, former State Department Director of the Office of Far Eastern Affairs until his job was given to hard peace advocate John Carter Vincent, an old China hand who was later targeted by the McCarthyites, testified on 15 September 1951 in connection with the IPR hearings in the Senate. He unabashedly reported Occupation hearsay—he was not in Japan in late 1945—regarding the alleged morale boost given to the Japanese Communist Party by Norman and Emmerson in effecting the release of "communists." Shortly thereafter, secret RCMP records show, Herbert was asked by External to supply a rebuttal to Dooman's testimony for the RCMP, Superintendent McClellan in particular, who then forwarded the rebuttal to the FBI and the State Department.

Norman's testimony before the RCMP is virtually identical to that which he gave six months later in affidavit form for Emmerson's Loyalty Board hearing, again making clear that he and Emmerson acted on orders from General Thorpe. In both statements, he makes clear that other officers, including Lieutenant Colonels Davis and John Irving, accompanied Emmerson and him on the second trip to the prison, that "these trips were undertaken on the orders of General Thorpe," and that after the trips he "duly filed [reports] in Headquarters" and submitted copies to External Affairs.[11] Yet despite Emmerson's factually identical account of the episode being accepted by the State Department and the FBI, and his loyalty reaffirmed, and despite External's acceptance of Norman's account, he was forced to repeat his account under secret questioning in an RCMP interrogation in January 1952.[12] This, fourteen months after he had been given a clean bill of health. The Willoughby legacy clung on like a whining infant. The reason, no doubt, is that this episode was not treated in isolation of other unsupported allegations. Willoughby had cast his anti-communist net widely, linking Herbert to many others beyond the old China hands crowd.

It is important to realize just how widely Willoughby did cast his net, as well as the criteria he used to fish suspected communists from the troubled seas of Occupied Japan. By showing this we gain a better understanding of the horrible reality that all the ingredients of "McCarthyism"—guilt by association, presumption of guilt, a lack of respect for free speech and independent thinking, and so on—existed well before February 1950, when the tormented Senator from Wisconsin made his famous speech in Wheeling, West Virginia, sending America deeper into a decade of Cold War hysteria. But a few words about the fanatical "fisherman" himself.

Charles A. Willoughby was born in Heidelberg, Germany, in 1892, the son of Frieherr (Baron) T. von Tscheppe-Weidenbach and his wife Emma Willoughby von Tscheppe-Weidenbach, originally of Baltimore, Maryland. According to one account, relying on Heidelberg records, there is serious doubt about his claims to aristocratic birth. Regardless, his family arrived in the United States when Willoughby was eighteen years old, at which time he enlisted in the Army under the name of Adolph Charles Weidenbach. Bright and aggressive, young Adolph Charles rose quickly through the ranks, reaching the rank of captain by the time MacArthur, who was then Field Marshal of the Philippine Commonwealth, met him. MacArthur brought Captain Willoughby, who now sported a new name as well as custom-tailored uniforms and a monocle, to the Philippines, eventually promoting him to Assistant Chief of Staff for Intelligence. It was in the Philippines that Willoughby became intimate with a number of wealthy Spanish *caudillos,* many of whom were ardent admirers of fascist Francisco Franco. Willoughby learned to share their admiration of Generalissimo Franco. John Gunther, in his book *The Riddle of MacArthur,* reported that in Tokyo one evening Willoughby rose to toast "the second greatest military commander in the world, Francisco Franco" (MacArthur being the first). Spain, said Willoughby, is "a cradle of supermen."[13]

A super-patriot at best, a fascist at worst, Willoughby approached his job as chief of counter-intelligence in the Occupation with the single-minded intention of helping MacArthur to make Japan into a Pacific bastion of anti-communism. His obvious enemies were the Soviet Union and its presumed Japanese communist puppets. But, in addition, Willoughby believed that "leftists and fellow-travelers [had been] hired in the States and unloaded on the civil sections [G-1, headed by Courtney Whitney] of general headquarters," meaning that he also faced an "internal enemy." To identify them, Willoughby writes, G-2 relied on "derogatory reports from various security agencies in Washington" in building a case against such characters as part of the process "to get rid of these people." One principal criterion for identifying "leftists and fellow-travelers" was association with the Institute of Pacific Relations. His other criteria included derogatory FBI reports, derogatory G-2 reports, derogatory local investigations, derogatory State Department reports, membership in the communist party or in "communist-front organisations" (of which the IPR was counted as one), local "Red press contacts," or local "Russian contacts."[14] According to Willoughby, Herbert Norman was guilty on at least six counts.

Willoughby felt that his job was made especially difficult by Washington's policies of coddling leftists, foreign and domestic. As he put it, "Long before McCarthy became nationally known, the silhouette of Soviet espionage and communist penetration in the Far East had been sharply etched in intelligence channels—only to be ignored or suppressed in Washington."[15] He wrote those words several years after suffering an official Army and State Department rebuke for irresponsibly identifying the wrong people—innocent people—in the wartime Soviet espionage ring operating in Tokyo.[16] Like McCarthy later, Willoughby felt that the State Department housed "New Dealers" of leftist sympathies and had even forced them on MacArthur's Occupation. Norman doubly fell into this category, first because he had been hired by Thorpe, whom Willoughby suspected of being soft on communism, and secondly, because Herbert's nationality quite literally made him "un-American."

In the fall of 1946, though Willoughby had to suffer passively the presence of Allied Soviets in Japan and MacArthur's democratic acceptance of the resurrection of the Japan Communist Party, he believed he did not have to tolerate the presence of left-wingers in the Occupation's employ. He therefore prepared a "Secret" memorandum for MacArthur entitled "Leftist Civilian Employees of GHQ." At that time he could list nine Occupation employees with "known leftist tendencies or who habitually associate with leftist [newspaper] correspondents." Prominent among the journalists were Joseph Fromm, Mark Gayn, "Canadian-born" David Conde, and Andrew Roth of the left-leaning *Nation*. Eventually Willoughby was successful in getting Roth and Gayn expelled; Norman happened to be friendly with all four reporters.

Besides their connections with suspicious journalists, Willoughby also argued that "leftist employees" were guilty of "having seriously misdirected the policies of the United States by attempting to discredit the Yoshida Cabinet and thereby promote the interests of the Japan Communist Party." Curiously, as already shown, MacArthur in fact was a chief detractor of Yoshida, as was Norman, because of Yoshida's numerous attempts to employ wartime reactionaries and to circumvent democratic Occupation reforms. MacArthur, of course, transcended politics in Willoughby's eyes, but Norman and G-1 personnel critical of Yoshida did not: their criticism of Yoshida was sufficient to prompt questions of loyalty. Willoughby accused these same nine G-1 employees, and Norman, of threatening the "security of classified information," though not in one single case did he document the bases of his suspicions.[17]

Willoughby's autumn 1946 report (about which more will be said shortly), was circulated to General Whitney in G-1 and to MacArthur, and met with serious criticism—from Whitney especially. Whitney regarded the September report as "an attack on the Section [G-1]". Willoughby's intra-G-2 memoranda made it equally clear that MacArthur did not find the report convincing. Bruised but not beaten, Willoughby issued a second report in June 1947, asserting that "subversive elements are employed in this Headquarters. Evidence is not only local, but is largely derived from U.S. reports," meaning that in the interim he had been in touch with G-2 in Washington and with the FBI. "We are vulnerable," said Willoughby, "exposed to proven international espionage and local maneuvers . . . and ideological penetration." Willoughby encouraged Whitney and MacArthur to jump on board: "The national trend is anti-communistic."[18] G-2 in Japan was merely following the trend, and, as if to admonish Whitney, "There is support in America for what

Taken sometime in the 1920s; left to right: Charles Holmes (who was best man at Irene and Herbert's wedding in 1935), Dr. and Mrs. Peter Millman, Herbert, and his sister Grace.

Above left: Howard and Herbert Norman, 1932.

Above right: Herbert, Irene Clark, and Howard, 1932.

Left: Taken in Japan in 1938; left to right: Grace, Mrs. Edgar Knipp, Mrs. Daniel Norman, Edgar Wright, Herbert, Reverend Daniel Norman, and Dr. Edgar Knipp. The Knipps were very close friends of the Norman family.

Norman with chargé d'affaires D'Arcy McGreer in Tokyo sometime during internment, December 1941 to June 1942.

General Douglas MacArthur and Norman in Tokyo after the war.

Norman (third from left at the top of steps) as Head of the Canadian Liaison Mission to Occupied Japan, with members of his staff; taken in front of the Canadian Embassy in Tokyo, 1946-47. Irene Norman is standing on the steps, third from the right.

Norman with a group of women who attended a memorial service for his father, Reverend Daniel Norman, in Nagano, 1947.

Irene and Herbert Norman greeting Mrs. Douglas MacArthur and the General's aide-de-camp, Colonel Sidney Huff, in Tokyo, at a Dominion Day reception, 1947.

Norman greeting General Z. Pechkoff, Chief of the French Mission to Occupied Japan, 1947. (Norman is suffering from tennis elbow; Pechkoff's right arm is missing.) *(U.S. Army photo)*

Norman, left, with Lieut. General G.G. Simonds of the National Defense College and J.H. Leemon, supervisor of the British Commonwealth Cemetery; taken at the Cemetery, Yokohama, in June 1947. *(U.S. Army photo)*

Norman with Prime Minister Yoshida, Australian High Commissioner Macmahon Ball, and the P.M.'s aide, 1949.

Norman greeting Minister of External Affairs Lester Pearson as he arrives in Tokyo to confer with MacArthur, January 1950. *(U.S. Army photo)*

Norman with a tennis partner in Tokyo, taken while on leave from New Zealand, 1955.

Herbert and Irene Norman, with staff of Commissioner's office in New Zealand, taken at a farewell reception before Norman's departure to Ottawa for reassignment to Egypt, May 1956.

Norman presenting his staff to President Nasser of Egypt, September 1956.

The Normans' residence on Boulos Hanna Street, Cairo, taken by the author in 1984.

The Wadi el Nil Building on el Sad el Ali Road, Cairo, taken by the author, 1984.

Herbert Norman's gravestone, beneath a cypress tree, in the Protestant Cemetery, Testaccio, Rome.

I am doing; don't make the mistake of being soft on communism."

The principal difference between his September 1946 report and the June 1947 one is the deletion of three names from the original list and the substitution of two new ones. Also in the second report, Willoughby expanded his checklist of wrongdoing for demonstrating communism to twenty-one criteria. He added such items as membership in or affiliation with such organizations as the Washington Committee for Democratic Action, the American Friends of the Chinese People, and "IPR affiliation with the New Deal." After each name appearing on his list of "Leftist Personnel in GHQ," Willoughby placed an *x* beside the criteria that was applicable. Though not one of his eight individuals named in the June 1947 report was "guilty" on all counts, Willoughby identified "the case of [Andrew Jonah] Grajdanzev as typical."[19] Grajdanzev was found "guilty" on six counts, among them: having an FBI record, a Military Intelligence record, "local communist affiliations, and IPR affiliation." Thomas A. Bisson was presumably an example of an extreme case, since according to Willoughby he was "guilty" on eleven counts. And a final example, that of Miss Beate Sirota, who was not deemed important enough to rate inclusion in the master list at all, but was instead simply reported on separately, gives some indication of what constituted a "small fry." To examine each case in turn is instructive.

Grajdanzev, working for the Local Government Division in Government Section (G-1) as a research analyst since January 1946, was kept under surveillance between 8 June and 28 June 1946. He came to the attention of G-2 because of his Russian name and his Russian birth, his friendship with several of the newspaper correspondents mentioned above, his past work for IPR, and because his employment references included two IPR members, E. C. Carter and Owen Lattimore. Initial investgations showed that he "attempted to descredit the Yoshida Cabinet"; that he secured copies of several books written by one Japanese "anti-communist" named Kawai Yoshinari, Yoshida's Welfare Minister, that led to the purging of Kawai; that he had once sought but failed to gain employment with the Office of Naval Intelligence ("but was not engaged because of his Russian background and leftist reputation"); and that he obtained a position with the Office of Strategic Services (OSS) "partly through the influence of the Owen Lattimore, well-known leftist . . ."[20]

For Willoughby the evidence of such leftist "tendencies" warranted extensive surveillance. The results of G-2's spying on Grajdanzev are intriguing: he "took his meals alone"; he "spent a considerable amount of time in his room, presumably writing, and received very few visitors, most of whom were Japanese"; he visited a small printing shop close to the American Embassy, to whose owner Grajdanzev was overheard saying, "Tell Kurita to send a letter to the newspaper protesting about the —— of Japan"; he was spied upon while taking Japanese language lessons; a "letter in Russian was taken from the wastepaper basket in his room at the Dai Ichi Hotel," though the report said the letter was signed "Anna" and addressed to "Dear Andre," and its content "appears to be entirely [a] personal affair."

The inescapable conclusion drawn from surveillance: "As a result of this surveillance, no positive evidence of subversive activity was found," though, not to be denied the right to legitimize G-2 suspicions, the report concluded, "but subject's movements and habits are of such an unusual nature as to warrant consideration." Surveillance may have failed, but "intelligence gathering" did not: "particularly significant" is the fact that Thomas Bisson is a colleague of Grajdanzev, that Bisson is also "a product of the leftist Institute of Pacific Relations," leading Willoughby to conclude that "there exists in the Government Section in the persons of subject, Bisson, and others, a small leftist group or 'cell' which is aggressively attempting to discredit all but Communist and leftist Japanese elements and to compromise the present policies of the United States in Japan." Worse yet for Grajdanzev, Willoughby was not reluctant to assert that the "evidence" "strongly suggests the possibility that subject has been developed as a long-range

Russian agent and that his primary purpose in GHQ is to provoke confusion and chaos . . ."[21] An impressive leap of faith.

Willoughby's almost religious zealousness in hunting down suspected communists explains his anomolous conclusions about Grajdanzev that the evidence can not sustain, indeed, that are even contradicted by subconclusions embedded in the report, such as "no positive evidence of subversive activity was found." Such is the character of McCarthyism. Once having arrived at such damning charges about Grajdanzev, it becomes easier to duplicate them in "similar" cases, such as Bisson's. Indeed, the "evidence" against Bisson reads very much like that marshalled against Grajdanzev, barely necessitating even a change in "subjects'" names. One of Bisson's crimes was associating with Grajdanzev, his colleague in G-1; another was having "criticized the Yoshida Cabinet as being reactionary and as an obstacle to democratic development"; another was membership in the IPR, "long under leftist if not Communist control"; and another, Bisson's references included Edward Carter, Secretary-General of the IPR, and Phillip Jessup, a Columbia University Professor of Law who, in 1950, when serving as Ambassador at Large, was characterized by McCarthy as having an "unusual affinity" for Communist causes.[22] As Bisson was a close personal friend of Herbert Norman, and also, like him, an academic who specialized in Japanese studies, the Bisson case is an important one for providing clues about G-2's investigation of Norman.

As a publishing Japanologist, Bisson's views were, quite literally, an "open book," available to anyone who sought to peruse his writings. Apparently Willoughby instructed his officers to do just that. Their findings, based on reading "both magazine articles and books" written by Bisson, "indicate that he has consistently entertained strong anti-Japanese sentiments, while being friendly toward Russia and China, particularly the Chinese Communists, although his sympathies toward Russia and China have been somewhat overshadowed by his extreme hostility toward Japan." In addition, Willoughby is especially condemnatory toward what he calls Bisson's "virtual obsession" with the *zaibatsu*. "In his recent book, *Japanese Wartime Economy*, published in 1945 under the auspices of the Institute of Pacific Relations, subject argues that the Zaibatsu were even more responsible for the war than the Japanese militarists."[23] Nowhere in their analysis of Bisson's writings is any mention of historical context, namely that "extreme hostility" toward imperialistic Japan was the norm among Asianist scholars, indeed, most westerners since 1931, when Japan had invaded Manchuria as prelude to its 1937 war against China. Nor is there any indication that most Occupationaires, including MacArthur, attributed Japanese aggression in large part to *zaibatsu* monopolization of wealth in the prewar period. McCarthyism is after all, ahistorical.

Yet for Willoughby, Bisson was guilty of much more than anti-Japanese sentiment. Bisson also made the mistake of "being in contact with" members of the "leftist cell" of journalists at the Tokyo Press Club, including Joe Fromm, Mark Gayn (then with *The Chicago Sun*), Gordon Walker (*Christian Science Monitor*), and David Conde (Reuters). "Leftism" in the case of these journalists meant nothing more than reporting instances of the "Japanese . . . circumventing SCAP's efforts to democratize the country"; this was Fromm's point, a fact that no intelligent observer disputed in 1946. Bisson had made the same observation "a few weeks earlier" than the Fromm report and the fact that the two men knew one another and shared the same mistrust of Japanese conservative rulers was sufficient in Willoughby's view to attribute Fromm's "negative" reporting to Bisson's influence.[24]

Bisson did more than simply "convert" impressionable journalists to his negative opinion of Japanese reaction; he also "had a long record of association with "Communist front organizations," among which were the American Committee of Anti-Nazi Literature, the American League for Peace and Democracy, and a nameless wartime organization appealing for the boycott of Japanese goods; too, Bisson made the "mistake" of signing his name to an "Open letter for Closer

Cooperation with the Soviet Union" in 1939. The list of his "crimes" is endless: Bisson wrote an article for *Soviet Russia Today*, was a member of the editorial board of *Amerasia*, was the editor of a research bulletin called *USSR in the Far East*, was associated with *China Today*, and even held union membership once upon a time. Finally, and perhaps most damning, if tone counts for much, "Subject is known to be on exceedingly close terms with Tsuru Shigeto, an extremely leftist Japanese who was arrested before the war by the Japanese police for his activites with the Japan Communist Party and the Young Communist League." Through Bisson, the report concludes, Tsuru "is able to inject his views into the work of SCAP and exercise a direct influence in Occupation policies."[25]

On even closer terms with Tsuru, and the person who introduced Bisson to Tsuru, was Herbert Norman. Later, the FBI would assert, without providing reasons, that Bisson was Norman's secret IPR contact in Japan in 1946, for what purpose Hoover's hounds did not say. And to make the triage complete, Willoughby asserts in a secret report about Norman, "The trend of this whole initial report is Norman's association with Tsuru. That is the hub around which the inquiry rotates."[26]

Follow the "logic": Grajdanzev is a "long-range Soviet espionage agent," he is friendly with Bisson who is guilty on more counts of disloyalty than anyone else employed by G-1 and who serves as a conduit for Tsuru's communist views to make their way into SCAP policy; Bisson got to know Tsuru through Tsuru's old Harvard communist friend Herbert Norman, who also happened to assist in the release of notorious Japanese communists, who exerts considerable "influence" over old China hands in the Occupation, and who is finally posted in August 1946 as head of one of the Allied missions. What do you get from this complex intermeshing of communist conspirators? The answer, as Willoughby concluded, ". . . Norman was a communist espionage agent."[27]

Such "evidence" against Herbert Norman is clearly indirect; the direct "evidence" will be examined momentarily.

But for now it is important to understand that the man making the charges was as close ideologically to the fascists that his Army had just defeated as one can possibly imagine. The last G-2 case to be examined, that of Miss Beate Sirota, should make this charge against Willoughby even more apparent.

The Sirota report, written by Willoughby himself, was never intended to see the light of day in the form in which Willoughby left it before passing it on to his assistant, a Dr. Spinks. It is not difficult to imagine why. Willoughby identifies Sirota as an "expert" (his quotation marks) who was involved in the purge of right-wing village headmen. Willoughby's contempt for her reputed "expertise" is apparent early in his report to Spinks: "The 'expert' is about 26 years of age—rather young. A comparatively recent graduate of a Pacific Coast college—a general course. No evidence there of specialization, of any kind. here *[sic]* are literally thousands of graduates, of such small colleges; no one in their right mind,*[sic]* considers them an 'expert' of anything, rather apprentices of some career, or some job. *[sic]* this expert happens to know Japanese—but so do hundreds of *nisei* [second-generation Japanese-Americans] ad *[sic]* other members of military linguist teams. She is a woman, a girl of no particular distinction . . . . Her parents are Russian emigres, from Kiev via Austria. Obscure begininngs, obscure itineraries."

For Willoughby, most important about Sirota is that she is Jewish, Russian, and essentially stateless: She is "certainly not American; and her familiarity with American standards, thoughts and ideals are those hastily acquired, at an immature age, thru *[sic]* being sent to the States, for an education." "They are Jewish." They arrive in Japan during the war via Shanghai, "where they work mysteriously and precariously. Shanghai, that focal point of intrigue and espionage . . . . They run into a Jewish clique . . . One Jew recommends another [for a job]." And then, inexplicably, Willoughby tries to weave Sirota and her family's fate into the Sorge spy ring: "Then we come across the crazy quilt of the Sorge spy case. Sorge, international spy, working for both the Russians and the Germans. A story in itself." The seeming *non sequiturs* continue: "From that period [Sorge case, 1941–44], we find that 'expert' almost psychopathic in her hatred of the police and the neighborhood authority. She is childish in her glee, at being able to vent her fury, her suppressed hatred, in a position as 'expert on the purge of neighborhood officials'....[his ellipses] a stateless jewess, *[sic]* a hastily acquired citizenship, wielding the power of the United States and the prestige of MacArthur."[28]

Sexist, chauvinist, anti-Semite, and conspiracy theorist extraordinaire, Willoughby shows his 'character' best in discussing his intentions to rid the Occupation of Sirota.

Despite, or perhaps because of, being a first-generation American himself, Willoughby's suspicions about the loyalty of naturalized Americans, especially those with Russian backgrounds, were not limited to a few individuals, such as Grajdanzev or Sirota. In his way of thinking, finding several suspicious cases warranted blanket indictments against everyone else who shared similar family backgrounds. Hence, in addition to the individual case studies of the sort described above, Willoughby also commissioned more general studies, such as one identifying *all* "foreign elements employed in General Headquarters." This study, dated 5 March 1947, begins: "Russian and Russian-satellite backgrounds of civilian employees present a potential threat of leftist infiltration detrimental to the interests of the United States and constitute a security risk." The study observes that of "304 foreign nationals employed in GHQ, 28% are either of Russian or Russian-satellite backgrounds." Their family heritage, in his view, makes them "unquestionably susceptible to Soviet and Communist influence . . ."[29] In a related report, this one dated 28 January 1947, he further observes that ". . . the incidents *[sic]* of leftist activity is much higher among personnel with Russian and Russian-satellite backgrounds than among other individuals." Willoughby also states that "seventy-one leftist cases" are "now in the active file of G-2." Omitted from this report, but certainly significant in light of the Sirota case, it appears that substantially more than half of those who were named by Willoughby for "leftist activity" were Jewish Russians or Jews from "Russian-satellite" nations.

Willoughby's tendency to issue blanket indictments was not restricted to national background or, apparently, religion. In a 1 March 1947 report, Willoughby indicts the Institute of Pacific Relations in a significant prelude to the Senate's McCarran Committee attack on the IPR in 1950–51. Indeed, it is clear that the McCarran Committee—which also went after Herbert Norman in the same years—relied heavily on the substance, if not the language as well, of Willoughby's G-2 investigation of IPR. As will be discussed in a subsequent chapter, Willoughby secretly sent his IPR records to Robert Morris, attorney for the McCarran Committee, before he left Japan.

Norman was, of course, one of the more distinguished Japanologists among the IPR ranks: he had published with them, had contributed to its journal *(Pacific Affairs)*, represented the organization in Japan during the Occupation, and maintained many close personal relationships with IPR's officers and personnel.

Willoughby's judgment of the organization was venomous: "To all outward appearances it is a sedate, scholarly, respectable research institute," but "from its establishment in 1925, the IPR has been under the control of Communists and fellow-travelers." It is "a high-powered leftist pressure group, the main objectives of which are to give a leftist bias to American public opinion in regard to Far Eastern Affairs and to develop and plant 'Far Eastern Experts' in American universities and colleges and in United States Government agencies." Its "ruling clique"—"the four most active and vocal commissars are fellow-travelers and communists"—consisted of Edward Carter, Frederick Vanderbilt Fields, Harriet Moore, and Owen Lattimore. These four, Willoughby says, "cleverly concealed its leftist aims and the leftist character of its administrative control."

Its two chief organs, *Pacific Affairs* and *Far Eastern Survey*, according to Willoughby, "reveal a consistent and subtle propaganda line aimed primarily at building up communist influence in the Far East." Anyone publishing in these journals is egregiously accorded "expert status" and is thereby "groomed" for placement "in many key positions in Government agencies." Further, "by the effective use of the system of mutual recommendations," the "ruling clique" has succeeded in placing "its leftist proteges" in "wartime agencies." One such example cited is the OSS, the CIA's wartime predecessor, which, it should be recalled, tried to recruit Herbert Norman. (One has to ask, with so many leftists influencing wartime policy, how did the Allies manage to win?) In any event, Willoughby supports his claims by citing the names of Grajdanzev, Bisson, Lattimore, and several others.

It should by now be evident that given the nature of Willoughby's views, Norman would quite naturally fall under suspicion: he was not an American, he was associated with IPR, his duties in late 1945 necessarily meant associations with Japanese communists, and he was friendly with a great many American "leftist" personnel in G-1. In Willoughby's view, any one of these was sufficient to prompt investigation but when considered all together they demanded more than investigation, i.e., they demanded first Norman's exposure, then his dismissal, and finally his prosecution.

Absolute precision about the time periods of different G-2 investigations of Norman is not possible, given the degree to which extant G-2 records have been censored. Nonetheless, it is clear from the uncensored portions that Willoughby was co-ordinating his different investigations with the FBI. The record of the FBI investigation of Norman is quite clear: after the Tsuru Affair investigation was closed in 1942, the FBI did not recommence its investigation of him until 16 October 1946, roughly two weeks after Willoughby submitted his first report about "leftist personnel" in G-1 and just two months after Herbert assumed his new post as head of the Liaison Mission. The official category used by the FBI for him was "Security Matter"; this classification continued to be used until 11 March 1947, when the case was dropped, probably at the request of G-2 which, in a 10 December 1950 inter-office memorandum concerning Norman, refers to "the possibly damaging old study on leftist infiltration into this Hq which I was directed to impound."[30] The inference is clear: he had been one of those targeted in the autumn 1946 investigation that had so outraged General Whitney.

The focus of that investigation, and the wide range it assumed, is dealt with at some length in a 30 November 1950 Military Intelligence memo from Tokyo to Washington, concerning Willoughby's "long held suspicions of Dr. Norman" that had been confirmed in a 22 November letter. Willoughby also refers to an August 1950 letter from Washington, which in turn refers to "new" information garnered from "the Canadian authorities" and from "the Federal Bureau of Investigation."[31] Hence, by August 1950, two months before his recall to Ottawa, Herbert had become the subject of a combined Canadian-American inquiry.

A great many names are mentioned in this 30 November communiqué, but, as noted earlier, two names in particular prove important in light of subsequent events: Tsuru and Halperin. Willoughby writes that in the past "Norman's connections with Tsuru Shigeto have been the subject of interest here." He makes the assumption that "the group of young instructors and graduate students at Harvard who met for the study of American capitalism from the Marxist point of view," quoting portions of an FBI report, might be "the same persons who have held rather high positions here as economic advisors or consultants . . ." The G-2 letter then lists a great many names of "the persons [who] are somehow connected with either Norman or Tsuru or both," adding that "all of them have come to our official attention before, some of them have been the subjects of extensive 'loyalty investigations,' and the organisations or groups mentioned seem to be common to all the persons involved."[32] The list, it should be mentioned, is cited for purposes of eliciting from Washington more information about the individuals mentioned, but, again, on the assumption that the names have some connection with Norman, Tsuru, or both.

Among the more important names, at least with regard to

demonstrating guilt by association, are Bisson, Edward Carter ("he has long been a friend of Norman"), "Canadian-born" David Conde, Eleanor Hadley (connected with IPR and "an associate of Norman's while she was here [working for the Occupation]"), John Service (who, with Emmerson, it mistakenly asserts, "made an abortive attempt to hasten the return to Japan of certain Japanese members of the Yenan group"), Owen Lattimore, and Andrew Grajdanzev. Halperin's name appears in connection with Mr. and Mrs. Philip Olin Keeney, "known Communist[s] and courier[s]." The report states that "We know that Keeney and Tsuru knew each other here." This leads to the question, "Could this lead to Keeney having been associated with Isidor [sic] Happerlin [sic]? With Norman?"[33]

Herbert had been recalled by the time of this speculative naming of names, due to the RCMP's and External's concerns about his connection with Israel Halperin, who had been indicted but exonerated in the Gouzenko affair. As G-2 had been made privy to Ottawa's suspicions, it was not simply grasping at straws in posing questions regarding suspicious associations. But by the spring of 1947, when the FBI and presumably G-2 had closed their investigations of Herbert, at least for the moment, a determination had been reached that, given the evidence, Norman no longer deserved to be considered a "security matter." No doubt playing a part in this was the MacArthur-Whitney repudiation of Willoughby's "damaging old study on leftist infiltration." But also playing a part was a secret State Department summary of Herbert's character that gave him security clearance.

The State Department report, dated 29 June 1948, characterized Herbert as a "moderate liberal," as one "who enjoys the confidence and respect of his superiors," and as "an American—as opposed to a British-Canadian." It notes that he is "objective and academic, but at the same time a practical man, having many interests outside his special field"; it adds that "one source" credits him with having "excellent judgment" while another says that "he is misled by superficial appearances." So far as the Occupation is concerned, the report says that Norman "has expressed his warm endorsement of the policies of General MacArthur."

Since a copy of this report appears in Army Intelligence records, it must be assumed that Willoughby had access to, if not possession of, it. The fact that its contents are all drawn from "confidential" interviews conducted during 1946 or 1947, means that it must again be assumed that Willoughby had good reason to know of the generally high regard in which Norman was held during, if not before, the time when Willoughby commenced his investigation of him.

Why, then, did Willoughby (and the FBI, which also had access to this positive information) persist in the investigation of Norman? The answer is that Willoughby was one of the purer *products* of his time. His very *raison d'être* was to suspect the worst of human beings; to, when in doubt, assume that associations with IPR members, Japanese leftists, or G-1 "New Dealers" meant at least culpability if not guilt in Cold War espionage. This is not its progenitor. There are two other pieces of evidence, not cited in either the FBI or G-2 reports on Norman, perhaps because of censorship, that might explain Willoughby's bulldog pursuit of his "case." This evidence has to do with Israel Halperin.

As already mentioned, Halperin was one of several Canadians arrested in early 1946 by the RCMP as a result of the testimony of Igor Gouzenko. Though eventually acquitted of any wrongdoing, supposedly because of the refusal of an alleged co-conspirator to testify against him, Canadian and American spy-chasers nonetheless remained convinced that Halperin had been guilty of spying for the Soviets during the Second World War, along with at least one other Canadian— Hazen Sise—who was later named by American "spy queen" Elizabeth Bentley. Central to the Canadian and American suspicions about Halperin's guilt was his personal notebook containing the names and addresses of friends, which had been seized as part of the investigation. Among the names in the notebook was Herbert Norman's, mentioned seven times in all, each with a different address and beginning in Cambridge, Massachusetts, where both Halperin and Herbert had been Harvard graduate students. (With them at Harvard, and likewise listed in Halperin's notebook, was Tsuru. See Chapter 10.)

While it might be reasonable to assume that in 1946 the RCMP would have immediately investigated everyone listed in Halperin's notebook, at least in Norman's case it is obvious that they did not. The fact that his name appeared in the notebook did not become relevant for the RCMP until September of 1950, when the FBI first argued the importance of that inclusion which, in turn, led six weeks later to Herbert's recall to Ottawa from Japan.

This fact is important in light of evidence showing that in July 1946, the FBI undertook its own investigation of at least one other person whose name appeared in Halperin's notebook. The person investigated was Norman's friend, Lorie Tarshis, born Lorie Singer in Toronto.

An FBI report dated 29 August 1946, referring to an investigation of Tarshis completed the month before, begins, "Subject's name found in address book of Israel Halperin, a known Soviet Espionage Agent, who was recently apprehended in Canada." The report further notes that Tarshis "was a friend of Shigeto Tsuru, a Jap who was repatriated to Japan June 18, 1942." Also of significance, it says of Tarshis, "Subject and his wife appeared on list of members of NORTH AMERICAN SPANISH AID COMMITTEE." An additional item mentions that "on page 36 of this address [book]," and here the document is censored.[34] It seems reasonable to assume that on page 36 of Halperin's notebook appears the name of Herbert Norman. Regardless, at this early date, the FBI had begun its own investigation of Norman, separately from any G-2 one.[35] Hence, however tenuous, a connection is nonetheless established among Herbert, Tarshis, Tsuru, and Halperin, with, again, Halperin identified as "known Soviet Espionage Agent." Too, since Herbert participated at Harvard with both Tsuru and Tarshis in what the 1942 FBI report on the Tsuru Affair called a "Marxist Study Group," which also allegedly included Robert Bryce, the FBI was well on its way to developing a significant "Canadian connection" with

Soviet espionage that went well beyond the Gouzenko revelations.[36]

These connections, by themselves merely suggestive, take on added importance in late summer 1950 with the Klaus Fuchs case. Fuchs was a German-born naturalized British scientist, on loan from Britain since 1943 as part of the Allied war effort, who had worked at the U.S. Atomic Laboratory at Los Alamos, New Mexico, on the development of the atom bomb. In February 1950 the FBI had aided British intelligence in uncovering Fuchs's participation in atom bomb espionage. The FBI's part in uncovering Fuchs had come as a result of cross-referencing Fuchs's name, which also appeared in Halperin's notebook, with a tip from a British informant who had been engaged in atomic research in England. By May of 1950, the FBI had been able to expand its investigation of other names in Halperin's notebook. A few short months later the Fuchs-Halperin connection had quite clearly resulted in a second look at the other names appearing in the Halperin notebook, leading to FBI correspondence with its RCMP counterparts regarding Herbert Norman.

A 14 October 1950 letter from Arnold Heeney of External to Hume Wrong, then Canadian Ambassador to the United States, helps to show just how far the connection had been developed by the FBI. Heeney begins: "As a result of the discovery in the Halperin notebook of Fuchs' name, the FBI have in the past month been making an elaborate study of that notebook, and following up names in it. As a result of this procedure, they have made a number of inquiries of the RCMP." Heeney points out that External is trying to find "reasonable explanations of the various points," and that the RCMP "have held off as long as they can making a report to the FBI" while External looks into the connection. Heeney also says that "almost incredibly [the FBI] had not realised Herbert Norman's present position," nor, "curiously," had the FBI noted "mention of Norman's name in connection with the Senate Committee's Inquiry in April [1950; see below], the fact that Norman was lent to General Thorpe . . . , and the fact that Norman was at one time in the employ of the Institute of Pacific Relations."[37]

Besides the importance of the Fuchs-Halperin-Norman connection, several other facets of the Heeney statement are noteworthy. Clearly the FBI was withholding from the RCMP knowledge of how much it already knew about Norman, possibly in order to test how forthcoming Canadian security people would be. By August 1950, the FBI and Willoughby's G-2 in Japan were freely exchanging information about Herbert, comparing notes about his connections with IPR and his employment with Thorpe, although it is true that nothing in the uncensored record indicates that the Senate inquiry warranted special attention. And, of course, the FBI had learned of his present position in Japan through its exchanges of information with Willoughby. What truly is "almost incredible" is that Heeney could have been naïve enough to think that the Americans had not done their homework.

The point worth emphasizing here is that Norman's recall from Tokyo, to which Heeney refers in his letter to Wrong, was prompted by a disingenuous FBI and a frightened External which, according to Heeney, worried that Hoover might take "precipitous action, including, perhaps, publicity." Equally important to observe, as had Willoughby and the FBI, External also had reached the conclusion that Norman's work with the IPR and with Thorpe were potentially damaging pieces of "evidence." But the important difference between the Americans and the Canadians in this instance is that Heeney assumed Herbert was innocent until proven guilty— "Norman Robertson will give him an opportunity of answering questions arising out of the evidence"; and elsewhere in the letter, "it is our hope that on his return, it will be possible to find a reasonable explanation of indications, which on the face of them, are awkward"[38] —while the FBI, relying on its own and Willoughby's suspicions, presumed Herbert's guilt.

The process that resulted in his recall and subsequent grilling by the RCMP began in the 1950 Senate hearings in Washington, two months before the outbreak of the Korean War. Herbert, for his part, learned about the Senate hearings by May of that year, getting his first intimation that his fate was being dealt a decisive blow by events that were unfolding in McCarthy's Washington.

His name first became public on 20 April 1950, in the Tydings Senate Committee hearings investigating Senator Joseph McCarthy's allegations that a number of State Department Far Eastern experts had been disloyal to the United States. The hearings began in March and ended in June, and the chief target of McCarthy's accusations and of the Subcommittee's inquiry was Norman's old friend, Owen Lattimore. Among the cast of characters who testified were J. Edgar Hoover and General Eliot Thorpe. Hoover lent the hearings his and the FBI's credibility while Thorpe testified as a witness in defense of Lattimore's loyalty, a defense he extended to include the IPR.[39] It was during the questioning of General Thorpe that Herbert's name was introduced. Senator Hickenlooper asks:

"General Thorpe, were you connected with the preparation of an intelligence report in connection with a man named Norman shortly before you left China and came over to Japan and came back to the United States, whose report was submitted to General Willoughby?"

Thorpe: Norman? I don't recall the name.

Hickenlooper: You don't recall a man by the name of E. Herbert Norman?

Thorpe: Oh, yes; yes, sir. He is the Canadian representative. Oh, yes.

Hickenlooper: That is the fellow. Were you associated with Mr. Norman in preparing a report that was transferred to Mr. Willoughby shortly before you came back to the United States [in 1946]?

Thorpe: Not that I know of. Dr Norman was associated with my section in SCAF *[sic]* Headquarters until he was appointed Canadian representative on the Far East Commission, that is correct, but I don't remember ever making a report on him, sir.

Hickenlooper: Did he make a report which was filed with you for transmittal to the proper channels on the political situation in Asia?

Thorpe: Not to my knowledge; no, sir. That must have been after I left.

Hickenlooper: I am asking about shortly before you left.

Thorpe: No, sir. So far as I recall, I do not remember that.

Hickenlooper: I am not necessarily assuming such report was made, but following up my question, a report which was submitted to you and which you approved and transmitted on to General Willoughby.

Thorpe: Not to my knowledge. I was not under General Willoughby. I reported directly to the Chief of Staff [MacArthur], and did not report to General Willoughby. I had no occasion to transmit reports to him.[40]

Suffice it to add that the questioning continues three more rounds in the same uncertain vein, without establishing anything substantial regarding a report of any sort, or anything more about Herbert Norman. What makes the questioning important, aside from Norman's name being introduced in such a damaging context, is the obvious deduction that the Senate McCarthyites had already drawn, having been informed of Willoughby's suspicions of Norman, which most likely had gotten into Hickenlooper's hands via an FBI source. (Note that from the time of this first McCarthyite committee until the 1957 subcommittee which sealed Herbert's fate, the FBI issued repeated denials of illegally providing the legislative branch with information regarding security cases.)

Although nothing directly damning about Herbert had been mentioned in the Thorpe interrogation, Canadian Ambassador to Washington Hume Wrong was sufficiently alarmed by the very fact that Norman's name had been mentioned in this context that he cabled Secretary of State Heeney the next morning. Most of the cable was a summary of Thorpe's testimony, though Wrong ended his cable by referring to Hickenlooper's being questioned by reporters following adjournment about the reference to Norman and refusing to comment; and with the more ominous remark that Lattimore's defense counsel, Abe Fortas, suggested to newspapermen "that Senator Hickenlooper's line of questioning about Norman had indicated a desire to establish a link with the Canadian espionage enquiry" (i.e., the Gouzenko affair).[41]

A week later, the head of the American and Far Eastern Division, Arthur Menzies, with Heeney's approval, cabled Norman in Tokyo to report on the Hickenlooper questioning of Thorpe. The cable ended with two remarks, one an oblique warning, the second an implicit, albeit sympathetic, query: "I am inclined to think that no useful purpose would be served in issuing a statement here at this time." And, "I should like to add that we are all distressed that your name should be raised in this way without any explanation being given as to what Senator Hickenlooper was driving at."[42]

Norman accepted the warning about not lending credence to the episode by commenting publicly, and he also took the query to heart. He cabled Heeney on 2 May 1950: "I appreciate your thoughtfulness in informing me regarding Hickenlooper's question. I had not, repeat not, heard of it before but I was puzzled by an inquiry I had from General Willoughby's office a week ago asking whether I knew anything of a rumour that Thorpe had been reassigned from these Headquarters 'because of some report.' I was entirely ignorant of any such rumour and it was my impression that Thorpe left here with the highest respect of his own officers and of General MacArthur and in fact was decorated for his services." He then summarized his 1945 work for Thorpe before adding, "I am also completely at a loss to explain Hickenlooper's query. It may possibly be that he had heard some rumours of bad feeling between Thorpe and Willoughby while the former was in Tokyo and hoped in some devious or accidental manner to have this matter aired, hence discrediting Thorpe as a witness in the case."[43] Herbert's supposition has reason to recommend it, since Thorpe was testifying as to Lattimore's loyalty—McCarthy's "test case" for proving communism had infiltrated the State Department; yet if Hickenlooper had been in receipt of Willoughby's suspicions, then his intent was not so much to discredit Thorpe as to show that foreign service officers from Allied nations were, just as Lattimore was suspected of being, in the employ of Moscow.

In any event, Norman ended his self-defense with the admission, "Naturally I am disturbed that Hickenlooper should have chosen my name and am puzzled how he came to have it, particularly when it is not a relevant issue at all. I entirely agree with you that no useful purpose could be served by any public statement."[44] As it turned out, however, a public statement was simply forestalled by one year.

As discussed above, the earliest mention of a date when G-2 in Tokyo and G-2 in Washington began comparing notes about Herbert is August 1950, cited in the 30 November letter from Willoughby to Washington. On the other hand, Washington and Ottawa did not begin comparing notes until 8 September when Hoover initiated communication with the RCMP. From the flurry of internal RCMP documents about Herbert that was generated over the next two years, what becomes clearer than anything else is the crucial importance that both the FBI and the RCMP placed on the fact that Herbert's name appeared in Halperin's notebook.

From a secret RCMP memorandum entitled "The Norman Case: Some Factors and Considerations," it is apparent that the initial 8 September letter from Hoover caused the RCMP genuine embarrassment. Mention is made that in 1947 the FBI "made some investigations at Harvard because of the appearance of Norman's name in the Halperin notebook, but closed their file without reporting to us." Clearly the reference is to the wider investigation including Tarshis that is discussed earlier. The RCMP report goes on to note, "When Norman's name came before the Senate Committee [Tydings Subcommittee] it is easy to understand the FBI's interest and desire to get all the facts they could; indeed they may have felt a little remiss in not pursuing the 1942 [Tsuru apartment] episode a little more closely—thus in the same way that we feel somewhat remiss in not following the Halperin entry more quickly." "More quickly" means after four years!

The RCMP self-criticism continues: ". . . we cannot feel too satisfied over the fact that Norman's name was not picked out of the Halperin notebook earlier." And then the obligatory excuse: "The only thing that can be said in explaining the failure to process the Halperin diary names sooner is the bulk involved and the fact that work arising from report of the Royal Commission on Espionage [Kellog-Taschereau] was taken up in order of its apparent importance with regard to the facilities available."[45]

RCMP self-deprecation stems from its embarrassment at being shown the relevance of Canadian-generated evidence by the American FBI. The admission is an important one, for it was made sometime after Norman's death in 1957. The report itself is undated, but reference to his death, almost seven years after Hoover first contacted the RCMP, makes it clear that the report is a retrospective account of RCMP failings in its handling of "the Norman case." More about Canadian spy-chasing in Chapter 12; here we will restrict ourselves to the events leading up to his recall, based upon what "evidence" was *then* available.

The copy of the 8 September Hoover letter obtained by me from the FBI, using the Freedom of Information Act, is heavily censored, and an attached "Deleted Page Information Sheet" reveals that six pages of the document were withheld entirely. But by consulting the RCMP records, the contents of both the censored FBI letter (two pages in length) and the deleted six-page attachment become easily discernible. First, Hoover's letter identifies Norman as a "Security Case-C" (C meaning communist) and notes that a carbon copy has been sent on to the Foreign Service Desk for eventual transmittal to the State Department, which would be forced to deal with the diplomatic aspects of the case. Second, the letter refers to the suspected link between Norman, Halperin, and the

Fuchs case. And finally, the six omitted pages are copies of Special Agent reports regarding first the Tsuru apartment affair and second the results of the FBI's investigation into names listed in Halperin's notebook. Related to the Tsuru material is collateral evidence regarding Herbert's participation at Harvard in the "Marxist study group" as well as "specimens" of his handwriting obtained from the Harvard University registrar.[46]

The first recorded Canadian reaction to Hoover's 8 September letter by responsible officials in Ottawa came in a 15 September letter from George Glazebrook to Lester Pearson, who was then at the United Nations in New York with the Canadian delegation. Glazebrook opens his letter by referring to an "awkward situation" that he is handling with the advice of Norman Robertson and in the absence of Arnold Heeney. "Inspector MacNeil of the Special Branch of the RCMP came to see me yesterday. He had received in the ordinary way an inquiry from the FBI about Herbert Norman. The FBI's interest in this arose out of their study of the Halperin Notebook."

Glazebrook goes on to remind Mr. Pearson that "when you saw the photostat of the Notebook [1946?] . . . you ran across references to Herbert Norman, and my impression from your remarks at that time was that this was one of several innocent people mentioned in reference to addresses and social engagements. Not surprisingly, the references are seen differently by the FBI."[47]

And here, succinctly summarized, is the crux of a problem that would not be solved even *after* Norman's death: different Canadian and American perceptions regarding what constitutes suspicious or disloyal behavior.

Glazebrook also mentions the FBI's reference to "a Japanese scholar" in Herbert's background who "was far to the Left." No doubt this refers to Tsuru. Glazebrook expresses concern over the likelihood of the FBI pushing its investigation of Norman to a speedy conclusion before External has a chance to find "satisfactory explanations." He assures Pearson that he is doing his best to contain the situation by limiting the number of people involved and further indicates that the RCMP is being supportive.

On the basis of the Hoover letter, however, the RCMP began immediately to probe more deeply into Herbert's past. On 29 September it sent External a brief summary of their findings. In the RCMP material that I obtained, two names linked to Herbert are excised, although as this information ultimately found its way into the Senate Subcommittee on Internal Security (SISS) records which I examined in Washington in August 1983, I am able to fill in the blanks, here denoted by parenthetical enclosures: "Letter to External— setting forth information received from (Sise)—together with reference on (Frank Park's) desk pad and report of Secret Agent dated 20–2–40 this included the information that we had failed to connect the Prof. Norman mentioned in Secret Agent's report with Egerton Herbert Norman."[48] Hazen Sise had been identified in 1945–46 by Elizabeth Bentley, and Park was a Montreal lawyer once active in a wartime Soviet friendship organization; Chapter 12 tells more about both men.

Between 29 September and 11 October, the RCMP expanded its investigation, by now labeled "Top Secret," and reported to Glazebrook on the latter date about new information it had gathered. It reported that one of the addresses under Norman's name and listed in the Halperin notebook was Herbert's father-in-law, Harry Clark of Hamilton. It further reported that at Herbert's wedding, the best man had been C. P. H. Holmes, data on whom is excised in the RCMP record, though in the SISS record it is reported that he was a "well known communist."[49] But most important, at least for American investigators later on, is a reference to a statement attributed to Gouzenko, made before the Royal Commission, that has Soviet spy Colonel Zabotin being asked by Moscow if he knew "a person by the name of Norman." Zabotin answers "No," and the RCMP concludes that, "It would appear that NORMAN is the surname of a person in whom the Russian Intelligence Service had an interest."[50]

Three days later, on 14 October, Heeney writes to Pearson notifying him that Norman had been cabled and ordered "to return by air within a week." He ended his short note with a depressing, albeit realistic, assessment: "I am very much afraid that even if we satisfy ourselves of Norman's innocence, *we will never be able to satisify the Americans.*"[51] (Emphasis mine.) Another letter, this one from Glazebrook to Pearson, suggests that Norman had been told by the RCMP why he was being recalled. Hence, his recall came as no surprise: according to author Charles Taylor, Herbert had told his brother that during his last months in Japan he believed that his secretary, who was "dating" an officer from G-2, had been spying on him.[52]

Herbert cabled External on 16 October, acknowledging receipt of the 14 October cablegram ordering him home and notifying the Department of his planned arrival in Ottawa on 21 October. Meanwhile in Ottawa, plans were being made for Norman Robertson to begin preparation for leading the questioning that would commence three days after Norman's return. Getting him back as quickly as possible was seen as vital since External thought it likely that "in view particularly of the unfortunate attitude taken by Hoover as a result of the Fuchs incident," "precipitate action, including, perhaps, publicity" was likely to result. External did not want Herbert unprotected in Tokyo should this happen. Steps to ensure that untoward publicity would not arise were taken quietly through External's contacts with the State Department, hoping that State might co-operate "in avoiding a storm which can only do harm." Some comfort was derived from the unsupportable hope that "the State Department will realize that Norman is a scholar of international reputation" and might understand, therefore, that his "academic tastes" led him, "in his younger days," "like undergraduates of the '30's, [to] flirt[ing] with Leftist ideas."[53]

Though these early, pre-recall letters are careful to avoid presuming guilt, there is obviously an internal debate going on. While hoping for State Department understanding and co-operation, there is nonetheless a realization that "the evidence now brought before us . . . *is in part a different na-ture.*"[54] *(Emphasis mine.)* Heeney tells Wrong on 14 October, "There are in the Halperin Notebook seven references to Norman. Some of them described him as 'Herb Norman' and one bracketed him with a certain Sliget Tsuru *[sic]* who appears to have been a Japanese Communist. The FBI have also mentioned an attempt by Norman to get possession of books and literature of a Communist nature left by Tsuru on his return to Japan in 1942. There is also evidence that Norman has associated with various Communists on what appears to be more than a basis of casual friendship."

Of course it was impossible for responsible External members to ignore the accumulated FBI and RCMP (and, indirectly, the G-2) evidence; yet, again, External officers tried hard to avoid presumption of wrongdoing. Heeney writes, "At the moment, we are assuming nothing, except that it is proper to withdraw him from his responsible and confidential work pending a further examination of the situation."[55] In fact, responsible External officers feared less a finding of Norman's guilt than they did Washington's inclination to advertise presumed guilt. On 17 October, for example, Wrong contacted the American Deputy Under-Secretary, Freeman Matthews, and concluded from their conversation that "he will be able to talk privately to Hoover" about External's desire for "avoidance of publicity."[56]

Lester Pearson went a step further. In a phone conversation with Norman Robertson, Pearson asked that the RCMP report *not* be transmitted to Washington until he had had a chance to see the file (Pearson was still in New York). Pearson soon learned, however, that the RCMP had already sent the report, dated 17 October. In retrospect, Pearson's request was wise. It was the 17 October RCMP report that followed Norman to his grave, the report that was filled with errors and unsubstantiated allegations, the one that the RCMP itself later disavowed, but the one that the FBI secretly gave to SISS and that served as the basis for the Senate's public allegations against Norman in August 1951. It was, so far as the FBI and

SISS were concerned, received truth, a decalogue of misdeeds, suspicious associations, and treasonous ideas.

What this RCMP report and every other later, amended report did was to define Herbert largely in terms of his associations, in terms of whom he knew rather than in terms of what he had actually said and done. Remarkably, *nothing* in any American, or External, or RCMP document dealing with his loyalty was concerned with what he actually reported as a diplomat, even with how he *might* have influenced Canadian and/or western foreign policy for better or worse; nor was there any evidence of how he acted as a presumed Soviet agent. More tragic still, who Herbert actually was—his behavior, his personality, his writings—both official and unofficial—or his thoughts, his beliefs, his being, had no relevence in the investigations carried out. Herbert Norman as a person had been lost in the maelstrom of accusations. For many influential people, after October 1950, *he* ceases to exist except in terms of the *other*, of the suspect. He becomes a "case," a political abstraction, a non-being. He is no longer a diplomat, a scholar, or a scholar-diplomat; he is no longer an official representative of Canada with a *verifiable* record of service, a written legacy of official reporting that can be sifted for evidence of misrepresentation, of misdeeds, of disloyalty. In fact, what he did in the performance of duties assigned by his government becomes irrelevant. He is overtaken instead by external forces—the FBI, G-2, the RCMP, External, SISS, and other acronyms denoting impersonal powers—that seek to legitimize their own function of crying wolf by finding wolves. Herbert understood this and fatalistically despaired of the reality six and one-half years later. Friends and supporters likewise despaired but acknowledged their helplessness to rectify the dehumanization of Herbert Norman. Glazebrook summarized External's thinking on the eve of Herbert's recall from Japan: "We are hopeful with our knowledge of Norman's character and intellectual interests that the various connections which he had with communists or near communists can be explained to our satisfaction. We are, however, far from hopeful that we can persuade the Americans, particularly Hoover, to reach a similar conclusion."[57]

Herbert Norman's destiny was consigned to the hands of Washington's most famous anti-communists. The hell that awaited this victim of political persecution lay open, just barely in the future, and nothing could close it. The 17 October RCMP report was in Hoover's hands, its secrets and lies about to be shared with Senate witch-hunters. Herbert Norman was doomed.

CHAPTER 7

"A MAN WHO MIGHT HAVE EXISTED"

"Norman seemed to us as safe as a house: the last man they'd suspect."
Charles Woodsworth, *Ottawa Citizen,* 14/8/51

en months passed from the time of Herbert Norman's recall from Japan until allegations of being a communist were made public. During that time he had been, in effect, "arrested," "tried," and "exonerated" by his department, declared innocent of any wrongdoing and, in External's own form of restitution, restored to duty and promoted to Head of the American and Far Eastern Desk in Parliament Hill's East Block. His loyalty properly acknowledged and his status confirmed, the personal agony that Herbert had been forced to endure was seemingly at an end.

But of course, as we know, the nightmare had only just begun. As foreseen months before by George Glazebrook, there was little hope that Canada could "persuade the Americans, particularly [J. Edgar] Hoover" that Norman's "various connections which he has had with communists or near Communists" could be explained to their satisfaction.[1] As predicted, Canadian exoneration had little currency among the American intelligence people, and absolutely no deterrent value for publicity-minded Senators who had invested their political careers in the public process of "naming names." In August 1951, "Herbert Norman" was a name waiting to be named.

Once he was "named" for public consumption, Canadian

authorities proved, regretfully, to be two-faced. Publicly they protested Norman's innocence and denounced the American anti-communist pillorying of one of their own, but privately they lent sufficient credence to American accusations as to begin anew their investigation of the man. Quiet scholar-diplomat that he was, anxious to avoid publicity, Herbert refrained from denouncing Canadian government hypocrisy: he continued to desire to be a public servant. But privately he lamented the never-ending assault on his character and the blows to his emotional stability. "Innocence is not enough," he later confided to a friend, adding, "You can't wash off the poison of a smear."[2]

He now understood the sorrowful observation of his friend Owen Lattimore who was being attacked publicly in early 1950 and who recorded his "kangaroo" trial in his July 1950 book, *Ordeal By Slander:* "The charges against me built up a circumstantial picture of *a man who might have existed.* I was not that man, but those were the charges I had to refute. If I was not careful, I might fall into a trap. People might think I was trying to defend myself against *real charges.*" [3] (Emphasis mine.)

Like the proverbial "wife-beating" charge, the accused had to consciously moderate his reply, lest he seem too defensive and therefore guilty. And in Herbert's case, to extend the analogy, it was vital that he not *appear* to feel guilty for long ago having abused—verbally, psychologically, wishfully—his "wife," though in his mind all the while conceding that perhaps he *could* have behaved differently and "better" to-ward her, if only history could be rewritten. "Circumstantial pictures" of the sort mentioned by Lattimore, after all, are never totally misdrawn—a certain reality is accurately por-trayed—but they can be entirely misunderstood if the view-er's vision is obstructed by a preconceived notion of what the picture *should* look like. More concretely, involvement in communist movements in the 1930's could appear in the 1950's as "wrong," particularly if the accuser had no sense of history, context, or appreciation for the exegencies of circumstance.

Norman's accusers in the autumn of 1950, in the autumn of his short life, bore the man no malice, just suspicion. Theirs was an evil thoroughly banal, obliged as they were to follow impartial procedures for investigating suspicious characters that unfailingly and implicitly, by their very nature, maligned the "subject's" character. It could not be helped: duty is duty, and perhaps more consciously followed when, as in this case, the American patron arrogantly suggests that its Canadian client has not fully met his obligations to be dutifully suspicious.

So, Lester Pearson's last-minute request to withhold the RCMP security report of 17 October from the FBI until he had the chance to review its findings arrived in Ottawa too late to be honored. And so it begins: Americans less trusting and more fearful of communist evil begin a process that stage after stage denied basic civilized protections to the presumed communist suspect. In walks the missionary's son, frightened and fearful of secular authority.

The basis of the joint RCMP-External interrogation of Norman after his return from Japan was the 17 October RCMP report that had been sent on to the FBI. Probably no other report about him, whether Canadian or American, proved as influential and ruinous as this one; its contents haunted him for the remainder of his life. Although its most damaging elements were largely discredited by the RCMP's subsequent 1 December report, which was shared with the FBI and eventually accepted by some American intelligence people, Senate witch-hunters continued to rely on the 17 October report as if it were the final word on the matter. In short, the Senate kept alive a damaging and partly erroneous report that the official representatives of the Canadian government not only disavowed and overturned, but also requested be disregarded by the Americans.

The report is five pages in length and consists of eight separate segments; it is signed by R. A. S. MacNeil, Inspector, "for Officer in Charge of Special Branch" and is classified "Top Secret."[4] Segment 1 is three lines in length, totally censored. Segment 2 is a straightforward biographical sketch of Norman. Segment 3 is a full citation of General Thorpe's letter of fulsome praise of Norman's sterling character and accomplishments in the early period of the Occupation, quoted in part in Chapter 4. Segment 4 treats the Senate inquiry of March 1950, in which Norman's name was mentioned in Senator Hickenlooper's questioning of Thorpe (again, discussed in the preceding chapter).

Segment 5 is divided into three subsections and, so far as the Americans were concerned, introduces the most damaging evidence because it connects Norman with suspected "Soviet agent[s]." Section "a" refers to a person, whose name is excised, who "is believed to hold high office as a secret member of the LPP" (Labour Progressive Party) and is "a suspected Soviet Agent." Reference is made to the person's "desk pad" which was seized in May 1948 and which contained two entries, one to "Herb Norman" and another to "Herby Norman," both accompanied by telephone numbers. Secret Senate documents, filed away deep in Senate Internal Security Subcommittee files, tell of Frank Park's "desk pad" seized in May 1948 and showing Herbert's name and telephone number.[5] Significance of the evidence aside, it is clear that the FBI passed on the "Top Secret" report to Senate McCarthyites, *in violation of* Canadian requests for confidentiality.

Section "b" of Segment 5 discusses an RCMP "secret agent" report of February 1940 which "reported that one, Professor Herbert Norman, who at that time was attending Harvard University and was connected with McMaster University in Hamilton, was a member of the Communist Party of Canada." The secret agent further reported that Norman wished to return to Canada in order to teach at University of Toronto or Queen's University. Yet it is also noted that "some enquiries" made then showed that "there was no record of any Herbert Norman having been a member of the faculty of McMaster University, nor were any former members of the staff at McMaster known to be at Harvard at that time." Additionally, "no positive identification" of Herbert with the subject of the agent's report could be made.

Part "c" relates the details of a presumed link between

Herbert Norman and the "Norman" mentioned by Soviet defector Gouzenko. "Gouzenko, in his testimony before the Royal Commission, stated that in 1944 Moscow asked Colonel Zabotin [Red Army Intelligence (GRU) officer in Ottawa] if he knew a person by the name of Norman. Zabotin replied that he did not." Reference is then made to two other Canadians, whose names are blackened out in the RCMP report. Of one of them, Pavlov, NKVD (KGB) agent working under cover as an Embassy official, is reported to have told a Lieutenant Colonel Motinov, "He is ours, don't touch him." Given the number of letter spaces excised, four, it is virtually certain that one of the men was Hazen Sise or Frank Park, a deduction strengthened by collateral evidence that will be discussed later; the identity of the other man is given in a Senate document, quoted just below. Regardless, this section of the report concludes, "There is no connection between xxxx and Norman other than the assumption on the part of Zabotin. It will be noted that Moscow did not confirm this assumption. It would appear that Norman is the surname of a person in whom the Russian Intelligence Service had an interest. It is, however, impossible to make a definite identification."

Connecting Norman with Soviet agents, even if tenuously and without factual support and conceding that the connection was highly questionable, nonetheless did terrible damage to his reputation in the eyes of the Senate McCarthyites once they got hold of this material. In the Senate file on him—again, which I examined in uncensored form—there are two references to this alleged connection. One is an undated memorandum that begins, "This is purported to be an excerpt from page 23 of the report of the Canadian Royal Commission on Soviet espionage (from the testimony given by Gouzenko)" and ends with, "The above given quotation from the report of the Royal commission should be checked for accuracy." The quotation appears to be a biased and distorted fascimile of the material quoted in the RCMP report. The quotation reads: "When Moscow asked of Zarubin if he knew a certain Norman, he answered that he did not. Then Motinov and Zarubin thought they had identified him. They asked Pavlov about the man they had in mind and Pavlov said, 'Don't touch Norman. We work with him.' Zarubin then telegraphed the capital that that 'Norman about whom you asked is N. Freed and the neighbors [code name for NKVD, the Soviet secret spy organization] are busy with him.' The capital did not answer."[6]

It seems obvious that the faulty memory of the author of this Senate report confuses the name Zabotin with Zarubin. The N. "Freed" identified, according to an FBI document, is "Norman" Freed, which helps to explain another sentence in the RCMP report: "It seems unlikely that they would offer a Christian name [Norman, as in Norman Freed] of a person previously unknown to them for checking." To wit, the RCMP was leaving open the possibility that the "Norman" being referred to was not Freed but Herbert. And in the most damning of sentences attributed to the Russians, "He is ours, don't touch him," the Senate report changes the statement into, "Don't touch Norman. We work with him."[7] By concluding its "quotation" of the Royal Commission report by using only the initial *N* before Freed's surname, a fatal conclusion identifying Herbert with the "Norman" that Zarubin/Zabotin mentions, is left unfixed. But however one chooses to interpret the Senate's transmogrification of the RCMP or Royal Commission reports, the result is nonetheless one of confusion and uncertainty regarding Herbert Norman. The very fact that this document found its way into the Senate files, and remained there in uncorrected form twenty-five years after Herbert's death, further suggests that the Senate had made up its mind about him. And it also shows the FBI to have been lying when it issued, two weeks after Herbert's death, a disclaimer: "The FBI has not made available to the Senate Internal Security Subcommittee any reports or files or information pertaining to the late Dr. Egerton Herbert Norman." This lie came from the master dissembler himself, J. Edgar Hoover.[8]

Segment 6 of the October RCMP report concerns "an investigation [that] has been carried out in Toronto, Hamilton and Ottawa" regarding the accuracy of the addresses and phone numbers for Norman appearing in the Halperin notebook. Results of the investigation show: 1) that Halperin misspelled "Friel" Street where Herbert lived between 1943 and 1946; 2) that a second address refers to the headquarters of the Women's International League for Peace and Freedom, based at Charles Street in Toronto between 1940 and 1949; 3) that one of the telephone numbers listed against Norman's name was that of the Far Eastern Division of External; 4) that another address is of Herbert's father-in-law, Harry Clark, of Hamilton, who is identified as "devoted to attending football and hockey games and other sporting events"; and 5) that a partially excised passage dealt with C. P. H. Holmes, identified only as having been born in Japan in 1910 and having served as "one of the witnesses" at Herbert's and Irene's marriage in August 1935. A full two thirds of the remainder of this page is censored, but since the full report was passed on to SISS by way of the FBI, its content is known. The SISS document uses *exactly* the same wording in introducing Holmes's name before identifying him further as "a communist and active in the Communist underground in Ottawa."[9] Here the remainder of Segment 6 of the RCMP report is censored; but the SISS report was not.

The SISS report identifies, in about the same amount of space censored in the RCMP document, other people with whom Norman had some "suspicious" connection. The SISS report notes that Herbert "was associating in 1940 with Donald H. McCrimmon and Hilka Hormavirta, known communists." Hilka Hormavirta was Irene Norman's chiropractor, and Donald and Mrs. McCrimmon were casual social acquaintances in Ottawa's wartime social circles.[10] Additionally noted was Norman's connection with "Frances [Frank] W. Park, a Toronto lawyer and suspected Soviet agent who is believed to hold a high office as a secret member of the Labour Progressive Party of Canada and who was the National Director of the National Council for Canadian-Soviet Friendship at a time when Communist control of that organization was public."

Frank Park is further identified by Harry Ferns in his book *Reading from Left to Right*.[11] Ferns states that in the autumn of 1944 when Park worked for the Canadian Information Service he was quite openly a communist. Ferns also tells how Park had "dug around" the Gouzenko evidence and had discovered that the Russian defector had named Ferns in connection with spy-scientist Alan Nunn May, but hastens to add that Gouzenko had misidentified Ferns not only as a friend of Nunn May but also as a person connected with a "research laboratory in Montreal." Neither allegation was true. In any event, as should be self-evident, avowed communists like Park, who resigned from government service to promote friendship with Canada's wartime allies, the Soviets, were unlikely recruits for Soviet espionage, not to mention the more relevant fact that the extent of his only *known* connection with Herbert was a telephone number on a desk pad.

Segments 7 and 8 of the October RCMP report simply offer assessments of Norman's character— ". . . [he] has always been of the scholarly type . . .; enjoys an international reputation as a leading scholar in Japanese history"—and notes that he has been recalled from Japan immediately.

Despite an understandable disgust over Hoover's lie about not passing information on to SISS, we can be grateful now, though only for the sake of the historical record, that the RCMP report made its way into SISS hands. We can be less grateful for the fact that the 1 December RCMP report that discredited the October report never found its way into SISS files, or at least into extant files. We can be even less grateful that the file was passed on in the first place, that Lester Pearson's belated attempt to prevent the transmission failed, and that the RCMP apparently gave the FBI unrestricted access to its files on Herbert, as a 24 November 1953 "Top Secret" memo from Arnold Smith to Pearson reveals: "Glen Bethel [Hoover's Ottawa agent] had full access to all the transcripts, etc. without any limitation."[12] The transmission belt of suspicion worked with deadly efficiency, producing an outcome as uncertain evidentially as the unhealthy suspicion that energized it. And so Norman, lover of human freedom, was pulled into the suspicion-ridden circle of interrogators whose task it was to ascertain his loyalty.

Irene Norman recalls that "the 1950 interrogation never ended. Herbert got no support from Pearson; Hume Wrong was his biggest supporter. It was as bad as the March-April 1957 period."[13] Herbert entered into a Raskolnikovian world of "crime and punishment," never knowing when he would be called in to answer charges, the content of which he could only suspect but never know for certain. The questioning began a few days after his return on 21 October; officially it ended six weeks later, but it never ended in his apprehensions, ones which were painfully validated by a second round of questioning that began in January 1952.

Unlike the 1952 questioning, there is no transcript of the October-November 1950 interrogation, very likely indicating that a stenographer was not present, an assumption apparently confirmed in a memorandum by George Glazebrook that details the findings of the first day of questioning, 24 October, conducted by himself and Norman Robertson. Other than this one report, all the others are detailed summaries of findings which are in turn summarized in the 1 December 1950 report to the FBI exonerating Norman of any wrongdoing.

Glazebrook's report on day one of questioning makes clear that the hub of the enquiry revolved around the Fuchs-Halperin connection. Klaus Fuchs's name, as did Herbert Norman's, appeared among the dozens upon dozens of names found in Halperin's notebook. Glazebrook records, "Norman admitted knowing Halperin since his college days at Toronto where they lived in nearby rooms. His most recent contacts with Halperin, he said, were after he returned from internment in Tokyo [1942], and before going back to Tokyo in 1946." Norman said that he saw Halperin "some six or seven times" and that "his own association was that of a former college friend, and the wives had common domestic interests." Glazebrook asked the obvious: ". . . why, when the inquiry by the Royal Commission on Espionage was instituted, and Halperin's name was known to be involved, he had not let the Department know of his acquaintance with Halperin?" The answer: "Norman replied that he had worried about this point a great deal, and had come to the conclusion, on the assumption that the Department would know, from the evidence, of his association with Halperin, that he should not himself raise the question." Both Robertson and Glazebrook then pointed out that had he "done so at that time, his position would be easier to explain now." Herbert could only "agree that he had made a mistake, but added that since his conscience had been clear, he had not felt then that to mention the matter would be the wise course." The Ontario syndrome at work—a neurotic concern for appearances? The privacy-minded, shy scholar, hoping against hope that the connection might escape official scrutiny? Or did he have something to hide?

For the records, reports Glazebrook, Norman "stated categorically that he was not guilty of passing information of any kind," that his conduct while with the department "had been meticulously careful," and that "his own conscience was quite clear." When asked if he had ever been a member of the Communist Party, "he categorically replied that he had not." He confessed only to having "had associated with radical undergraduate groups" while at Toronto, to having "been a member of the League for Social Reconstruction in Toronto, and of a social group at Cambridge, and he mentioned individual communists in Cambridge he had known." Norman falsely claimed to have ended all radical political activity and associations once he got to Harvard but truthfully asserted that after he entered government service he had been "careful not to indicate the particular work in which he was engaged."[14] With a full decade of External service behind him, and communism now an abstract and academic concern equally far removed in time, he spoke according to what was relevant to him there and then. He would not tell his questioners about his private letters to Howard, announcing membership in the Party, offering an apologia for Stalin's repression, and lamenting the deaths of communist friends; these were *his* experiences, important in his past but irrelevant now, and therefore they were not to be shared with External or anyone else.

What he thought more relevant was how he had distanced himself from outspoken former comrades whose association he no longer valued nor any longer needed. Herbert had his own proof, though he did not offer it then, knowing enough to conclude that in the saying of it he would open a new can of worms. But he must have recalled how three years earlier, when in England, he had snubbed Cambridge Party member Victor Kiernan, who mournfully recalls the incident today.[15] Or how he brushed off Phillip Jaffe, the *Amerasia* editor who was indicted for treason in 1945, when Jaffe had called on him in Ottawa late in 1943.[16] Too, he might have defended himself by telling how he had been courting and supporting Douglas MacArthur just months before. But Norman could not be self-serving in such a situation; to do so would seem defensive or irrelevant at best, and suspicious at worst to his questioners, so he instead told Glazebrook that "he would be willing to resign if that was thought to be the right course." ". . . he fully recognized the embarrassing position in which developments placed the Department, and was most anxious not to harm the Department."[17] A company man, whose Japanese sense of honor, or Ontario syndrome's concern for appearances, was sensitized to shame—*he felt no guilt*—Herbert was ready to sever himself from his company for the sake of the company; it was the honorable thing to do.

Honor of this sort would likely have been perceived by his questioners as egoistic self-indulgence or as political escape in the context: national security was at stake, not to mention the credibility of Canada's intelligence apparatus in the eyes of its American patron. So the questioning continued, and Norman persevered.

As mentioned above, no reports about each day's interrogation exist, apart from the first day's questioning. But a report entitled, "Studies in Communism, Re: Egerton Herbert Norman," and dated 27 November 1950, provides a clear indication of the content of the six-week-long interrogation sessions.[18] The report suggests that the questioning was broad

and wide-ranging, covering every phase of his life. His readings of Marx, Lenin and Trotsky at the University of Toronto,
his ties with the Cambridge University Socialist society and
with John Cornford, his association with Tsuru at Harvard
and with the "study cell" there. The conclusion: ". . . by
this time [1939] Norman had been studying communism for
approximately five years and irrespective of the extent, he
must have been partially conscious of the object of the [Har-
vard] study group. To accept less would place him in the
category of being politically naive, or worse, a fool. He is
said to be neither."

Norman is quoted as stating that the "Russian practice of
socialism . . . was not to his liking and the purges was one
of the several deciding factors [in his break from commu-
nism]. In his opinion . . . the British approach to democracy
is superior to all other forms." This, he claimed, was the
conclusion he had reached while at Harvard, adding that
"Not only had he *not* accepted their [communist] theories,
but the history of the Far East demanded practically all his
time." In New York, while with the IPR, Herbert said, he
associated with *all* sorts of Far Eastern experts, "both those
of the left and the right," including several "communists."
By the time he joined External, "his academic interest in
communism had apparently waned," limited to "association
with some of that ideology."

His association with Halperin, which he asserted to be
entirely apolitical, is not disbelieved—"there is the possibility
it is correct"—in view of the findings of how the principals
in the so-called spy ring operated according to the Royal
Commission report. A connection is noted between Halperin
and Tsuru, and the FBI report about how Norman attempted
to gain possession of Tsuru's books is mentioned, though
finally his version of the story is also accepted, attributing
the FBI version to a "misunderstanding." Why this finding
is important, given the centrality of the episode (as discussed
in the Introduction to this book), requires elaboration.

Norman's version of the Tsuru apartment episode is not
detailed in the November 1950 report, but it is discussed at

length in a 13 May 1957, "Top Secret" report, written by "J. L." (Jules Léger?) and entitled "Memorandum for the Minister." On page one, all but the first line is excised, probably because it was a verbatim quote of an FBI report; but the opening line reads: "You asked for a note on the circumstances surrounding Herbert Norman's attempt to acquire the library of Tsuru." Page two opens with:

"After interviewing Norman [1952?] and further enquiries, it was determined that Norman, when he was being repatriated in 1942 from Japan, an exchange of internees took place in Portuguese East Africa. When he disembarked there he was met by Tsuru. During a brief conversation Tsuru offered Norman his library at Harvard and suggested contacting xxxxxxx, a former economist at Tufts attached to the Wartime Production Board in Washington. [The description fits Lorie Tarshis perfectly.] (xxxxxxx was at one time and may still be a communist.) [*This* description does *not* fit Tarshis.] This Norman did. Subsequently he proceeded to Harvard and began searching for the library, a portion of which he found in various parts of the University. Norman claimed he knew nothing of the contents of Tsuru's apartment and had merely gone to that address, as well as the others, in an attempt to gather together the promised library. He generally confirmed the discussion with the FBI agents but with slight variation. These variations were regarded as insignificant and required no elaboration. Norman told us that his interest in the library was twofold: he desired it for both his work and his further study of Japanese history. Norman retained his interest in the library right up to 1950 and remarked that what the FBI had possession of was something entirely separate."[19]

What this latter sentence no doubt refers to is the English and foreign-language materials included in Tsuru's library. In a Boston-originated FBI report, dated 16 October 1946, the contents of the library are identified as "a nearly full series of Senate reports on the United States munitions hearings, reports on neutrality matters, reports on labor investigations, and extensive literature in five languages, Japanese, Russian, German, French and English; quantities of Communist propaganda, correspondence regarding the Young Communist League, the League Against War and Fascism, the Harvard Teachers Union, and the Communist Party Workers School." The list goes on to include several "Marxian publications" and reference to Tsuru's private correspondence, including a letter mentioning the "Marxist study group" at Harvard and a particular paper on "American Imperialism" written by Herbert Norman; despite months of effort to locate this paper, according to FBI records, it was never found.

An internal FBI memorandum from D. M. Ladd to L. L. Laughlin, dated 23 August 1951, clarifies a number of previously unanswered questions regarding the episode. The report notes that "the material left by Tsuru . . . was examined by Bureau agents on November 8, 1942. The day following the examination, Egerton Herbert Norman contacted the Bureau Agents and attempted to secure from them the property of Tsuru." The report repeats the allegations of earlier ones, namely, that Norman lied initially in claiming to be on an official government mission before amending his story with the truth, that his interest in the books was personal. But no less important, here it is revealed that Norman had initiated contact with the FBI, which suggests that there was nothing surreptitious, let alone conspiratorial, in his attempt to get Tsuru's books. This fact is *not* reported in RCMP documents dealing with the episode, which means that the FBI probably did not share this valuable piece of evidence with its Canadian counterparts. Neither, apparently, did the FBI share another extremely important conclusion it reached about the content of Tsuru's books and articles, namely, "it was determined that they [the documents found in Tsuru's apartment] were of no particular value from a security viewpoint."[20] In short, the FBI purposely mislead the RCMP by making it appear, first, that Herbert had been "caught in the act" of trying to sneak out Tsuru's documents, and second, that the documents had some sort of security value.

Probably because the FBI was not forthcoming about the episode with the RCMP, in the 13 May 1957 Canadian "Memo-

randum" about the episode, there appears a handwritten notation in the margin that asks, "does he not deny
misrepresentation?" If this notation fairly reflects the lingering doubt that Norman's superiors had about the episode,
the FBI's "disinformation" had to have contributed to the
problem—though it would appear that perhaps Herbert's
statements to his government might also have contributed.
The "Memorandum" continues, "The library he referred to
was entirely in the Japanese language and while it probably
contained a few Japanese Marxist books they certainly did
not reflect the character of the library. He [Norman] could
not reconcile the statement of the FBI that the library was
mainly communist. The collection in which he was interested
was principally concerned with Japanese history."[21]

If we allow Herbert the benefit of the doubt, then he sought
to retrieve only that portion of the library which was written
in Japanese and was concerned with Japanese history, perhaps
that included the very books that he used in writing his dissertation since we know Tsuru lent significant assistance to
Herbert's thesis work. Further, since we know that some
portion of the library consisted of Senate and U.S. government reports—hardly communist material—and that all the
material had no "security value," then the episode seems
anything but suspicious. From the FBI's point of view, however, the fact that one of its agents claimed that Herbert
misrepresented himself initially, and that the library, quite
apart from its content, belonged to an assumed communist,
thereby automatically giving it "security value," makes it
appear that Herbert was up to no good.

So which was it? There is no convincing argument in Norman's favor that will satisfy "conspiracy theorists." The inclination is to believe government officials, the FBI in this
case, rather than the individual being accused. Yet there *is*
collateral evidence that favors Norman. According to Harry
Ferns, Norman related the details of the episode to him in
the autumn of 1943, about one year after the event and, in
Ferns's words, "long before the U.S. Senate or anyone else
thought fit to consider it." Ferns relates a story very similar

to the one that the Canadian "Memorandum" quoted above recounts, but with two important differences. First, Norman's initial contact with anyone in trying to acquire Tsuru's library was with the janitor of Tsuru's apartment building. The janitor would not let him into the apartment, so Herbert encouraged him to "consult the Cambridge police and the authorities of Harvard University . . ." and said he would return the following day. When he did, Herbert found two FBI agents waiting, one of whom was "hostile and aggressive": "Who the hell are you and what the hell do you want?" Norman answered with a lengthy self-introduction, saying he was an employee of the Canadian government, a friend of Tsuru and so on, but when the hostile agent attacked Herbert for being "an alien," he answered by explaining, in Fern's words, "Canada was at war with Japan in the same way as the United States was, and that he had no intention of harming the United States." Ferns adds, "The other FBI agent had to explain to his colleague that Canada was indeed at war with Japan."[22]

If the episode went as Ferns remembers it, then the alleged "misrepresentation" by Norman at the outset, i.e., that he was a Canadian official on secret government business, is explained in his favor: the hostile and ill-informed FBI agent, who had already examined the "communist" literature, inferred from Norman's explanation the lie that he expected. First, here was a foreigner trying to secure the red-tainted possessions of another foreigner, and an enemy at that. The agent did not know Canada was an ally, and thus assumed the worst of Herbert at the outset, construing his introduction of himself as a devious misrepresentation, assuming that anyone who wanted to gain possession of "communist" literature would perforce do so secretly. As Norman eventually got the chance to explain why he wanted Tsuru's books, the suspicious FBI agent interpreted this as a guilty admission of someone "caught in the act." Likely, it was the hostile and aggressive agent who wrote up the report that became the basis of the Canadian's FBI file. (What is not resolved by the Ferns story is the FBI report that says Norman contacted the Agency originally, rather than the janitor; this may be a result of faulty FBI records, or confusion regarding Herbert's suggestion to the janitor that he contact the authorities for authorisation to take possession of Tsuru's books.)[23]

Skeptics might question whether Ferns's account is to be believed; they might assert that Norman was simply covering himself in the fall of 1943 in anticipation that this episode might later return to harass him. If so, it should be remembered that at this time, in Ferns's words, "he was just as much as a Marxist as I was," meaning that, assuming Ferns's reading of Herbert's ideological stripe as of 1943 was correct, Norman had no reason to dissemble about the episode.[24]

But even if this does not suffice to convince the skeptics, the "J. L." memorandum ends in such a way as to suggest that Herbert's superiors had decided that his version of the story was credible enough to warrant protection from the press: "As you know the line we have taken with the press is that Norman did not misrepresent himself to the Bureau but merely said that he was employed by the Department which would be a natural thing to say. We have also told Blair Fraser [a newspaper journalist] and others that his interest was in the library as such and not in Mr. Tsuru's personal belongings and that this was because of Norman's interest in Japanese history."[25]

In light of the "1950" reference date in this memorandum, it seems fair to conclude that "J. L.'s" findings on the Tsuru episode were based on the October 1950 questioning. To return, now, to its principal findings as they were discussed in the 27 November 1950 "Studies in Communism" report.

The report also records Norman's admission of meeting Park "on three or four occasions" and does not dispute his contention that the two men were merely social acquaintances. Similarly, Herbert admits of knowing Zabotin, having met him once at a diplomatic get-together, but adds that he reported the meeting with the Russian in an "official memorandum of the conversation." He says much the same about his connection with Pavlov, Second Secretary of the Soviet Embassy in Ottawa. (Howard Norman remembers inviting

Pavlov, Herbert, Halperin and others to a dinner party at his Ottawa apartment in late 1943; Howard organized the party "in the spirit of Canadian-Soviet [wartime] co-operation."[26] And in this regard, Herbert "can offer no explanation for this piece of information [regarding the "Norman" mentioned in the Royal Commission report] given by Gouzenko." His interrogators concluded that "there seems to be no answer to the evidence given by Gouzenko" about the "Norman" in question.

All this relates directly to Herbert's own testimony. No less important is the concluding section of the document entitled "Comments." This section dwells on whether Norman was as "politically naïve" as he seems to have been. "Many of his explanations could be accepted as logical and reasonable providing he is politically naïve." In fact, the judgment that he was "naïve" *is* ultimately made, and passed on to the FBI, yet this "Secret" RCMP report leaves alive the possibility that the truth might be otherwise: "Should such [Norman's naïveté] not be the case, it could be assumed he was quite conscious of the dubious political aspirations of their [communist groups] associates." But it further notes that "there is no evidence . . . to suggest disloyalty." It dismisses the alleged Soviet connections by asserting that "by virtue of his position, [he] was one who had access to information of interest to the government of the U.S.S.R." The bottom line, and that which was reported to the Americans: "The worst possible conclusion we can arrive at is the very apparent naïveté in his relationship with his fellow men."[27] Washington ignored this conclusion.

What Washington got in the 1 December report from T. M. Guernsey, Special Inspector for the RCMP, was a detailed accounting, five single-spaced typewritten pages, of all the evidence and findings of the 27 November report just quoted. This "Top Secret" document is identified as "further to our memorandum of October 17, 1950," and emphasizes at the outset that "a most intensive investigation has been carried out with the kind assistance of xxxxxxxxxxxx." "Special investigative methods" were used, perhaps alluding to the assertion that "unconsciously, he has been subjected to other methods," and the document finally asserts that an in-depth "assessment of Norman's personality" has allowed them to arrive at "an impartial assessment."

Emphasis is placed on Norman as "a scholar of high standing," and on his rating by External as "one of its ablest officers." Yet the "undeveloped faculty" that has got him into trouble is "he clearly lacks any shrewdness in judging individuals." He is portrayed as the classic egghead: "astute in the subjects in which he is versed, . . . naïve in his relationships with man." Herbert was too trusting: "He has frequently failed to properly assess his social acquaintances but rather accepted at their face value all those who interested him without being conscious of their ideology." Norman, in short, liked people for what they *were,* not necessarily for what they believed: "It is apparent that he either cared for a person or not according to the personality reflected by the individual." But in Washington's eyes, at best this RCMP assessment makes him a "dupe." The *coup de grâce*: "It is apparent this *undeveloped* part of Norman's personality *partially* explains his associations with those of the left." (Emphasis mine.)

The personal associations most deserving of record to the RCMP's FBI counterparts are "those, many of whom are on the left, with knowledge of the Far East." The familiar litany begins: Tsuru figures prominently; Norman's "failure to assess Tsuru as a Marxist, in our opinion, is one of the many examples of Norman's naïveté, as another scholar [Bryce? Tarshis?] who knew Tsuru at the same time readily identified the latter as a Marxist economist." Of course Norman knew Tsuru to be a Marxist. One has only to recall the letter he wrote to Howard that mentions the "brilliant Japanese Marxist" with whom he had become acquainted. Clearly, Norman misled the RCMP in this regard, as he did as well about his conclusion, in the words of the RCMP report, "that communism was not the answer to world problems by the time he entered Harvard." Revisionist historian that he was, Norman could easily and without guilt employ values that he held in 1950 in order to rewrite or explain the past. Clio's once shapely figure sags with time.

The RCMP also told the FBI that it accepted Norman's account of his attempt to acquire Tsuru's books. "We are completely satisfied that his overtures for the library in no way referred to the communist literature and correspondence found in Tsuru's apartment. We are also satisfied his claim of the library was for the purposes previously mentioned ["for both his work and his further study of Japanese history"]." Yet, Washington remained unsatisfied and, as we shall see in Chapter 10, called on Tsuru to testify against Norman in late March 1957.

About Norman's connection with Halperin, the FBI is told that Herbert was aware during their undergraduate days that Halperin was "a socialist, never a communist and [that] it was with great surprise that he learned of Halperin's involvement in the espionage cases." In the RCMP's judgment, "his statement is confirmed in the document quoted on page 48 of the Report of the Royal Commission in which Lunan reported to Rogov to the effect that Halperin was 'definitely not labelled with any political affiliation'." That Norman's name appeared seven times in Halperin's notebook was reported to have been reasonable in Herbert's view because he would "have no reason to deny giving an address should Halperin request," given the casual nature of the relationship. The RCMP concludes on this score, "We feel satisfied that Norman was quite innocent of Halperin's covert political and espionage activity." (Though exonerated, Halperin was really guilty in the RCMP's view.) Apparently, the FBI accepted this judgment, though its legislative counterpart, SISS, did not, free as it was to interpret secret documents passed into its hands by the FBI in any way it chose.

And for good reason, it would seem, assuming that SISS also got hold of this 1 December report. Seeds of doubt had been planted. In its amended report the RCMP opined that "the 'Norman' referred to [in Gouzenko's testimony] is very probably none other than E. H. Norman." And although it concludes that "we are of the opinion that Norman was never

developed, consciously or unconsciously by the Russians ...
"— they were probably just "talent-spotting"—"the identity
of Norman will never definitely be known..." Not unless,
of course, you are a Senator of SISS and convinced that Gouzenko's ambiguous testimony has greater credibility than an
RCMP judgment.

No such tentative language is offered regarding the "Secret
Agent" report of 1940 that identifies a "Professor Herbert
Norman" as a communist. On this score the RCMP states
emphatically that "the information given is one of either mistaken identity or unfounded rumour by an unidentified sub-
source."

Similarly, several other cases of questionable associations,
names deleted, "have been cleared up to our satisfaction,"
including the one person with a four-letter surname who, as
mentioned earlier, served on the "Wartime Information Board"
and can only be Hazen Sise or Frank Park. Sise was employed
by the National Film Board, Park by the Canadian Information Service. Here the RCMP dutifully reports that Norman
"only met xxxx on several occasions, knew little of him, and
nothing of his political ideology." "We are of the opinion
that Norman is sincere in the explanation of his relationship
with xxxx." Too, the RCMP easily dismisses the relevance of
Herbert's childhood acquaintance with Charles Holmes.

The report concludes: "There has been no evidence uncovered which would indicate disloyalty on the part of Norman. The worst possible conclusion we can arrive at is the
very apparent naïveté in his relationship with his fellow man."
A request, honored in the breach, follows, ". . . the information supplied you concerning the case be restricted for the
information of xxxxx."[28]

References in the report to subcategories such as "5(f)"
would seem to suggest that the "enclosure" noted at the
bottom of the 1 December report can only mean the 27 November "Studies in Communism" report discussed above.
Assuming this is the case, the conclusion about Norman's
naïveté must have been read by the FBI and SISS as a weak
apologia. In the latter report, despite a tentative clearance,

he is described as neither "politically naïve" nor as a "fool," on the assumption that his eyes must have been open to the sort of people he associated with. Contradictorily, he is pictured as a man who judged people according to appearances rather than ideological substance. But if you are a true believer in the McCarthy crusade to root out "communists," at home and abroad, then you assume that a friendly government has behaved in all too friendly a way toward a smart Harvard Ph.D. who has since his youth known the "wrong" people and has had access to the "right" secret intelligence information. In short, you assume the worst, you assume guilt rather than innocence, especially if you see imbedded in an RCMP intelligence report unresolvable contradictions. "National security" is too precarious to permit trust to be invested in a report that forgives because of some misguided humanistic attempt to understand the suspect in terms of his "personality."

And on top of unsatisfied suspicions, there rests the habit of trust invested in America's own infallible security agency and its pope, respectively, the FBI and J. Edgar Hoover. With all of his power, his resources, and his indefatigable energy in keeping America safe from communists, Hoover, not some Scot in the RCMP, is to be trusted. After all, Canada was a second-rate power, a weaker cousin of the U.S., northern and cold, and with no atomic secrets of its own to protect. Nonetheless, the FBI *was* correct in *assuming* that Norman had lied, at least about certain particulars, even though it had *no* concrete evidence to support its assumptions, but it was American arrogance in the end that discounted the findings of an ally and friend.

Regardless, Canadian officials were satisfied with Herbert's trustworthiness and loyalty. Arnold Heeney, Under-Secretary of State for External Affairs, wrote RCMP Commissioner S. T. Wood on 1 December thanking him for the report clearing Herbert and "concur[ring] in your findings which satisfactorily remove any security risk which may have been suggested by certain information . . . ." Heeney also announced to Wood that, effective 4 December, Herbert was being reassigned as head of the American and Far Eastern Division.[29] Even so, External was taking no chances. On 4 December External asked that the RCMP issue a formal security clearance for Norman in his new capacity; it did not come until six weeks later, on 23 January 1951.[30] Though there is nothing in the written record to explain the delay, it seems fair to speculate that the Mounties were willing to forgive the past but reluctant to trust a future which would place Herbert at the center of U.S.-Canadian relations at the time of the Korean War. An entire censored paragraph following reference to the security clearance by the RCMP would seem to lend credibility to this suspicion.

Norman, of course, would have seen the delay in this light, positioned as he was as head of the American and Far Eastern Desk but denied access to intelligence information until late January. This awkward delay could only have enhanced his sense of gloom. As noted earlier, Irene Norman recalls that for the two of them this period "was as bad as the March–April 1957 period."[31] That winter they fought against the gloom that had overtaken their household by attending concerts, by entertaining, and by spending quiet evenings at home reading. "We tried to keep ourselves together," she remembers, which was especially difficult for her because "Herbert was keeping the details [of the interrogation] to himself."[32]

Not entirely. Robert Bryce, then Secretary of the Treasury Board, recalls taking long walks with Norman, during which he would tell about how the RCMP pressured him to reveal the names of left-leaning friends. Bryce remembers that his friend saw his problem as balancing loyalty to his government against loyalty to his friends. Bryce concludes, "Herbert was loyal both to his friends and to his government."[33]

Still, Herbert tended to turn into himself during this and other periods of difficulty, wishing to protect Irene from the tawdry details, just as he had done during the Harvard era of political activism. But the price of internalizing the problems posed by the external world was apparent to his friends. One recalled recently how he witnessed Herbert crying in one of the halls of the East Block following one particular interrogation session.[34] Another remembers Herbert's description of what for him had been "psychological torture": how questions to which he felt he had given full answers would be abruptly reintroduced days later; how certain portions of the case against him were seemingly settled and then raised once again; how the irregular scheduling of sessions threw him off balance; how he never knew exactly when the phone in his apartment would ring and a dark voice would issue a polite command to appear for another round of questioning.[35] Perhaps these are the tactics referred to above in the 1 December RCMP letter to the FBI where it is reported that "unconsciously, he has been subjected to other methods [of interrogation] . . ."

Norman spent his "home leave" being questioned, and his "unspent leave" and "annual leave" (all together, from 23 October to 9 February) recovering from the ordeal. He and Irene stayed then with his sister and brother-in-law, Rev. and Mrs. R.C. Wright. When the ordeal was over, his old friend and protector, Hume Wrong, then Ambassador to Washington, invited Norman down to get him away from Ottawa for a short while in early April. Herbert followed this holiday with a short trip to London in June to begin discussing the Commonwealth position on the Allied peace treaty with Japan. On his return he was quickly scuttled out of Ottawa for a tour of duty in New York as the Acting Permanent Representative at the United Nations, replacing John Holmes, for an "indefinite period."[36] In short, External was giving Herbert assignments that kept him away from his *nominal* position as head of the American and Far Eastern Desk.

The reasons are not hard to imagine. As later revelations make clear, Washington was not happy that Norman had been given a position that gave him access to Washington secrets. Moreover, Washington's displeasure over Herbert's standing became especially acute after the defection of Guy Burgess and Donald Maclean in May of 1951. Thereafter, several U.S. Senators secretly speculated on a possible link between Norman and the two British defectors, as did the RCMP, which investigated the possible link with the assistance of Britain's M.I.5. Too, by this time, SISS had found in Phillip Jaffe a secret informant who was willing to supply additional derogatory information about Herbert, including his suspicion that he was a homosexual.[37] In Canada, on the other hand, the RCMP was dutifully recording secret testimony claiming that Herbert kept a mistress while in Japan. In brief, though he had been officially exonerated of any wrongdoing or disloyalty, unofficially—which is the realm of most McCarthyite machinations—Herbert was still a suspect.

As we will see, these developments unfolded in the year between his exoneration and his removal as head of the American and Far Eastern Desk and his politically safe appointment as head of External's Information Division. Midway in this period, the American suspicions of Norman finally went public, when, in what must have been an engineered, staged, and orchestrated move, SISS produced a witness who was willing to say publicly what the McCarthyites had been uttering privately: that Herbert Norman was a communist.

CHAPTER 8

"COMMUNIST"

Upon the brink of grief's abysmal valley . . .
So dark and deep and nebulous it was
Try as I might to force my sight below
I could not see the shape of anything
. . . .
to think that souls as virtuous as these
were suspended in that limbo, forever!
. . . .
I came into a place where no light is.
Dante, *Divine Comedy: Inferno, Canto IV*

On 7 August 1951, Herr Doctor Karl August Witt-fogel was testifying before the Senate Internal Security Subcommittee (SISS) and was naming the names of fellow Asianists who, unlike himself, had not publicly recanted their false belief in communism. He was speaking specifically about members of a "communist study group" who had met under his intellectual leadership in New York in the summer of 1938. In replying to SISS counsel Robert Morris, who was asking about the identities of the study group's participants, Wittfogel said, "There was a talented and pleasant young man who was studying in the Japanese department at Columbia. His name is Herbert Norman."

Morris: Was he a member of this study group?

Wittfogel: Yes.

Morris: To your knowledge, did he know it was a Communist study group?

Wittfogel: Yes, it was obvious.

[242]

Morris: To you?

Wittfogel: I think it was obvious in general.

Morris: Was it obvious therefore that he was a Communist?

Wittfogel: Yes.[1]

Clearly expecting this answer, Morris immediately began to read into the record material dealing with Herbert's ties with the IPR, the chief concern of SISS in that session.

"Yes." The word had been imminent in the chain of events leading up to Wittfogel's testimony; all that had remained was the public uttering of it, and thus did Norman "come into a place where no light is." The period of emotional darkness that he had painfully endured after his recall had at least been kept secret, out of the public limelight, but now the suspicion, transmogrified into alleged fact, had been made public, forcing those who had quietly exonerated him to loudly protest his innocence before the world, an American-centered world in which allegation alone was frequently sufficient to ruin careers and to destroy lives.

Lester Pearson moved quickly to repair the breach, too quickly for some, and issued on 9 August a strongly worded objection to the "unimpressive and unsubstantiated" charges against Norman. Without offering any but the vaguest indications of temporal reference, saying only that "reports [had] reached the department which reflected on Mr. Norman's loyalty and alleged previous association with the Communist Party," Pearson's defense left the false impression that the "reports" might refer only to the Senate's inquiry of two days earlier. Pearson simply noted that "these reports had been carefully and fully investigated" and "as a result . . . Mr. Norman was given a clean bill of health."[2]

Pearson had not wanted to make public the earlier, secret investigation of Norman, for Norman's sake, and so he left ambiguous the nature and timing of these "earlier reports." But in keeping the reasons for the government's renewed confidence in Norman private, Pearson unwittingly opened the door to public skepticism over the apparent alacrity of the security clearance of Herbert. Harold Greer's column in the *Toronto Star* just one day later makes this clear.[3]

SISS members clearly ignored Pearson's protestations of Norman's innocence. Throughout the next month Norman's name was repeatedly brought up in the IPR hearings, during the questioning of General Willoughby, Owen Lattimore, Eugene Dooman, and John K. Emmerson. Even as late as March 1952, his name was being resurrected in SISS testimony.

Norman, luckily, was in Ottawa at the time of Wittfogel's SISS appearance, although officially he was posted at the United Nations, serving as Acting Permanent Delegate, a position he took up on 26 June and the tenure for which was deemed "indefinite" by External.[4] Shortly after being named and defended, Norman left Ottawa in early September for the San Francisco Peace Treaty as Pearson's chief aide; following the conference he returned on 11 September directly to Ottawa. This was a change in plans ordered by Pearson, who wanted to spare Herbert the discomfort of returning to New York to face a publicity-hungry American press. Norman's personnel record shows that this change in plans forced him to relinquish his New York apartment a month early, but in compensation, and as an official endorsement of confidence in his loyalty, he was reinstated as Head of the American and Far Eastern Desk, much to the chagrin of the Americans. To anticipate somewhat, a short while later Norman was divested of this position due in part to insistence of the Americans, though the divestiture was carried out unceremoniously in a feeble attempt at face-saving by his government.

Norman learned about Wittfogel's testimony, as well as that of Willoughby, from a "confidential" cable from a member of the Canadian delegation to the UN who explains that William Holland of the IPR "telephoned to ask me to pass on to you the following information" regarding the Senate testimony. Herbert reacted by writing up a self-defense in a "Memorandum for Mr. Glazebrook," which he classified as "Secret" and dated 13 August. This memorandum is three pages in length and addresses the five major charges made against him during SISS hearings.[5]

About Wittfogel's claim that he "attended a Communist study group in Cape Cod or New York," Herbert writes, "he is definitely telling a lie." He says that he had known Wittfogel and had "had a few conversations" with him and even "treated him with considerable deference" in light of Wittfogel's academic standing, but recalls that the conversations were of "an academic nature, although contemporary Far Eastern affairs might have come into it." He adds that he did not know "Moses Finkelstein," whom Wittfogel says was a leader of the study group, and further asserts that "it can be categorically denied that I was present at any student group, Communist or otherwise, at Cape Cod in 1938 or 1939 or for that matter at New York."

He then dealt with that part of Wittfogel's testimony into which Robert Morris inserted a memorandum written by Edward Carter, then Secretary-General of IPR, to Owen Lattimore regarding the transmission of secret material from New York to Tokyo by way of Norman at the Canadian Legation; this was in 1940. Herbert writes, "I would like to say that no one in the IPR approached me with such a proposal. I could not therefore have consented to it and I did not transmit any material between the Japanese and New York IPR."

A related allegation, introduced by Morris into the IPR hearings, refers to Carter's suggestion that Herbert write for *Pacific Affairs* while in External's employ and use a *nom de plume,* which SISS regarded as highly suspicious. Norman says that he had been asked "from time to time" by the IPR to write different articles "of an historical nature" and that he did so after returning from Japan in 1942, but that "in each case they were cleared by the Department." He then refers any doubters to his "immediate chief" at that time, a Mr. Stone, who "undertook to have the final draft [of the articles] cleared for me." He similarly reminds his superiors that he only published his book on Ando Shoeki after receiving department approval.

Regarding the fourth Wittfogel accusation, that Herbert had attended the same communist study group with alleged communist Lawrence Rossinger, he openly admits knowing

Rossinger, but says he did not meet him until the 1945 IPR conference held at Virginia Hot Springs, about which the department was fully apprised.

Finally, he deals with the general issue of his relationship to the IPR, which SISS carelessly labeled a "communist front organisation." Herbert says that in his third year as a Rockefeller grantee, "I made use of the IPR facilities for reference work, etc. and the understanding was that they would publish my monograph." This, he says, was his "only direct connection with the IPR," and with its officers, William Holland and Phillip Lilienthal.

Ottawa was apparently satisfied with Norman's answers to the SISS-initiated charges and on the following day, 14 August, sent a "confidential" memorandum to the State Department expressing the Canadian government's "regret and annoyance that their counsel [SISS's Morris] went out of his way to drag Mr. Norman's name into their hearings." Ottawa further asked that any such suspicions in the future be dealt with confidentially through the State Department, not through Congressional committees.[6] Ottawa's request, although reasonable and fair, was naïve in its assumption that the American executive branch might attempt to prevent legislative excesses in this period of Cold War hysteria. Norman's name had been mentioned in SISS hearings too often—thirty-six times according to SISS—for easy assention to Ottawa's request.[7]

Ottawa's protest was not just naïve, it was also hopeless. By August of 1951, in the electrically charged Cold War, when anti-communism had taken on all the features of a secular religion with McCarthyites serving as its profane priests and grand inquisitors, the fundamental constitutional separation between the legislative and executive branches had ceased being honored, save in the breach. Norman's "case" makes this point very clearly. Robert Morris, the person who orchestrated the Wittfogel testimony, could only make his allegations with "moral" certainty because members of the executive branch were channeling information about the Canadian diplomat to him. And, as we have seen, much of this information originated from the good offices of the RCMP.

Chief among the executive branches funneling information to Morris was Army Intelligence and in particular General Willoughby. A Secret Army Intelligence report, dated 1 July 1957, which tried to explain in the aftermath of Norman's death just how Congress got hold of Army information, says, "On 10 May 51, one crate, containing classified documents, presumably two footlockers each bearing a certificate of supoena *[sic]* by the US Senate Judiciary Committee, room 424-C Senate Building, Washington, DC, was transported on the airplane Bataan . . . ." The same report, entitled "Egerton Herbert Norman," also shows that secret testimony from Lieutenant Colonel Roundtree, Willoughby's assistant, confirms that the contents of the footlockers were "data on the Sorge case" and "data . . . pertaining to the Japan Council, Institute of Pacific Relations, *because of the interlocking nature of the two cases.*" (Emphasis mine.)[8] As shown earlier, there was no proven connection between the IPR and the Sorge case, except in Willoughby's demented mind. Morris, in receipt of such fantastic conclusions about Norman, however, had no apparent reason to doubt the conclusions of the Army's number-one intelligence person in the Far East. One has also to wonder whether Morris lent even greater credibility to this Army "intelligence" report in light of the knowledge that copies were also sent to the CIA, the State Department, and the Army in Washington.

Another lengthy Army report that examines how Morris got possession of Army intelligence files concludes that "the derogatory information about SUBJECT [Norman] contained in the FBI memorandum was turned over to the Senate Internal Security Subcommittee by General Willoughby *on a personal basis.*" In other words, no subpoena was involved, Willoughby was simply trying to help Morris and SISS to prosecute/persecute Norman.[9]

This latter quote makes important reference to FBI material that found its way into the Willoughby report and hence into

Morris's questioning of Wittfogel. The "FBI memorandum," which figures so decisively here, is the one dated 1 November 1950, which is itself based *almost entirely* on the faulty 17 October RCMP report. Willoughby used the 1 November FBI report to write his "definitive" 11 April 1951 report on Norman, which is the one he forwarded to Morris. That report, entitled "Summary of Information, Subject: Edgerton [sic] Herbert Norman," had been prepared "by the Far East Command as an inclosure to a Special Report, Subject: Japan Council, Institute of Pacific Relations."[10] Besides reaching Morris's hands, according to a secret 3 June 1957 Army report, Willoughby also sent copies to his friend, Major General Bedell Smith, then head of the CIA. This latter report, and another dated 22 April 1957, make clear that Willoughby's reasons behind the wide dissemination was his fear "that Norman [was] being considered for the position of U.S.-Canadian Intelligence Liaison Officer," which can only mean, given the time reference, his sensitive appointment as head of the American and Far Eastern Desk in External while the Korean War raged on.

To cut through this confusion: Morris's questioning of Wittfogel on 7 August 1951 was based on the 1 November 1950 FBI report, which combined its information about the Tsuru apartment affair with the faulty 17 October RCMP report, all of which found its way into Willoughby's 11 April 1951 report that sought to connect the Japan branch of the IPR and the wartime Sorge spy ring with Norman. Inasmuch as the most important, albeit misshapen, link of this twisted chain is Willoughby, a 30 November 1950 memorandum from Roundtree to Willoughby helps demonstrate the degree of Willoughby's tenacity. The memorandum refers to a recent communiqué from Washington about Norman, the contents of which are deemed "interesting but inconclusive." The focus of the Washington report was the Canadian's connection with Tsuru. Recall, now, that by the time of this memorandum Norman had already been recalled to Ottawa and had not yet been named as head of the American and Far Eastern Desk. But for Willoughby, Norman's removal from action was not enough: the memo says G-2 had "obtained on a practically full-time basis five agents from Tokyo area" to work exclusively on the Norman case. In addition, Roundtree reports of conducting a "thorough search of G-2 files" for derogatory information, as well as conducting "research on the Japan Council of the IPR" in order to establish "Norman's contacts, associates, etc." And finally, mention is made of refocusing "this whole initial report [on] Norman's association with the Japanese Tsuru."[11]

Since there exists no follow-up report on the outcome of all this laborious "intelligence" work, it is probably safe to assume that their labors came to naught. But Willoughby's suspicions could not be quelled. Apparently unable to dig up any additional derogatory information about Herbert, he followed the path of least resistance and fell back on Norman's links with the IPR, with its members in the Occupation, and on the FBI/RCMP material. Morris got it all.

Morris was getting even more from a confidential informant, Phillip Jaffe, one-time editor of *Amerasia,* which was cited by the California Committee on Un-American Activities in 1942 as "communist initiated or controlled." Jaffe was himself indicted in August 1945 on a charge of espionage conspiracy, was convicted and fined $2,500.[12] He confided to Morris in 1951 that his old "friend" from the late Thirties, Herbert Norman, had spurned him in 1943, and as a consequence, says Morris, Jaffe "has had a sort of grudge against N. Felt he had been slighted by being dropped." Jaffe confirmed for Morris the communist credentials of Norman, and even suggested "it was possible that N. was a homosexual." In addition, said Jaffe, as of 1942, "he and Irene weren't getting along well and might get a divorce."[13] SISS files on Herbert are filled with such gossip, in every case *unsupported* by corroborating evidence, which perhaps explains why Morris did not rely *publicly* on such evidence in his vilification of Herbert. But neither did he mention letters such as the one from William Canning of Babylon, New York, who tells of attending the "Marxist study groups" of Finkelstein and Wittfogel but adds, "Herbert Norman did not attend these sessions so far as I can remember."[14] Neither did Morris place much stock in Finkelstein's SISS testimony of 28 March 1952, when Finkelstein, who by then had changed his name to Finley, told Morris that he "never met him [Norman] and [I] never heard his name until I saw it in Wittfogel's testimony."[15]

Official Canadian protests, coupled with strongly written editorials in Canadian newspapers that denounced the witch-hunt in terms such as, "The Smear Comes North" or "The Contemptible Attack on Mr Norman"[16] as well as behind-the-scenes pressure by Canada's diplomatic delegation in Washington eventually saved Norman from being forced to resign or worse. Regarding diplomatic pressure, for example, W. D. Matthews, minister in the Canadian Embassy, met with State Department officials on 14 August and threatened to make public the privately communicated protest quoted above if the U.S. government failed to respect the principle of confidentiality.

Norman was likely told about efforts on his behalf, and may have felt sufficiently vindicated and protected. He told Mr. C..B. Fahs at a reception at the Indonesian Mission in New Rochelle on 17 August that he felt "the matter can be cleaned up," although he confessed to being worried that the press might be giving the "wrong impression" by quoting out of context. He told Fahs (who secretly reported this conversation to someone in the Senate Judiciary Committee) that "it is all a matter of guilt by association, due to his period of work with the Institute of Pacific Relations." In addition, says Fahs, "he had realized even then that there were doubtful elements in the IPR and too close association was not desirable."[17]

If indeed Norman adopted such a reasoned attitude to the problem, whatever confidence he had in his assumption that the matter would be "cleaned up" disappeared by early the next year. As he was soon to discover, on 28 December 1951, the RCMP received word from England that he had been a communist while at Cambridge. Round two of interrogation began in January 1952.

By the time the second round commenced, Norman knew

that the untoward publicity generated by the SISS hearings, as well as the American pressure to remove him from his post as Head of the American and Far Eastern Desk, had damaged his career and probably his credibility with at least several of his superiors. How could he conclude otherwise? Even as Lester Pearson was publicly expressing his unqualified confidence in his loyalty, Herbert was quietly being divested of all responsibility for overseeing Canada's American Desk. On 15 September 1951, just four days after his return from the San Francisco Peace Conference, M. Cadieux of the Personnel Division noted in a secret memorandum that Escott Reid had gotten Herbert's agreement the day before to "complete the foreign policy survey" undertaken but left uncompleted by another officer. This new assignment was little more than busywork for Herbert; for External's part it appeased the Americans while permitting Canada to sustain the pretense that it was not caving in to U.S. pressure. Cadieux writes, "On paper . . . he will remain the head of the American and Far Eastern Division, as his removal from that post might induce some persons to believe that we have lost confidence in him and that we are transferring him to a straight research job." While it is true that as early as 27 July, before Wittfogel's testimony, this change in assignments had been discussed, it is equally true that the timing of the change and the expressed need to minimize the perception that "we have lost confidence in him" unquestionably stemmed from the embarrassing public exposure of Norman's past.[18]

Norman knew what was happening. He had read newspaper accounts of other witch-hunts in the United States. He could read for himself the transcripts coming out of the Senate hearings, such as, for example, the remark that Robert Morris made to General Willoughby on 9 August: "He [Wittfogel] identified as a member of a Communist study group and as a member of the Communist Party [*sic:* Wittfogel never said this] Herbert Norman. Herbert Norman is today, Mr. Chairman, Chief of the American and Far Eastern Division of the Department of External Affairs of Canada. *That is a place of great importance.*" (Emphasis mine.)[19]

Hence, in mid-September, Norman was effectively removed from this "place of great importance" and made into a researcher. Meanwhile, the RCMP had been carefully monitoring the revelations emanating from SISS testimony, recording, for example, Wittfogel's testimony, Morris's claims, and Dooman's allegation that Norman and John Emmerson "had released two communist leaders and had driven them to their homes" in late 1945. The mere recording of such testimony—already denounced by Pearson—suggests that the RCMP believed it relevant. This was bad enough, but then, according to the RCMP chronology of the "Norman case," several pieces of information about him were received in October and November which were not passed on to External until early December; the content of the new information had been blackened out in the official records but a fair guess as to the content can nonetheless be made.[20]

It might have concerned the mid-August testimony of America's favorite spy queen, Elizabeth Bentley, which identified the IPR as "red as a rose"; or it might have concerned Bentley's allegations that two "high-ranking" Canadian government officials had "contact with communist espionage agents in the United States" during WWII. (This is how the Canadian government got the news from the FBI.[21] The *New York Times* vaguely identified the "agents" as members of a "friendly government.")[22] Bentley, in fact, had named two Canadians—Lester Pearson and Hazen Sise, but for the public, uninformed about the identity of the two Canadians, it was probably reasonable to assume that the now well-known Herbert Norman must have been one of them; indeed, as will be shown later, several influential witch-hunters mistook Sise for Norman.[23]

Regardless of the content of the new information received by the RCMP, there is no guesswork concerning the startling information that came from Great Britain's counter-intelligence unit, M.I.5, in late December, alleging that Norman had been a communist while at Cambridge.

History repeats itself—Herbert was forced to relive the horrendous interrogation experiences of just fifteen months earlier, yet this time, perhaps, with the knowledge that the evidence could not be dismissed as easily as had been the wild ravings of professional American witch-hunters. After all, Britain's record of reasoned civility toward suspects in the Cold War lent credibility to the charges.

What information came from Britain in late 1951 is mentioned in the RCMP's "Brief of Information and Investigation," an undated listing of evidence, and Herbert's reply to same, that appears to be inclusive through early 1952, the date of the last dated reference. The relevant item here refers to an allegation from a British source (name excised) who claimed that Norman had been friendly with Communist Party member Victor Kiernan at Cambridge and had co-operated in organizing what the RCMP terms the "Indian Students' Secret communist Group" at Trinity College.[24] As seen in Chapter 2, this allegation was in fact true.

But what prompted its being mentioned in late 1951, as the RCMP records make clear, is a note from Canada's High Commissioner in London to George Glazebrook in External. The cable is dated 8 September, just a month after Wittfogel first named Norman. It begins: "I had a telephone call last evening from a contact in xxx and the purpose of this call was to find out whether Mr. E. H. Norman had attended Cambridge University." After learning the answer was yes, the "xxx contact said that they held a compromising letter involving 'E. Norman' who had apparently been at Cambridge in 1934 and 1935." The letter was described as "of very considerable significance."[25] The High Commissioner's "contact in xxx" promised to send it on to the RCMP. Though the letter is not included in the RCMP file, subsequent questioning of Norman makes clear that it concerned his political organizing work with Indian students at Cambridge and/or his friendship with Party members Victor Kiernan and John Cornford.

Nor was this the only new piece of suspicious evidence coming in the wake of the Wittfogel testimony. Brigadier Fleury, posted in the Occupation in the late Forties, had come forward in late August to report, "in strict confidence," a piece of gossip he had heard in Tokyo from "a high ranking

U.S. Officer" regarding the "real" reasons for Norman's recall a year earlier. Fleury also reported that, at a dinner party in Tokyo, news that Norman was a "Communist or fellow traveller" was discussed openly, and at another dinner party, at which Herbert and Irene were in attendance, the same charge was leveled in Herbert's presence.[26]

More ominous yet, although never commented upon by the RCMP but which had to be reconsidered in light of the M.I. 5 letter, were two anonymous letters that came in the immediate aftermath of the May 1951 defections of spies Guy Burgess and Donald Maclean. Written on "Minister of National Health and Welfare" stationery, and addressed to MP Paul Martin, the informant said that Burgess, Maclean, Norman, and himself were classmates at Cambridge where Herbert had been "engaged in Communist activities." In his first letter of 8 June to Martin, the informant pointed out that "since . . . Maclean recently visited Ottawa in his official capacity the association of these various facts could or could not be significant." In his second letter of 11 June, he elaborated:

> One of these men [Burgess] is an expert on Far Eastern Affairs in the British Foreign Office (a job similar to that held by my friend in Ottawa [Norman]), plus the fact that the other Englishman (Maclean) visited Ottawa recently, could mean that the three were known to each other, and also that they could have been in touch with each other on problems common to their work and that my friend, no matter what his view is now, could possibly be in possession of a clue which could possibly contribute to clarifying the mystery of the disappearance of these two men.[27]

So, as the wolves began catching the scent of the wounded prey, the Mounties began accumulating new evidence that went some distance toward denying Norman his right to work in his government's employ. With the Americans expressing concern over Herbert's sensitive position, with new suspicions being voiced in the wake of the Wittfogel testimony, and with British involvement,[28] a new round of questioning was inevitable. Finally, on 4 January 1952, Inspector

Guernsey of the RCMP wrote Glazebrook about a classmate of Norman's, at both Toronto and Cambridge, who had "observed Norman associating with a group of students [at Cambridge] interested in communist affairs and theories."[29] Herbert stood precariously "upon the brink of grief's abysmal valley."

It seemed to Glazebrook, then with Defence Liaison in External, that enough new evidence had accumulated to warrant another interrogation. In a secret memorandum to Mr. Heeney, dated 18 January 1952, Glazebrook summarized External's newly modified position toward Norman in these words: "The effect of the new evidence and subsequent conversation with Mr. Norman is, in broad outline, as follows: 1) It shows that at one time he was, in effect, a Communist in opinion. 2) The evidence states that he was an active member of the Party with a particular job. 3) The evidence introduces new Communists who were alleged associates. 4) It extends the period of Communist belief to some undefined point after he left Cambridge for Toronto [1935]." Glazebrook called for a "re-examination" of the older evidence in light of the new; and he advised that External should anticipate problems the Minister (Pearson) might confront, publicity problems in the event Norman's loyalty was questioned in the House, and problems with the United States, not least of which was the anticipated American uproar "if it so happened that Norman's duties required him to work with them on highly sensitive material." On the latter issue, Glazebrook further noted "a similar problem arises in the United Kingdom as in the United States if Norman were to work with them."[30]

Glazebrook hastened to add, almost gratuitously, in reviewing the position of External, that "there has been at no time any suggestion of disloyalty during the period in which Norman has been in the Department." Yet Glazebrook also raised the possibility that Herbert might have "attempted to influence policy to the left in the period before this case broke." A hand-written notation in the margin beside this latter point, perhaps Pearson's, adds, "this must be tackled."[31]

Glazebrook emphasized several other issues as well. First,

assuming exoneration, the question of whether Norman "can be freely posted," given the position of the U.S. and the U.K.; second, in the event Herbert resigned and accepted an academic appointment, how would the public perceive his resignation; and finally, Glazebrook realistically pointed to the troublesome effect of possible American publicity, namely, that "the 'where there is smoke there must be fire' argument will always pop up." His recommendation, really a repetition of one made fifteen months before: "Our real problem at the moment . . . is to make up our own minds whether Norman effectively broke with Communist thinking before he entered the Department." Once before they had decided this question in Herbert's favor, but now, Glazebrook realized, even "if the answer to this question is favourable, we must still consider whether it would be in his best interests, as well as ours, that he should remain indefinitely in the Department." The anonymous hand-written notation at the bottom of the page raised a related issue—even if he is found "trustworthy," if it is true that he was once a member of the Communist Party, should he be given access to classified material?[32]

The assumptions that underlay the questions, the doubts, and the concerns of External all boded ill for Herbert. It was a "Catch-22": he could be found "loyal" but nonetheless untrustworthy, or at best limited in his value to External since the Americans and the British had expressed serious reservations about his reliability. Guilty or innocent, he was "tainted," and no sort of positive evaluation by External and/or the RCMP would ever change that.

A thirteen-page report, listing all the unanswered questions about Norman, was prepared around this time—groundwork for the interrogation to follow. Testimony from old friends, observations about how he had modified earlier testimony regarding associations with left-wingers, the SISS hearings, Brigadier Fleury's confidential report, the Halperin notebook (which assumes renewed meaning), the Tsuru connection, the Gouzenko claims, Herbert's relationship with Frank Park, his general "connection with communism" based on his testimony—all these were counted as relevant issues that Norman would have to address once again. Indeed, in private, pre-interrogation conversations with Glazebrook in early February, Herbert had been very forthcoming on all these issues, perhaps hoping that the entire mess might be put to rest in such a way as to make unnecessary the RCMP questioning. He even went so far as to say that "it would be accurate to describe [me] as a communist during [my] second year at Cambridge," insisting nonetheless that he never joined the Party despite efforts by his mentor John Cornford to recruit him. Herbert also insisted that though a contemporary of Guy Burgess, he knew only the name and not the man, whose reputation he described as "undesireable." He also insisted that he had never met Donald Maclean. He did admit to visiting Victor Kiernan at Cambridge in 1947 while in England for an IPR conference, but added that he stayed away from Cambridge and Kiernan when in England in May 1951 for purposes of discussing the Japanese peace treaty with Foreign Office counterparts.[33]

Norman had been forthcoming, more so than ever before. It must have required immense courage—or reflected terrible fear—to confess to Glazebrook that he might have been described as a communist in 1935. Naïvely, Herbert seemed to believe that by being *more* truthful than he had been in late 1950, by omitting *less* information about his past political affiliations, the "rewards" would somehow be greater, that perhaps he would be commended for his honesty, would be forgiven, and his credibility fully restored. He seemed not to recognize that Glazebrook's *duty* was to be suspicious, to assume that disclosures of this sort were never total, to assume guilt until innocence could be unambiguously established. Hence, Glazebrook wrote Heeney on 6 February, after Herbert had told "all," "I told Norman our difficulty in reconciling evidence concerning his active work for the Communist Party with his own [1950] explanation."[34] With that revelation, Herbert no doubt finally realized that truth told late is perceived as lies told earlier.

Superintendent George McClellan, Inspector Guernsey, and George Glazebrook faced Norman behind closed doors in the East Block beginning 26 February. The transcript of the interrogation is twenty-six pages in length; one can only speculate on the amount of time it took, but no speculation is required to observe how painfully inarticulate Herbert became under pressure, how lengthy and self-justifying, even defensive, his answers to their questions were. No counsel was present to advise him to keep his answers short and to the point.

The questioning began with McClellan introducing Guernsey, who said he would confine his questions to "your days at Cambridge," to the relationship with John Cornford, and to a number of other people, one of whom is clearly Lorie Tarshis who was linked with Halperin, had attended Toronto and Cambridge, and had taught at Tufts University in Boston while Herbert was at Harvard. (It appears that the reason for the RCMP introducing Tarshis's name was an FBI report linking him with Halperin.)

When asked whether he thought Tarshis had been a communist, Norman said he was not, but was on the left as "far as Hitler was concerned," though was not pro-Soviet. The other Toronto contemporary who had gone to Cambridge and then to Harvard, also identified as an economist, was Robert Bryce, about whom, it seems, Herbert was also asked (the name is excised). Again Herbert says "he," too, was not a communist. He did admit to knowing the New Zealander Maclaurin, too, but dissembled when he described Maclaurin as "a member of the Conservative Club," and added, "I don't know what happened to him, except that I did hear later that he was later killed in Spain."

Herbert admitted to knowing several others whose names were raised by his questioners but denied knowing others (all the names are blackened out). He also admitted having known one fellow who was connected with the League Against War and Fascism in Toronto and said that he had "a slight connection with it for a few weeks." He added that his interest in the group was short-lived because he feared for his reputation and because his university studies and his teaching at Upper Canada College were so demanding. Then, when asked bluntly whether he had been a member of the Communist

Party, Herbert said no, confessing only to having had an interest in Marxism. He denied "wittingly or consciously" knowing anyone in the British Communist Party, said he never told anyone he was a member, but did admit to talking "quite recklessly in those years[:] in a way I was very carefree and did not weigh my words."

Norman admitted to having been a member of the Cambridge Socialist Society, but denied (falsely, according to Kiernan), that he was in charge of organizing colonials (Indian students) for the Party. He said that Cornford tried to interest him in this work, "but nothing came of it from my point." He told of knowing a number of "Asiatics" in the Socialist Society but claimed that Cornford "never proposed that I should engage in secret work, go to India or get connected with the British Communist Party and I didn't have any dealings with it at all."

The questioning shifted abruptly to Norman's connections with Tsuru. When asked to "say [what] he was," he replied that Tsuru would only admit to being a Marxist and got angry at any suggestion that he was a Communist. When his interrogators asked Herbert to explain the difference, a difference, *not incidentally,* that was central to his own ideological identity in the late Thirties, he answered: "Well, I took it [the distinction] to mean he wasn't interested in political activities of any kind and that he didn't wish to follow the party line." Today, we might describe Tsuru and Herbert as "armchair Marxists," intellectual Marxists who abhor political activism.

Midway through the interrogation, just before the four men broke for tea, Norman asked to make a statement, in order to explain himself and his political views and friendships.

I have been interested in politics of all kinds, and oriental students and their views and so forth. Kept up my interest in the Far East, but since I got more matured, and particularly since I got in the Government Service, despite that period, I have maintained what I consider a discreet and loyal attitude and have tried to make use of what knowledge I have gained on oriental things—personal knowledge and what you're reading, for the interest of the government. If I had remained in academic life as I intended to do after having won the Rockefeller Fellowship [1936], naturally I would have gone into research and writing . . . . [in] those years before I was in Government had I known certain Indians, Chinese, or anyone you wish to name [as] leftwing, I wouldn't necessarily have liked him for being leftwing, but I wouldn't have been afraid to know him because he was.

Norman must have known that it was impossible to explain, let alone justify, his youthful radical political views to anyone who had not been a part of the anti-fascist movement of the Thirties, so he explained himself in *human* terms, in terms of his human attraction to different people whom he could admire and respect for *who* they were and not necessarily for *what* they believed or advocated, though as he shortly thereafter acknowledged, his intellectual curiosity made everyone potentially worth knowing. He said as much when trying to explain his association with certain left-wing Chinese: "I would be very interested to hear what a Chinese had to say—whether it was critical of his government or was for it—it wasn't up to me to make any decisions *about the man.*" (Emphasis mine.) Curiously, Glazebrook, the only intellectual among Norman's questioners, did not quite accept this view; he asked: "Wouldn't you make any decisions [about the man]?" Replied Herbert: "I might say he was a windbag, or he is fanatical and, therefore, a bore, or that he is very well informed."

He neglected to define what "well informed" meant, though the astute Glazebrook must have suspected that, at least for that period in Norman's life, it meant a radical/progressive political outlook. Glazebrook queried, "Wouldn't this *[how the man presented his views]* be getting some reflection of the information you were getting from him?" Norman was caught, and his answer shows him at his worst: "Oh, yes, I am assuming if the man had any intelligence and wasn't— and wasn't fanatical which is unpleasant in any shape or form— as I say if he had something interesting to say about [blank in original]. I am interested in that part of the world [China?], but after I came to the Government, I think—I tried to—I felt genuine loyalty to Canada. I was never aware of any temptation to do anything to the contrary to Canadian interests . . ."

Defensive, no doubt feeling beleaguered, perhaps intellectually uncomfortable with the difficult distinction between a man's personality and his beliefs, Norman struggled repeatedly thereafter to find the appropriate words to express his ideas and to explain his past behavior. One can only imagine that Glazebrook, at least, sensed the man's growing difficulties, and thus returned to the most important issue at hand: "Even if you admitted you were a member of the party at one time, or anything else, I am not saying . . . it will be much better to do that [confess?] in my own opinion." (Ellipsis in original.) With this, Norman inched even closer toward a confession: "Yes, in my Cambridge time I came close to it [joining the Party] and if I had stayed there another year I might have." Five years later, Norman "confessed" in words to that effect just before he took his own life.

Glazebrook at this point recognized that Herbert was weakening. He raised the Wittfogel allegation, then added: "A lot of people think, whether it is true or not, that there is some truth in those things and we get information from other sources quite independent." Herbert responded by informing his questioners about his relationship with the ex-communist German émigré, emphasizing that he met with Wittfogel only "three or four times" and then in the professor's office, solely for academic discussions. When asked why the Professor should lie and perjure himself, Norman generously suggested that Wittfogel was simply confused at best or at worst had misinterpreted several of his remarks about Chinese economic history to have "some kind of Communist slant." Norman offered the further observation that it was "curious business" that Wittfogel would be "the chief lecturer at the Finkelstein study group long after he, Wittfogel, ceased to be a communist." After a follow-up question, he added, "I am not trying to say he had any malice towards me, but

I think there is such a thing as being an obliging witness."
Glazebrook admitted the possibility.

Questioning proceeded along well-trodden paths of the
past—ties with leftists in Canada, the U.S., and England—
and was periodically interrupted with the question, "You
have never been a member of the Communist Party?" followed by Norman's by then nearly standard answer, "No,
I considered myself very close to it for about a year but I
didn't accept any posts or responsibilities." Finally Herbert
agreed that he might legitimately have been regarded as a
"fellow-traveller."[35]

Only that? His answer to everyone's favorite question simply does not square with his bold pronouncement to Howard
in 1937 that he had joined the Communist Party under the
"tutelage" of John Cornford. Had Herbert lied to Howard
in 1937, or was he lying in 1952?

In one respect the question is academic, i.e., worth debating but not worth fighting over. The most pertinent question is not whether he ever agreed to join the Party—there
were no card-carrying members in Cambridge in the Thirties,
according to Victor Kiernan and Margot Heinemann, Cornford's lover when Herbert knew them—but rather whether
out of loyalty to communism Herbert chose to betray his
government. There is absolutely *no evidence* of this any-
where, not in the RCMP, FBI, Army Intelligence, External
Affairs, SISS, or State Department files. Indeed, as late as 17
August 1951, FBI agent L. L. Laughlin in a memo to D. M.
Ladd writes: "No information appears in Bureau files which
would substantiate Wittfogel's allegation that Norman was a
Communist."[36] Nor, as already shown, is there evidence of
disloyalty or misrepresentation of fact in any of Norman's
official dispatches to Ottawa when he was in a position to
purposely mislead his superiors in such a way as to advance
the cause of the Soviet Union. Being in a position that could
advance "communist interests," whatever this means, does
not in itself mean that one did.

But in another respect, the question is anything but academic. It has to do with what kind of person Norman was,

especially in relation to his brother Howard. When Herbert told Howard he had joined the Party, Cornford had just been killed, Herbert was grieving over the loss, and was suffering the "survivor's guilt" that politically inactive "armchair Marxists" especially would be prone to experience. When Marx reminded his followers that the purpose of philosophical speculation was not to understand History/Clio, but to change it/her, he was preaching a sort of call to activism that a missionary's son could easily understand. But Herbert, unlike his father and his brother, was no activist. Symptomatic of his politically inactive personality was his answer to the 1952 allegation by the RCMP that he had handed out leaflets at the Toronto Exhibition for the League Against War and Fascism in 1935. He conceded that he was physically in Toronto then and therefore *could* have, but told his questioners that he emotionally—constitutionally—could not have: ". . . the reason that I am quite sure I didn't is that I don't remember and secondly a thing like that would be so painful to me. I hate anything like—handing out—well I've never— well I've never *done it*, standing on street corners handing out pamphlets. That's something I couldn't forget."[37] Norman was incapable of doing something so common. He loved humanity, as many leftists do, but could not bring himself to actually touch elbows with the man on the street.

An anecdote told by his niece Margaret, now a physician, helps make this point. She recalls traveling by bus to Ottawa during the early 1950s to visit her aunt and uncle just before entering university. She was met at the bus station by Herbert who immediately asked her how the trip went. She told the brutal truth, how an inebriated man sitting next to her urinated in his pants while he slept. Margaret vividly recalls today her Uncle Herbert's disgust and incredulity and infuriated response and how she concluded then that not only was he naïve, innocent, and removed from life's awful realities, but also that he was incapable of accepting such painfully human truths. Similarly referring to his naïveté, Margaret once remarked, "Uncle Herbert could not understand evil."[38]

Norman lived an ivory tower existence, protected from the

distasteful, the mundane, the pitifully human aspects of life, those aspects of existence which characterize the lot of ordinary human beings, with which he clearly did not identify. He wanted to save them, not mingle with them. Passing out political leaflets, preaching to public gatherings, these were the activities that his father necessarily performed, ones which Howard the missionary likewise "stooped" to do. Herbert Norman would have none of this. Forever the democratic aristocrat, his role was to lead by written example, not by rousing the rabble. A Cambridge man, a Harvard Ph.D., an author and a diplomat, a man who proudly rode in limousines and traveled long distances by ocean liner or by plane, a cultured *gentleman* who delighted in telling obscure historical anecdotes in the presence of refined company, of impressing his fellow enlightened souls with his knowledge of classical music and poetry, he was decidedly not the sort to stand on street corners and hand out political pamphlets.

Howard, on the other hand, followed in their father's footsteps and did precisely this, although he substituted religious pamphlets for political. Howard had chosen the familial "safe route" of proselytizing for God, of wearing five-year-old suits, of "making do." Herbert had repudiated this life course, had scorned God's missionaries, had rejected his father's life choices, and hence Howard's, in order more easily to justify his own. Howard was their father's son, Herbert was not; this was a bitter realization, one that called for unequivocal repudiation. Joining the Communist Party, or at least professing to have done so, served as a proud announcement that he was his *own* man. Herbert may or may not have joined; this was less important than making Howard, and hence his father, aware that he had chosen a *different* path, but one to which he was no less committed. Commitment means a lot to missionaries, religious or secular.

His commitment to a different, but ethically equal, if not (he felt) superior cause was frequently driven home in his correspondence with Howard. One of the bitterest exchanges between the brothers had to do with Herbert's caustic attack on the meaning of St. Paul, the epitome of divine revelation, in whose mission Howard believed strongly. Herbert repeatedly made light of Paul's conversion on the road to Damascus, ridiculing Howard for investing so much belief in so perceptibly absurd a story. It is for this reason highly relevant that Norman answered his interrogators' query in 1952 about when he *ceased* being a "fellow traveller" with the following:

> Well, I didn't have any sudden light on the road like St. Paul; maybe it would have been better if I had. But it was a slow process in which I gained intellect from maturity and I must have figured for myself that that tendency of mine was not motivated by any blind admiration of Russia. Even in my most solemn days such goings on there were very disturbing. The purges were very distasteful, to say the least.[39]

The intellectual always, he could reject the revelation of St. Paul as easily as he could reject, eventually, the belief that the Soviet Union was god. He told his questioners about baiting Cornford by taking a Trotskyite position, getting in response from Cornford the argument that "I was always interested in ideas of that sort, not necessarily leftist ideas." In his own defense he said, "I tried to keep an open mind on a variety of things and, therefore, I didn't wish to become fanatically wedded to any one of these theories. I thought life started getting too complex to just take a theory and superimpose on it and say 'now you get it.' It's a nice lazy way of doing it; I have many intellectual doubts about things."[40]

The perpetual doubter, the intellectual is: he/she can never accept received truth—religious or secular—for too long a time before looking for other, equally relevant truths. Norman realized what difficulty this caused him, as a servant of the government for which the *one* truth is the national truth: "I was continually trying to test my ideas against reality and so forth and I went through this phase and looking back now, although it's giving you considerable trouble, certainly me, I am not aware that I ever violated my duty to my Government, nor have I engaged in what might be called 'conspiratorial activities,' trying to pass secret messages off or anything or that sort."[41]

Doth he protest his innocence too much? Or is he trying to educate his interrogators about the workings of the mind of an intellectual? Neither they nor Herbert could then comprehend the personal "hidden agenda," the one inscribed in the religious tablet of his missionary background. Nor did either side seem to confront the obvious, existential fact that a middle-aged man, deeply into a career and a stable personal life, was trying to recall how he was as a youth with few ties other than those to his unbridled conscience. Life makes us all into revisionists, anxious to rewrite the past in order to make sense of the present. Clio, in this sense, is always raped by her suitors.

Norman could only recall his strong hatred of Hitler— "the most important impact in that phase of my life was the phenomenon of Hitler"—and his attraction to Cornford, "a bit of a prodigy" who seemed "to treat life free, easy, and gay." The leftists were "the more intellectual ones, the more lively ones," and toward them Herbert, a kindred spirit, was attracted. But for Glazebrook, at least partly taken in by the Cold War, what mattered was "not whether you incurred a disease, but what disease you had."[42] Communism as cancer: the roots of the metaphor go deep.

What could Herbert say to such an opinion? He said, "Yes, yes." Men like Glazebrook were in charge; Norman knew this. In 1952, communism was a disease, and the afflicted had to accept the judgment of society's judges, just as lepers once upon a time accepted isolation or stoning. His judges asked him, in the event of war with Russia, "what would you think?" Political outcast that he was, he of course said he would side with Canada, on the side of the judges.

The questioning degenerated thereafter, its items posed in simple-minded terms to evoke expressions of patriotism; Norman did not disappoint them, but he must have wondered about the sort of sheltered life that his antagonists had lived, about how little history they seemed to know, about how hateful they must be toward a historical force of which they seemed completely ignorant. The questioning ended with best wishes for Norman to enjoy a relaxing holiday. Herbert's final words: "I can relax because I know I haven't done anything wrong. I know how these things can come in now that my name has been in the headlines . . ." [43]

Thus ended the questioning. In late March Lester Pearson proposed closing the file and "regarding the enquiry as completed with a complete clearance for Norman." Yet the minister left open the possibility that the investigation would be renewed if "new evidence came to the RCMP . . . ."[44] No documents exist to tell whether Norman was told if all doubts as to his loyalty had been satisfactorily resolved. He did learn, however, that he was being reassigned from Head of the American and Far Eastern Division to Head of the Information Division, beginning in July 1952. This was a "safe" position—he must have concluded this much—where a former "fellow traveller" who had been declared, in Pearson's words, "an efficient and trustworthy member of this Department," could work without inviting the ire of the Americans or the British and the suspicions of his fellow Canadians. Officially, Herbert was not a "communist."

CHAPTER 9
DIPLOMAT

Remembering the past, perforce
He is a victim of remorse

Pushkin, *Eugene Onegin*

C leared but nonetheless tainted, forbidden from working in any post that would involve the Americans or the British, his stature as a diplomat diminished by embarrassing publicity, Norman was forced to languish as Head of the Information Division for nearly one year. Today Irene Norman can recall little that is memorable about this period of political isolation, and perhaps that is precisely what Ottawa had hoped. Out of sight, out of mind—such may have been External's reasoning. His internal exile was interrupted only by a short trip to Paris in December of 1952 to attend the North Atlantic Council meeting for Canada; this may have been seen as a safe way for Canada to redeclare to the Allies its confidence in Norman. He, too, may have seen the event in such a positive way, but if he did, then he did so ever so briefly. No sooner did he return than his mother died.[1] On the heels of his diplomatic nadir, Herbert was painfully reminded of his mortality.

A man of Norman's ability could hardly be allowed to languish indefinitely in a nondescript position with the department, and so he was resurrected, ever so safely, by being appointed as High Commissioner to New Zealand on 24 January 1953. New Zealand was no Tokyo, let alone Peking or Moscow, two other possible appointments mentioned just three years before, but at least it would put him back into the field. Yet as Pearson himself acknowledged in his memoirs, "New Zealand was an easy post and he was not subject to much working pressure." Privately, on 3 March, Pearson wrote to congratulate Herbert on the posting, adding, "It will not be as active a post as Japan, or as harassing as the Department, but I hope you will find it both enjoyable and rewarding . . . . I hope also that you will interpret the appointment as a renewed expression of the confidence of the Prime Minister and myself in you and in your service to our country."[2]

This would be Norman's "R & R," his busman's holiday. Ralph Collins, Canada's first ambassador to China and one of Herbert's contemporaries, described the appointment in this way: "For someone of Herb's calibre, being sent to New Zealand was a defacto 'rest and cure': it got him out of the limelight."[3] Not exactly. Upon announcement of his new position, the Second Secretary of the American Embassy in Ottawa filed a two-page report about Norman that included a lengthy reference to his problems with SISS; a copy of the report was sent on to New Zealand.[4] Neither would the RCMP take any chances: in its file on Herbert, the appointment was carefully noted, along with the words: "Recommended: Review Norman's activities in N.Z."

Norman understood that Ottawa's intent was both to indicate its "renewed . . . confidence" and to give him a restful break from the political difficulties that had troubled him so. He wrote to Pearson with heartfelt gratitude: "[I wish] to say how much it has meant to me to serve under you as Minister. From the personal or human [point of view], it has sustained me during the difficult last two years. . . . I am delighted to be given the responsibility of representing Canada abroad."[5] Despite his gratitude, Norman understood that New Zealand was neither an exciting nor demanding appointment. A letter of 9 April 1953, before his departure from Canada, informed him that he would have only a five-person staff in New Zealand, three of them clerks.

But for Irene the assignment was a godsend. The Normans left Quebec on 25 April, sailing first to Southampton on the liner *Scythia*, with ports of call in London, Paris, Naples, and Sydney, not arriving in Wellington until 21 July. "It was wonderful," she wrote friends in Ottawa, referring to the emotional release from the anxiety-ridden lives that they had endured for the past three years.[6]

Despite knowing that Wellington was his own particular Elba, Norman appreciated his life in exile for the first two years. In December of his first year, he had received a personal note from Pearson commending him for "how well you are doing in your new post"; Herbert wrote back to say how much he enjoyed the "atmosphere of tolerance and goodwill" in New Zealand.[7] He wrote Howard and academic colleagues in Japan about how his free time permitted more in-depth reading than he had done for years. He worked on a volume of essays in the philosophy of history that was published in Japan in Japanese. He assisted a graduate student of Ed Reischauer of Harvard in researching a doctoral dissertation, and he played more tennis than he had in years. He enjoyed an agreeable relationship with his staff. T. H. W. Read, who served under Norman until February 1954, remembers him as "just about the perfect head of post." Read reports that although "I am sure he was aware that the waves of the McCarthy [sic] investigation had reached and sensitized New Zealand," he still lived as "a man fully engaged in overcoming his current problems." Nonetheless, Read remembers Norman as "appreciative and invariably courteous" toward his staff, although he would frequently demand "five or six drafts" of his dispatches before sending them off to Ottawa.[8]

Read also recalls that Norman frequently socialized with two professors at the University of Wellington (on his arrival the *Wellington Evening Post* had described Herbert as "a scholarly High Commissioner," and indicated his interest in scholarly pursuits in New Zealand)[9] and the Australian manager of the Bank of New South Wales, Harold Holliday, with whom he frequently played "lawn tennis." But most of all, says Read, he was regarded as "an authority who could perhaps throw light on the potential of this recently feared enemy [Japan]," and therefore was called upon to give periodic briefings to the New Zealand cabinet.[10] And, with his reputation as an East Asianist, he twice delivered lectures to New Zealand universities during his three-year stay. Perhaps in recognition of his early role in making New Zealanders more aware and less fearful of Japan and East Asia, after his death a scholarship fund in East Asian Studies was established in Norman's name at the University of Wellington.

One of the speeches he gave at Wellington was the valedictory address to the class of 1956, focusing on New Zealand and its people. Ten single-spaced typewritten pages, it reveals the scholar's eye for the effect that climate has on a national character and the democrat's sensitivities for how poorly the prevailing white culture has treated the aborigines, the Maori. He paid tribute to the fundamental egalitarianism of the people and commended them for supporting the realistic strategic shift away from Great Britain and toward the American defense alignment, but without abandoning their tradition of "sturdy independence."[11]

Norman left New Zealand on at least three different occasions during his tenure there. On the first occasion he travelled with his wife to Samoa, leaving on 6 July 1954 and returning on 9 August. Canada's High Commissioner, R. G. Powles, had invited them for a three-week stay, but Norman so enjoyed the experience that they remained an additional two weeks.[12] The lengthy memorandum, twenty-one pages long, that he sent to Ottawa upon the conclusion of the trip is the best indication of the pleasure he derived from the visit. He writes like an anthropologist about the indigenous dignitaries they met and about the intricacies of the different islands' economies and traditional forms of rule; his report is a scholarly *tour de force*. One brief example: on Western Samoa he interviewed Tamasese, a Samoan aristocrat, whom he describes in tantalizing detail: "Tamasese is an impressive man both physically and intellectually. He is, like many Polynesians, a giant, about 6'6" in height and I should guess about 300 lb. in weight. His face impresses one as that of an elderly and amicable mastiff, with deep wrinkles and heavy jaws; but his ponderous movements and slow good-natured smile are not an index to his mentality."[13]

Besides this trip to Soamoa, Herbert visited Japan once and

went to Australia several times on diplomatic business. He
left by himself for Japan on 3 May 1955 and returned 21 June;
the purpose of the trip was to meet with his publisher, Iwanami, about his new book of essays, and to visit his brother,
for the last time as it turned out. A lengthy explanation to
Ottawa about his meeting with his publisher—he emphasized
that his book was "unrelated to current issues": "no contro-
versies are likely to explode when publication takes place"
since the book would be printed in Japanese—resulted in
permission from Jules Léger, Undersecretary of State[14] to
publish and a brief statutory leave of absence. And while in
Japan the two brothers visited for one last time. Howard
recalls lengthy but good-humored arguments the two had
about St. Paul, and an emotional confessional in which Herbert tearfully professed his innocence of any wrongdoing
against his government.

The leave in Japan was a concrete sign that Norman was
champing at the bit for a more meaningful appointment than
New Zealand. His normal tour of duty was not due to end
until 1957, but he was growing impatient with the enforced
rest and relaxation that New Zealand offered. He must also
have been wondering whether his future with External would
forever after entail sleepy little posts on the edge of the Pacific.
Happily, however, in March of 1955, he found reason to
write Pearson and broach the question of his future: an offer
had come from the University of British Columbia to organize its Far Eastern Studies Department. "It would not be
a fair question to put to you to ask what might be my future
in the Department, but I thought it proper to enquire whether
in your estimation I might continue to serve the Department
with increasing usefulness and in due time to undertake perhaps a rather more active type of work wherever the Department sees fit." He emphasizes that "I would rather remain
in the Department" but wonders what kind of role he can
expect in light of the "unfortunate publicity of the past year."[15]

Pearson wrote back immediately. His letter of 7 April 1955,
classified "Secret," opens with, "It was to be expected that
one of our universities would approach you to join its staff."

But he goes on quickly to say, "There is no doubt in my mind that as time goes by you will be asked to undertake more and more responsible jobs in the Department," citing Tokyo as a specific example. Pearson also empathizes with Herbert's "difficult decision." He says he will understand if Norman opts for the academic life, yet emphasizes "how highly you are regarded in the Department," and even leaves open the possibility that "if you decided to leave the Service I would hope that at a later date you could consider a posting with us." Pearson ends by declaring "I have committed myself much more than I usually do in writing this letter, but I did wish to let you have this expression of the very high regard in which I hold you."[16]

Concrete expression of Pearson's "very high regard" for Herbert came at year's end. On 22 December 1955, Norman received a letter from Jules Léger, broaching the possibility of a posting in Cairo. Norman replied on 5 January 1956, perhaps playing hard to get, remarking that although New Zealand was "rather quiet and isolated," it was "not without its charms and presents some opportunity for study and contemplation." But he ended his reply with a declaration that Cairo would be "a stimulating challenge" and that he would "be quite happy to move."[17] Pearson had delivered on his promise of a "more responsible posting"; Norman was thrilled, his wife remembers well. On 4 April 1956, exactly one year before his death in Cairo, the petition for approval of his appointment to Egypt, and concurrently to Lebanon, was approved. Just a month earlier, Herbert got the letter from Léger which told him to return to Ottawa via Cairo and the U.K.; he and Irene left New Zealand on 10 May by ship, stopped off in Cairo on 17 June, and finally arrived in Ottawa on 12 July. By then the Suez Crisis was beginning, so his briefing in Ottawa was cut short; he and Irene returned to the land of the Pharoahs on 19 August. He had less than eight months to live.

During his last five months in New Zealand, as he awaited official word of his reappointment to Egypt, Norman used

every spare minute to begin learning as much as he possibly
could about his next posting. For the scholar-diplomat, preparation meant reading books about Egyptian history, society,
culture, and transnational relations. Perhaps due to his intellect, or perhaps owing to a lifelong passion to understand
foreign cultures, within a short while after his arrival in Cairo
Norman had, according to those who knew him best, already
acquired the reputation for being something of a budding
Egyptologist.[18]

But no amount of reading and studying could have prepared him for the role he would eventually play in this most
contentious of times. The Normans arrived just a few weeks
after the nationalization of the Suez Canal by President Gamal
Abdul Nasser in what many regard as one of the first and
most dramatic assertions of Third World independence in the
postwar era. Nasser had decided to create an "Egypt for the
Egyptians," and this would mean taking possession of the
most obvious, not to mention profitable, legacy of British
imperialism, the Suez Canal. Egyptian nationalism, therefore,
was pitted against British imperialism, and Norman, as chief
representative of a Commonwealth nation, necessarily had
to stand on the side of the Queen, at least initially. Thus, he
and Irene entered a nation where they automatically were
guilty by association, where their nationality and their race
would only accentuate their foreignness. The times were tense,
the weather was dry, hot and miserable, the political climate
one of hostility and mistrust toward "Europeans"; Norman
arrived just in time to witness Cairo at its worst and try to
make sense of the chaos for Ottawa.

He took up his new position with a certain sort of intellectual baggage in hand: he was not unsympathetic to the
underdog image that Nasser had been cultivating, he respected Egypt's attempt to free itself from British control,
and was mindful of Egypt's precarious position of straddling
the gulf that separated the west from the east in the Cold
War, the gulf that, for its own convenience and profit the
developed world had dug between itself and the underdeveloped world.

The objective situation that he found was this: Nasser was inveighing against imperialism, that "great force that is imposing a murderous, invisible siege upon the whole region."[19] Nasser was calling for the "liberation" of the economic resources of Egypt from western control as a first important step in reasserting Egyptian sovereignty. Gaining control over the French-built and British-owned canal was a *sine qua non* for "liberation." From Britain's point of view, a narrow perspective shaped by its conquests in the heyday of its imperialist ventures, maintaining control over this vital waterway, through which a good portion of its trade went, was justified by reason of security, strategy, and commercial interests. When, in a *coup d'état* on 23 July 1953, Nasser seized control of Britain's "Achilles' heel," as the Canal was dubbed in a 1956 *Economist* article, Britain had never felt so vulnerable.[20] It dealt with the problem by signing an accord with Nasser's government in July 1954 that called for the withdrawal of British troops in the succeeding twenty months in exchange for an Egyptian promise to guarantee free passage through the Canal, as well as a promise to permit the reactivation of a British military base in the event that the Canal was attacked by an outside power and Egypt requested assistance. The 1954 agreement was a compromise: Egypt was rid of the British troops that had been stationed there since 1882, and Britain got assurance of the Canal's defense.

Despite the agreement, relations between Britain and Egypt had not improved. The main problem was Israel. Like the rest of his Arab neighbors, Nasser refused to accept the existence of Israel, while Great Britain and the other major western powers served, in varying degrees, as Israel's guarantors. Yet Britain also promised, in August 1954, to sell arms to Egypt as part of a larger strategy to ensure a balance of power in the Middle East that had been upset by Israel's victory over the Arab states in 1948. In February 1955, for what Nasser said were reasons of self-defense in response to an unprovoked Israeli raid against the Egyptian Gaza region, Egypt tried to buy arms from both Britain and the United States. The United States stalled and Great Britain attached

strings to the sale which they knew Nasser would find un-
acceptable. Nasser tired of waiting for western arms and in
September 1955 bought arms from Czechoslovakia on very
easy credit terms.[21] The Cold War had come to Egypt.

Reacting to the Czech arms deal, Britain and the United
States tried to keep Nasser in the western camp by offering
a $400 million loan to build the Aswan Dam across the Nile.
But in an American election year such aid to a country that
was buying arms from the eastern bloc and that had just
granted the Chinese communists diplomatic recognition, became too risky politically, so, on 9 July 1956, Eisenhower,
followed by the British a day later, withdrew the loan offer.
The Soviets then offered what the Americans and British had
falsely promised. But what was worse for the west, Nasser
expressed his outrage toward the western aid withdrawal by
nationalizing the Suez Canal Company. As Britain's Anthony
Nutting, foreign minister at the time, phrased Nasser's action, ". . . Egypt was not going to be pushed around by the
west."[22] The west, especially Britain, was outraged.

Nasser kept the Canal open, but Britain nonetheless rattled
its sabers. Egyptian control of the Canal was just one more
nail in the coffin of Britain's dead empire, a painful reminder
to the nation's more conservative elements that the glory days
of dictating policy to weak, "backward" countries were gone
forever. Britain retaliated in late July by freezing all Egyptian
assets; the United States and France followed suit. And suddenly Britain began denouncing Egypt for discriminating
against Israeli shipping through the Canal, a matter that the
west had largely overlooked for several prior years.

This was the situation into which Norman came in August
1956. His earliest cables reflect, as it turns out accurately, a
more realistic view of the situation than his British counterparts had offered. In an 8 September dispatch Herbert reported that, contrary to the British prediction that Nasser
would back down on the Suez Canal issue, given the pressures
being applied, the prospect was unlikely. Norman noted that
Nasser was acting "not on the basis of Egyptian interests
purely," but was behaving as he was for "pan-Arab reasons"

and in order "to maintain his prestige" in the Arab world. He reconfirmed these impressions following a private conversation with Egypt's minister of the interior on 16 October, stressing the minister's "passionate nationalist" feelings as well as his "strongly anti-communist" stance.[23] Herbert was saying then what most informed observers are only now acknowledging about the Middle East: namely, that devout Moslems are at best uneasy allies of the Soviet Union, at worst vehement enemies.

Norman makes this point convincingly in a dispatch largely concerned with the personality of Nasser and written just three days after his first meeting with the Egyptian president. In that cable of 6 September, which was circulated to all of Canada's major embassies abroad, he argues against the assumption that Nasser will take Egypt into the "Communist orbit." Nasser, he says, is as much an anti-communist as he is an anti-imperialist. Nasser must be understood in terms of Egyptian history, one of military defeats, of being conquered, of spiritual exhaustion, and of having values fundamentally antithetical to the west's. Neither should Canada or the west expect that Egypt would willingly follow the political practices of its mentor, Great Britain. Norman points out that from the Egyptian's point of view, from the point of view of the colonized, institutions like parliament and political parties are necessarily associated with *foreign* control; instead, he says, Egyptians are more supportive of the military since it secured Egypt's liberation from the corrupt monarchical rule through which Britain once operated its "protectorate."

He emphasizes, however, that under Nasser Egypt has not been reduced to a military dictatorship; the "unpleasant overtones" of typical militarist rule are not present in Egypt. Nasser is not a "ruthless dictator" and is not to be compared with Argentina's Juan Peron, for he lacks the "boundless egotism" of the South American dictator. Rather, Nasser suffers from the malady which Egypt as a whole exhibits: namely, a sense of inferiority *vis-à-vis* the west, meaning he desires only to be respected. Norman reports that Nasser claims his government to be strong but reformist, dedicated to a policy of internal reform that will eliminate the sort of popular discontent that is the basis of communist appeal. He adds that Nasser's pan-Arabism is, similarily, a means to buttress the Middle East from the communist appeal.

But lest his portrait of Nasser seem too accepting of Nasser's own claims, Norman interjects his own observations as well. He points out that Nasser's real goal is "Nasserism" within Egypt and throughout the Middle East. Not so much a product of egotism as "naïveté" and "provincialism," Nasser's projection of himself regionally is a reaction to the western imperial presence for generations, his inability to separate himself from the nation, and his desire to assert Egypt's independence and sovereignty in a world dominated by the big powers.

He also dwells on Nasser's less savory characteristics. He reports that Nasser sees himself not as a dictator, nor as a despot, but simply as an "authoritarian" who "rules with popular assent." Herbert opines that the truth is more complex. Nasser is an "opportunist" whose behavior is as much governed by emotion and intuition as by logic; that as a Moslem, Nasser evinces a distinctive sense of fatalism as well as the more dangerous trait of seeing himself as "an instrument of God." The missionary's son warns: "A man who believes he is both divinely inspired and led will probably be more inflexible in following a course that may prove disastrous than one who is more immediately aware of his own human frailty."[23]

Although based on only a 35-minute interview, in which Nasser did most of the talking, Norman drew seemingly vast unacademic conclusions about the man and his nation during this troubled period. Nasser, he said, was neither a communist nor a fascist, and fortified his point by comparing him with Stalin and Hitler. Egypt, he said, is in "a period of transition," a contradictory period wherein institutions and ideologies were still in flux and nothing was yet permanently formed. Do not, he warned, accept the notion of eventual communist domination—history would prove him correct—but instead understand that Nasser suffered from a "love-hate" relationship with the west: all he wants is to be "loved," to be respected as an equal, and since he has not gotten what he wants, he hates the west, a dangerous precedent, Norman warned, that the other Middle East nations might follow. He further cautioned that Nasser was too parochial for his words not to be taken at face value; in its sophistication, the west is reading too much into Nasser's words, looking for disguised "signals" in his pronouncements, and cited the British Cold War-inspired misreading of Nasser's declaration that he would accept development aid from *anyone*. Norman's plea is to tolerate Egyptian nationalism: it is, he says, an "irresistible force" that the world will have to learn to accept.[24]

But at the time it suited Britain's, and France's, intention to discredit Nasser by imposing a Cold War interpretation onto events in Egypt. When France invited Prime Minister Anthony Eden to a secret meeting on 14 October 1956, for purposes of planning a surprise attack against Egypt, with the Israelis leading the way, Eden jumped at the chance.[25] France initiated the meeting because it was concerned about Nasser's pan-Arab support for Algerian revolutionaries against French colonial rule. Israel, for its part, worried about Nasser's arms buildup, especially in light of his support for Palestinian guerrilla raids, launched from the Gaza Strip and the Sinai, as well as his blocking of Israeli shipping through the Tiran Strait. Thus, each for its own reasons, Britain, France, and Israel were begging for a fight.

It came on 29 October. According to plan, Israel invaded first across the Sinai, which would give Britain, under the terms of its 1954 agreement with Egypt, pretext to order both sides to withdraw from the Suez. Israel would demur, allowing the Anglo-French force to intervene in ordered to "save" the Canal from being damaged. The two powers would then intervene and claim to be "separating the combatants" and "extinguishing a dangerous fire," while actually they intended to take control of the Canal.[26] Their real hope was to topple Nasser, but under the guise of peacekeepers.

Once the Israeli and Anglo-French invasion took place, Canada adopted a neutralist position in reaction, choosing not to be a colonial "chore boy" for England, as one External Affairs document characterized Canada's stance.[27] Though it is impossible to prove, it can nonetheless be reasonably conjectured that Norman's early and reasoned dispatches, picturing Egyptian nationalism in a balanced way, were important influences in determining Canadian neutralist policy. Neither pro- nor anti-Nasser, his observations would only permit a reasonable reader to conclude that Nasser had not fallen into the Soviet camp, that he merely wanted Egypt's sovereignty to be respected, and Egypt's declarations of independence to be taken seriously.

External Affairs Minister Lester Pearson was just that sort of "reasonable reader," although more likely than not, Norman's communiqués from Cairo simply served as additional, supporting evidence in Pearson's moves to strike an independent foreign policy at this time. Canada had asserted its independence from Britain and the United States as early as the 1 November, all-night session of the United Nations General Assembly. That night the U.S. resolution calling for an immediate cease-fire and the withdrawal of Israeli and Arab troops to behind the Armistice lines (drawn in 1949) was naturally opposed by the French and English, who were joined by Israel, New Zealand, and Australia, though the resolution passed. Canada abstained, thereby separating itself from both U.K. and U.S. policy. Instead, Pearson called for the establishment of an international peace and police force under UN command. Two days later the British and French accepted Pearson's recommendation and the General Assembly voted in favor of the Pearson plan. Significantly, Egypt was among those nations which abstained. Nonetheless, on 7 November, Canada was among the first to offer its military to the UN peacekeeping force. Thereafter, commitment to the plan could not be separated from Canadian pride, a kind of investment of national ego upon which rode a new self-image of independent thinking.

On 8 November, Egypt finally agreed to permit a small

team of UN observers to enter the nation in order to watch over the cease-fire. Canada's General E. L. M. Burns flew to Cairo the same day to begin discussions with the Egyptian government about the introduction of a UN force. On 11 November Egypt agreed in principle to the entry of UN peacekeepers. But principle was one thing, practice another. Gun battles between Anglo-French and Egyptian forces occurred periodically; Israel and its European allies wanted more definite assurances about the UN force; and Moscow, rebuffed in its efforts to turn the peacekeeping mission into a superpower intervention, reported that Soviet "volunteers" were willing to help the Egyptian forces; the situation was chaotic, uncertain, explosive. United Nations Secretary General Dag Hammarskjöld flew to Cairo on 16 November, just a day after the advance units of the UN forces, composed of just ninety-five Danish and Norwegian troops, had arrived. Canadian troops in Naples, Italy, readied to move a few days later, but were forced to wait. Nasser would not let them into Egypt: guilt by association—Canada as a Commonwealth nation—meant that Nasser was prejudging Canada, calling into question its impartiality as well as its credibility. The author of the idea to use UN peacekeeping troops, Canada, would not be allowed to write its own script. In his memoirs, Lester Pearson summed up the problem: "Canada . . . had taken an entirely independent and objective position in the United Nations, not an easy thing to do given our close and friendly association with the British. Having taken this independent position, it would be very hard for Canadians to be told that their troops were not considered independent."[28] Norman's job was to convince Nasser of Canada's "independence," and, on the other hand, to help Ottawa understand just why this petulant dictator wanted to keep Canada out of Egypt.

Norman had laid the groundwork for good relations with Nasser during their first meeting on 3 September.[29] He informed the president that his reading about Egyptian history had sensitized him to its century-old problem of securing independence. Herbert also told Nasser that Lester Pearson was "sympathetic" to the economic and social reforms that Nasser was attempting. He reported that he left the first conversation impressed with Nasser, his desire for independence, and his strong sense of nationalism.

Herbert did not meet again with the Egyptian President until 9 December. In the interim, Nasser had balked at the suggestion that Canada's the Queen's Own Rifle regiment be included in the UN peacekeeping detachment. Norman had concluded that, in Pearson's words, "it was the constitutional issue (that is, our Commonwealth association) that raised doubts in Egyptian minds. . . ." Egyptian recalcitrance resulted in the Queen's Own Rifles being stranded in Halifax, anxiously awaiting orders to proceed aboard the *HMS Magnificent* to Egypt. Meetings between Hammarskjöld and Nasser, between Hammarskjöld and Norman, UNEF Commander Burns and Hammarskjöld, and between Norman and Burns finally resolved the problem, at least temporarily, by early December, when Herbert cabled Ottawa to say that Burns no longer felt he needed Canadian infantry but instead would want specialist troops. "It was disappointing to the Government and confusing to the public," wrote Pearson of the episode, "that our original offer of assistance had been altered."[30] Clerks rather than infantrymen would make up Canada's contribution to UNEF, a "typewriter army," said the Opposition in Parliament; face had been saved, but not without having been badly bruised.

But that it had been saved at all was at least partly due to Norman's second conversation with Nasser on 9 December. In this conversation, held at Nasser's El Abdin summer palace about twenty or so miles north of Cairo, Nasser explained that Canadian infantrymen might be seen by the Egyptian people, especially by right-wing Moslems, as a "foreign occupation"; personally, Nasser said, he did not worry about the integrity of the Queen's Own. For Norman's part, he lectured Nasser on Canadian history, about "the growth of our nationhood," about Canada's historical yearning to be independent; these were words Nasser could easily understand, and Norman claimed that Nasser listened sympathetically. He also reminded Nasser that Canada had gone out on a political limb in initiating the UNEF concept, in terms of its status and reputation with both the domestic and the international communities. Two weeks later, Burns informed Pearson that Canadian specialist troops would be welcomed.[31]

Whether the lecture on Canadian history helped convince Nasser to accept Canadian UNEF forces can only be guessed, but what is beyond doubt is that Norman dutifully facilitated understanding between the two governments at precisely the time when it was most needed. Pearson acknowledged as much in remarks made in March 1957 when he said of Herbert: "Indeed his record in the Canadian Foreign Service, and especially the work he did in Egypt, completely justified the confidence we placed in him. It can be said categoricaly not only that his despatches from Cairo were brilliant, but that they showed more than usual understanding of communist penetration in the Mideast."[32]

The best example of Norman's "brilliant despatches" is his 14 January 1957 cable, which he entitled "Egypt at the Crossroads." So insightful was this account that Ottawa asked four days later whether Norman would give his consent to its being shared with the Americans and the British; he assented.[33] The cable also shows that his eyes were open to communist influence in Egypt, another point that Pearson cited in praising him.

The context of Norman's remarks concerned Egypt's reaction to Eisenhower's failure to condemn the Anglo-French invasion, despite American support earlier of UN action to put an end to hostilities; Norman examined the Egyptian perception that American policy was in general cooling toward Egypt. Nasser wanted to be respected by the Americans as a leader of an independent nation that was free to accept aid from, and maintain political relations with, both the superpowers; he was not getting the respect he wanted. Making matters worse, the Egyptian economy was experiencing a down-swing, and the Israelis were continuing to occupy the Gaza Strip. Herbert was trying to place this situation against the backdrop of a secret British report, substantiated in large part by the Indian ambassador following a meeting with Nasser that concerned a reputed coup attempt against Nasser by Egyptian monarchists; and his own observations, culled from earlier reports, about the extremist Moslem factions that were similarly putting pressure on Nasser; and the growing pro-communist movement in Egypt that also threatened Nasser's rule. In short, he realistically portrayed Nasser as a leader who was forced to deal with a variety of constraining forced domestically, and imperialistic forces internationally. Nasser was a leader "at the crossroads."

Nasser, Norman warned, had been overcome by the "air of political stagnation," and had become "indecisive" in the face of internal criticism of his handling of the Suez Crisis. Trying to be a spokesman for "Third World" neutrality in the Cold War, Nasser realized that his credibility rode atop appreciation of his precarious position by all the nations involved—the United States, the Soviet Union, and the Arab nations he was trying to represent. Egyptian prestige was on the line, Nasser was "at a loss" how to salvage it in the face of American rebuffs, and surrounding him were domestic critics anxious to expose his failures.

Norman amplified on this communiqué in another one four days later. He re-emphasized that Nasser's prestige with more conservative Arab states had suffered as a result of his arms deal with the communist bloc; Libya, specifically, had fallen away from Nasser's leadership and was moving toward the west. Morocco, too, had made gestures toward the west and away from Nasser. Norman observed that since filing his last dispatch, Nasser had extended his nationalization policy to include more banks, insurance companies and import firms, but suggested that "emergent Arab nationalism," not communist principles, was behind the action. Implicit in his comments was the notion that domestic pressures lay behind the move: rural discontent, dissidence within the army, and Egyptian communists who shared Moscow's view that Nasser was expendable were all factors in Nasser's radical assertion of Egyptian sovereignty at the expense of foreign-owned firms.[34]

Nasser struggled on the horns of a dilemma, and Norman wanted Ottawa to appreciate the president's predicament. Similar concerns appear in his memorandum a day earlier, which reported on Nasser's interview with the editor of the Indian newspaper, *Bitz*. Norman's comments clearly reveal his objectivity. The interview demonstrated that while Nasser "has not shown himself to be a man of violence," his behavior was that of "a morose, turbulent, ill-adjusted teenager." Preeminently, Herbert said, Nasser is a "man of impulse and feeling," like most Arabs, and therefore must be approached with "careful and patient diplomacy" in order to achieve a relationship of "a reasonable degree of understanding and mutual trust." He pleaded with Ottawa to understand Nasser by putting itself in his "disturbingly subjective" position. The president is understandably "obsessed" with "national dignity and sovereignty," and quite naturally identifies the undifferentiated west with his European antagonists, Britain and France.[35]

Norman was building bridges across the cultural and political gulf that separated the west from the Arab Middle East; that of course was his job—a kind of communications broker—but he did it exceedingly well. Regardless of the behind-the-scenes effect that his words may have had in helping to secure peace for the Middle East, his wise analyses of the Egyptian situation had shown the conflict to be unrelated to the east-west conflict, but rather very much a part of what we today call the north-south conflict. Again, his view did *not* overlook the significance of communist activity in the region. In his 19 January 1957 cable, for example, he identified communist agitators as a potent threat to Nasser's regime, but as the empiricist scholar, he placed no less importance on the destabilizing effect of Moslem extremists, such as Anwar Sadat, whom Herbert characterized in March as "the eternal anarchist" possessing "rather destructive capabilities."[36]

These communiqués show that Norman gathered his intelligence from a wide variety of sources. He met frequently with the American and Indian ambassadors, both of whom had secure access to high-ranking Egyptian officials; he met with Egyptian corporation heads, members of the Egyptian foreign ministry, and Egyptian and foreign members of the press corps. Much of the intelligence-gathering he did himself; his own staff was small: initially, three foreign service officers and three clerical workers, expanded to eight and then, by January 1957, thirteen. His duties, moreover, became particularly onerous once his embassy undertook representation of Australian interests after that embassy was closed in a gesture of support for Great Britain. As well, Norman had the additional burdens of purchasing a new chancery in late January, and attending to security problems following a break-in in late February. And as hostilities heightened, the embassy had to cope with a massive number of requests for immigration visas.

All signs of the tensions of the times, which Herbert coped with personally by what had become his own peculiar survival techniques, namely, playing tennis on a regular basis at the Gezira Sporting Club, which figured prominently in his letters to family members, and entertaining friends and colleagues. His secretary at the time, Norma Nadeau, fondly recalls the 1956 Christmas party for the embassy staff at the Norman home. "We played charades late into the night; we all had a marvelous time, and I think Mr. Norman had thoroughly enjoyed himself as well. He loved charades and was great at organising games." She also recalls his scholar's zest for studying and reporting on events: "He was interested in everything and reported extensively to Ottawa; he appeared to be thoroughly enjoying himself."[37]

His second in command, Arthur Kilgour, who arrived in mid-February 1957, got a similar impression of a man glorying in the excitement of his duties. Kilgour recalls upon his arrival how Norman took him around to meet "people whom he judged should be known by his new deputy. . . . I recall the evident appreciation of others in receiving a call from Herbert Norman, the respect they had for his insight, and the enjoyment of his easy style and manner. Somebody remarked to me that for every call Mr. Norman made he received two." Kilgour also recalls being told by a newspaperman, "As far as I can make out, there are only three ambassadors who count in this town. There's the American; there's the Indian; and there's yours."[38] This impressed Kilgour, who remembers being even more impressed when on his first morning Norman was called upon by the American and Indian ambassadors and by the Canadian commander of UNEF, General Burns.

It may seem a *non sequitur* that Norman could derive pleasure from a posting that was tension-filled and entailed unceasing hard work, but it is not. The reason seems to be found in words that his friend, Egyptian businessman Omar Foda, recalls Herbert uttering during one of the social hours they regularly enjoyed: "After New Zealand, I'm happy to be back in the mainstream." Foda also recalls a remark made by his brother, Daoud, who was quite close to Norman. According to Daoud Foda, the Canadian, "very dignified, very serious," delighted in being the lone intellectual at get-togethers largely consisting of diplomats and business people. From atop his intellectual tower, supported by his diplomat's prestige, Norman could easily dominate. People hung on his words, he could be the center of attention when he so desired, and could warm himself in the sunny, admiring gaze of his audience, especially of the younger women, an impression reinforced by another Egyptian friend and government minister. Herbert, Foda says, existed on a "higher plane," and those around him seemingly delighted in looking up.[39]

Mundane earthly affairs kept him occupied, however. Such was the case in mid-March when a second crisis over Canadian participation in UNEF began, forcing Norman into his third and last meeting with Nasser. The context is this: in late 1956 the UNEF commander asked Nasser for permission to introduce a Canadian armored reconnaissance squadron to help patrol the Egyptian-Israeli border once the Israelis withdrew. Canada assented to the request immediately, but Egypt balked, initially because the Israelis had yet to withdraw, thereby making the request academic. But once the Israelis withdrew and still the Canadian contingent was kept waiting in Naples, it seemed to some observers that the second phase of the peacekeeping mission was imperiled. Hammarskjöld and Ralph Bunche both intervened to urge Nasser to relent, but to no avail. Then on 12 March, Herbert received a cable from Ottawa warning that a "major political storm" was brewing concerning the "delay on the part of the Egyptian authorities in approving a United Nations request for the admission" of the Canadian squadron.[40] Herbert was ordered to get Nasser's permission. He told Ottawa on the same day that he felt the problem was "technical," and not because the troops would be Canadian, as was the case the autumn before.

Norman acted quickly. On 14 March he phoned Nasser at his summer palace and received permission to call upon the president that evening. He drove to the palace alone. Late that night the two men conversed for several hours. What Norman said to Nasser was contained in his cable to Ottawa of the next day.

He told Nasser that his visit was *not* on Ottawa's instructions, but instead because he was worried about the "hostile tone" toward Canada that had characterized recent news reporting in Egypt. He assured Nasser that he simply wanted to clear up any lingering misunderstandings about Canada's role in UNEF. He warned Nasser that the government-controlled press's accusations that Canada was "imperialistic" would have negative repercussions in Canada, and insisted that Canada was sympathetic toward the problems of emerging nations. For his part, Nasser told Norman of his fears that Pearson was too pro-Israeli and had seemed to hint of the use of force to clear the Canal in his 6 March speech to Parliament. Nasser said that Egypt was tired of threats. Norman retorted with the claim that all Canada wanted was a "fair compromise," the best indication of which was the criticism that Canada's independent foreign policy was getting from both east and west. No less than Egypt, he argued, Canada was the victim of unfair press coverage by Cold Warriors, and Egyptian press accusations were not only unfair but also potentially damaging to the morale of Canadian troops. Nasser agreed. Norman then asked Nasser to issue a statement to the press which would correct the misimpressions about Canadian intentions. Nasser indicated in turn that he felt that the "misunderstandings" had been resolved, and told Norman to tell Pearson that Canadian reinforcements would be welcomed. He ended their interview by inviting Norman to "visit more often."[41] Herbert had won; Canadian troops arrived in Egypt five days later. Kilgour recalls that Norman returned from the interview "in good spirits—it was obvious that he had had success. . . ."[42]

Success for peace in the Middle East meant nothing in Cold War Washington. Even as Norman was meeting with Nasser, Senate McCarthyites were reintroducing his name into SISS proceedings. They knew nothing of his efforts in Egypt, nor would they have cared if they had known. He was a one-dimensional man in Washington—he was a communist. History was about to repeat itself; as Marx said, all important historical events occur twice, the first time as tragedy, the second time as farce. Farce, when political, is the theater for victims.

CHAPTER 10

VICTIM

I am struggling with words.

Jean-Paul Sartre, *Nausea*

Do you expect more from these avatars?

E. L. Doctorow, *The Book Of Daniel*

His loyalty to his government had been affirmed and reaffirmed, privately in December 1950 and February 1952, and then publicly in August 1951 and March 1957; the last occasion immediately followed SISS's resurrection of the old charges. But not by words alone did Ottawa profess Herbert Norman's loyalty: twice Herbert had been assigned highly responsible diplomatic posts and had himself performed in a highly responsible manner. Nonetheless, he was accused of disloyalty once more. On 14 March 1957, as before, he was accused of being a communist. Words uttered against him more than a half-decade earlier would not be laid to rest by anti-communists who refused to let McCarthyism expire. Instead, all the old "evidence" against Herbert was mechanically recycled in March 1957 by atavistic avatars, by men who dwelt in the past but who were themselves incapable of understanding its meaning.

For them, all the official declarations of loyalty in the world would not make Herbert Norman "innocent." For them, "innocence" meant something very different from "loyalty." "Innocence" meant one of two things: either the absence of a "security file" on an individual or the public recantation by a confessed communist of his "false" beliefs. Otherwise, the suspect was assumed guilty: once a communist, always a communist.

"Innocence" is absolute, one either is or is not. "Loyalty," on the other hand, is altogether too relative: one may be "guilty" of once having entertained, or even of still entertaining "false beliefs," but might still behave honorably and loyally on behalf of one's government. Too, judging "loyalty"—the gray area between guilt and innocence, if you will—was an exercise in subjective evaluation; ultimately, those who remain suspicious of an individual deemed "loyal" must then judge the judges, that is, decide whether those who rendered the judgment are themselves trustworthy.

For the FBI's part, Canadian government "judges" were not trustworthy. In a 24 April 1957 FBI memorandum, Canadian Justice Minister Garson is secretly accused of purposely omitting damning portions of the body of evidence against Norman. Similarly, the RCMP's "judgment" is questioned: "It appears that the RCMP's clearance of Norman was based primarily on their acceptance at face value of his statements to them."[1] In another FBI memorandum, J. Edgar Hoover accuses Minister for External Affairs Lester Pearson of having lied regarding the sharing of information about Norman with the United States government.[2] In short, the FBI, which did share its information about him with SISS, judged that it could not trust his Canadian judges.

And as for SISS, its spokesmen made much of the facts that intelligence agencies, both Canadian and American, had extensive files on Norman, and that neither he nor his government had come forward to challenge the Wittfogel allegation that he, Norman, was a communist. Complicating matters further, by mid-March 1957, when SISS renewed its attack against Norman, SISS counsel Robert Morris was arguing before State Department officials that the ambassador's official patron and judge, Lester Pearson, was himself a one-time communist agent and should be exposed as such. Although Morris yielded to the State Department admonition not to release this "information," Morris's considered opinion that Norman was a communist was only strengthened by the "knowledge" that he had been protected by an alleged communist.[3]

A cynic—whom I would define as anyone who has had

the experience of having read thousands of pages of "intel-ligence" agencies' reports—might argue that the State De-partment did not do a better job of forcing SISS to keep harmful testimony against Norman from being publicized because it decided that the sacrifice of one Canadian ambassador was a fair trade for preserving good relations with Canada's Min-ister for External Affairs. The simple empiricist, on the other hand, would point out that the "goods" they had on Norman were far more compelling than the unsupported testimony of Elizabeth Bentley against Lester Pearson, and thus would reason that rules of evidence should permit prosecution in the one case and permanent postponement in the other. Judge the facts for yourself.

The evidence against Herbert Norman was reintroduced on 12 March in SISS hearings and was made public two days later, on the same day that he was meeting with Nasser. He himself learned the bad news on 15 March; he told an embassy staff person, "Their (the committee's) principle is to knock a head whenever it comes up."[4]

Norman was referring to his name being mentioned during the SISS questioning of his old friend, John K. Emmerson. At the time Emmerson was Deputy Chief of Mission in the American Embassy in Beirut, Lebanon, but was in the States on special assignment to the UN General Assembly and was awaiting reassignment to the American Embassy in Paris. Emmerson was told that his appearance before SISS concerned "testimony about you and certain documents of yours" that had "accumulated" since 1951. Robert Morris led the ques-tioning, and he began by asking Emmerson to go back to his "general assignment in Yenan . . ." and his work with the Chinese and Japanese communists who were there during the Second World War.[5] It was evident that Morris wished to rehash the old issues of how China had been "lost" and how Japanese communists had been repatriated to Japan from China during the Occupation.

In the latter context, Herbert's name was introduced re-garding the release of communists from Japanese prisons. Morris then asks Emmerson, "Do you have any knowledge that Mr. Norman, the man you talked about, was a Communist." Emmerson answers, "I had no knowledge whatsoever." Undeterred, Morris reads into the record the Wittfogel testimony; Emmerson responds, possibly in order to impress his questioners, possibly in order to deflect the hostile questioning, "He is presently Canadian Ambassador to Egypt."

Morris tries to continue, but is interrupted by Senator Jenner: "You say he is now Canada's Ambassador to Egypt?" Morris's assistant McManus then interrupts, asking whether ". . . you know if he was in Egypt when Donald McLean [sic] was over there?" Jenner betrays his ignorance, McManus his suspicions of a communist espionage conspiracy; and the other Senator present, Watkins, belatedly asks for reconfirmation from Emmerson that Norman is in fact presently in Egypt. Old concerns are then raised: whether Emmerson knew about efforts to make Norman "the official intelligence liaison between Canada and the United States"; about his heading the American and Far Eastern Desk; and about his ties to communism in general and several suspected communists in particular. Tsuru's name is also brought up, Emmerson mentioning that the Japanese economist is currently at Harvard; two weeks later Tsuru will be questioned by SISS.

Morris, without notice and out of context, reads into the record "from a United States Government executive agency security report" (FBI) material dealing with Norman's recall from Japan "when his government discovered certain communist connections, specifically with Israel Halperin, a Canadian citizen of Russian parentage, who was one of the principals implicated in the exposed Soviet military intelligence operation in Canada." Morris does not mention that Halperin was acquitted, nor does he say anything to suggest that the substantive basis of the report from which he was quoting—the 17 October 1950 RCMP report which was central to the 1 November FBI report—had subsequently been overturned by the 1 December 1950 RCMP security clearance. Instead, Morris implies a Canadian cover-up when he mentions that the Canadian government had prevented Gouzenko from testifying before SISS. He then proceeds to itemize all the pieces of "evidence" against Norman contained in the faulty 17 October RCMP report.[6]

Despite a promise from SISS to keep the Emmerson testimony private, despite a Canadian government request to respect its right to investigate its own officials, the Emmerson testimony of 12 March was released to the press just two days later. One day later, Norman learned about Emmerson's testimony from the Egyptian vernacular press. On the same day Pearson stood before Parliament to denounce SISS charges, and one day later the State Department issued a statement affirming its confidence in the Canadian government's selection of its representatives, thereby distancing itself from SISS. For his part, Pearson sent the substance of his remarks in Parliament, along with Opposition leader Diefenbaker's supportive comments, to every major Canadian Embassy in the world, including Cairo. Pearson's 15 March cable read in part:

> This record contains a great many innuendos and insinuations that Mr. Norman was a communist. We knew all about these charges which were made years ago in Washington, DC, as a result of which Mr Norman was subjected, in his own interests and in the public interest and with his own approval and full co-operation, to a special and exhaustive security check, the results of which were announced in two press releases . . . A result of that check, Mr. Speaker, our confidence in Mr. Norman's loyalty was not weakened in any respect. Nothing he has done since has affected—unless to increase—the confidence we have in him as a devoted, efficient and loyal official of the Government, who is doing extremely important work at a very difficult post in a way which commands my whole-hearted admiration and deserves my full support. These slanders and unsupported insinuations against him contained in this USA senatorial subcommittee report we can treat with the contempt they deserve.[7]

Stronger words of support Norman could not have hoped for. No hedging here: Pearson had defended Herbert before his ambassadorial colleagues around the world, before the Canadian Parliament, before the Canadian people, the American people and government, and before the world. If that was not enough, Jules Léger sent a personal note to Herbert on the same day, expressing heartfelt moral support. His colleagues in the embassy likewise indicated their support. In Kilgour's words, after being "upset when the information was first received, he continued to carry out his work normally," especially after he received the Pearson telegram.[8]

Arthur Kilgour recounted six days after Herbert's death that although the ambassador carried on with his normal duties, and although "there was no sudden and drastic change in his behavior," there nonetheless appeared signs that "he was preoccupied." His secretary, Ms. Nadeau, "found him somewhat tense"; Kilgour noticed that "he appeared unwilling or unable to take any detailed interest in drafts or questions we wished to discuss"; and at one diplomatic reception, "he appeared to several people to be quite upset."

Quite apart from the Washington trouble, the times were stressful in themselves. To his brother Howard he wrote about how "very hectic" his life was, how "intense and exacting" his work was, and about the "strain on one's patience" that living conditions caused.[9] Herbert wrote Ross Campbell in External on 12 March that "Life remains hectic—I think Nasser enjoys a good crisis—I'm getting a bit weary of more than one a week." Too, he worried that he would soon have to return to Beirut, where he was accredited as minister, for an inspection of the embassy there; he had not been in Beirut since early November, so the trip was long overdue. As well, he was keeping important scheduled appointments with people like Stavropoulos, Hammarskjöld's assistant, and with the Greek and Indian ambassadors. He also had to get personally involved in untangling the public relations mess over the alleged shooting at a Palestinian by a Canadian UNEF soldier.[10] In short, his diplomatic responsibilities did not cease, nor could he easily shirk them, once the SISS trouble started up.

As mentioned, the reassuring telegram from Pearson and the letter from Léger had helped Herbert keep an emotional lid on the McCarthyite pressure cooker. He cabled Under-

Secretary Léger on 19 March in order to express his appreciation for their support: "I have sent a personal msg to the minister expressing my deep appreciation for his remarks in the House of Commons on allegations against me. I wish also to thank you most warmly for your thoughtful and helpful tel." He told Léger that he had decided not to issue a statement to the press, to say simply that Pearson had clarified the whole issue, and that "as far as I was concerned it was a closed incident."[11]

His government was in fact trying very hard to put an end to the affair. On 20 March the embassy in Washington transmitted Ottawa's formal protest to the State Department. Dated 18 March, the note from Ambassador Heeney restated that "Mr. E. H. Norman, the Canadian Ambassador to Egypt, [is] a high and trusted representative of the Canadian Government." Addressed to Secretary of State John Foster Dulles, the note continued: "The irresponsible allegations to which I refer, and which in any event would concern matters to be dealt with by the Canadian Government and not by a Subcommittee of the United States Senate, were contained in the textual record . . ." of SISS's press release on 14 March. The Heeney note reminded Dulles of Norman's security clearance following similar allegations, issued back in 1951. And in very tough language, Heeney said, "I am instructed to protest in the strongest terms the action . . . . This procedure is both surprising and disturbing because it was done without the United States Government consulting or even informing the Canadian Government and without taking account of relevant public statements made earlier by the Canadian Government."[12] Attached to the note were Pearson's 9 August 1951 press release that gave him a clean bill of health, and a 16 August 1951 statement from Pearson asking that the names of Canadians "should not be made public but that the normal practice of sending them to the Canadian Government through normal diplomatic channels" should be followed.

SISS was notified of the official protest and on 20 March met with three State Department officials to discuss its significance. Robert Morris and William Rusher represented

SISS, Rod O'Connor, Robert Cartwright and Ernest Lister represented State. O'Connor opens with a declaration that "derogatory information against foreign officials of a friendly government" should, as the Canadian protest note requests, go to State. Morris retorts by reminding O'Connor that "Canada knew about our testimony concerning Norman and *there has been an exchange of information.*" (Emphasis mine.) Morris then reads "a secret memorandum to the group." The content is not told in this SISS document, but it might be inferred that it concerned an RCMP-FBI accord on the exchanges of security information about individuals, and that Morris, who refused to acknowledge a difference between what executive and legislative investigatory bodies were doing in the common battle against communism, concluded that SISS should not feel constrained. Morris's next remark seems to permit such a conclusion. "Because a foreign national crosses the trail, must we stop our investigation? What about Tsuru? We still have to ask him about it." The remark suggests both that Morris will not respect a "separation of powers" between executive and legislative, and that he had already arranged for Norman's old friend, Tsuru Shigeto, to testify about Norman.

O'Connor tries to remind Morris of the problem: "Let us go over the executive with you and then we can determine," but Morris interrupts with one of his most telling remarks: "We operate on such a close margin, we can't wait for it to be presented to the Canadian Parliament and then wait for their decision. *We would go out of business economically.*" Morris seems to be saying that the business of witch-hunting depends on finding "witches" to hunt, that funding, and perhaps more broadly, public support, is contingent on the speedy and decisive naming of names.

Morris goes on the offensive. He "read Elizabeth Bentley's testimony of 14 August 1951 concerning Pearson to the group." He asks, "What would you do with this? Release it?" And here O'Connor explains American pragmatism at its worst/best: "I am sure that would blow us out of the water on our northern border. The release of that kind of testimony would get us into a terrific jam with our Canadian friends." O'Connor requests, and Morris tacitly agrees, to hold up the Bentley testimony on Pearson's alleged wartime Soviet espionage activities.

Morris has several other items on the agenda. He asks O'Connor to "check with the FBI on the truth and the accuracy of our evidence on Norman." O'Connor assures Morris that "the information furnished us recently from the FBI is nothing more than you have." The remark permits several interpretations: first, that Morris has been cut off from the FBI source that has been feeding SISS with information about Norman; second, that the old, pre-1957 evidence from the FBI is still all that anybody has, and that the State Department is merely confirming the accuracy of what had been passed on to SISS years before; or three, that Morris is admitting, implicitly, that he is still working against Norman on the basis of 1950's evidence. Sorrowful reality, whatever the case.

"The third thing," says Morris: "What do you suggest about how to protect the United States security against Norman. The FBI knew about [Alger] Hiss and [Klaus] Fuchs but nothing happened until it was brought out. In this case Norman and Emmerson had what looked to us like an emergency meeting [in Beirut in late October 1956] and they got together. We still do not know what happened. Emmerson wants to change his [12 March] testimony. What do we do about it? You tell us." O'Connor merely replies, "Not about our guy (Norman)." Morris answers, "About Norman too." The latter point refers to the reason for the meeting, namely, the Canadian protest to prevent Norman's name being brought up again. It is important to observe that by not objecting at that point, the State Department representatives tacitly acquiesced to Herbert's name being introduced in the second round of questioning of Emmerson that was to take place the next day. No less important, Morris was placing Herbert Norman in the ranks that Alger Hiss and Klaus Fuchs occupied, which can mean only that despite knowing nothing yet about the purpose of the meeting between Norman and

John Emmerson in Beirut, Morris had prejudged both men as guilty of some sort of conspiracy.

Morris suggests reasons for his certainty of Herbert Norman's guilt in a parenthetical comment that follows: "Morris points out that no Canadian official approached Wittfogel who gave Subcommittee original information concerning Norman." When reminded of the problems with the Canadian government arising over publicizing Norman's case, Morris retorts: "What about Burgess and Maclean? Should we clear through the British Government? What is the standard?" O'Connor's answer is weak: "I think what we are talking about are friendly allied governments . . . As far as the Communist countries are concerned, unload your guns and fire away." Finally, Lister intervenes, "If there is any more public reference of Norman we are at trouble with Canada." He then reminds the assembly, "Pearson is a hero. Right now he is cooperating to the fullest extent with our government in defense contracts."

It would seem that little had been resolved regarding the Canadian protest over the renaming of Herbert in SISS hearings; Pearson, however, had been spared.[13]

Norman's name was again introduced in SISS hearings on 21 March, the day after Morris met with State Department officials, during Emmerson's second appearance before the committee. He was there at his own request in order to clarify and to elaborate on a number of issues raised on 12 March. Much of the session revolved around his relationship with Herbert Norman and their meeting in Beirut in late October.

As Emmerson reports in his memoirs, *The Japanese Thread*, during his *first* session with SISS, "instead of allaying the committee's suspicions, I succeeded in creating new ones. I mentioned that Norman and his wife had been with my wife and me for about two hours on the day he arrived in Beirut by ship from Cairo" (four days before he presented his credentials, which took place on 31 October). Emmerson says, "Due to some kind of mental block, I could not remember how we got in touch with each other, stating that we never corresponded." After testifying the first time he recalled that Herbert had written him from New Zealand in April 1956 with the news that he would soon be in Cairo; Emmerson adds that they had not corresponded in the ten years since "we both had served in Washington."[14] Emmerson writes that he was told by a State Department friend that his 12 March testimony had been excellent except with regard to the Beirut meeting with Norman. On his own initiative, therefore, he contacted Morris to ask for this second hearing of 21 March. Between the first testimony and Emmerson's request for a second, Morris violated the agreement reached at the first session, that Emmerson's testimony would be kept confidential and would not be released to the press. Naturally, Emmerson went into the second, therefore, skeptical of another SISS promise to respect confidentiality. (To anticipate, Morris also released the transcript of the second session on 28 March. The topic of the hearing was entitled "Scope of Soviet Activity in the United States.")

In his second hearing, Emmerson recalled for the subcommittee that his Beirut meeting with Norman took place on 27 October, one day before his own departure for Washington. He told about receiving the spring 1956 letter from his friend, announcing the new assignment in the Middle East, and about learning from the Canadian chargé in Lebanon of the date of Herbert and Irene's arrival. He offered that he had left the Canadian chargé a note for the Normans, asking that they "drop by our house for lunch." The get-together of the two couples lasted about two hours, which Emmerson described as "entirely a social one."[15]

So far as things political were discussed, Emmerson remembered that Norman mentioned his security clearance in 1951 and the fact that he had supplied Emmerson with an affidavit in 1952 concerning their interrogation of the Japanese communist prisoners in late 1945. In Pavlovian response, Morris and company reintroduced the details of the episode. It was in this context that Emmerson made his only damning statement about Norman, though arguably without malicious intent. He was recalling the interrogation of a Japanese socialist in 1945 during which Herbert "made some statement which appeared to agree with the general thesis which this man was proposing." Yet Emmerson quickly thereafter noted, "But it did not indicate to me that Mr. Norman was a member of the Communist party, or that he was a Communist."[16]

Even more damning "evidence" of Norman's left-wing sentiments was elicited by the subcommittee on 26 and 27 March from his old friend from Harvard, Tsuru Shigeto. Tsuru, as mentioned above, was in the United States that year as a visiting lecturer at Harvard, a fact the subcommittee had learned during round one of the Emmerson hearings. A reasonable reading of Tsuru's testimony suggests that he did not testify as a "hostile witness."

Tsuru pretty much told the subcommittee what it wanted to hear, and made it easy for SISS interrogators to lend credibility to his testimony by picturing himself as a reformed Marxist. His confessional included admission that he had "overstepped the limits of propriety in my associations"; that he had "committed excesses"; that he had been guilty of "youthful indiscretions"; and offered the self-serving claim that "I have become increasingly critical of Marxism, let alone communist political policies." If that were not enough to establish his anti-communist credentials, he added, "Although I would not in any way condone my youthful indiscretions during my student days, I consider that this experience enables me to hold to my present views with greater strength and confidence and to challenge Communist doctrines more effectively."[17]

With his sins confessed, his attempt at redemption included the admission of knowing a great many names of people who interested the Subcommittee, most of whom were acquaintances of Herbert Norman. Canadians Robert Bryce, Israel Halperin, and Lorie Tarshis are mentioned as former Harvard acquaintances; T.A. Bisson and several others from the Occupation period, all names found in Willoughby's suspect list, Tsuru also identified; from the IPR, Tsuru named Bisson again, as well as Frederick Field and William Holland; likewise, *Amerasia* figures, Phillip Jaffe and Owen Lattimore, are singled out. At the end of the lengthy listing, he is asked, "Have you given the committee the names of all the persons which you knew [to be?] or had reason to believe were Communists?" The question is ambiguous, but Tsuru replies, "Yes," thereby permitting any reader of his testimony to decide who in the list were simply people he knew, and who were communists.[18]

Not surprisingly, the subcommittee members reserved an inordinate amount of time for the topic of Tsuru's relationship with Norman.[19] Tsuru discussed the materials that he left behind in his Cambridge apartment when he was repatriated and which his friend had later gone to claim. He also confirmed the existence of the Marxist "study group" at Harvard which had included Robert Bryce and Herbert Norman. And worst of all, although probably true, Tsuru said that Israel Halperin "was introduced to me, I believe, by Mr. Norman. The year I cannot remember quite exactly, but possibly around 1937." The portion of the FBI report on Norman which deals with Tsuru's SISS testimony identifies Halperin as "the same one involved in the Canadian espionage case in 1946." [20] Ironically perhaps, Tsuru further pointed out that it had been Bryce who had introduced him to Norman.

The Canadian Embassy in Washington cabled Ottawa the day after Emmerson's second-round testimony was released, which coincided with press reports about Tsuru's testimony. The three-page cablegram began: "Despite the efforts which have been made by the State Department, the publication yesterday, on the basis of the subcommittee's decision, of further testimony taken in closed session in the hearings on the case of John Emmerson on Mar 21 clearly indicates that the subcommittee remains in full control of its extraordinary procedures, and is unlikely to drop this case or to acknowledge in any way that its methods are at fault." It outlined options regarding how the government might react to SISS disclosures, although it recognized that the State Department's inability to control SISS meant "we need not be too optimistic of the effects of our representations."[21]

By then, Norman also had ceased hoping that SISS could be controlled. On 25 March he had received a letter from an External Affairs colleague, Frederick Palmer, who had enclosed a newspaper clipping about Emmerson's first testimony before the Senate Subcommittee. The clipping referred to Morris's promise to continue his investigation of the Canadian ambassador despite Pearson's protest in Parliament. The letter from Palmer began by reminding Herbert of the 1951 publicity, "about your association with Communists... and I believe as a result you went back to Ottawa and subsequently to New Zealand." Palmer went on, "At that time I was surprised that you were moved from New York. It was my feeling that *if the Department had any faith* in Herbert Norman they would have left him there, no matter what McCarthy and his associates might have said." Palmer added, "I hope the Department really does something this time to clear you for all time." (Emphasis mine.)[22]

The tone of the letter was friendly and sincere, but its effect was exactly opposite to what Palmer probably intended. Kilgour recalls that the receipt of the letter and the clipping "marked perhaps a turning point" in Herbert's behavior. Prior to receiving this news clipping, he knew only what Ottawa had told him, which emphasized its support, and what little that had been reported in the Egyptian press. As a result he felt reasonably secure and protected. The Palmer letter and the news report forced a change in attitude. He told Kilgour, "Those people in Washington are still after me." Thus, he realized finally that Pearson's protection was insufficient. Pearson could not protect him from his past. Norman told Kilgour of how he had written a "testimonial upholding Emmerson's character" years before (1952) and now feared "in reopening the Emmerson case, [SISS] had found this document in the Emmerson file and it had probably 'enraged' them."[23]

But that was not all that concerned him, according to Kilgour. Norman painfully recalled the 1950 and 1952 RCMP investigations and how his acquaintance with Owen Lattimore and with other "various people" had been discussed but thankfully had been kept secret. But now, Kilgour said, he "indicated that . . . the Committee in Washington might be able to reveal apparently new information [and this] disturbed him very much." Norman knew that the FBI had fed information to the RCMP, according to Kilgour; so perhaps now he worried that the RCMP had reciprocated by sharing with the FBI the transcripts of the earlier interrogations. This could be the "new information" that he spoke of.[24]

After this conversation on 25 March, Kilgour says that Herbert's behavior changed alarmingly. He ceased the practice of meeting with Kilgour first thing each morning; at public gatherings he "scarcely took part in the conversation and in fact did not appear to be mentally with us"; and "he began closing the door to his office and lying on the chesterfield." Several of the embassy staff believed him to be ill. One of the local servants, says Kilgour, was asked on 29 March to "open the door going onto the roof of the chancery building" and watched as Norman "spent some time walking around the roof looking over the sides, particularly at the corner above the garage which is the highest point."[25]

On the same day the Cairo vernacular press reported that the Senate Subcommittee had questioned Tsuru two days earlier. Kilgour states that the news was kept from the ambassador and that, as far as he knew, "Mr. Norman never learned that the committee had already commenced making further inquiries about him." Yet Mrs. Norman told Kilgour after her husband's death that he had told her "that the committee probably would eventually interview the professor" because he knew that Tsuru "was temporarily working at Harvard." A hand-written margin notation beside this remark of Kilgour's concluded, Norman "must have been in touch with him [Tsuru]."[26]

Herbert finally spoke with Kilgour at length on 3 April about the Senate investigation, and admitted how it "had got him down"; he also recalled how "tiring" the ordeal had been in 1950/1952. He told Kilgour that he had concluded then that the RCMP "obviously had been fed with material from the FBI." In this context he recalled a luncheon with John

Foster Dulles in Tokyo, during which Dulles made the point that Alger Hiss's single mistake was in not cooperating with the FBI. And now he worried that he would be recalled to Ottawa for another "prolonged inquiry" that might conclude that "he was not properly cleared" years before. Exactly what Norman meant by this was clarified just two days before his death in a remark he made to an Egyptian doctor, who later told Kilgour "that Mr Norman felt that he had let the Canadian Government down because it previously had said that he had never been a communist but now he was afraid that a committee in Washington might show that he had *almost* been a communist."[27]

"Almost a communist": like "almost pregnant," the idea would be funny were it not for the tragic consequences. Norman's concern over what the subcommittee might conclude was echoed in words that Tsuru offered to the subcommittee in his own defense: "I acted like a Communist, I spoke and wrote like a Communist. But . . . I never was a member . . . ."[28] Such fine distinctions properly belong in gentle academic society; they are the sort of distinctions that debating clubs might argue over; they are also the sort that Norman naïvely offered to his RCMP questioners in 1952 when he tried to explain the difference between a Marxist and a communist. But for men out to save the "free world" from the "red menace," men of the sort whom Grant Goodman identified as "truculent cheerleaders of repression,"[29] the communist enemy could only be an undifferentiated, duplicitous, and implacable foe about whom no fine distinction between "almost a communist" and *a* communist should be accorded. What the enemy thought, how it saw itself, what excuses it offered for past behavior—these were of no consequence.

Herbert Norman of course realized this. He felt that Alger Hiss "probably had been framed, . . . that *his only mistake* had been that he said he didn't know Whitaker Chambers and he couldn't go back on that statement." (Emphasis mine.)[30] Herbert's *only mistake* had been in first withholding the full truth from his questioners in 1950, in leaving them with the impression that he had simply been naïve in his past associations, and in being quiet once they accepted that explanation. He had capitalized on his reputation of being an intellectual, an academic, not really cognizant of this world, as one who built human relationships on the basis of ideas rather than personalities. The truth had been otherwise: Herbert had been attracted to communism not simply because its representatives were the best and the brightest in the two Cambridges of the 1930s, but also because he had become a religious apostate in search of secular figures who promised a humanist sort of salvation. Cornford, Tsuru, perhaps even Wittfogel—such men offered the intellectual vision and leadership, even charisma, that the missionary's son needed in order to fill the spiritual vacuum left by his wilful departure from his father's holy mission.

Norman had spoken the truth when he told Howard in 1937 that he had "loved" Cornford and that under his "tutelage" had joined the Party. He had lied to his RCMP interrogators in early 1952 when he told them that he had resisted Cornford's overtures to join the Party. But in the fifteen years that separated truth from lie, he had found another, equally emotionally satisfying truth that lent meaning to his life, an ethical structure that respected his intellect and abilities—External Affairs. His career as a diplomat had turned the truth of 1937 into a lie by 1952, if not well before. His Canadian interrogators instinctively accepted this; his American persecutors steadfastly remained indifferent to the fact, because in their paranoiac seizures they were ignorant of the human being. As a result, Norman would have to pay dearly for what Tsuru called "youthful indiscretions."

CHAPTER 11
SUICIDE

There is but one truly philosophical problem, and that is suicide.

Albert Camus, *Myth of Sisyphus*

But I suggest, gentlemen, that the difficulty is not so much to escape death; the real difficulty is to escape from doing wrong, which is more fleet of foot.

Plato, "The Apology"

On the morning of 2 April, two days before his suicide, Ambassador Norman left his home unusually early for the apartment house of his friend and personal physician, Dr. Halim Doss. The drive from the official residence in Dokki to Doss's eight-story building in Zamalek took no more than ten minutes. Norman arrived at Doss's building, Soliman House, on the west bank of the Nile, sometime between 7:30 A.M. and 8:30 A.M.

He entered the antiquated lift, the size of a broom closet, and ascended to the doctor's penthouse apartment. Czech-born Mrs. Doss met him at the door and quickly asked the reason for the early visit. The ambassador explained that he wished to return a book that Dr. Doss had lent him. Incredulous at so strange an excuse at so strange an hour, she looked the visitor over closely and concluded that something was awry: he appeared abnormally and visibly upset, and frenzied in his behavior. She explained that her husband was then readying himself for work and invited him to take a seat before asking whether something was wrong. She disbelieved his speedy denial and offered him a cognac, which Norman gratefully accepted. She sat quietly with him as he sipped the drink.

Norman broke the awkward silence by asking the whereabouts of the apartment's verandas. Puzzled, Mrs. Doss uncomfortably reminded him that he had seen them many times, but nevertheless offered to escort him to the verandas on the second floor of the apartment. Upon seeing that the first of the two verandas was enclosed in glass, built in order to fence in the Dosses' young children, Norman asked if he might see the other. Mrs. Doss was at a loss to understand why, but humored him. The other was enclosed in wire mesh. There they stood in silence for a few moments before Norman asked whether he might have a glass of water from the kitchen downstairs. When she returned, Norman was sitting on the sofa, bent over, with his head between his hands. Again she asked if something was the matter, and this time he explained that he had come to their apartment with the intention of killing himself. His lackluster attempt at suicide was his last cry for help.

Dr. Doss cancelled his morning classes at the University of Cairo's School of Medicine and spent two hours in conversation with his friend. Norman spoke about many things, about SISS allegations, about the 1950 RCMP investigation, about his relationship with Lester Pearson, about his childhood, about his ties with communism, about the suicide notes he had already written, and about his fears of the future. Dr. Doss listened patiently and carefully, and can recall today with precision the content of he conversation. The story he told me in Cairo in November of 1984 closely matches the remarks he made in confidential interviews shortly after Norman's suicide both to Arthur Kilgour and to officials of the American Embassy, at least one of whom was an operative for the Central Intelligence Agency (CIA).

Dr. Doss asked Herbert why he was fearful, so fearful as to contemplate suicide. Norman recounted for Dr. Doss the American case against him, relating in detail the charges made by Robert Morris and members of the SISS, that he was a communist. In Doss's words, Norman claimed that he "was as near to having been a communist without being a communist as one can be." He recalled his associations at Cambridge and the known fact that his name had appeared in the private phone book of Halperin, an alleged spy for the Soviets. Herbert related in some detail the ordeal he had suffered upon his recall from Japan in 1950, "the most gruelling experience of my life," according to Doss. He told Doss that he had refrained from naming former friends and associates during the RCMP investigation, but had told his interrogators enough to make clear that he had been a fellow-traveler if not a full-fledged communist. Herbert added that the "clean bill of health" that Lester Pearson had pronounced in 1951, following the first SISS allegations, had been "misleading." In retrospect, with the same hindsight boasted by several Conservative MPs in April 1957, Herbert wondered out loud before the doctor whether Pearson should not have played the press game differently in 1951 and told the whole truth. Regardless, on 2 April 1957, Norman insisted that he could never again endure the "gruelling experience" of a third RCMP interrogation, and speculated on the prospect of an FBI attempt to "frame him."

Doss's reaction to these admissions was to query whether Norman was a religious person who believed in guilt. Doss even asked whether he "was the son of a preacher," believing that to get Norman to see that there existed experiential reasons for his "guilt" would eventually serve to set the man's mind at ease. Doss also recommended a leave of absence, arguing that enforced rest was preferable to the ruination of a career. Norman demurred, however, denying that Christianity was an issue in his thinking and dismissed the suggestion that a short holiday would improve matters.

Nothing had really been resolved save that Norman's resolution of suicide had been postponed, having found an objective, ready listener. He chose to close their morning meeting with an invitation to Dr. Doss to visit with him and Mrs. Norman that afternoon so that the discussion of suicide could continue in the presence of the one person who would be most affected. Doss agreed.

Today, Dr. Doss does not believe that the afternoon meeting, lasting from 3:00 P.M. to 5:30 P.M., between the three accomplished very much, although Mrs. Doss recalls her husband returning from the meeting and telling her that the question of "committing Herbert" to a mental institution had been broached but quickly rejected because it would mean a speedy end to his career. She also recalls today, as does her husband, that a prescription of sedatives and rest was agreed upon and that another meeting among the three of them should take place two days later. According to Doss's testimony given to an American Embassy official after Norman's death, he later personally delivered the sedatives to the Norman residence. Today Doss recalls that he tried phoning Norman on the morning of the fourth but failed to contact the ambassador because the embassy phone number had been changed in the interim. Doss tried a second time that morning, but by then it was too late.

Between the early morning meeting alone with Doss and the afternoon meeting with Doss and Irene, Herbert met in his office at the embassy with King Gordon, then working for the United Nations Information Centre for the Middle East. Gordon had been in Egypt since November and had visited with the ambassador frequently. He commented in a letter to Lester Pearson three days after Norman's death about their relationship in 1956–57. Gordon wrote: "I got to know him much better and my appreciation of him and affection for him deepened enormously. I felt he was the one man in Cairo I could talk with in complete confidence and understanding." "In these talks," Gordon adds, "there was no 'other side' of Herbert that came out. The man was transparently sincere and of complete integrity." These qualities, Gordon maintained, were apparent to "Egyptian friends and officials" and adds, "there was no one among the diplomatic corps for whom they had a higher regard and esteem."

Gordon recalls visiting Norman on Tuesday, 2 April, with the purpose of discussing recent developments in the Suez Crisis, but was surprised to discover that "Herbert showed no interest" in them. But when Gordon mentioned the "Senate business," the ambassador "opened up immediately and it was obvious where he was living." Of course, Gordon had no idea that earlier that morning Norman had half-heartedly tried to end his life, but Gordon was sufficiently sensitive to his friend's state of mind to know that he had fallen into a very deep depression. His letter to Pearson relates the depths of that depression as no other document of that period or recent interview with survivors can.

Gordon listened to Norman with an assumption that he claims—and this is supported by the words of others close to Norman—was shared by others: "All of us saw Herbert as he had been, temporarily upset, but essentially the gifted, balanced rational human being that this [suicide] could never happen to." I mention this now, before examining Gordon's recollections in detail, because his words betray the sort of Christian bias about suicide that I will discuss later in this chapter: namely, that only an irrational, unbalanced person would commit suicide. As I intend to demonstrate, Norman's decision to kill himself was the rational choice of a free human being who saw his self-destruction as the best if not the only way to honor his obligations while simultaneously ending his personal torment.

Gordon recalls Herbert's first words once the conversation shifted from political developments in Egypt to the "Senate business": "King, I have never been so depressed in all my life as I have been during these last weeks. I'm glad you came because you are one of the few people that I can talk to freely about it." Much of what he related to Gordon, assuming as I must that Gordon's interpretation is correct, is a more detailed account of what he had told Dr. Doss earlier that morning.

Gordon wrote:

The first thing that became clear was that he was convinced that the revival of the old charge and Morris's subsequent threat that nothing would interfere with the investigatory work of the Committee was a sure indication that a new investigation was going to be pressed. He spoke of his experience last time when his security clearance was being conducted, admitting that no inquisitorial methods were employed but just with terrible thoroughness. He was convinced that his

RCMP file had been handed over to the FBI and dreaded what the FBI working with the Senate Committee might do by pulling information out of context and giving a distorted interpretation of the information contained there.

In short, Norman *knew exactly* what the Washington witch-hunters were doing.

Gordon emphasizes: "There was no question of his fearing that new information might be brought out: in fact, he mentioned with some satisfaction the thoroughness of the last investigation although confessing the harassing physical and psychological ordeal it had been for him."

What Gordon writes to Pearson next is extremely important because his words address a CIA claim that Chapman Pincher makes much of in both his *Their Trade Is Treachery* (1981) and his more recent *Too Secret Too Long* (1984) which accuses Norman of spying for the Soviets. Pincher emphasizes the CIA claim of Norman admitting to a doctor (Doss) that he was fearful of the prospect of a Royal Commission inquiry which would force him "to implicate 60 or 70 Americans and Canadians and that he couldn't face up to it and was going to destroy himself." Pincher's entire case against Norman in his first book rests on this CIA quote and it is clear that in his second book he writes with this quote in mind (the "new" information Pincher adds in his second book, based on Anthony Blunt's testimony to M.I.5, will be addressed in the final chapter). No less important, the CIA's later investigation of Norman, conducted after his death, co-ordinated with the RCMP, largely rests on a presumption of guilt suggested by the above quote when taken out of context. The Gordon-Norman talk of 2 April places Herbert's fear in context.

Gordon continues: "He did think that other people might be involved, unjustly, by distorted use of information in his file. He was quite aware that there had been in the past no bounds to the iniquitous conduct of such investigations when there was a deliberate attempt to 'smear someone's reputation.' "

It is clear that Norman understood the nature of the anti-communist beast. He rationally concluded just how evil McCarthyism could be, that it would distort information about an individual to "prove" its presumption of guilt. Nothing irrational or "unbalanced" here. His eyes were fully open to smear tactics. It was one terrible thing that he had been victimized by such tactics, but it was quite another for friends, innocent friends, to be implicated for what he by then regarded as past mistakes, or "mistaken views" as Pearson later termed Norman's affiliation with communists. Herbert knew exactly what action he alone could take to prevent other innocents from being victimized and to put an abrupt end to his own victimization.

His concern for the welfare of his friends is revealed elsewhere in the Gordon letter to Pearson. "He was acutely aware of his position in the Department and as a representative of Canada in a very sensitive post. He had the feeling that the Department might be embarrassed if a senior official were to be involved once again in the unsavory activities of the Senate Committees." And Gordon's next words clarify a doubt long plaguing Norman's defenders, i.e., whether he felt adequately supported by Pearson: "He was fully aware of the complete backing of the Department and extremely grateful for your [Pearson's] statement [in his defense]. But he felt that neither the Department nor the American Administration could head off anything if the Committee were determined to press a new investigation."

King Gordon is here describing a fully rational person in complete grasp of his faculties; Norman knew how to figure a cost-benefit analysis of his predicament. He knew of the damage he might cause his department, he understood the perspicacity of the subcommittee, he knew and appreciated his department's support, and he fully comprehended the department's and Eisenhower's limitations in influencing the "legislative" branch of the American government. Yet the fact remains that Gordon, who knew Norman so well, who admired his rationality, could not reassess Norman's death except in terms of a logic that relied upon a Christian moral code rather than the Socratic, or even the feudal Japanese code of honorable suicide. Gordon, like so many since, was blinded by his own cultural understanding of suicide, while others less sensitive than Gordon took suicide as tantamount to an admission of guilt.

Aware of his own powerlessness before evil characters intent upon Manichaean manipulations of others' lives, Norman concluded to Gordon, "King, I wakened the other night suddenly with the phrase going through my head: 'Innocence is not enough.' I have, I believe, served the Department with complete integrity. I have been completely scrupulous and discreet in everything that I have done and said in carrying out my job. But that is not enough. If this thing comes up again, I don't think I can go on. I would sooner get right out and go on a farm." Or in today's parlance, "buy the farm." A wish for death was preferable to psychological torture, to being put in a position where he would have to hurt his friends, knowing good intentions count for naught in a world dominated by witch-hunters. Peace is death; death is peace.

Gordon could not even begin to entertain such a thought, nor could anyone closely associated with Norman. Hence, Gordon tried reassuring his friend, reminding him that the renewal of the charge was incidental, that McCarthy had fallen from grace in the American public's eyes, that the FBI was distancing itself from Morris and company, that Morris himself was a "vicious little man" who should not be taken seriously. Norman, thought Gordon, was consoled by these utterances and emboldened by the advice not to "harbour these anxieties." But Gordon also thought afterwards that "Herbert had gotten himself into a solipsistic state in which he believed that evil forces were converging upon him and there was no escape." Such was Gordon's conclusion after Herbert's death. After the fact, suicide, in such circumstances, seems the result of a solipsistic state of mind; before his death, Norman, ultra-rational character that he was, would "return to normal" in Gordon's words of hope. Gordon could not understand that in the late 1950s the rational view of a victim of McCarthyism was solipsistic, although he could nonetheless intellectually admit that this was a possibility: "In our talk, he kept reverting to the evil character of these investigations and of the men who carried them out. He spoke of evil as if it were an incarnate thing, . . . as something capable of destroying life, of destroying the world. Unfortunately, much of what he said fell into its true perspective only after he died."

During his afternoon meeting with Dr. Doss and Irene on 2 April, Herbert had promised not to do "anything drastic" without again consulting with his wife and the doctor. It may have been that the discussion with them, and with King Gordon that day was sufficiently cathartic to make him think twice about suicide. It is easy to imagine that he *wanted* to be dissuaded from the act of self-destruction, yet at the same time, given his suicide two days later, it is also easy to assume that their intervention had merely convinced him to postpone the inevitable. The fact that he discussed with Irene the idea of taking a leave of absence and accepting one of several invitations for a visit from concerned fellow ambassadors posted in Europe, suggests that he seriously entertained the thought of choosing life over death. Yet at the same time, according to a confidential memorandum from Owen Roberts, the Third Secretary in the U.S. Embassy, to the State Department, Herbert persisted in discussing suicide with Irene, concentrating on "the various means of doing it—such as slashing his wrists, gas, or jumping." The memorandum makes clear that Irene "had hoped that the discussion had served to let him talk the matter out of his system."

It would seem that Herbert was still of two minds. The effects of indecision were obvious to the U.S. ambassador, Raymond Hare, who recounted for the State Department a meeting with Mrs. Norman to "discuss the circumstances surrounding her husband's death" three days after his suicide. Mrs. Norman recalled that Herbert had been "unable to sleep for days except by the use of sedatives" and that "his physical and mental condition had become increasingly alarming."

Irene told Ambassador Hare that "in view of her husband's

nervous state, she had tried to distract him by encouraging him to go out as much as possible and also by spending long hours, particularly at night, with him in order to attempt to occupy his attention and also to leave him alone as little as possible." Such was her plan on their last evening together.

On the evening of 3 April the Normans joined others in the diplomatic community at the Odeon Theatre in Cairo for a special showing of the Japanese film *Mask of Destiny,* sponsored by the Japanese Embassy. Before the showing, the Normans dined with Egyptian businessman Daoud Foda, his American wife, and Arthur Kilgour at the Semiramis Hotel. Kilgour and Foda's brother today recall that while the conversation was light and superficial, Norman was glum and uncharacteristically silent, opening up only to discuss the drafting of a telegram to Ottawa for a planned leave of absence.

According to Mr. Mounir Abdul Malik of the Egyptian Foreign Ministry, an eyewitness who sat immediately in front of Norman at the theater, the ambassador's entrance into the movie house was extraordinarily odd. He says that Norman parted company with Irene, the Fodas, and Kilgour to move alone to the very front of the theater and take a seat in the second row immediately behind him. Malik knew Herbert well, both officially and unofficially, and thus greeted him the moment he became aware that Herbert had sat down behind him. But, in Malik's words, "Herbert looked ahead vacantly and did not acknowledge the greeting." Malik says today that Norman was completely "oblivious" to his surroundings and totally self-absorbed. During the movie, Malik says that Herbert frequently emitted spontaneous utterances of surprised agreement with statements made by the film's major characters.

The theme of *Mask of Destiny* has been discussed by several writers who have treated Norman's suicide on the assumption that its fatalistic message must have deeply affected his thinking. A similar conclusion was reached by Colonel Alfred Ashman, an Army attaché in the U.S. Embassy who knew Norman well in Japan between 1945 and 1948, and who attended the movie that night. As Ashman wrotes in a confidential memo to U.S. Ambassador Hare:

> In retrospect the story of the film may have had some influence on the working of Ambassador Norman's mind at that crucial period since he committed suicide the following day. In brief the film depicted a Japanese mask maker who was depressed because, in spite of numerous efforts, he had been unable to produce a mask for a certain Japanese nobleman which carried within it the spirit of the nobleman concerned. In other words, each of his efforts ended with a mask "without life." The nobleman insisted, however, on taking the mask and shortly thereafter met his death during an assassination attempt by a rival faction. Recovering the mask, the mask maker realizes that this actually has been his greatest masterpiece since he had been able to foresee death.

Malik claimed that after the showing of the film Norman not only suddenly acknowledged Malik's presence but was smiling, clearly in better spirits, and very aware of others in the theater. Ashman, however, recalls that in departing "the Ambassador waved in a preoccupied sort of way and went on."

After the film, the Normans went back with the members of their dinner party to the Semiramis Hotel for a nightcap. Reportedly, conversation was lively, Norman was cheerful, causing his friends and wife to think that the grim message of the movie had served as a kind of emotional catharsis.

But, according to Dr. Doss, who after the suicide discussed this with Irene, when the couple returned home, Herbert confided to his wife that he saw the movie's message as a "sign." Seemingly, Irene interpreted this as a positive sign, not as an implicit promise to end his life. She, even more than the others in their party that evening, was anxious for Herbert to recover his emotional balance, hoping that, in King Gordon's words, "his thinking would return to normal." She probably heard what she wanted to hear when he spoke of the movie being a sign. In any case, Irene was exhausted from the evening's activities and from all the previous anxiety-filled days, so she retired shortly after returning home, leaving Herbert alone to compose, unknown to her, another series of suicide notes. Eventually he took a light sedative and slept soundly, though not for long.

He awakened early the next morning and went to his study shortly after breakfast. When Irene joined him, Herbert announced that he intended to walk several blocks for exercise before meeting his chauffeur for the customary drive to the embassy. At about 8:30 A.M., he said goodbye.

He left from the front door of their large two-story residence on Boulos Hanna Street, turned right on the sidewalk, and walked perhaps 200 yards to where Boulos Hanna met el Sad el Ali Road, turned left and walked another 200 yards to the Wadi el Nil Building, which overlooks the Nile River. He had been there many times, either to visit the Swedish Legation on the third floor, its ambassador's private suite on the eighth floor, or the apartment of his Egyptian foreign ministry friend and fellow classical music lover, Mr. Malik, on the second floor. Entering the front door, he went immediately to the lift, took it to the top floor where Ambassador Brynolf Eng's penthouse apartment was, and then crossed the hallway diagonally to the stairwell leading to the roof. Upon reaching the roof he walked to the east side, the side facing the Nile and the Indiana Hotel across the road. From the southeast corner of the roof, he could easily see his residence to the north.

The morning of 4 April was sunny and warm, perhaps 80° F already. Norman removed his coat, his glasses, his watch, and his cufflinks, and took from his coat pocket two suicide notes written the night before and that morning. He folded his coat and placed the notes on top of it, weighting them down with a small stone he found on the roof. Likely he surveyed the scenery, looking back to his home where Irene busied herself with household chores. A protective wall, about four feet in height, separated him from the edge of the roof. He mounted it and stepped over onto the concrete awning, itself about four feet in depth. Across the way he watched a woman window-washer, suspended by ropes from the roof of an apartment building. He looked down and watched people walking to work. He paced, waiting for the sidewalk to clear. According to witnesses, he paced for ten minutes.

That morning his friend Abdul Malik was at home, sitting on his second-floor veranda directly under the place where the ambassador was now pacing. Malik had injured his foot several days before and had aggravated the injury the previous evening out at the Odeon Theatre, and, consequently, he called in sick that morning. He sat sipping his morning tea while watching pedestrians go to work.

At about 9:00 A.M., the window-washer across the way caught Malik's attention. Fascinated by the danger of her work, he watched as she maneuvered to swing herself to the next window, noticing that in the process she had turned herself around to face his building. He fixed his eyes on hers as she suddenly looked upward and screamed. He watched her terrified eyes move quickly downward and then saw a body fall directly in front of him. The body fell face down, striking the Swedish minister's parked Volvo at the curb.

Disbelieving his own eyes and still hearing the fading cries of the window-washer, Malik groped to put his hands on his cane, got himself up, went to his door, and proceeded to the exit at the front of the building. He was the first to arrive on the scene. The face of the body was unrecognizable but he instinctively guessed who it was. Within seconds, a limousine driver arrived, parked near the body, walked toward the bloody scene, and began wailing. Malik knew this driver: he worked for Herbert Norman. Malik ordered the driver to return to the ambassador's residence; then he limped back to his apartment and phoned the police. When they arrived, he escorted them to the roof of his building, and showed them the spot from which Norman must have jumped. There he found the ambassador's coat, his watch, his glasses, his cufflinks, and the notes. Now he understood what his instincts had dictated moments before: Herbert Norman had killed himself.

The official coroner's report read: "The deceased, Mr. E.

Herbert Norman, Canadian Ambassador in Cairo, died from multiple comminuted fractures of the skull bones with lacerated brain, fractures of ribs, pelvic bones, both arms and legs with internal haemorrhages."[1]

As the two epigraphs to this chapter indicate, there are "at least" two competing philosophical attitudes to the act of suicide. Camus better than Socrates understands and explains how even in an impossibly bleak situation the individual should nonetheless celebrate existence as a good unto itself. Life, however much objective conditions abuse it, is always worth the living—"One must imagine Sisyphus happy," says Camus in the ultimate line of his essay—because he derives delight even from the endless struggle itself. Though "the worm [may dwell] in man's heart," forcing him away from "lucidity in the face of existence to flight from light," the "healthy" man will always vomit forth the ugly worm of despair and suicide in favor of rational understanding and existential celebration of human activity. In short, for Camus the act of suicide can only be a pitiful confession "that life is too much for you or that you do not understand it." This is an unforgivable weakness, a moral capitulation by an unhealthy soul to the view that life is simply absurd or unfair; it is something that the "healthy" man would reject absolutely.[2]

Camus' interpretation of suicide is Christian-like for its unbridled optimism about the Job-like qualities of the human spirit; Camus would have his "healthy" man affirm his morality by embracing horrific torment in the name of existence.

Socrates, on the other hand, whose writings Norman studied and wrote about, counterposes to Camus' view a perspective that makes suicide into an ennobling act of self-sacrifice for some larger social good. While Camus in the Judeo-Christian tradition places the individual—privatized, alienated, alone—onto the center stage, Socrates, freed by his pre-Christian culture and his epoch from such historically limited values, places the individual into a larger social context. Thus, Socrates can justify suicide as the act of a right-thinking, fully socialized individual.

Norman, as well as anyone, showed his appreciation of the Socratic position in his 1948 essay entitled "Persuasion or Force." In this essay he reviewed the story of how Socrates committed suicide in order to solve the dilemma between, on the one hand, protecting his presumed right of free speech against a state overly fearful of sedition and, on the other, his civic obligation to obey the laws of the state of which he was a citizen. Through suicide Socrates reaffirms the citizen's right of speech and accepts, even effects, the state's punishment for seditious preachings. Socrates died the good death, in Norman's view, remaining true to himself and true to the laws of the state.[3]

Norman's view of Socrates as a right-thinking, fully socialized individual who opts for a noble death that enables him to respect all his commitments is not very different from the traditional Japanese view of suicide as a noble act. One need only inspect Ivan Morris's *The Nobility of Failure* to gain a fair perspective on the numerous Japanese heroes who chose suicide rather than dishonor their feudal relationship with lord or nation. Suicide for one Japanese hero after another is a higher good deserving of praise rather than condemnation.[4]

Socrates' views on suicide are not far removed from the feudal Japanese view: suicide at its best was a noble act of self-sacrifice intended to preserve a higher social good, whether a personal relationship with one's lord or a civic relationship with one's state. Norman, as classicist, Japanologist, and agnostic, probably thought of suicide in these terms. Although undoubtedly Herbert chose to end his own life in a period of deep despair, anxiety and fear, he nonetheless had carefully considered in a most rational way the effect that this act would have on all those near to him. His death act, then, was not the desperate deed of a pessimist or nihilist, but instead the rational choice of a man intent upon defending his own honor, the honor and reputations of those whom he represented, and the ultimate emotional well-being of those for whom he cared most.

But if we set aside the philosophical perspective, then suicide becomes mystery, terrifyingly concrete yet incomprehensibly abstract. We strain our imaginations and tax our rational faculties to make sense of the act, knowing it to be unnatural because it contradicts the most fundamental *grundnorm* of all, that life is better than death, that survival and the desire to live is intrinsic to our humanity. Emotionally we must recoil from the act of suicide, and in the process reaffirm our own rationality and human nature by denouncing suicide as irrational and unnatural. Yet still the mystery remains.

It is not enough to be able to relate the preceding events to the act itself, the external forces impinging on the subject's mind, because we know that other human beings have confronted obstacles and problems no less severe and still opted for survival. So we turn to the psychiatrists, the psychologists, the sociologists, and others for a convincing explanation. We learn how to distinguish between altruistic suicide, egoistic suicide, and anomic suicide and are quick to conclude that these Durkheimian classifications classify but do not explain; they merely provide a sense of intellectual order in the face of an act that still seems to defy human reason. Ultimately we may resign ourselves to accepting Alvarez's conclusion that "The real motives which impel a man to take his own life . . . belong to the internal world, devious, contradictory, labyrinthine, and mostly out of sight." But as rationalists we grope for greater insight into "the internal world," and arrive at Freud's conclusion: ". . . the ego can kill itself only if, owing to the return of the object-cathexis, it can treat itself as an object—if it is able to direct against itself the hostility which represents the ego's original reaction to objects in the external world."[5] In killing himself, Herbert killed McCarthyism.

But is Freud's internal world in all its generality the same as Norman's specific world on the day he elected to destroy himself? Did Herbert Norman take his own life because he could not eliminate the lives of his tormentors? Frustrated in his desire to enact his aggressive impulses against others, did he turn his aggression against himself? And if he did, how do we then classify his suicide? Was it egoistic, anomic, altruistic?

Whether or not we can agree with Freud's interpretation, and even if we can accept one or more of Durkheim's classifications, are we not still left with questions that, once asked, keep the mystery alive? Why did Norman not direct his aggression outward? Why did he not turn to others for succor in his time of greatest need? Why did he not recapture his individual identity by simply resigning from External? Why did he not rationally assess the weakness of his enemies and elect to live? The mystery indeed lives on, although in the immediate aftermath of his death, the reasons for his suicide seemed only too obvious to his family members, friends, and critics alike.

Two days after Norman's death the flag-draped casket bearing his body was flown to Rome for cremation and burial. Earlier the same day the diplomatic community in Cairo had gathered at St. Andrew's Church for a memorial service. Before Irene Norman and most all of Cairo's diplomatic corps, the Reverend R. A. Stewart tastefully avoided mentioning the Augustinian ban on suicide or Egypt's Islamic laws against the act, remarking that "Foolish persons declare that there are sins which God cannot pardon . . . but who are we that we should dare to set bounds to the reach and effectiveness of God's forgiveness?"[6]

The secular authorities, excepting the McCarthyites, were no less forgiving in the many apologias offered in the days that followed Herbert Norman's death. Indeed, among the many government officials—Canadian, American, Egyptian—and the journalists who commented on his death, there was widespread consensus that he was blameless for his suicide and guiltless of the SISS charges; conversely, the Senate Subcommittee was made to bear full responsibility for "driving" him to commit suicide.

The period of mourning coincided with a hostile public reaction against SISS. The sacred and the profane occupied in unequal measure the thoughts and emotions of family, friends, colleagues, officials, and journalists who joined publicly in undiluted condemnation of SISS while each mourned, privately in his or her own way, the tragedy of Norman's premature and unnatural death. In Japan, Herbert's older brother Howard could say only, "I was terribly shocked. I loved him dearly. It is a tragedy." Sister Grace, wife of Reverend R. C. Wright, permitted grief to give way to understandable sisterly rage, saying : "They [SISS] hounded him to death."[7] True to character, Irene grieved quietly, refraining from making any statement for public consumption, choosing instead to accompany her husband's body to Rome for cremation and burial before going on to England where, on the advice of External Affairs, she remained secluded for two weeks with friends before unobtrusively slipping into Canada free from the public eye.[8]

Norman Robertson, in Rome on assignment for External Affairs, was given responsibility for arranging cremation and burial in Rome's Protestant Cemetery in Testaccio. Irene's choice of a Rome burial site over Canada came as a surprise to Herbert's relatives and Canadian friends, but her reasons were her own. "I liked the idea of Rome. There was no plot in Ontario more appropriate." Herbert and Irene had visited Rome in quieter and better times and felt, very likely, as Norman Robertson wrote, that "Testaccio is a beautiful and memorable place." About the burial, he said, "There was no service, no ceremony, nobody but Berlis and Claude Roquet from the Cairo Embassy and the very nice old Italian who looked after this burying ground for more than forty years. He had found a spot beneath a big cypress—a yard away from where Shelley and Trelawney lie, and he had a small camellia bush ready to plant above it."[9]

The lonely solemnity of his burial in Rome contrasted with the noisy memorial service held the same day in Ottawa at Chalmers United Church. Television and press cameras lined the entrance as the Prime Minister, the Chief Justice, External Affairs Minister Pearson, the diplomatic corps, and large numbers of friends and admirers entered the church. In a confidential telegram to the State Department, Livingston

Merchant, the U.S. ambassador to Canada, also in attendance, wrote that the service "testifies additionally to public interest and likelihood [that his is an] issue which holds highly charged appeal to latent anti-United States feeling, particularly in federal election campaign, [and] will not be allowed to die out quickly."[10]

Merchant was correct. Anti-American feelings were expressed not just in Ottawa that Sunday morning. In New York, from the pulpit of the Episcopal Church, Dean James Pike compared Norman's death with Christ's in his sermon, "Did Jesus Have to Die?" Pike declared that SISS had "hounded him to death," that like Christ's persecutors, the Sanhedrin, Norman's tormentors were "doubtless good fathers, gentle companions, kind to animals," but afflicted nonetheless with "the blindness that comes with power" and were guilty of "the all too American conviction that we are omnipotent, omnicompetent and infallible."[11]

Memorial services for the Canadian diplomat in New Zealand and Japan later intoned the same sort of criticism with a zealousness no less bitter for the tragedy they lamented. Alleging "assassination by slander" as the cause of his death, both New Zealanders and Japanese friends nonetheless expressed their sadness in positive fashion by creating scholarship funds in Herbert Norman's name.[12]

Outrage rather than grief, however, was the dominant emotion expressed around the world, especially in Canada. University of Toronto students, on 6 April, dressed in white sheets, gathered at the center of campus, and burned effigies of Senators McCarthy and Eastland and of Special Counsel Robert Morris. Elsewhere, the United Steelworkers issued a resolution, accusing SISS of "indecent, arrogant, bully behavior." Columnists for different newspapers in Canada variously wrote of "calumny that drove Mr. Norman to suicide," of "murder by slander," quoting CCF leader Alistair Stewart, and of "character assassination." One London newspaper wrote of the "slimy tentacles of unproven charges," while the *Melbourne Herald* said it was "persecution which led to his death." Pearson tried to be more precise in a remark quoted the day after Norman's death, attributing the suicide to "the combined effect of overwork, overstrain, and the feeling of renewed persecution on a very sensitive mind and a not very robust body [that] produced a nervous collapse."[13]

Pearson's explanation is important because it was the first from someone who knew Herbert well and who attributed the cause to internal, psychological factors in combination with the obvious, precipitating, external cause of SISS allegations. Among columnists, only Harold Greer, writing for *The Toronto Star*, and Joseph Fromm, writing for *U.S. News and World Report* from Cairo, where he had known Norman, made the internal-external connection. Greer suggested in a 6 April article that Norman "was, really, not tough enough for the kind of diplomacy practised today," adding that his "political naïveté" about McCarthyism left him vulnerable to its worst effects. Norman's first secretary in the Cairo Embassy, Arthur Kilgour, touched upon the same connection, from which Fromm took his lead, in a comment made to reporters on the day of the suicide: "He was a very sensitive man who took this sort of thing harder than perhaps most men would."[14]

In brief, as the connection between Norman's emotional frailty and the rigidity of the charges against him was being made, the public was left with the clear impression that a stronger man might have endured, that Norman had been vulnerable only because he was a "sensitive" intellectual, and that a tougher, less tender soul would not have taken the extreme step that Herbert had.

Pearson truly believed what he said: he was not simply speaking for public consumption, though that may have seemed the case at the time since, having begun the race for the Prime Ministership, Pearson was anxious to distract public attention away from this case and redirect it toward less emotional issues, especially after Diefenbaker, on 12 April, in Parliament questioned Pearson's veracity in his portrayal of Norman as innocent. But in a private letter to an old friend, then living in Kentucky, Pearson spelled out clearly what he thought the real reasons for Norman's suicide were:

The Ambassador's mind had given way under terrific pressure of never-ending work plus, and this was very important, the revival of old charges against him that he was a communist. He was a very sensitive man, too sensitive in fact, and the revival of these charges after four or five years of immunity from them was too much for him. *He had completely atoned for Communist illusions and mistakes* when he was a student by 16 years *[sic]* of devoted and valuable service in our Department, but there were those who kept hounding him, and I hope that they are now satisfied. [Emphasis mine.][15]

Privately, then, Pearson repeated what he was saying publicly. Norman had had a nervous breakdown; his mind had "collapsed"; he was too sensitive, too emotionally vulnerable, despite his *atonement;* the suggestion that persecution following on the heels of immunity broke his spirit can only be read as a psychological explanation for his suicide. In short, SISS provided only the external stimulus for the internal breakdown that was inherent in Norman's personality.

And thus, after accepting the certainty of SISS calumny, a concerned public also had to confront the tainted specter of a weak, over-sensitive, vulnerable and once-upon-a-time guilty individual, guilty, that is, of "Communist illusions" for which, in Pearson's words, he had atoned. Such is the enduring image of Norman the suicide which confronts us today. It is a strong image, reinforced by years of a "red scare" that repeatedly spits forth socialist apostates, self-confessed sinners, from Elizabeth Bentley to Karl Wittfogel to Tsuru Shigeto, who were forgiven, even praised, by self-righteous officials and a socialized citizenry that gloried in morbid confessionals. Norman, indeed, is almost a metaphor for a worst-case scenario of a red-turned-loyalist in the Cold War whose chief mistake was to forgo a public confessional and the demeaning process of begging for forgiveness in the form of denouncing his former communist friends.

Curiously it was a cultural difference between Canada and the United States that permitted Norman to forgo the public cleansing that earmarked the likes of Wittfogel, Bentley and Tsuru. In America the rites of political purification had to be conducted in the (sometimes) open chambers of the Congress and then in the always-open pages of the media. In Canada, forgiveness—the individual's "atonement" for past "mistakes"—came behind the closed doors of the East Block, where only officialdom had to be convinced of the suspect's loyalty. Once "cleared" and given a "clean bill of health," as Norman was in late 1950, a career could be kept intact. Yet despite this important cultural difference in attitude toward method, the two nations nonetheless had in common a Christian attitude about *purpose* —in both nations the rites of purification were obligatory.

But Canada, once it had divested itself of a degree of its sovereignty by sharing privately garnered information about one of its citizens with the publicity-minded U.S., ultimately and necessarily became compromised by American methods. This picture is, moreover, glossed with even brighter colors once it is recalled that Pearson, under Diefenbaker's persistent, Americanlike questioning in Parliament, felt compelled to disclose Norman's youthful flirtation with communism on 12 April, barely a week after Herbert's suicide.[16] Once this happened, the Canadian media began to resemble the sensationalist U.S. press, pointing the finger at Pearson while giving greater credence to McCarthyite allegations against Norman.

Once Lester Pearson had conceded a degree of truth to the American (and now Diefenbaker) charge, albeit stressing that Norman's associations were only of historical significance, he opened the floodgates of reassessment of what was quickly becoming "the Norman Case." "The Norman Tragedy," replete with nationalistic sentiments of righteous indignation over American smear tactics, had been transmogrified into a "case." Arthur Blakely, for example, writing for the Montreal *Gazette*, attacked Pearson's credibility in a series of three articles which suggested that Pearson may have been guilty of covering up Norman's communist associations. So strong was the case that Blakely made against Pearson that Pearson himself felt obliged to defend his support of Norman in a lengthy 18 April *Gazette* article. In his defense, Pearson emphasized that Herbert had come to regret "those earlier associations" and that *if* he had known that Herbert had kept "strange ultra-leftwing associations" while in the employ of External, then he (Pearson) would be "unworthy to be a minister of the Crown and should resign."[17] For those already convinced that the SISS changes were even partially accurate, Pearson's *second* public defense, couched in the conditional, raised more serious doubts about the truth of the matter and therefore contributed to a speedier transformation of Norman's death from a tragedy into a case. McCarthyism had come North—differing methods of handling "security cases" faded into irrelevance in the face of the shared purpose of rooting out communists.

Nevertheless, Pearson's psychological explanation for Norman's suicide was not immediately or even later contradicted by most journalists, whether friends of foes. Indeed, at the time, in the heat of anger and outrage against SISS, an explanation other than the one given by Pearson seemed unimaginable. Yet, curiously, very little public attention was given to the two suicide notes left by Herbert atop the el Wadi building, first allegedly quoted in part in the Canadian press immediately after his death and then quoted *in toto*, again, allegedly, by the New York *Daily News* on 18 April, only to be repudiated by Pearson a day later.

The *Globe and Mail* on 5 April printed what purportedly were the two suicide notes. The first was to his wife: "I kiss your feet and ask you to forgive me." The second was addressed to Swedish Ambassador Brynolf Eng: "I have no option. I must kill myself for I live without hope." The article said the notes were written on embassy stationery and "apparently" made no reference to the Senate allegations. It is important to observe that no Canadian official denied the accuracy of *these* purported suicide notes.

Then on 18 April, the New York *Daily News*, under Jerry Greene's byline, quoted what it claimed was the "complete text of the two suicide notes left by Norman," adding that the newspaper had passed the notes on to SISS. (One must wonder where the *News* got the notes: from SISS, the State

Department? the CIA? the FBI?) According to the *News* account, Herbert wrote to Irene:

Dear Wife: Farewell to you, my beloved, and to my family. I wanted so much to tell you all about my troubles during these last few days of my life because I think of you as my spiritual partner but I finally decided to bear them alone and not distress you. I also wanted to tell you before going out this morning of my intention to commit suicide but I changed my mind at the last minute, feeling it would be better for you to learn of my death—afterwards. I have no more hope in life, no more future. Please forgive me my love, for ending my life like this. I feel I don't deserve to kiss your feet.
Farewell my beloved. Best wishes to my family.

Herbert.

In fact, the note he left to Irene, confidentially reported to Ottawa on 5 April by Kilgour, read, simply:

Dearest and purest and kindest. I am not fit to live. I am not fit to kiss your feet. You are in a world apart, so pure and merciful and compassionate. I cannot live with myself any more. I am without hope or deserving any sympathy.

Herbert.[18]

The second note, also found atop the el Wadi Building, was addressed to Ambassador Eng. The *Daily News* account read:

I wanted to spend some time with you during these last few days of my life and tell you about what has been worrying me but am afraid that even in this letter I cannot bring myself to tell you [the] true reasons that impel me to commit suicide.
I have decided to die near your home. I know this may cause you some trouble and I am sorry but you are my best friend.
Farewell.

Sincerely,
Norman

In fact, the note, whose handwritten original appears in RCMP files, reads:

Mr. Eng, I beg forgiveness for using your flat. But it is the only clear jump where I can avoid hitting a passerby.

E.H.N.[19]

Pearson lost little time in denying the authenticity of the *News*'s two alleged suicide notes. On 23 April, Clyde Blackburn of the *Globe and Mail* wrote that Pearson had allowed him to see but not to quote from the Eng note as a way of discrediting the *Daily News* version. Blackburn wrote: "The text of the note as seen by this correspondent contains no reference similar or in any way related to that published by the *News*." Blackburn makes clear that he was not allowed to see the note to Mrs. Norman, but concludes his article by referring to unnamed Canadian government officials who said that the note to Mrs. Norman "was just as much at variance with their facts as was the Eng note version." Pearson himself explains in his memoirs that, "I had seen the original letter. It was very personal and very pathetic, and bore no relation to the published version." He makes clear that he chose Blackburn to validate his claim because the letter "was too intimate" to "table in the House."[20]

Pearson also makes clear in his memoirs that the American "unfriendly press" versions of the notes implied that Norman's mysterious so-called "true reasons" for killing himself, as cited in the purported Eng letter, lent credibility to the charge of communism and/or treason, and perhaps even a Pearson cover-up in 1950–51 for a fellow-traveller and friend.

The actual notes to his wife and to Eng do not say much about the state of Herbert Norman's mind at the time of his death, nor do they offer reasons for his fatal act. These are to be found in the three other notes that Herbert left behind in his study and that therefore were kept out of the media's hands. One was addressed to his brother Howard, another to Howard and his wife Gwen jointly, and a third note, left unaddressed, was found by Mrs. Norman later on the morning of the suicide. She subsequently turned the note over to Arthur Kilgour, who in turn shared it with the American ambassador to Egypt, Raymond Hare. This is important because it proves that the American government had possession of Norman's declaration of innocence but nevertheless chose to discount it later when trying to prove that he had been a communist, if not a spy.

Hare offered a résumé of the letter to the State Department in a communiqué dated 26 April. It reads:

> The ambassador expressed the hope that he would be forgiven for the act he was about to commit and hoped that the Deity would also pardon him, if indeed that were possible. He went on to say that he had never betrayed his own or any other government and that he had never violated his oath of secrecy. If he had made any mistake it was having confidence that his innocence would in itself bring his difficulty to an end. Now he realized how naive he had been and that he would continue to be "pelted" with charges of which he could not foresee the end. He had now come to a point when, if he had ever been disloyal or knew of disloyalty of others he would say so. (NOTE: The obvious meaning here was that if he had any confession to make, there would be no point in not making it now. I asked Mr. Kilgour if this was his understanding. He said it was.)
>
> Finally, in the same vein as at the beginning of the letter, the Ambassador regretted any embarrassment which he might be causing to his government and to his wife, who had been better than he deserved.[21]

Hare's account is, in fact, a reasonably accurate rendering of that which Kilgour reported verbatim to Ottawa on 6 April, and whose original, hand-written draft appears in the RCMP files:

> I am overwhelmed by my *consciousness of sin*. May god in his infinite mercy forgive me if He will.
>
> Time and the record will show to any who is impartial and not wont to make every unsolved case stick to my name, that I am *innocent on the central issue*— i.e. I have never conspired or committed an act againt against the security of our state or of another state—Never have I violated my oath of secrecy. But how the issues will be obscured and twisted! But I am too tired of it all. The forces against me are too formidable,

even for an innocent man, and it is better to go now than to live indefinitely pelted with mud—although so much of it will be quite incorrect and false. My loved ones will regret this act but I believe they will understand the reasons for it. In utter humility I beg their forgiveness.

The Department will be greatly distressed at the possible implications of this—but I trust in an exhaustive and fair minded study which will uphold my innocence. At a moment like this which is beyond the reach of human [illegible]ment and because I dearly love Canada and my work in the Department I would freely confess any breach of security made by me, or of which I knew. Too many words—and I am too tired [to write more?] woe. Illusion has been my besetting weakness, naivete my chief flaw. I thought innocence of any act against security was enough—how naive! The Department is too well aware my error—but crime no—that I have not committed. I commend to the warm sympathy of my friends my dearest wife of whom I am utterly unworthy and yet throughout all trials and bitter disappointments has sustained me.

E.H. Norman

This suicide note contained none of the ambiguity of the *Daily News* accounts, and perhaps for this reason its content was not leaked to the press by the State Department. The State Department apparently did not wish to contradict the SISS attempt to create a perception of Norman's guilt, because despite the knowledge and possession of Hare's report, it cooperated in releasing, albeit on a restricted basis, a damning CIA report that *did* seriously impugn Norman's loyalty. The content of this report was partially quoted in a late-April issue of *U.S. News and World Report* and is cited in full in the next chapter.

Another suicide note, addressed to Howard alone, has been quoted in full by Charles Taylor; its confessional tone echoes that of letters Herbert wrote his brother years before and suggests that he sought to mitigate the awful effect that his "sinful" form of death would have on his missionary brother:

I am overwhelmed by circumstances and have lived under

illusions too long. I realize that Christianity is the only true
way. Forgive me because things are not as bad as they appear.
God knows they are terrible enough. But I have never betrayed my oath of secrecy. But guilt by association as now
developed has crushed me. I have prayed for God's forgiveness if it is not too late.[22]

Taylor mentions another, separate note, addressed to Howard and his wife Gwen jointly, which "asserted his complete
innocence" and reads: "My Christian faith, never strong enough
I fear, had helped to sustain me in these last days."

Howard Norman later told me that in letting Taylor see
these two notes, he felt like a "ghoul dancing on my brother's
grave," and said he deeply regretted allowing anything so
private see the light of day. He said this to me in answer to
my request to see the notes for the sake of verification.[23]
While he declined to open the suicide notes to me in 1978,
he did quote from one in a 1984 letter to me. The one line
he cited was: "I have lived with illusions too long and I now
know that Christianity is the only true way."

Howard quoted from the two notes in greater length when
writing Lester Pearson on 22 April 1957. In addition to the
lines quoted above, Herbert had written: "There are forces
bent on my destruction— and I am *not suffering from a
persecution complex.*"[24] How, then, might these three notes
be interpreted?

Charles Taylor, who knew only about the two notes to
Howard and Gwen, and not about the ones to Irene and Eng,
dismisses the possibility that Herbert was simply offering
words that he knew would console his brother, and suggests
instead that Herbert did in fact recant "illusions which he
derived from Enlightenment humanism" in favor of "reaffirming his Christianity."[25] I do not agree and neither does
Herbert's wife, Irene. For Howard's sake she has refrained
from ever telling her brother-in-law that to the end Herbert
remained the agnostic that he had been since his stark discovery in the Calgary TB sanitorium that God was a convenient fiction for the physically ill or alienated individual,

for people who coped with their mortality by attributing to a non-existent god all the powers that man himself is capable of realizing but is reluctant to grasp.

What Taylor perhaps does not see is that Herbert Norman was a kind and considerate agnostic who would go to any lengths to protect his loved ones from the sort of pain that he had recently been forced to endure. While it is of course true that in three of his five suicide notes he asked for "God's forgiveness," he may have simply been asking for Howard's forgiveness. Whether this was the case or not, he knew the magnitude of his sin, whether at that moment he was thinking as a Christian, as a humanist, or as a humanist reared in the Christian tradition. But even if in his final days he sought refuge in the comfort of his family's religious grounding, even if he was "reaffirming his Christianity," this does not mean that he rejected his humanistic principles. The two sets of values, with the humanist most definitely derived from the Judeo-Christian tradition, are not incompatible; there is no "zero-sum" relationship between them.

The "illusions" that Norman faced, then, were not ones "derived from Enlightenment humanism," but were, as he himself said, ones derived from the belief that "innocence of any act against [national] security was enough." His naïveté had been brutally punctured by the "formidable force" of McCarthyism. And it is perhaps a tribute to his humanism, certainly to his intellect, that he understood that it was not the individual McCarthyites who were working against him— he did not name any one of them—but rather the destructive "force" that these men simply represented and, yes, served. He had not become disillusioned with man or with particular men, but rather had despaired of the possibility of overcoming the inhuman, malevolent, McCarthyite "forces bent on my destruction." Like most "isms," McCarthyism is a political force that respects neither God nor Mammon, let alone individuals. Born in fear, nurtured in hate, and acting in the conviction of moral certainty, McCarthyism reduces complex human beings to simple categories, *friend* or *foe*. Identified as *foe*, Herbert concluded ". . . it is better to go now than to live indefinitely pelted with mud . . ."

In composing his suicide notes, Herbert provided only partial reasons for his despair: his fear that McCarthyite attacks would never end, that guilt by association would "crush" him, that the future could hold no promise of vindication. These fears account for Herbert's despair, but not for his choice of self-destruction. Camus' Sisyphus helps us to understand this much, inadequate though this may be. But Norman's Sisyphean despair was compounded by feelings of fear and anxiety as well—fear of a "retrial" of the 1950-52 RCMP interrogation and anxiety over the effects on his friends that such an investigation would likely have. Would Sisyphus have continued to will his existence if he had had to cope with fear and anxiety as well as despair? Or would he not have wisely and humanely placed his head beneath the rolling monolith, praying for a quick end to life's unbearable torments?

Norman's death notes can not answer these questions, but the words of the two people psychologically closest to him can.

Irene is unequivocal: Herbert killed himself in order to protect his mentor in External, Lester Pearson. He knew that Pearson knew the truth about his youthful political "illusions," and also understood that for Pearson to be compelled to "cover up" for him again, as he had in 1950–51, might destroy Pearson's political career. Norman had told Dr. Doss of his regret that Pearson had not revealed the full story seven years before, and he told Irene that he must "help Mike Pearson."[26] That meant not just Pearson's political future, but also Pearson's political present, at the United Nations, in the Middle East, in Egypt, where the risky Pearson peace-keeping proposals might be discredited if it was learned that a former fellow-traveller was representing them. Norman thought that his sacrificial death would save Pearson.

Doss lends credibility to this view. In a 23 April 1957 conversation with Owen Roberts, a counsellor in the American Embassy, held before witnesses, Doss said, "The Ambassador [Norman] stated several times that he wanted to finish up the affair in a way that could not be overlooked."[27]

Suicide would make the kind of political statement that his tormentors would neither be able to ignore or respond to guiltlessly. The act of self-sacrifice on the altar of duty would silence them.

Her last conversations with Herbert allow Irene no other conclusion today, and allowed no other conclusion then. She told King Gordon, three days after Herbert's death, "Perhaps if it results in bringing an end to this kind of thing, it will have been worthwhile."[28] These sound like Herbert's words.

For all her sensitivity and native intelligence, Herbert's dearest wife tended to vocalize the thoughts of her husband, as I suspect she did then when speaking with Gordon. For twenty-two years she had been the brave "stoic" in a marriage with a frightened and sensitive egoist; it was always her role to provide emotional balance to his otherwise terrified existence, especially after 1950. She had been Herbert's closest friend and most reliable confidante in their last years, and treasured these two roles. She remained contented to be an extension of her husband's mighty ego, and after its mortal disappearance, to be its dignified spokesperson. Today she still sees his suicide as an unselfish, heroic, but stupid act because she feels that the one person he most wanted to protect was undeserving of that ultimate act of self-sacrifice. Pearson, she feels, abandoned Herbert at precisely the time when Herbert most required reassurance. And she points to the irony of the fact that Pearson's letters of reassurance, most needed by her husband at the time that she and Dr. Doss were attempting to restore his emotional balance, arrived too late to be of use. Pearson wrote two letters just before Norman's death, both expressing reassurance and confidence in his loyalty and in his work. On 29 March, Pearson wrote:

Dear Herbert,

I have been very glad to pass on to Mr. Diefenbaker, as requested in your telegram of March 19th, your appreciation for the way in which he referred to the renewed allegations of the United States Senate Committee.

I hope it will be some comfort to you to know that there seems to be almost unanimous public repudiation here in

Canada of the sub-Committee's "smear." The enclosed press clippings are a fair sample of newspaper opinion. You might also like to know that among others I have had a very warm letter from Sir Avary Gascoigne voicing his disgust at the suggestions made in the United States and paying the highest tribute to your talents and character.

With warmest regards,

Yours sincerely,
L.B. Pearson.

Very likely, this letter, classified "Personal and Confidential," did not arrive in time as it was apparently sent as regular mail. So, too, with the following letter, dated 3 April, and classified as "Secret and Personal":

My dear Herbert,

I am sorry not to have replied before this to your letter of March 5, which I found a very illuminating commentary on the Egyptian reaction to the position we took during the Assembly and especially in my statement of February 26 on the Israeli withdrawal issue. We have greatly appreciated and valued your regular reports on this and other matters, and we are particularly grateful to you for the good missionary work you are doing in acquainting President Nasser and his associates, not to speak of the Egyptian press, with our general attitude towards Middle Eastern questions. I look forward to a talk with you on all these matters in about a month's time if, as I hope, I am able to attend the meeting of Middle East heads of mission which we hope will take place after the Ministerial meeting in Bonn. I gather that the Department will shortly be sending you a further message on this.

With all good wishes to yourself and Irene,

as ever,
Mike Pearson.[29]

Irene privately criticized Pearson for failing to be more supportive. Howard instead wrote to Pearson on 22 April in order to *explain* his brother's death. Howard tells Pearson that he intends to submit his account to *The United Church Observer*, but only with Pearson's approval. Pearson eventually opposed publication, although by that time Howard himself had decided against submitting his apologia. The letter, which he entitles "My Brother," is clearly heartfelt and very emotional, and he tells of writing it after receiving the "two [hand-written] farewell notes" from Irene, who mailed them from seclusion in London. Howard's letter reflects what Gwen Norman refers to as "the Ontario Syndrome," or a strong tendency to be overly concerned with public appearance, a trait repeatedly ascribed to the personality of Herbert and Howard's mother.

Howard begins, "I am writing this primarily for the people of the United Church of Canada, because it must seem dreadful to many of them that the son of one of their missionaries and a high Canadian diplomat should have taken his own life; and to correct some of the more lurid touches in the 'Time' account." He then lists three reasons for his brother's suicide. "First, Herbert was sick with overwork." Pearson of course reached the same conclusion in assigning cause, but Howard is more specific, listing Herbert's many routine official duties, the extraordinary ones due to the Middle East Crisis, and Herbert's correspondence "mentioning illness two or three times." As related reasons, Howard might have added his brother's tendency to fatigue due to being overweight (around two hundred pounds) and the unrelenting heat; his anxiety over the climate of racial hostility toward "Europeans"; and his unprecedented use of sedatives.

The second reason Howard cites was the heavy burden of "the tragic issues of the crisis . . . He had a keen political mind and imagination and a tender heart," referring to Herbert's humanist tendency to take to heart the misery of all the people most affected by the Suez Crisis and his ideological predisposition to root for the Egyptian underdogs. Howard summarizes Herbert's empathetic quality by citing the disciple Paul in this regard: "And apart from all these things, there is the daily presence upon me of my anxiety for all the churches."

But the bulk of Howard's letter to Pearson concerns the third suspected reason for Herbert's suicide: "Herbert had a personal burden to bear. In 1933 he went to Cambridge University and . . ." Here Howard reveals, and justifies, Herbert's conversion to communism. He says, of what he terms Herbert's "ten years of ideological confusion," "To some people it is a shameful thing that a close relative has been 'red'." But then Howard explains why *his* truth is otherwise. Howard cites history—Hitler, the breakdown of capitalism, depression, impoverishment, the widespread conversion to communism by "some of the most brilliant and bravest men in England at that time"—to explain and justify Herbert's politics. Then Howard poses the question that so many thereafter asked when raising the problem of Herbert's loyalty:

> The question is not "what did Herbert believe in the thirties," but what did communism do to him?

Howard's answer is credible for reasons he himself mentions:

> I can say out of a close and intimate knowledge, for we discussed everything freely, and in perfect trust, that his integrity remained constant through all the changes in his thinking. (I speak the truth as a minister of Jesus Christ.) He had a passion for truth—did he not delight in digging for it in history?— and over the years honest thinking and a scrupulous conscience never deserted him. Before he was summoned to Ottawa in 1950 to be investigated, he told me, brother to brother, alone in the room, that he had never betrayed his trust in the Canadian diplomatic service.

Except for the details of his marriage, Norman had spent a lifetime of sharing his most secret and intimate thoughts with Howard—the brothers were, as he had characterized his relationship with Howard in the Thirties, "attuned so closely that you can imagine what I felt . . ." Here Howard was more than imagining—he was asserting his brother's innocence—and thereby dismissing as fatuous the idea that only a guilty man would end his life—based upon forty-seven years of mutual sharing, intimacy, upon the evidence in the two notes of farewell, and upon Herbert's 1950 and 1954 private declaration of innocence in Tokyo when they last met.

For Howard, then, it was not disloyalty that explains his

brother's self-destruction, but instead it was Herbert's fear that his "youthful indiscretions"—Tsuru's admission exactly—would continue to haunt him, as Howard explains here:

> As he grew away from communism and advanced in the government service, he grew more anxious about his youthful indiscretions. I thought he was morbidly anxious and—heaven forgive me—was mildly contemptuous of his timidity in this respect. But he did not underrate his enemies. As the reports about him from Washington in mid-March went around the world, there may have been coldness or suspicion in the diplomatic corps in Cairo to feed his fears. Sometime before his death it had become a fixed obsession with him that he must go to Ottawa again to be investigated.[30]

"Morbidly anxious" of being caught in a disreputable lie—disreputable for both Herbert and Lester Pearson, who shared in the lie after 1950—and of the likely political consequences, Herbert *chose* death. That the "lie" should have to be forgiven as "youthful indiscretion," rather than as a simple *datum* of individual experience as Pearson initially understood his communism, never quite occurred to Herbert in these terms, struggling as he was with the force of McCarthyism. From the vantage point of chaotic, war-torn Cairo, it was not evident that this most recent blast of McCarthyism was the last. Yet Norman knew enough to hope that his death might just temper, if not quell, the paranoiac force following what he hoped would be "an exhaustive and fair minded study that would uphold [his] innocence."

That was Norman's ego speaking. His ego put him in the center of history. It was inflated enough to entertain self-destruction, well-formed enough to believe that his misfortune could be addressed by him alone, foolish enough to conclude that he might improve history by putting an end to his own, and naïve enough to imagine that his "case" would be resolved by his government in his favor. But if his ego was oversized, and maybe too much a reflection of the "Ontario Syndrome," it did not totally emasculate his rational faculties: he identified McCarthyism for the evil that it was, however solipsistic this seemed to his friends and family, and concluded, quite rationally, that he could prevent it from destroying him, and others, by destroying himself. Quite rationally, as well, Norman attempted to anticipate the grief and guilt his death would provoke among family and friends by expiating any reason for such emotions in his final letters. He understood that his choice of the most self-centered of all manners of dying would leave the survivors feeling alone, neglected, alienated, abandoned, and betrayed. His notes attempted to ameliorate, even pre-empt their guilt by assuming it all for himself. Ambassador Eng got an apology, Howard got a reaffirmation of Christianity, his government got reassurance of his loyalty, and Irene got a declaration of love. Incidentally, Canada got *both* a hero-as-victim and a dead "communist." Nineteen-fifty-seven was an election year. Everything was debatable.

CHAPTER 12

"SPY"

Doomed for a certain term to walk the night,
And for the day confined to fast in fires
Till the foul crimes done in my days of nature
Are burnt and purged away.
    William Shakespeare, *Hamlet* (spoken by the Ghost)

A diplomat is dead. The world cries "foul play" and the Americans who drove him to his death react with words and deeds of self-justification. In Canada, according to John Sawatsky, "RCMP headquarters openly and unapologetically rejoiced at his death."[1] For some people, his self-destruction was taken as additional evidence that the cause of exposing him was just, that the end he met was fitting, an admission of guilt, a concrete sign that he must have been a communist, perhaps even a spy. But not everyone was convinced. And so, seeking vindication, those who killed him continued to search for the evidence that would, for once and for all, convict him on the stage of world opinion.

The search was furious in its pace, outlandish in its method, secret in its procedure. But the simple fact is, more evidence against Herbert Norman was gathered after his death than during his life. The Norman case, therefore, was not laid to rest upon his death; it lives, even today, in the extant files of almost all the intelligence agencies, Canadian and American. "Counter-espionage cases [like his]," says James Jesus Angleton, the CIA's number-one spy-chaser for nearly two decades, "are not perishable items."[2] Or as another former agent—this one the CIA's station chief in Ottawa in the early Sixties and assigned to the Middle East at the time of Norman's death—put it, "A file has no age."[3]

"Counter-espionage"—was Herbert Norman a spy? On 15 May 1958, barely more than a year after his death, the MP from Vancouver East asked the Secretary of State for External Affairs to address a reputed CIA report filed from Cairo that attributed Norman's suicide to a fear of having to face a royal commission inquiry that would force him "to implicate 60 or 70 Americans and Canadians. . . ." The minister was queried whether such a commission was then considered or "is now being considered. . . ." The following day the minister replied with a simple "No" to both questions.[4]

The doubt that had prompted the MP's query had not been erased by the minister's terse reply. Doubts about Norman's loyalty linger today for similar reasons. No royal commission, no official investigation, and no real answers explaining his guilt or innocence, save for Pearson's protestations in Parliament in the immediate aftermath, have resulted in periodic visitations of allegations of "foul crimes" against his nation and the west by professional and amateur spy-chasers. As recently as 12 January 1985, Peter Worthington, then Toronto Sun columnist, lent credence to the allegation that Herbert Norman might have been a spy for the Soviet Union.

Worthington is not alone in holding fast to his suspicions; he is only the most recent to express them. Chapman Pincher, for instance, has strained to prove that Norman "had been a long-serving Soviet spy who had faked his break with communism to gain entry to the diplomatic service as a 'mole'."[5] Michael Straight, long-time editor of the New Republic and one-time Cambridge Party member and "Apostle," similarly suspects that Norman may have been recruited as a "mole" while at Cambridge.[6] And a former highly placed CIA agent asserts unambiguously that Herbert Norman "was a conscious agent of the Soviets for a significant period of time."[7]

These are not mean-spirited people who instinctively cry "wolf" for no good reason. Their suspicions are not without empirical foundation, nor in every case are their minds shackled to the anti-communist monolith of Fifties McCarthyism. Rather, they share the knowledge of the Cairo-originated CIA report that informed the query by the MP from Vancouver East in 1958; and they are worldly-wise to the realities of Soviet espionage. The latter results in an attitude which deems it judicious to abandon the maxim of English-speaking justice—innocent until proven guilty—in favor of a presumption of guilt in espionage cases until, and only until, innocence can be proven. Simply put, in their view the burden of proof is placed on Norman's defenders. No doubt, too, they would strengthen their case by arguing that Norman's employ in the government, thereby giving him the opportunity to damage national security, justifies the presumption of guilt and the abandonment of traditional canons of justice.

But their case against Norman does not rest on this alone. They point out that the "fourth man" in Gouzenko's "ring of five," Anthony Blunt, named Norman during his M.I.5 interrogation in the early Sixties; they say that at least one Soviet defector of the same period likewise pegged Norman; and they make much of the fact that it would have been physically possible for Norman to have met with spy Donald Maclean before his defection to the Soviet Union in 1951, or with Maclean's partner, Guy Burgess, British Far Eastern expert. Finally, they allege that External Affairs, and Lester Pearson specifically, orchestrated a cover-up of Norman's illicit activities.

Implicit in their charges, as in the query of the MP from Vancouver East, is the need for a complete investigation of the Norman "case." Of course, it will be remembered that Norman himself, in his final written words, his "last will and testament," if you will, had asked for "an exhaustive and fair-minded study" which he felt certain would prove his innocence. Curious though it is, even if Worthington, Pincher, and Norman's other detractors knew about Norman's "deathbed" request, it is unlikely that they would regard his plea as evidence in his favor. The purpose of this last chapter, therefore, is to defend Norman's innocence, to answer the charges leveled by his detractors, to get at the truth.

The truth—which should probably be rendered upper-case T—is hard to nail down. The path is labyrinthine; and it is complicated by the "wilderness of mirrors"—Angleton's metaphor to describe the plots and counterplots of Soviet espionage—that surround the many different pictures of Herbert Norman that are offered by those who have made it their business to spy upon him. The Truth is furthered complicated by the very profession of those who claim to know what the Truth is: their *job* is to suspect the very worst of their "subjects," to assume guilt rather than innocence. For them to assume otherwise would be to deny their own *raison d'être* and perhaps jeopardize their nation's security. As one former CIA agent who dealt with the Norman case put it, "Herbert showed a predisposition toward communism," and whether he was "a white sheep, a pink one, or a black one," you must suspect him because he had "peculiar associations."[8]

The old, raggedy suspicions hang on Norman's back like a threadbare cloak. Again, says Peter Worthington in lending credence to Chapman Pincher's accusations, "I've written a fair amount in the past about the intertwining lives of Norman, Pearson, and Gouzenko. Pearson remains the biggest mystery. Why did he lie or mislead about Norman's background? Why did he lie to the public and media when he tried to prevent Gouzenko from testifying to the Americans? What about Elizabeth Bentley who claimed she was a courier between Norman and Pearson and Soviet Intelligence?" He does not stop there; he cites Pincher's suspicion that Herbert Norman "worked for the KGB in all three postings [Japan, New Zealand, Egypt]"and furthermore gave the North Koreans "the green light to invade South Korea in June, 1950." He additionally cites Pincher's alleged attribution of Blunt's remark that "Herb was one of us. . . . meaning a recruit to Soviet Intelligence and not just a homosexual."[9]

There is a danger imminent in taking all these charges against Norman seriously: by responding to each, you run the risk of giving them greater credibility than they deserve. Indeed, it is hoped that by this point in the book most readers will have decided in favor of Norman's loyalty, if not his innocence. Yet it would be understandable if some readers remain unconvinced, especially older ones who have over the years read and reread the charges against Norman in a variety of forms. It is to the yet unconvinced that the following information is largely addressed.

The case that Herbert Norman was a spy in the Soviets' service is based on two cases of mistaken identity and on one instance of guilt by association. Importantly, one of the two cases of mistaken identity and the one instance of guilt by association interlink. They are welded together in the person of Lester Pearson. Critical in showing this fact is Pearson's FBI file, #65–60356.

Pearson's file contains 475 references to the man as of 12 April 1957, though the file continues on through 1968. Throughout most of this period Pearson's case is labeled an "espionage-R" matter, meaning that he was suspected of spying for the Soviets. The relevance of this fact for the Norman case is obvious: if Pearson was a spy for the Soviets, and if Norman was the communist that some people claimed, then Pearson's public defense of Norman's loyalty meant that he was simply protecting a member of his spy ring.

An excellent indication that this view persisted, even well after Herbert's death, is a letter that J. Edgar Hoover wrote to U.S. Attorney General Robert Kennedy in 1963, following Pearson's election victory. Referring to "important security evidence," Hoover wrote: "Pearson was heavily involved in the Herbert Norman case. Norman was the Canadian Ambassador who was identified by excellent witnesses as a Communist."[10]

In 1963, Hoover's best evidence that Pearson was a pawn of the Soviet Union was his defense of Herbert Norman. That defense, please recall, went back to August 1951, following Wittfogel's allegations.

Within a week of the SISS trouble, publicity-conscious Elizabeth Bentley, who had been naming names for several years, told Hoover or one of his minions that she had something to add to earlier testimony. The "something" was that during World War Two, when Pearson was posted in Washington, he fed information to someone whom Bentley alleged was a courier for the Soviets. The someone was Hazen Sise, Canadian Film Board representative in the Washington, D.C. Canadian Embassy. As the charge reads in Pearson's FBI file, "This is to advise that Elizabeth Bentley stated that Lester Pearson and Hazen Sise . . . were friendly in Canada and were connected with and moved in left wing circles in Canada before World War II. According to Bentley . . . in 1943 [Pearson] attended all top level meetings with British diplomats in Washington, D.C. At these meetings policy and political matters were discussed. Pearson would make this information available to Size [sic], who in turn would provide the same to Bentley. This type of contact was maintained for about 1 1/2 years in 1943 and 1944."[11]

For what it is worth, Bentley added a *caveat* regarding this information: "She also stated that she was only guessing but that she was of the opinion that Pearson either knew that the information made available by him was being given to an unauthorized person or that he was simply stupid."[12] Nothing about Bentley's guesswork appears in any later documents in his FBI file: the spy-chaser mentality does not easily accommodate guessing.

That Bentley waited until the fall of 1951 to name Pearson—by which time his name was in the news daily due to his defense of Norman—is curious since she first named Hazen Sise in 1949. On 6 June of that year the *New York Times* cited Bentley's testimony that said Sise was one of several who "were on the relay team that passed information to the Russians." (Sise immediately issued a denial.) Even the FBI noted this in one of the first memos appearing in Pearson's file: "The files of the New York Office fail to reflect that Elizabeth Bentley at any time spoke to Bureau agents concerning Michael Pearson [as his name was rendered for the next two years], Canadian Minister of External Affairs." [13]

But even if Bentley was telling the truth about the Pearson-Sise connection, what does Herbert Norman have to do with it? The answer is: "Nothing." Proof comes from Hazen Sise's FBI file, #100–364301. In it is a nine-page summary of Bentley's complete testimony given in secret in New York in mid-September 1951. Bentley answered the question: "Did

[you] ever hear of Egerton Herbert Norman? If so, details," with the one-word reply, "No."[14]

Why, then, do Worthington and others ask, "What about Elizabeth Bentley who claimed she was a courier between Norman and Pearson and Soviet Intelligence?" Simply, the answer is that when the story about Pearson funnelling wartime secrets to the Soviets during the war was first leaked, the name of the alleged intermediary—Sise—went unidentified. But since Norman's name had been in the news so frequently in recent months, the *assumption* was made that the intermediary must have been Norman.

Hoover did nothing to disabuse newspaper columnists of the notion that the guilty party was Norman, though of course he knew better. Perhaps he wanted to indict Norman in the public's mind in anticipation of later prosecution; speculation on this matter will yield few results. This is in any case less important than the effects—still obvious today in comments of the sort that Worthington has made—which cast an even larger shadow on the question of Norman's loyalty.

Mistaken identity convicted Norman in the mind of the public, but it was Pearson's defense of Norman that made both men guilty in the FBI's opinion. Here Norman suffered doubly, first because of the nature of Pearson's 1957 defense, and second because of Pearson's refusal in 1953 to permit Gouzenko—the man who, the FBI believed, named Norman—to testify in the United States.

In late 1953 the Americans made much ado about Canada's, and Pearson's, reluctance to let Igor Gouzenko testify in the United States about Soviet espionage. Who, the Americans were asking, was Pearson trying to protect by denying them access to this most important Soviet defector? One American journalist went so far as to charge Pearson with sabotaging efforts to pinpoint Soviet intrigue in North America and suggested that Pearson's reasons were to protect himself. Thence began, in the newspapers, the Bentley story that Pearson passed information to the Soviet allies during the Second World War.[15] Secretly, Hoover was then writing memoranda for internal FBI consumption about "inaccurate statements made by Pearson [which] were quite annoying," accusing Pearson of misrepresenting both the Harry Dexter White case—White, a Treasury Department employee for whom Pearson once wrote a letter of recommendation, was then under consideration for appointment to a White House position[16] —and the SISS request for interviewing Gouzenko, resurrecting in the process the Bentley allegations of two years earlier. The details of each case are less important than the conclusion which Hoover was drawing, namely, that Lester Pearson's behavior seemed to be confirming Bentley's accusations. Remarkably, when Canada announced on 24 November that it would permit Senate investigators to interview Gouzenko *in Canada,* with Pearson emphasizing Canadian-American cooperation in fighting "subversion," Hoover recorded nothing for the record.[17] Pearson, however, then in New York to speak to the English-Speaking Union, opened his speech with expressions of pleasure that "nobody is going to ask me, I hope, 'Why don't you make Mr. Gouzenko appear for questioning?' or "When did you cease to be a Communist?'."[18]

The more recent allegations against Pearson and, by McCarthyite extension, Norman (or vice versa), such as Worthington's, have their origins in this late 1950s period, but they assume greater importance following Norman's death. The reason in part lies in *how* Pearson chose to defend Norman in Canada and how in turn his defense was interpreted by influential figures in Washington and Ottawa. Pearson's "mis-defense." as some would have it, resulted in the generation of even greater suspicion of Norman and of Pearson himself. More precisely, his handling of Norman's suicide refers to the Worthington question, "Why did he lie or mislead about Norman's background?" The unstated assumption is that Pearson tried but failed to effect a cover-up of Norman's alleged perfidy.

As mentioned in the preceding chapter, Pearson lent his voice to the public outcry against SISS in the immediate aftermath of Norman's death. No less did Opposition Leader

Diefenbaker join the chorus of anti-American dissent in that federal election year. Pearson took his outrage a step further in his 10 April address to Parliament, linking Norman's death with the larger issue of American violation of Canadian sovereignty: "The issue before us . . . is not only the tragedy of one man, victimized by slanderous procedures in another country and unable to defend himself against them. There is the broader question of principle involved—the right, to say nothing of the propriety, of an agency of a foreign government to intervene in our affairs in such a way as to harass one of our citizens who held a responsible and important position in the service of our Government."[19]

Pearson was prepared to practise what he was preaching: he told Parliament that earlier in the day the Canadian ambassador to Washington had delivered a note of protest that threatened "not to supply security information concerning Canadian citizens to any United States Government Agency" unless assurances came from the American executive branch that all such information would in the future be withheld from "any committee, body or organisation over which the Executive Branch of the United States Government has no executive control. . . ."[20]

This may have been a political maneuver on Pearson's part. On 6 April Diefenbaker told Parliament, "let us once and for all tell the United States that jurisdiction of these Senate Committees is in the U.S. It does not take in Canadians. Let us tell Americans they have no business condemning Canadians." A "confidential" telegram from the American Embassy in Ottawa to the State Department saw Pearson's 10 April threat to withhold security information as "meeting political exigencies" and trying to take "the wind from opposition sails."

But if Pearson had won the first round, Diefenbaker won the second and more important. On 11 April, Diefenbaker pointed out that in 1951, when Norman was first named by SISS, "instead of the Canadian Government standing up and asking for proof rather than suspicion, it took the action of transferring Mr. Norman from the United Nations to far-off

New Zealand." Pearson reacted on 12 April, or rather over-reacted by offering more information about Norman than he ever had before. Admitting he was departing from normal practice, he said that "Mr. Norman as a university student many years ago was known to have associated quite openly in university circles with persons who were thought to be communists or who appeared to behave like communists," but then went on to reassert his confidence in Norman's loyalty.[21]

In being open, fair, and honest, Pearson opened the door for Diefenbaker to charge in: the Opposition leader asked whether the SISS allegations "were untrue and unjustified and have no basis in fact?" Pearson reasserted Norman's loyalty, and Diefenbaker correctly pointed out, ". . . the answer is an equivocal one" and with this he begins to question whether Pearson's 10 April threat to withhold security information from the U.S. was wise.[22]

More than enough had been said. Within days editorial opinion began to change. The *Globe and Mail* wrote about "The Pearson Case" following the minister's subsequent admission that some of the information used by SISS was of Canadian origin; and a *Montreal Gazette* writer, Arthur Blakely, attacked Pearson for lack of candor about Norman's youthful associations, prompting the minister to publish embarrassing clarifications in that newspaper. The U.S. ambassador in Ottawa told it as it was on 15 April in a confidential telegram: "Believe Pearson's improvised and shaky handling of the debate on Norman Case . . . has developed nagging doubts in Canadian public's mind as to validity government's expressed faith in Norman. . . . It appears now that the government in its anxiety to assuage public indignation over the Norman case, and to counter opposition exploitation of issue in election campaign, has been placed by opposition in position of seeming protest too much." Smugly, it seems, the American ambassador concluded, ". . . opposition criticism of government for overly harsh attitude toward US in this case has put government on defensive and will tend to make Norman case *opposition versus government* issue rather than

Canada versus US issue." [23] (Emphasis mine.) In short, Diefenbaker's Opposition won, as did the U.S.; Pearson lost, as did Herbert Norman's short-lived reputation as the victim of a smear campaign. Less than a month later, the American ambassador cabled home: "Norman affair has virtually disappeared from Canadian press" and observes, "Some editorials contained overtones of regret for previous strong anti-US attitudes." And finally, "Government itself having made damaging admissions regarding Norman past more eager than ever to let matter rest." He noted the forthcoming election, the 10 June election which, as it turned out, Diefenbaker won handily.[24]

Thus, Pearson did not lie or mislead the public about Herbert Norman in 1957—that he did in 1951 by withholding information that did not, in his opinion, pertain any longer to the question of Norman's loyalty; rather, he was too honest following Herbert's death. He had provided one piece of uninterpreted data about Norman's youth that, even in the waning years of McCarthyism, was sufficient in the public's mind to cause doubt about Norman's loyalty. Pearson did not seem to understand that the intelligent distinction he was able to make between past "guilt" of adhering to communism and present loyalty to government was incomprehensible to many. Pearson's mistake, Herbert's loss. And for spy-chasers everywhere, the whole affair smelled of a bungled cover-up.

But assume for the moment that Pearson was, as Elizabeth Bentley once put it, "simply stupid" about the realities of the communists' mode of operations, that Pearson's intellectual distinctions were contradicted by actual "mole-ish" Soviet-sponsored infiltration by characters like Norman. This is the Pincher/Worthington claim, that Herbert dutifully carried out the Soviet grand design while serving as a diplomat in Japan, New Zealand, and Egypt. In order to respond, it is necessary to re-examine previously offered evidence in this suspicious light.

How, first, might the case be made that Norman served the Soviets while posted in Japan? Spy-chasers would point out that in his first tour of duty, 1940–42, when he served as a language officer, he maintained his links with the "communist front" organization, the IPR; that in his second tour of Japan duty, late 1945 to early 1946, when he worked for Occupation counter-intelligence, he assisted in the release of communists; and that in his last tour, as Head of the Liaison Mission, he subtly tried to influence Canadian policy against U.S.-designed Occupation reform and, more damning yet, passed on information to the Soviets that led to the North Korean invasion of the South.

Information given in earlier chapters refutes such a claim. Herbert never tried to conceal his ongoing ties with IPR; throughout the Forties he published with External's permission some of his most important scholarly work under IPR auspices; furthermore, he openly attended two of their international congresses during this decade and he helped to re-establish the Japan branch of the IPR after the war. He showed no signs at all of trying to hide his IPR connections, institutional and personal, until, that is, he was named in the course of the 1951 Senate hearings on the IPR; only then, as he told C. B. Fahs, did he try to distance himself from the "doubtful elements" in the organization.[25]

About Herbert's role in releasing Japanese communists in October 1945, it need only be repeated that he did so on MacArthur's orders, albeit with great conviction in the justice of the order, and that this episode only became an element of suspicion once Occupation authorities "reversed [the] course" of democratic reform and began suppressing the Japanese communist movement. In General Willoughby's mind, Norman's role in the release was sufficient to indict him for espionage.

There is no doubt about the third, Japan-related charge: Herbert did try to influence Ottawa's thinking on Occupation policy, but, as I have shown, Herbert's dispatches to Ottawa consistently reflected a bias toward democratization, which was, after all, one of the central stated goals of the Occupation and of official Canadian policy. That his views, and Ottawa's, did not change when Occupation policy changed to accommodate Cold War fears of international communism

reflects a consistent belief in the strength of open and democratic nations to better withstand the communist appeal.

This latter observation partly explains how Herbert could
contradictorily both support censorship of the Japanese communist press and criticize the suspension of civil liberties once
the Korean War began. The contradiction is not unusual for
liberals, who necessarily stand in the middle of the ideological
spectrum and find themselves forever trying to effect reasonable compromises between the polar appeals of social justice
and conservative notions of law and order. War simply ac-
centuates the contrasting appeals, forcing liberals like Norman to hope that the suspension of liberty will be as short-
lived as the war itself, knowing in their hearts that the best
long-term strategy in combating communism is individual
freedom.

Of course, this view of "Norman the liberal" hardly squares
with the charge that he helped push the "green light" button
for the North Korean invasion of the South in June 1950. If
this charge is believed, then it is necessary to see his support
for censoring the Japanese communist press as a duplicitous
ruse for hiding his treasonous behavior. Those who believe
this will point to volume two of Pearson's memoirs in which
he recounts his and Herbert's meeting with MacArthur in
Tokyo in early February 1950, when this "most imperial,
proconsular figure," in Pearson's words, privately told the
two Canadians that Korea "was not vital to our security."[26]
Conspiracy theorists would have it that Norman passed this
most remarkable statement on to the Russians, who then
could, in full confidence and without fear of American re-
tribution, unleash the North Koreans. But as pointed out,
the American Secretary of State was then publicly saying
about the insignificance of Korea for western security what
MacArthur was uttering *privately* to Norman and Pearson.
In short, the Soviets need not have relied on "intelligence-
gathering" by Norman; they had only to read the American
newspapers to get that kind of information. And, quite likely,
for secret confirmation they had only to rely on one of their
real moles, Donald Maclean or Guy Burgess. Hence, even if

it is granted that Herbert Norman had both motive and opportunity to betray his nation, the deed would have been at best unnecessary, at worst, redundant.

But might not he have worked to undermine the western alliance while serving in New Zealand? Not according to his dispatches. Lengthy reports on Samoan culture and speeches to university graduates about the virtues of studying East Asia, and queries to Pearson regarding his uncertain future with External, even hints that he might resign and begin an academic career—these are hardly the stuff that spies are made of.

But the Middle East is a different story altogether. Hotbed of international intrigue, Soviet penetration, emergent Arab nationalism, and sometime host to the likes of Kim Philby and Donald Maclean, the Middle East presented conditions that were ripe for a reputed Soviet spy to alter world political forces in favor of international communism. Yet it has been shown through Norman's dispatches, his criticism of Nasser, Emmerson's recounting of the Beirut meeting between the two men *and* their wives, and Norman's indefatigable efforts to defuse the Suez Crisis, that he had indeed earned the high words of praise that Pearson used to describe his work in Egypt.

What about the CIA report that cast "reasonable doubt" on Norman's loyalty? The report, or at least that part quoted by SISS in treating "The Norman Case," reads: "The CIA has a file on E. Herbert Norman which contains a dispatch from Cairo dated in April, which dispatch puts its source as the most reliable that it has. The dispatch says that the night before Norman plunged to destruction he had dinner with a doctor. He told the doctor that he was afraid that Prime Minister St. Laurent was not standing behind him, that he was afraid there was going to be a Royal Commission inquiry, and that if he were called he would have to implicate 60 or 70 Americans and Canadians and that he couldn't face up to it and that he was going to destroy himself."[27]

Errors or omissions in the report first: the "doctor" is clearly Doss; Norman did *not* have dinner with him the night before his death; according to Doss, in 1984, and in his interview with the American ambassador in 1957, nothing was ever said about St. Laurent or a "Royal Commission inquiry"; nor anything about implicating "60 or 70 Americans and Canadians." To repeat, in one of his suicide notes, Norman said that he *hoped* some sort of official investigation would take place and would exonerate him. What is accurate in the CIA report is that he did discuss his plight with the doctor, that he did eat dinner the night before his suicide, and that he had professed his intent to kill himself. What is very debatable about the CIA report is his alleged motive for suicide, i.e., whether fearing his own exposure and that of friends drove him to self-destruction, or whether, as argued, for a multitude of reasons, self-interested as well as other-interested, he chose to put a decisive end to his personal torment in a way "that could not be overlooked."

What is not debatable is that SISS, which quoted the CIA document, decided on the meanest possible motive for self-destruction. An internal SISS memorandum written shortly after Norman's death shows this much. On a request from SISS legal counsel, Robert Morris, research director Benjamin Mandel found a "legal precedent" which showed that only a guilty man would kill himself. The case, which dated back to 1830, was tried in Salem, Massachusetts, site of earlier witch trials, and was entitled *Commonwealth v. John Francis Knapp and Commonwealth v. Joseph Jenkins Knapp.* Prosecuting attorney was none other than Daniel Webster. The case centered around the murder conspiracy of the Knapp brothers in league with one Richard Croninshield in the killing of "Captain White, a respected member of the community of Salem." As the trial began, Croninshield committed suicide, so Webster's task was to convince the jury that Croninshield killed himself only to escape prosecution. Webster argued, "An attempt at suicide may be construed as an attempt to flee and escape forever from the temporal consequences of one's misdeeds." There is, Webster argued, "No refuge from confession but suicide, and suicide is confession." Suffice it to add Webster won the case.[28]

But the SISS did not rest its case against Norman on legal precedent alone. In a secret document never made public, SISS constructed a chart showing the "parallel . . . careers of Norman, [John Stewart] Service, Emmerson, [George] Atcheson [MacArthur's State Department adviser in the Occupation], [John Carter] Vincent, and [John Paton] Davies," all "far eastern experts" whom the notorious pro-Nationalist "China Lobby" had singled out as responsible for the "loss" of China to communism. Morris was convinced that a conspiracy at the highest levels of the Canadian and American governments had placed these same experts in the Middle East "just before the Communist advances there" and that Pearson was involved. Unfortunately for Morris, the chart showed that their careers were anything but "parallel," and so the disappointing results were never made public.[29]

Today Morris is as convinced as he was then of Norman's guilt as a spy for the Soviet Union and cites the CIA memorandum quoted above as crucial evidence against Norman. Difficult as it is to reject totally the high degree of confidence he places in this dispatch, his Websterian tortured logic notwithstanding, countless hours were spent by me in tracking down its origins. Efforts took me to Cairo and thence to several of the CIA officers who served there in 1957. Two different prominent Egyptians, one of whom was Dr. Halim Doss, the "doctor" referred to in the CIA dispatch, confirmed that there were at least three CIA officers planted in the American Embassy in Cairo, one of whom lived on the bottom floor of the Doss apartment building and was a close acquaintance of the doctor. His name is Charles "Chuck" Cremeans. Cremeans writes, "I can't remember when it was that I was told the theory that he [Norman] had been in some way involved with the Communist movement and had feared the CIA knew of it and might expose him. It probably was Halim Doss who told me this. I never heard this story from anyone else, as far as I can recall. A great deal that was unexplained in Cairo in those days was attributed to the CIA in one way or another."[30] Whether it was Cremeans who spoke with Doss, or whether it was Richard Klise or Robert

Stookey, both identified as CIA case officers in Cairo in April 1957, working under the guise of foreign service officers, the doctor's report on the reasons for Norman's suicide was mangled in transmission to Washington, as Cremeans' testimony suggests when contrasted with either the American ambassador's report on Norman's death (see the preceding chapter) or Doss's own testimony to me in 1984. That the dispatch was accurately quoted in the SISS report is beyond doubt— the CIA counter-intelligence officer in Langley, Virginia, who looked after the Norman case has verified this much—but as his confidential testimony shows beyond a reasonable doubt, what the dispatch said was erroneous as he, too, admits that he was under the impression that Norman uttered his fear of a royal commission investigation to the doctor over dinner the night before his death.[31] In fact, only Arthur Kilgour Mrs. Norman, and the Fodas had been present.

It is possible, of course, that Norman had unwittingly expressed his fears at a dinner party at which Cremeans was present several evenings before his suicide, and that the report transmitted to Washington was simply mistaken about the time of Norman's admission and not about its content. But, then, why did the American ambassador to Cairo, whose report was based on extensive interviewing of Norman acquaintances, not correct the mistake? It thus appears that Cremeans or one of his colleagues reported second- or perhaps even third-hand information, based on "the theory that Norman had been involved with the Communist movement and had feared the CIA knew of it and might expose him." It is well to remember that the CIA's business in Cairo, as elsewhere, was to report on rumors and suspicions, and not necessarily to confirm their accuracy. Too, assuming that CIA officers in Cairo thought as Morris did, and believed that suicide is tantamount to guilt, reporting what they had *heard* from Doss or anyone else was their responsibility. A "reasonable doubt" had, after all, existed, and the dead Norman would never be able to refute their allegations.

Indeed, for those people who were inclined to see Soviet advances as a result of treachery within the American or

Canadian foreign service establishment, Herbert Norman's name served as a convenient foil in the years that followed. Since he was never really cleared, since Pearson's protestations of Norman's innocence quickly lost credibility since Diefenbaker, after winning the 1957 election, backed away from the case and the principles of sovereignty that it had raised, since the principal force that had destroyed Norman, the Cold War, remained very much alive, and since for intelligence agencies cases like his "have no age," in the succeeding years Norman's name periodically popped up in the news, or his case was secretly re-examined by counter-espionage people, whenever Canada or its representatives were linked with American (or British) Cold War concerns.

A year after his death, for example, when SISS released its annual report which named Robert Bryce as the person who introduced Norman and Tsuru at Harvard, the Norman case was briefly resurrected, as was the same sort of public furor. This time, however, it did not last. In May 1958, Bryce was secretary to the Diefenbaker Cabinet and Clerk of the Privy Council, a highly valued public servant who was not about to be sacrificed to one of the last of the McCarthyite ritual slanderings. Appropriately, the Diefenbaker government and the Canadian press expressed outrage that yet again the American executive branch was permitting SISS to defame another Canadian official so soon after the Norman imbroglio. External Affairs Minister Smith protested in the House of Commons on 14 May against such "innuendos against Canadian citizens," Bryce quickly declared that he had nothing to hide, and the government reminded the Americans of the 10 April 1957 note that threatened the withholding of security information. But this time around, both nations were anxious to avoid a pitiful repeat performance.

SISS defended itself by citing, among other things, the Cairo CIA dispatch on Norman as a means to justify its recent report on Norman, and emphasized that Bryce was only a "sideshow" to the whole affair. Indeed he was. As a 14 May 1958 FBI memorandum makes clear, the FBI did not even realize who Bryce was or the high position he held, nor did SISS itself. The memo's source is SISS counsel, Jay Sourwine; and the memo is addressed to Associate Director of the FBI, Clyde Tolson. The memo expresses surprise that mention of Bryce's name "has caused quite a storm in Canada . . . it turns out that Bryce was [sic] secretary to the Canadian cabinet."[32]

That the "storm" was of short duration, however, can be attributed to behind-the-scenes discussions between Canadian ambassador to the U.S., Norman Robertson, and State Department officials. A Mr. Jandrey of State met with Robertson on 15 May and "expressed the hope that this matter would not attract great attention in the Canadian press and would die down in a matter of days. He felt that its rapid fading from public attention would be the best thing that could happen." Robertson apparently agreed, but also asked whether State "was in a position to offer an apology." Jandrey, the record shows, did not reply.[33]

With the defusing of the "Bryce Affair," the Norman case ceased to attract public attention. For the next twenty years, virtually nothing about Herbert Norman was mentioned in the mainstream press; one had to go to radical right-wing publications to read anything. Commander William Guy Carr wrote *Red Fog Over America* in 1960, in which he tried to connect Norman with "the continuing Luciferian conspiracy" and something called "the order and sect of the Illuminati."[34] But in 1968 onetime SISS counsel William Rusher wrote *Special Counsel,* an embarrassingly effusive love fest for people like Robert Morris and Benjamin Mandel of SISS. He added no new information but did offer nasty speculation. Referring to the accusation that SISS's actions motivated Norman's suicide, he suggested that "as a Communist, Norman might (for all we knew at that moment) have had a dozen different reasons to commit suicide—blackmail, for instance, or imminent danger of exposure as a spy—that had nothing whatever to do with the actions of our Subcommittee." Just as damning, Rusher lends credence to the speculation that Herbert Norman was the "Soviet spy" identified by Elizabeth Bentley who fed wartime secrets to the Kremlin.[35]

This latter allegation was not new, of course. As Rusher

himself reports, it was first reported just three days before Norman ended his life, but then his name was not mentioned. Rusher simply assumed that it was Norman, not Hazen Sise, who had been named by Bentley. But in 1966, Conservative MP Gordon Churchill retrieved the story in order to defend Diefenbaker's handling of the 1960 Sevigny-Munsinger case. (Diefenbaker's Associate Minister of Defense, Pierre Sevigny, had a sexual relationship with Gerda Munsinger, a Montreal prostitute with alleged underworld and espionage connections.) Tit for tat, the Conservatives could as easily use a so-called security case like Herbert Norman's in order to discredit Liberal criticism. In this case at least, the FBI's assessment of the incident was correct. The agent in Ottawa reported to Hoover that in dredging up the Norman case, the Conservatives had effectively stonewalled the Liberals' attempt to embarrass the Conservatives: "It was the consensus of persons talked to that the members of Parliament will not be in any mood for further mudslinging. . . ."[36]

Neither, as it turns out, was the public exposed to "further mudslinging" of the sort that had left Herbert Norman's name dirtied for more than a decade after this last incident. What dirt that was flung thereafter all happened secretly, and it all concerned the question of whether Herbert Norman had been a Soviet "mole."

First made public by Chapman Pincher, the claim that Norman was a mole rested largely on a statement allegedly made by Sir Anthony Blunt sometime between 1964 and 1972, when he was being questioned by two M.I.5 officers, Arthur Martin and Peter Wright.[37] Blunt's reputed testimony against Norman should be placed in the larger context of the other claims Pincher makes in supporting the allegation that Norman had been recruited by the KGB. Pincher repeats the unsupported assertion that Norman was a homosexual, identifies, but does not name, Tsuru as "a Japanese Marxist who lived in Washington," recounts the false allegation that Tsuru's apartment contained "secret reports" that Norman had tried to secure under false pretenses; claims that Elizabeth Bentley, a "courier for Soviet agents," had "named Norman" (for what, he does not say); says that Norman was "publicly identified with communism in 1951" in SISS hearings that "were conveniently branded as witch-hunting"; asserts that only due to Pearson's protection, "Norman escaped serious investigation"; gives the impression that following this episode, Norman was sent as "Ambassador to Japan" before being posted to New Zealand and Egypt; avers that "there seems to be little doubt that he worked for the KGB in all three postings"; cites James Barros regarding the allegation that Norman's role "went far" in contributing to the North Korean invasion of the South; and offers a version of Norman's suicide which, for all its errors, should be quoted verbatim:

> Following increased suspicions, Norman was recalled to Ottawa in 1957 for "discussions" but prior to his departure, which had been arranged on a pretext, a CIA man in Cairo imprudently encouraged him to speak of his links with the Russians. Norman is then said to have remarked, 'I can't go back to Ottawa because, if I did, I would have to betray too many people.' That night he jumped to his death from the roof of the apartment block where he had a flat and killed himself. Either he had guessed the purpose of his recall or he had been surreptitiously told of it.[38]

Pincher concludes his badly flawed account of the Norman case with the claim that it was "one of the first to be analysed in detail by the Featherbed team [an RCMP counter-intelligence unit] which concluded that he had been a long-serving Soviet spy who had faked his break with communism to gain entry to the diplomatic services as a 'mole.'"[39]

There are as many as a dozen errors of fact in the one-page Pincher account, not to mention several incredible assertions, such as that Norman was a "known homosexual" (known by whom?), that he "escaped serious investigation" (does Pincher not know about the two RCMP interrogations?), and that "he worked for the KGB in all three postings" (no evidence is offered). It may be true that the "Featherbed team" reopened the Norman case in the early Sixties, as Pincher says, because in the RCMP file there is one undated sheet with the words, "Code named xxxxxxx [word excised]," and according to Mrs. Norman, RCMP officers appeared out of the blue at her apartment in 1964 in order to question her about Herbert's past[40], but in the released RCMP file there is nothing to verify the Pincher allegation that "Featherbed" concluded Norman was a "mole."

Nonetheless, this latter allegation was taken seriously by, for example, the *Globe and Mail* (28 March 1981) and *Maclean's* (6 April 1981) as indicated by their uncritical citations of Pincher's first book. Unwittingly, both publications strengthen the credibility of Pincher's reporting by doing as he did, namely, by reporting the allegations against one-time Canadian ambassador to the Soviet Union, John Watkins, alongside the Norman case.

As mentioned long ago, this is the second instance of mistaken identity. Briefly, Pincher alleges that Watkins "had been the victim of a KGB blackmail operation after agents had exploited his homosexuality."[41] Watkins was first identified but not actually named by Soviet defector Anatoli Golitsin sometime in 1961, and apparent confirmation that he *may* have been targeted for blackmail by the Soviets came when a second defector, Yuri Nosenko, named him in 1964. The RCMP interrogated Watkins, who supposedly confessed that he was a homosexual but denied serving the KGB; Pincher admits in his latest book that "The records show that Watkins did not serve as an agent of influence . . ." and that the RCMP, after twenty-six days of interrogation, "were convinced of his innocence." It mattered little to Watkins, however, as during one last interrogation session, he died of a heart attack.[42]

Although exonerating Watkins of spying, Pincher uses his case as a lead-in to Norman's, using the allegation of "homosexuality" as the common denominator. In Pincher's view Watkins was a confessed homosexual whom the Soviets tried but failed to secretly employ and Norman was a "known homosexual" successfully recruited by the Soviets at Cambridge, and, implicitly, kept in the Soviets' employ partly through threat of exposure of his homosexuality. Parallel cases, in that sense, but by admitting one man, Watkins, was innocent, at least of spying, Pincher enhances his credibility in accusing the other.

Apparently unknown by Pincher, the parallel quality of the charge might even be strengthened by citing the FBI file on Watkins, file #100–33811–3. It opens no later than 8 August 1951, at the same time that Herbert Norman was named by SISS for the first time, and continues through 15 October 1963, the date of the last *released* entry. Too many pages of documents have been withheld to opine on the question of why Watkins was first investigated, although it is clear from references to FBI interviews with former colleagues at Cornell University that his "loyalty" had been questioned by someone. Yet document after document attests to his loyalty, his trustworthiness, his "good character and associations," and his "dependable, highly-cultured, intellectual, well-read, and modest" nature. From the FBI's point of view, the worst testimony against him was that he was "liberal and progressive to the extent he supported social reforms of Franklin D. Roosevelt." It appears that this was the finding that Hoover reported to the CIA in late September 1951, when the case was closed; it was not reopened until late 1963, presumably on the merits of the statements made by one or more Soviet defectors.[43]

Like Norman, Watkins was an academic (Ph.D. from Cornell in 1944, specializing in Old Norse and Icelandic language and literature), held progressive views, was recruited into foreign service work, and was Canadian. Similar backgrounds, parallel careers, both suspected of disloyalty, and both "killed" as a result of suspicions held by "intelligence agencies."

Also in common, both men were suspected of having been susceptible to Soviet blackmail, one because he was a reputed homosexual, the other because he attended Cambridge in the early Thirties (Pincher is the *only* "student" of Herbert Norman who alleges homosexuality). Their lives were linked in the minds of intelligence people, in life inasmuch as August 1951 marks the FBI's serious questioning of their loyalty, in death inasmuch as the resurrection of charges of spying for the Soviets is traceable to Pincher.

But there is more that unites the two men. Clare Edward Petty, the CIA counter-intelligence officer who made the case that James Angleton was a Soviet agent, who gave evidence to the RCMP about Golitsin's and Nosenko's comments on Canadian moles, and who was involved in the investigation of John Watkins, says that "Golitsin's generalized and Nosenko's very detailed information about the Watkins case was the basis for my own interest in and review of the Norman case."[44] Watkins' was the principal case; Norman's, he says, was "a historic matter dealing with a whole epic of post World War II espionage cases." Interest in the Norman case, he claims, stemmed from "a follow-up on the Watkins lead." And Petty's review of the historic interest in the Norman case leads back to "flat, clear-cut evidence" that "substantial material was going out of the Washington office of the [Canadian] embassy" during the Second World War.[45] In short, Petty confused Norman with Hazen Sise, just as so many others have done, and, no less important, reviewed the Norman case in the early Sixties *because* the Soviet defectors' testimony about Watkins resembled the suspicions that American intelligence agencies had long held about Herbert Norman. Once having confused Norman's identity first with Sise and then with Watkins, the Agency proceeded to investigate Norman because he had a "basis for a relationship" with Donald Maclean; and second, that Norman had been linked with both Tsuru and Halperin; and finally because, like Norman, Guy Burgess was similarly concerned with "Far Eastern matters." He added that the (erroneous) dispatch from the CIA station chief in Cairo immediately following Norman's death was also a major reason for their suspicion.

Petty is not saying much that is different from what a onetime Angleton assistant in the CIA, who requests anonymity, points out: Norman "had a predisposition to be a [Soviet] agent," but adds that in the end, "his is a case with no head or tail."[46] Of course, rather than give Norman the benefit of the doubt, the CIA was obliged to regard him with

the greatest of suspicion. Mistaken identity, *bases* for relationships and "predispositions" made Herbert Norman into
a CIA case—at least on this score.

On another score entirely, which the CIA took into full
consideration, there is the testimony of two self-confessed
Soviet agents, Michael Straight and Anthony Blunt.

Michael Straight confessed to the FBI in 1963 about how
he had been recruited in 1934 at Cambridge to spy for the
Soviets. This in turn, once the FBI told British counter-intelligence, led to the questioning and confession of Sir Anthony Blunt of the same crime. (The confessions did not
prevent Straight from working for the Nixon administration
or Blunt from serving as the Queen's art historian.) The
public exposure of Blunt did not come until 1979, with the
publication of Andrew Boyle's book, *The Fourth Man*, or
the public confessional of Straight until he published his
memoirs, *After Long Silence*, in 1983. [47]

Blunt, we already know from Pincher, supposedly named
Herbert Norman as "one of us"; Straight claims privately
(not in his book) that "I assume they [the CIA and FBI] had
my version [about Herbert Norman's Cambridge politics] in
1963, since my comments almost certainly included him." [48]
If Straight's memory seems cloudy, it is. In the few words
he devoted to discussing Norman in his autobiography, he
gets his facts wrong; in his first letter to me, dated 30 May
1983, he addresses very tentatively the question of whether
Herbert Norman was a "mole." "Was Herbert, to my knowledge, a mole? First, let's agree on what we mean by 'a mole.'
The term in its present usage is defined by John le Carré: 'A
mole is a deep penetration agent, so-called because he bur-
rows deep into the fabric of Western imperialism.' Obviously, Herbert, as a student, was not a 'mole' in that sense."
Straight goes on: "Was he than a mole in the sense that the
term was used in Cambridge communist circles in 1935? That
is a question which I cannot answer with any conviction."
He says that he knew "ten or fifteen 'moles'" of the sort
who, "for reasons of discretion, did not attend college cell
meetings, parades, demonstrations and fractions." He adds,

"my *impression* was that Herbert was in this category; that I knew him to be a student communist, but that in the course of 1935 he ceased to attend Trinity cell meetings." (Emphasis mine.)

Straight recalls Norman's connection with the Indian "colonials," but can only recall that Kiernan, who succeeded Norman in organizing the Indians, was "either a mole, *or* was charged with briefing and generally keeping in touch with 'moles'; specifically Indians, whose status as colonials might have been undermined had they been openly identified as communists." In the earlier chapter "Student," we saw that Kiernan was and is today quite open about his and Norman's work with the Indian students.

Straight contrasts Norman with real moles, *i.e.*, those who "in preparation with a life spent underground, as a secret communist," "like John Cairncross [who] were presumably instructed to go underground as students in preparation for becoming Soviet agents within the British government." Who recruited them? Straight asks. Burgess recruited Blunt, but, he adds, "Blunt definitely did not recruit Herbert; nor, I'm sure, did Burgess. That leaves James Klugmann, the leader of the student communist movement with John Cornford."[49] Yet both Klugmann and Cornford, to use Pincher's dichotomy, were not "covert communists" and neither, presumably, were their converts.

The distinction is important. Burgess, Maclean, Philby, and Blunt, as well as suspected "fifth man" Leo Long, the film company executive who confessed when Blunt did,[50] were "secret communists" who fairly qualify as "moles"; open communists, like Norman, Kiernan, and Klugmann, do not by reason of their very openness.

Perhaps for this reason, Straight is extremely tentative about the degree of Norman's involvement. "I did know Herbert at Trinity, but not very well." And after discussing whether he was a mole, "My position is thus one which can hardly be relied on. . . . I cannot offer you any evidence to support the view that he was recruited for underground activity by [Klugmann]." Yet he avers, "I believed that many of the

Senate witnesses—Bentley, Massing, Chambers, and the defectors—were telling the truth." Could it have been that once having known Norman, but not well, at Cambridge, knowing him to be an associate of people like Straight's close friend, John Cornford, and believing all the negative publicity about Norman in the 1950s, that Straight offered the name of a dead man in 1963 as a *possible* mole? [51] Very likely, it seems, given his recollections.

Straight's secret testimony to the FBI led to the questioning of Blunt. The question is whether he, being quizzed upon the basis of the information supplied by Straight, was asked a leading question about the deceased Herbert Norman and offered Norman's name in the spirit of co-operation and in the desire to please his questioners and thereby end his own ordeal.

The question is difficult to answer, perhaps impossible for those committed to entertaining notions of Herbert Norman's guilt. But first be aware that Blunt and Burgess did not reappear at Cambridge until Herbert Norman's second and last year there. Blunt returned as a lecturer, Burgess as a graduate student, and hence at least in academic circles, they were far removed from Norman's world. Be aware, too, that Herbert was an outsider to their "Apostolic" group, that neither man is ever mentioned in his private correspondence (which did not hesitate to name Cornford), and that Straight maintains that Herbert did not attend cell meetings that year. Know, too, Pincher admits that Blunt during questioning did not hesitate to name dead men ("Blunt was prepared to volunteer information about several of the Cambridge Ring's associates and helpers who were dead.")[52]

Knowing these facts, we must assess Blunt's "confession" about Norman in terms of Pincher's claim. And since Blunt is dead, and his M.I.5 interrogators—Arthur Martin and Peter Wright—refuse to answer my questions, for validation of Pincher's claim it is necessary to turn to Blunt's biographer, Cherry Hughes. She wrote to me in 1984 "that Wright has admitted that Blunt may have lied to him—and I know that he did." Based on extensive interviews with Martin, she adds about Norman, "Arthur thinks he was not homosexual[,] just I suspect from a gut feeling—nothing more." The strongest evidence that she and Martin can offer in support of Norman's alleged "mole" status is that "Herbert Norman was involved in espionage for the Russians—he seemingly gave a partial admission of guilt to a CIA officer when he was in Egypt."[53] This sounds like the faulty CIA report cited and discredited earlier.

Straight's tentativeness, Hughes's questioning of Blunt's honesty (also an issue raised by Pincher[54]), and Martin's reliance on the faulty CIA report all add up to a level of uncertainty that makes it at best unethical to accept the notion that Herbert Norman was a "mole," at worst libelous.

But our case need not rest on this alone. We can return to known facts about his life and career that make the point of his innocence in an even more convincing manner. Herbert did not seek a career with External Affairs; he was recruited. His affiliations with Marxists and communists up until 1939 were open, his connections with the "communist-front organisation," IPR, were likewise open, as were his friendships with its members. His early writings had an unapologetic Marxist slant, his later work an unmistakable liberal bias. The Wittfogel claim that he participated in a secret Marxist study group is contradicted by two of its participants, Finley/Finkelstein and William Canning. During his second interrogation by the RCMP in 1952, he finally admitted the full degree of his participation in the communist movement at Cambridge. External, as a result, reaffirmed its belief in his loyalty. And one of his suicide notes clearly expressed the hope for a full-scale inquiry into the question of his loyalty—a deathbed "confession," if you will, protesting his innocence—which should indicate at least a guiltless conscience.

Suicide was the most obvious way to protest his innocence of the American charges, the only way to end his ordeal by slander, innuendo, and suspicion that he rationally understood would never end. Herbert Norman knew that innocence was not enough; death, he felt, would be.

Appendix I
RCMP Document, dated October 11, 1950

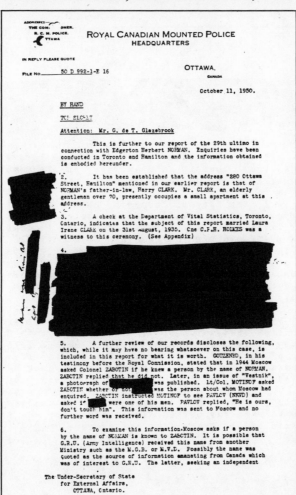

ADDRESSED TO
THE COM ONER.
R. C. M. POLICE.
OTTAWA

ROYAL CANADIAN MOUNTED POLICE
HEADQUARTERS

IN REPLY PLEASE QUOTE

FILE No. 50 D 992-1-E 16

OTTAWA,
CANADA

October 11, 1950.

BY HAND

TO: SLOULT

Attention: Mr. G. de T. Glazebrook

This is further to our report of the 29th ultimo in connection with Edgerton Herbert NORMAN. Enquiries have been conducted in Toronto and Hamilton and the information obtained is embodied hereunder.

2.   It has been established that the address "280 Ottawa Street, Hamilton" mentioned in our earlier report is that of NORMAN's father-in-law, Harry CLARK. Mr. CLARK, an elderly gentleman over 70, presently occupies a small apartment at this address.

3.   A check at the Department of Vital Statistics, Toronto, Ontario, indicates that the subject of this report married Laura Irene CLARK on the 31st August, 1935. One C.F.H. HOLMES was a witness to this ceremony. (See Appendix)

4.

5.   A further review of our records discloses the following, which, while it may have no bearing whatsoever on this case, is included in this report for what it is worth. GOUZENKO, in his testimony before the Royal Commission, stated that in 1944 Moscow asked Colonel ZABOTIN if he knew a person by the name of NORMAN. ZABOTIN replied that he did not. Later, in an issue of "Vestnik", a photograph of ████████ was published. Lt/Col. MOTINOF asked ZABOTIN whether or not ████ was the person about whom Moscow had enquired. ZABOTIN instructed MOTINOF to see PAVLOV (NKVD) and asked if ████ were one of his men. PAVLOV replied, "He is ours, don't touch him". This information was sent to Moscow and no further word was received.

6.   To examine this information.Moscow asks if a person by the name of NORMAN is known to ZABOTIN. It is possible that G.R.U. (Army Intelligence) received this name from another Ministry such as the N.C.B. or M.V.D. Possibly the name was quoted as the source of information emanating from Canada which was of interest to G.R.U. The latter, seeking an independent

The Under-Secretary of State
    for External Affairs,
        OTTAWA, Ontario.

Enc.

- 2 -

check on the source, would ask their Canadian representative, ZABOTIN, if NORMAN was known to him. It seems unlikely that they would offer a Christian name of a person previously unknown to them for checking. Both ████████ already were known. Again, ZABOTIN and MOTINOF did not ask if PAVLOV knew a person by the name of NORMAN but the discussion apparently centred around ████ There is no connection between ████ and NORMAN other than the assumption on the part of ZABOTIN. It will be noted that Moscow did not confirm this assumption. It would appear that NORMAN is the surname of a person in whom the Russian Intelligence Service had an interest. It is, however, impossible to make a definite identification.

for Commissioner.

TOP SECRET

(100-159485-83)

                    b7C

      It is noted that in his testimony before the
Senate Internal Security Subcommittee, Public Session,
March 27, 1957, Shigeto Tsuru said:

      "I knew (Israel Halperin) as an instructor of
mathematics at Harvard University....he was introduced
to me, I believe, by Mr. Norman. The year I cannot
remember quite exactly but possibly around 1937." (The
witness then went on to confirm the fact that this individual
was the same one involved in the Canadian espionage case in
1946 because he recalled being interviewed concerning his
knowledge of Halperin by U. S. Government representatives
in Japan.) (Page 5030-31, Volume 100)

      Tsuru was the subject of an extensive security
investigation instituted by the Boston office in November,
1942, upon receipt of information that he had left a large
quantity of material in his apartment in Cambridge,
Massachusetts, when he was repatriated to Japan in June,
1942. This investigation disclosed that nearly half of the
material left by Tsuru was communist literature and propaganda.
An address book also was left behind which included his
contacts through the United States and other countries and
which contained Norman's name and address.

                                b7C b7d

50   TOP SECRET

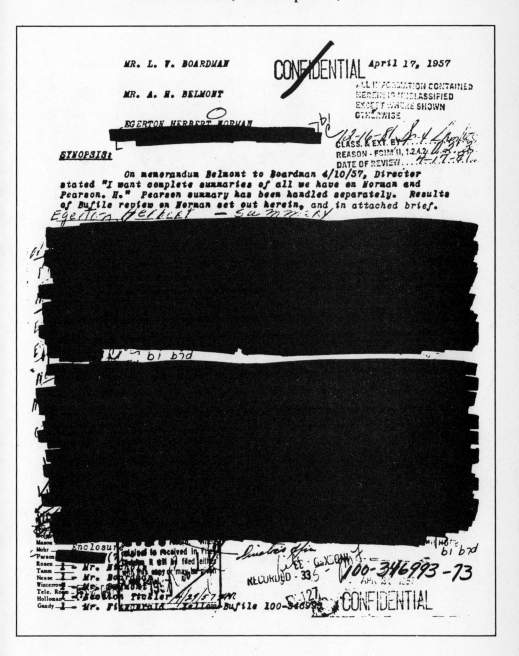

MR. L. V. BOARDMAN   CONFIDENTIAL   April 17, 1957

ALL INFORMATION CONTAINED
HEREIN IS UNCLASSIFIED
EXCEPT WHERE SHOWN
OTHERWISE

MR. A. H. BELMONT

EGERTON HERBERT NORMAN

CLASS. & EXT. BY
REASON - FCIM II, 1.2.4.2
DATE OF REVIEW

SYNOPSIS:

On memorandum Belmont to Boardman 4/10/57, Director stated "I want complete summaries of all we have on Norman and Pearson. H." Pearson summary has been handled separately. Results of Bufile review on Norman set out herein, and in attached brief.

Egerton Herbert — Summary

100-346993-73

RECORDED - 33

CONFIDENTIAL

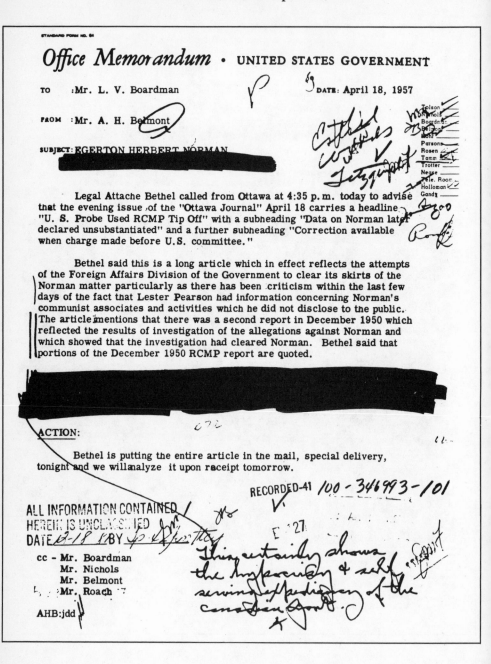

Office Memorandum • UNITED STATES GOVERNMENT

TO : Mr. L. V. Boardman

FROM : Mr. A. H. Belmont

DATE: April 18, 1957

SUBJECT: EGERTON HERBERT NORMAN ▓▓▓▓▓▓▓▓▓▓▓▓▓▓▓▓

Legal Attache Bethel called from Ottawa at 4:35 p.m. today to advise that the evening issue of the "Ottawa Journal" April 18 carries a headline "U.S. Probe Used RCMP Tip Off" with a subheading "Data on Norman later declared unsubstantiated" and a further subheading "Correction available when charge made before U.S. committee."

Bethel said this is a long article which in effect reflects the attempts of the Foreign Affairs Division of the Government to clear its skirts of the Norman matter particularly as there has been criticism within the last few days of the fact that Lester Pearson had information concerning Norman's communist associates and activities which he did not disclose to the public. The article mentions that there was a second report in December 1950 which reflected the results of investigation of the allegations against Norman and which showed that the investigation had cleared Norman. Bethel said that portions of the December 1950 RCMP report are quoted.

██

ACTION:

Bethel is putting the entire article in the mail, special delivery, tonight and we will analyze it upon receipt tomorrow.

RECORDED-41 100 - 346993 - 101

ALL INFORMATION CONTAINED
HEREIN IS UNCLASSIFIED
DATE 2-18 8 BY ▓▓▓▓

cc - Mr. Boardman
     Mr. Nichols
     Mr. Belmont
     Mr. Roach

AHB:jdd

NOTES

Introduction

1 The "Tsuru apartment episode" is discussed a half-dozen different times in the pages that follow, each time from a slightly different angle and in a different biographical context. That it was central to the FBI's assessment of Herbert Norman's "loyalty" is evident in that Agency's eighty-five-page "Summary of Information" dated 17 April 1957.

2 Tarshis's file, as obtained through the Freedom of Information Act, is woefully incomplete; Bryce's file number is cited in several Norman FBI file documents.

3 Thus Tsuru describes his Marxist leanings of the late Thirties before the United States Senate, Subcommittee to Investigate the Administration of the Internal Security Act and Other Internal Security Laws of the Committee on the Judiciary, 26 and 27 March 1957; importantly, as shown in Chapter 10, Tsuru's own accounting of his library, which Herbert tried to obtain, conforms with Herbert's account; see pp. 3742–43. Hereafter this Subcommittee is referred to as SISS (Senate Internal Security Subcommittee).

Chapter 1—Son

1 Correspondence, 3 March 1937.

2 W. H. H. Norman, "Norman of Nagano: A Biography of the Rev. Daniel and Mrs. Catherine Norman" (unpublished ms., 1964), p. 40.

3 Ibid., pp. 39–40.

4 Ibid., p. 82.

5 Cyril Powles, "E. H. Norman and Japan," in Roger W. Bowen, ed., *E.H. Norman: His Life and Scholarship* (Toronto: University of Toronto Press, 1984), p. 17.

6 Daniel Norman died in London, Ontario, on 19 June 1941 at age seventy-seven. (United Church Archives, Toronto.)

7 Gwen R. P. Norman, *One Hundred Years in Japan 1873–1973*, Part I (Toronto: United Church of Canada, 1981), p. 213.

8 "Norman of Nagano," pp. 155,156; correspondence to author, 23 January 1978.

9 "Norman of Nagano," pp. 21–22, 26, 128.

10 Ibid., pp. 128, 130; correspondence to author, 17 September 1984.

11 Ibid. Howard writes of his mother ("Norman of Nagano," pp. 156–57): "Her gentleness inspired confidence and intimacy"; "She was . . . constitutionally timid . . ."; "She was a 'home-body'."

12 "Norman of Nagano" amply describes Daniel's many virtues; Gwen Norman comments on Kate's "Ontario Syndrome" in correspondence 17 September 1984; and Howard sums up his mother's character (p. 157) when he writes, "'What will people think!' she would say to us; or, 'What will people think of Father and me if you do that? Parents are always blamed if their children go wrong.' She was fearful that Father would be misunderstood and frequently tried to restrain him." Also see Powles, "E. H. Norman and Japan," in Bowen, pp. 17–18.

13 "Norman of Nagano," pp. 11–12, 57–58, 118.

14 Powles, "E. H. Norman and Japan," in Bowen, p. 18.

15 Correspondence, 21 September 1926.

16 *One Hundred Years,* p. 160.

17 Takizawa Shiro, "The Memory of Herbert Norman," a speech given at a memorial meeting held in Tokyo, 4 May 1957; unpublished ms., translated by Okubo Genji; correspondence, Howard Norman, 11 March 1985 and 23 January 1978.

18 The two other "Musketeers" were Keith Armstrong and Donald Macleod, although some friends from his childhood include Charles Holmes; correspondence, Egerton Armstrong (Keith's brother), 7 September 1978. Macleod recalls, "We were somewhat more adventurous, perhaps, than average and imaginative, chiefly Herbert. We discriminated between fair and unfair (in our opinion) authority and resented the latter" (correspondence, 26 June 1978). Correspondence, Nellie S. Newman to author, 3 September 1978 and 14 August 1978; J.K.W. Ferguson, 26 February 1978; D. Macleod, 26 June 1978. Correspondence to author, 26 February 1978.

19 "Norman of Nagano," p. 12; Macleod (n. 18 above) writes of the "Three Musketeers," "Perhaps we read a bit more widely than some others, certainly Herbert did."

20 Correspondence, 21 January 1923.

21 Correspondence, 14 February 1923. "Norman of Nagano," p. 163.

22 Correspondence, 25 April 1922.

23 "Norman of Nagano," p. 165.

24 *Red and Grey,* (Kobe, Japan: Canadian Academy), p. 25.

25 Correspondence, 8 October 1926.

26 Correspondence, 11 April 1927.

27 Correspondence, 11 June 1927.

28 Correspondence, 27 June 1927, 11 April 1927.

29 Correspondence, 25 July 1927.

30 Ibid.

31 Ibid.

Chapter 2, Student

1 Jon Clark, Margot Heinemann, David Margolis, and Carol Snee, eds., *Culture and Crisis in Britain in the 1930s* (London: Lawrence and Wishart, 1979), p. 21 (Introduction by James Klugmann).

2 *Red and Grey: 1926*, p. 11.

3 Ibid.

4 Correspondence, 11 July 1927.

5 Transcripts and college records furnished by Victoria College Registrar, Kenneth Thompson, 12 December 1984. Correspondence: Berna Cleaver, 12 April 1978; Correspondence, W. J. Musgrove, 16 April 1978; Pauline McGibbon, 21 April 1978; Lois Darroch, 18 April 1978; Margaret Waugh, 24 April 1978.

6 Interview with Lorie Tarshis, Toronto, 29 March 1978.

7 Correspondence, 14 January 1932.

8 Ibid.

9 Ivan Avakumovic, *Socialism in Canada: A Study of the CCF-NDP in Federal and Provincial Politics* (Toronto: McClelland and Stewart, 1978), p. 53.

10 Correspondence, 7 April 1932.

11 Ibid.

12 Ibid.

13 Ibid.

14 Ibid. (italics mine).

15 Correspondence to author, William Grant, 23 July 1979.

16 Ibid.

17 Correspondence, 14 January 1932.

18 Interview, Ottawa, 11 November 1977.

19 Support for this view can be found in Herbert's testimony to RCMP interrogators during questioning in early 1952; see Ch. 8.

20 Heinemann, *Culture and Crisis*, p. 116.

21 T. E. B. Howarth, *Cambridge Between Two Wars* (London: Collins, 1978), p. 15.

22 Correspondence, 9 October 1933; 21 October 1933.

23 Interview with the Registrar, Trinity College, Cambridge, 7 November 1984;

Herbert's roommate's name was William James Henderson.

24 Correspondence, 21 October 1933.

25 Herbert's Trinity College transcript shows that he scored a "Class II, division 1" in his "Historical Tripos, Part I," in 1935, although in his "Preliminary in History" the year before he had earned a "Class I, division 2." Registrar, Trinity College, Cambridge.

26 Correspondence, 9 October 1933.

27 Ibid.

28 Interview, Toronto, 29 March 1978. Norman did not, however, neglect old friends whose political views differed. J. K. W. Ferguson, a former Canadian Academy classmate (although two years senior to Norman) was studying with the Department of Physiology at Cambridge in 1933–34. Dr. Ferguson recalls, "Herbert was caught up in the intellectual ferment of communism. He lectured me at length about his convictions, not I think with any hope of converting me. I was an interested but altogether too detached a listener." Ferguson also remembers inviting Norman to dinner, along with a Nazi named Schriever, but Norman left the dinner party early. Correspondence to author, 2 February 1978.

29 Interview with Lorie Tarshis, Toronto, 29 March 1978. See Kiernan, "Herbert Norman's Cambridge," in Bowen, *E. H. Norman,* pp. 27–45.

30 *New York Review of Books,* 31 March 1982.

31 Klugmann, *Culture and Crisis,* p. 35.

32 Correspondence, 3 March 1937; and Kiernan's letter to author, 24 October 1978.

33 Correspondence: Lorie Tarshis, 1 March 1978; Victor Kiernan, 24 October 1978. Kiernan in Bowen, *E.H. Norman,* pp. 40–41; and interview with Margot Heinemann, Cambridge, 7 November 1984.

34 James Cornford to author, 19 May 1978 and Christopher Cornford to author, 11 June 1978. Telephone interview with H. S. Corran, 6 November 1984.

35 Telephone interview, 6 November 1984.

36 Correspondence to author, 16 July 1978; and interview, Cambridge, 7 November 1984.

37 Michael Straight, *After Long Silence* (New York: Norton, 1983), p. 229 (Straight says Norman "killed himself after he was arrested in Canada"). Correspondence to author, 30 May 1983.

38 Interview with Lorie Tarshis, Toronto, 29 March 1978; with Margot Heinemann, Cambridge, 7 November 1984.

39 Correspondence, 21 October 1933.

40 Ibid.

41 Ibid.

42 Correspondence, 3 March 1937.

43 Public Archives, Ottawa, RG 32 C2, Vol. 338, file 1261, part one.

44 Correspondence, 21 October 1933; and Holmes's FBI file, 105–18139.

45 SISS files, National Archives, 73-A–1375 ("E. Herbert Norman"); undated memorandum says that on 27 March 1957, Dean Rusk mailed photostats of Norman's fellowship reports to Nelson Frank of the U.S. (District?) Courthouse, who in turn sent them on to Robert Morris, counselor for the Senate Subcommittee on Internal Security.

46 Okubo Genji, *Hābāto Nōman Zenshū, IV* (Tokyo: Iwanami, 1978), pp. 542–43; Norman's personnel record shows that on 5 July 1939, he received a temporary appointment as a Japanese Language Officer.

47 Norman FBI file, #100–346993, "Summary of Information," 17 April 1957; Hoover to [deleted], 3 November 1950.

48 Interview with Lorie Tarshis, Toronto, 29 March 1978; correspondence from J. K. Galbraith to author, 7 April 1981; correspondence from Paul Sweezy to author, 9 November 1980; Norman FBI file, Hoover to SAC, Boston, 3 November 1950.

49 Correspondence, 15 January 1937.

50 Kiernan, "Herbert Norman's Cambridge," in Bowen, p. 44, n. 4. Correspondence, Christopher Cornford to author, 11 June 1978. Interview with Lorie Tarshis, Toronto, 29 March 1978.

51 Correspondence, 4 February 1937.

52 Ibid.

53 Ibid.

54 Ibid.

55 Correspondence, 3 March 1937.

56 Correspondence, 4 February 1937.

57 Correspondence, 3 March 1937.

58 Ibid.

59 Ibid.

60 Ibid.

61 Correspondence, 5 April 1937.

62 SISS files; Rockefeller fellowship records refer to a request made in May 1938 to spend the next academic year at Columbia University in order to work with Professor Borton.

63 Public Archives, Ottawa, RG 32 C2, Vol 38, file 1261, part one.

64 Interview, Toronto, 29 June 1978.

65 SISS files, National Archives, Washington, D.C., Wittfogel to Benjamin Mandel, Research Director, 22 August 1951; note, too, that the Rockefeller fellowship records state that Norman spent the summer of 1938 in Japan with his parents, rather than in Hamilton, Ontario.

66 SISS files.

67 SISS files, Rockefeller report.

68 Interview, Ottawa, 11 November 1977.

69 Public Archives, Ottawa, RG 32 C2, Vol. 38, file 1261, part one.

70 SISS files, undated memorandum; Hugh Borton was also interviewed by the FBI.

71 Public Archives,, Ottawa, RG 32 C2, Vol. 38, file 1261, part one.

72 *Steppenwolf* (New York: Bantam Books, 1963), p. 25.

Chapter 3—Scholar

1 New York: Institute of Pacific Relations, 1940; a bibliography of Norman's published writings appears in Roger Bowen, ed., *E. H. Norman: His Life and Scholarship* (Toronto: University of Toronto Press, 1984), pp. 201–02.

2 New York: Institute of Pacific Relations, 1943, p. xii.

3 Public Archives, Ottawa, RG 32 C2, Vol. 338, file 1261, part one, 21 December 1942, regarding American offer to employ Norman in "political warfare"; and file 339, letter of 12 May 1945 (from External Affairs to Washington) regarding the British attempt to second Norman to their Far Eastern Intelligence Unit.

4 Elsewhere I've made the argument that Edwin Reischauer is the only American who has come close to equaling Norman's scholarly and diplomatic accomplishments, but it should also be pointed out that it took Reischauer longer to gain equal breadth and depth. See Bowen, *E. H. Norman*, p. 3.

5 Senate Internal Security Subcommittee [SISS] files, National Archives, Washington, D.C., 73-A-1375 ("E. Herbert Norman"), file #3, contains sketchy and ideologically critical "reviews" of Norman's writings. Noteworthy about *Japan's Emergence*, for example, are references to IPR Secretary General Edward Carter and Tsuru Shigeto in the book's Foreword; "communist references" to books written by Soviet scholars (e.g., pp. 40, 87, 134); and a citation of a Wittfogel article ("Wittfogel was then [at time of publication] still pro-communist.") Similar critiques of Norman's publications are found in the FBI "Summary of Information," 17 April 1957.

6 See Bowen, Part Two.

7 Correspondence, 15 May 1933.

8 Toyama Shigeki, "The Appreciation of Norman's Historiography," in Bowen, pp. 122–37, says Norman "was *not* a Marxist," yet also points out that Norman wisely relied on the research of a good many Japanese Marxist historians in his

own research.

9 Edwin O. Reischauer, "Perspective of a Lifelong Friend," in Bowen, p. 10 and p. 12, n. 5, makes this point, as does Charles Kades, one of several architects of the post-war Japanese constitution (see Ch. 4).

10 *Tokyo: Transactions of the Asiatic Society of Japan*, 3rd Series, Vol. 2.

11 The most scathing attack on Herbert's scholarship, though it does not directly impugn his linguistic ability, is George Akita, "An Examination of E. H. Norman's Scholarship," *Journal of Japanese Studies* 3,2 (1977): 375–419.

12 His annual Rockefeller Foundation records are in SISS files, see n. 5 above; and see *Japan's Emergence*, p. xiii.

13 See n. 11 above.

14 Permission was granted on 6 October 1941; see Public Archives, Ottawa, RG 32 C2 Vol. 338, file 1261, part one.

15 Akita, "Examination," p. 418.

16 "E. H. Norman, Modern Japan, and the Historian's Agenda," *The Japan Interpreter* 10, 3/4 (Winter 1976): 374.

17 Ibid.

18 *Japan's Emergence*, p. 8.

19 Ibid., p. 9.

20 Ibid., pp. 156–57.

21 Ibid., p. 4.

22 Ibid., p. 47.

23 Ibid., p. 143.

24 Toyama in Bowen, p. 123. See n. 8 above.

25 Ibid., p. 124.

26 *Soldier and Peasant*, p. 39.

27 Ibid., p. vi.

28 Ibid., p. 56.

29 *Japan's Emergence*, p. 47.

30 *Soldier and Peasant*, p. 57.

31 Ibid., p. 53.

32 *Feudal Background of Japanese Politics* has been reprinted in John W. Dower, ed., *Origins of the Modern Japanese State: Selected Writings of E. H. Norman* (New York: Pantheon, 1974), p. 320 (Dower edition).

33 After Herbert's death, William Holland sent *Feudal Background* to British

Japanologist Ronald P. Dore who was asked to review the manuscript for possible publication. Dore wrote in 1962, "Too much of this ground has been covered before in a more measured and scholarly way—and in greater detail—to make it worth publishing as a whole. . . . And there is also the general question of the tone and assumptions reflecting the atmosphere of the time it was written."

34 *Feudal Background,* p. 320 (Dower edition).

35 Ibid., pp. 353–354. Regarding presumed loyalty to IPR, documents kept in the Butler Library at Columbia University (Pacific Relations, Box 18, Box 31, and Box 41) show regular correspondence between Norman and IPR General Secretary Edward C. Carter, starting in early 1938 and concluding in late 1940. Usually quite formal and businesslike in tone, most of the correspondence concerns Norman's writing and research, especially his *Japan's Emergence.*

36 Dower, *Selected Writings,* pp. 91, 92.

37 Ibid., pp. 91–93.

38 *Ando,* p. 1.

39 Ibid., p. 7.

40 John Whitney Hall, "E. H. Norman on Tokugawa Japan," *Journal of Japanese Studies* 3,2 (Summer 1977): 373–74.

41 *Ando,* p. 45.

42 Ibid., pp. 17–18.

43 Ibid., pp. 183–84.

44 Ibid., pp. 321.

45 *Pacific Affairs* 23, 1 (March 1950): 93.

46 Ibid.

47 Hall, "E. H. Norman," *op. cit.,* p. 373.

48 Collateral evidence suggesting that Herbert's ability to read Japanese remained underdeveloped is the testimony of Hani Goro given on 4 May 1957, "On the Occasion of a Memorial Meeting" following Herbert's death. Hani recalls that in the 1940–41 period, "he came to me and asked me to read my book on the Meiji Restoration to him. I agreed and thus began to read it to him every afternoon for two or three weeks, always until it was dark." Translated by Genji Okubo, unpublished ms., p. 11.

49 In Bowen, p. 10.

50 Correspondence, 1945–50, *passim.*

51 External Affairs (hereafter EA) 9281–40C–23, 1 October 1946.

52 Bowen, pp. 143–54, esp. p. 154.

53 Bowen, p. 157.

54 Ibid., pp. 156, 158, 159, 165, 168; and see Ch. 2.

55 Two of the essays from this volume appear in Bowen.

56 Quotes taken from "History: Its Uses and Pleasures" and "Shrine of Clio"; "Shrine" is printed in Dower, pp. 103–08.

57 Norman FBI file, esp. "Summary of Information," 17 April 1957.

Chapter 4—Japanologist

1 Sidney Katz, "What Kind of Man *Was* Herbert Norman?" *Maclean's*, 28 September 1957, p. 87.

2 Charles Taylor, *Six Journeys: A Canadian Pattern* (Toronto: Anansi, 1977) p. 124.

3 Herbert remained in "War Services" work until his transfer to East Block on 5 January 1945; he began counter-intelligence work on 1 September 1942 (memo for Mr. Wrong); 25 June 1943, "Statement of Duties"; and 5 January 1945 memorandum, all in Public Archives RG 32 C2, Vol. 338, file 1261, Ottawa.

4 Remar to Langer, CIA (OSS), 21 July 1942; also in the CIA files is a 4 November 1942, letter of introduction from Minister Counsellor Lester Pearson to Col. "Wild Bill" Donovan, head of the OSS, introducing Norman and offering his services as a "liaison" between counter-intelligence people in Washington and Ottawa. This presumably puts Herbert in Washington just four days before the Tsuru apartment episode (see "Introduction") in Cambridge, Massachusetts.

5 Public Archives, Norman, 21 December 1942.

6 Public Archives, Norman, 4 August 1943.

7 Mackenzie King to Pearson, Public Archives, Norman, 30 March 1945.

8 Public Archives, Norman, undated memo.

9 Quoted in Keenleyside to Robertson, 13 September 1945, EA 104CD–311.

10 Boston: Little, Brown and Company, 1945, p. 38, n. 4.

11 Norman correspondence to wife, 25 September 1945; Hume Wrong to Keenleyside, 20 October 1945, EA 104-C–34; and EA 201 miscellaneous, 22 October 1945.

12 *Japan's American Interlude* (Chicago: University of Chicago Press, 1960).

13 Pearson to MacArthur, 9 February 1949, MacArthur Memorial Library, Norfolk, VA (RG-5: SCAP, Diplomatic Section, Canadian Mission); Norman to Pearson, Public Archives, Norman, 21 October 1948.

14 For SCAP order 93 (SCAPIN) of 4 October 1945, see *Political Reorientation of Japan, II* (Washington, D.C.: U.S. Government Printing Office), p. 464; (SCAPIN 548), pp. 479–81.

15 Dooman testified before SISS in August 1951 as part of the Institute of Pacific

Relations hearings, conducted by SISS, p. 748; see Ch. 10 for Emmerson testimony.

16 Edwin O. Reischauer, *Japan, Story of a Nation* (New York: Knopf, 1974), pp. 228–29.

17 Department of State, 740.00116 PW/11–1745, 5 December 1945 (cover letter), 17 November 1945 (Atcheson to Secretary of State); and 5 November 1945 (Norman to Atcheson).

18 Dale Hellegers, "The Konoe Affair," in L.H. Redford, ed., *Legal Reform in Japan* (Norfolk, VA: MacArthur Memorial, 1977), pp. 174–75.

19 See n. 17 above.

20 Public Archives, Norman, 18 March 1946.

21 PA, Norman, 31 January 1946; King's acknowledgment is dated 26 February 1946.

22 Unpublished ms., 4 March 1946.

23 Pearson papers, Public Archives, Ottawa, MG 26 N1, RG 32, C2, Vol. 338, file 1261, Part I. (Hereafter, Pearson papers.)

24 Kawai, *American Interlude*, pp. 51–52.

25 EA 104-C–01, 19 March 1946.

26 Ibid., and EA 50061–40, Vol. 3, 9 May 1946.

27 Unpublished ms., 4 March 1946.

28 EA 50061–40, Vol. 3, 9 May 1946.

29 Ibid.; also United Kingdom, Liaison Mission report, March 1946, p. 6, same file.

30 EA 50061–40, Vol. 2, 12 December 1945.

31 "Hard peace" advocates were generally found in G-1, "soft peace" advocates in G-2; Lattimore, for instance, as his 5 September 1945 letter to Keenleyside shows, identified himself with the "hard peace" position (see n. 9 above). Keenleyside said of his own position, "Although I would not describe myself as a "hard peace" advocate . . . I agree with the particular points made in Lattimore's note. What we need is neither a hard nor soft peace but a sensible one and the essence of such a peace seems to me to be the encouragement of all forces in Japan that will make for their *self*-liberation" (emphasis in original). Herbert's "hard peace" position, as quoted above, appears in EA 4606–40C, part one, 22 September 1944 (Norman to Keenleyside). Correspondence, Kades to Bowen, 18 January 1979. Kades served as Deputy Chief, G-1, between September 1946 and December 1947, and earlier (February 1946 to August 1946) as Public Administration Division Chief.

32 EA 4606–40C, part one, 22 September 1944.

33 Michael Fry, "Canada and the Occupation of Japan: The MacArthur-Norman Years," in *The Occupation of Japan: The International Context* (Norfolk: The

MacArthur Foundation, 1984), pp. 131–48; and Bowen commentary on same, pp. 155–57.

34 EA 4606–40C, 16 April 1946.

35 EA 8690–40, 14 May 1946.

36 Public Archives, Norman, 16 July 1946.

37 *Political Reorientation, II,* 756.

38 Ibid., also see MacArthur's autobiography, *Reminiscences* (Greenwich, Conn: Fawcett, 1964), pp. 308–71.

39 Dealt with at length in Chs. 6 and 7.

40 EA 4606–40C, part one, 12 March 1947.

41 Interview with J. J. McCardle, Ottawa, 16 August 1979. McCardle, who served as a language officer under Herbert, recalls six to eight meetings between Norman and MacArthur during each of his two years in Tokyo.

42 MacArthur Memorial, SCAP, Diplomatic Section, RG-5, Canadian Mission, 18 June 1947.

43 Ibid., 28 February 1949.

44 Correspondence, 18 January 1979; see n. 31 above.

45 EA 9281–40C, 1 October 1946; Herbert's cablegram announcing the request was sent on 30 September.

46 MacArthur Memorial, 23 November 1948.

47 EA 50061–40, Vol. 2, 8 November 1950.

Chapter 5—Democrat

1 Taylor, *Six Journeys;* Katz, "What Kind of Man"; Abe Tomoji, memorial meeting, Tokyo, 4 May 1957.

2 Interview with Lorne Berlet, Ottawa, 13 August 1979; interview with Omar Foda, Cairo, Egypt, 14 November 1984.

3 Interview, Tokyo, Japan, 14 May 1982.

4 Interview, Ottawa, 2 July 1983.

5 Fry, "The MacArthur-Norman Years" (typescript; a lengthier version of the edited paper appearing in source cited in n. 33, Ch. 4), p. 5.

6 EA 8620-G-40, 7 November 1946 (October Monthly Report).

7 Ibid.

8 EA 50061–40, Vol. 3/4–1, Keenleyside to Wrong, 10 October 1945. Keenleyside to Robertson, 4 September 1945.

9 EA 8690–40C, 20 December 1946. 21 November 1946.

10 EA 10858–10, 26 October 1949.

11 EA 8620-G-40, 3 October 1946. EA 1808–40C, 6 December 1946. EA 50061–40, 26 February 1947. Fry, "The MacArthur-Norman Years," typescript, pp. 14–17.

12 EA 8620-G-40C, 28 January 1948.

13 EA 4604–40, 5 December 1947.

14 Fry, "The MacArthur-Norman Years," typescript, p. 9. Toronto *Star,* 10 August 1951.

15 EA 8620-G-40C, 28 January 1948.

16 EA 50061–40, 22 March 1948.

17 EA 8620-G-40C, 19 March 1948 (italics mine). EA 8564-C–40C, 25 March 1948.

18 EA 4606-F–40, 19 January 1949.

19 EA 6605-AC–40, 1 November 1948.

20 EA 4606–40, 8 October 1948, and 20 December 1948.

21 EA 4606–40–20, 28 January 1949.

22 EA 4606–40–19, 28 January 1949.

23 EA 10463-B–40, 17 February 1950.

24 Ibid.

25 Ibid.

26 EA 4606–40–20, 28 January 1949.

27 EA 4606–40–19, 28 January 1949.

28 EA 4606–40–24, 3 March 1949; and Chalmers Johnson, *An Instance of Treason: Ozaki Hotsumi and the Sorge Spy Ring* (Stanford: Stanford University Press, 1964), pp. 65–66.

29 EA 4606–40–24, 3 March 1949.

30 EA 4606–40–24, 19 February 1949, and 3 March 1949.

31 EA 50061–40–4, 15 June 1949.

32 EA 50061–40–29, 18 March 1949.

33 EA 4606–40–24, 21 June 1949.

34 EA 50061–40–27, 1 August 1950.

35 EA 10463-B–40, 17 February 1950.

36 EA 4606–40–33, 27 April 1950.

37 EA 4606–40–27, 21 June 1950.

38 EA 50061–40–27, 1 and 2 August 1950.

39 EA 50050–40 5 and 16 September 1950. On sending a military representative to Tokyo, Escott Reid, in the document of the latter date, wrote, " . . . in view of close relations which Mr. Norman, Head of the Canadian Liaison Mission in Tokyo, has established with General MacArthur's headquarters, it would be mutually advantageous to both departments [External and National Defence] if the military representative were attached to Mr. Norman's staff . . . rather than being accredited independently to General MacArthur." Equally relevant, in a 13 September dispatch to Ottawa, Norman shows that he has accepted Mac-Arthur's bold prediction that the war would be over by Christmas; Herbert wrote, "It may be that the Korean War will not last many more months and the position [military attaché] will be merely a temporary one. . . ."

40 London: Sidgwick & Jackson, p. 418, citing James Barros.

41 Bruce Cumings, *Child of Conflict: The Korean-American Relationship, 1943–1953* (Seattle: University of Washington, 1983), pp. 44, 40–43, 47.

42 EA 50061–40–5, 24 May 1950.

43 EA 50061–40–33, 26 April 1950.

44 Cumings, *Child of Conflict*, pp. 49–50.

45 EA 11073–40–1 11 July 1950.

46 EA 50061–40–27 1 August 1950.

47 EA 4606–40 13 September 1950; see n. 36 above.

48 Pearson papers, 8 February 1950.

49 Pearson papers, Heeney to Norman, 22 February 1950; Norman to Moran, 14 July 1950; Moran to Norman, 18 July 1950.

Chapter 6—Suspect

1 Charles A. Willoughby and John Chamberlain, *MacArthur, 1941–51* (New York: McGraw Hill, 1954), p. 322.

2 RCMP files.

3 Emmerson FBI file # 121–23983. Although he was "cleared," as late as 1966, when he was being considered for a presidential appointment, history returned to haunt Emmerson. A 29 September 1966 FBI memo noted, "Emmerson was an associate of Herbert Norman . . . [and] an associate of John Stewart Service. . . ." Apparently Hoover himself carefully noted Norman's affidavit testifying to Emmerson's loyalty: a 1 April 1952 memo from Hoover to the State Department mentions receiving "through our Liaison Unit" something about Emmerson; the remainder of the document is censored, but given the timing of the memo—just after Herbert's affidavit—and its passage through Liaison, and State Department involvement, it is likely that Hoover was referring to Norman (Emmerson FBI file). Also see Emmerson's autobiography, *The Japanese Thread* (New York:

Holt, Rinehart and Winston, 1978), esp. pp. 314–16.

4 Edwin O. Reischauer, *Japan, the Story of a Nation* (New York: Alfred A. Knopf, 1974), p. 229; in his more recent *The Japanese* (Cambridge: Belknap, 1980), Reischauer uses the phrase "revolutionary reforms" (p. 108).

5 Emmerson FBI file, 13 August 1958; Norman Army Intelligence file, 3 June 1957. Also, Emmerson's Army Intelligence file, esp. several January 1951 reports, links Emmerson with Norman.

6 Emmerson FBI file, "Results of Investigation," 27 January 1958". (The date refers to the day Gen. Willoughby was interviewed and is embedded in the first paragraph.)

7 See E. J. Kahn, *The China Hands* (New York: Penguin, 1976), pp. 168–69.

8 Emmerson FBI file, Willoughby interview, 27 January 1958.

9 Ibid.

10 Ibid.

11 RCMP files, 21 September 1951.

12 RCMP files, 26 January 1952; see Chs. 7 & 8.

13 See Frank Kluckhohn, "Heidelberg to Madrid—The Story of General Willoughby," *The Reporter* 7 (19 August 1952): 25–30.

14 Willoughby, *MacArthur*, pp. 323; 323–24.

15 Ibid., p. 325.

16 Chalmers Johnson, *An Instance of Treason: Ozaki Hotsumi and the Sorge Spy Ring* (Stanford: Stanford University Press, 1964), pp. 64–65, 208–11. GHQ, SCAP, Willoughby to MacArthur, "Leftist Civilian Employees of GHQ," 27 September 1946, MacArthur Memorial, Norfolk, Va.; and Norman Army Intelligence file, 30 November 1950.

17 Ibid.

18 Memo for C-in-C,C/S, Gen. Whitney, from Willoughby, 7 June 1947, MacArthur Memorial; Army Intelligence files, 30 November 1950 Roundtree to Willoughby memorandum, and 10 December 1950, Willoughby to Lacey memorandum, make clear that the fall 1946 study was criticized; Willoughby refers to "the possibly damaging old study on leftist infiltration into this Hdq. which *I was directed to impound.*" (Italics mine.)

19 Ibid.

20 The Grajdanzev file is dated 15 January 1947; also to be found in the MacArthur Memorial Library, Willoughby papers, RG 23, Box 18, Series 2, part one.

21 Ibid.; Bisson's file is likewise dated 15 January 1947.

22 See also Thomas C. Reeves, ed., *McCarthyism* (Malabar, Fla.: Robert Krieger Publishing Co., 1982), p. 4.

23 Bisson file, 15 January 1947, MacArthur Memorial Library, Willoughby papers, RG 23, Box 18, Series 2, part one.

24 Ibid.

25 Ibid.

26 Norman FBI file, "Summary of Evidence," 17 April 1957. Army Intelligence Norman files, Willoughby to Lacey, 10 December 1950.

27 Emmerson FBI file, Willoughby interview, 27 January 1958.

28 Willoughby papers, MacArthur Memorial, undated report; see n. 20 above.

29 Willoughby papers, Willoughby to MacArthur, 5 March 1947.

30 Cited above, n. 18; the excised portions of this document are referred to the CIA, the originating source of the information, for freedom of information consideration.

31 Willoughby to Assistant Chief of Staff, G-2, Washington, 30 November 1950.

32 Ibid.

33 Ibid.

34 Tarshis FBI file (#100–19057), reported from Boston, 29 August 1946; curiously, attached to this document is verbatim testimony of Eleanor Hadley, taken in 1950, and reporting in very positive terms on Norman, Tsuru, and Bisson; the FBI provided no reason for appending the Hadley testimony to the Tarshis report.

35 "Brief of Information and Investigation," no date, claims "Halperin, a wartime Canadian army officer, was a Russian spy." RCMP files.

36 RCMP files.

37 RCMP files; a 23 May 1950 document in the RCMP files lists all seven "Norman entries in the Halperin notebook"; as it includes a reference to the 1942 Tsuru apartment episode, it appears the document originated from the FBI. Halperin is identified as a "Soviet Espionage Agent," language characteristic of FBI reporting. In any case, this would appear to be the first of many documents leading to Norman's recall and investigation. Just how serious the Fuchs-Halperin-Norman connection was can be guessed from the American press treatment of Fuchs at this time. Fuchs, said *Time* magazine (20 February 1950), "suffers from Communism's moral cancer." *Newsweek* (20 February 1950), not be be outdone, claimed, "Fuchs did not stand alone, for behind him . . . were tens of millions of equally fanatical and dedicated Communists." The FBI investigation of the Fuchs-Halperin connection included a lengthy interview of Fuchs's sister, Kristel Fuchs Heineman, in her hospital room in Westboro, Massachusetts, on 5 February 1950. "She denied that she had ever been visited by Israel Halperin." But she did say that she once had met with Halperin's wife, Mary, in the summer of 1947, although not in the presence of her husband. She states that Halperin *once* visited Fuchs when the latter man was interned in a German alien camp in Canada during the war (1940) (Special Agent B. F. Gordon to Hoover, 5 February 1950,

FBI file # 65–337–5). Former FBI agent, Robert J. Lamphere, who interviewed Fuchs for eleven days between 20 May 1950 and 2 June 1950, learned that Halperin's sole connection with Fuchs was that he had sent the interned man "some scientific articles or magazines." Lamphere concludes, "we became convinced that that ["Fuchs's name in the Halperin notebook"] had no Soviet intelligence connotation." Correspondence, 11 September 1984.

38 RCMP files, Heeney to Wrong, 14 October 1950.

39 U.S. Senate Subcommittee on Foreign Relations, 81st Congress, Second Session, pursuant to S. Resolution 231 ("A Resolution to Investigate Whether There Are Employees in the State Department Disloyal to the U.S."), 8 March - June 1950, pp. 566, 565.

40 Ibid.

41 RCMP files, 21 April 1950.

42 RCMP files, 28 April 1950.

43 RCMP files.

44 Ibid.

45 RCMP files.

46 Norman FBI files.

47 RCMP files.

48 RCMP files, to Glazebrook, and SISS files, National Archives, undated Subcommittee report. The "Secret Agent" later identified himself as Pat Walsh, one-time communist who by 1957 was a rabid anti-communist. On 25 March 1957, he wrote Pearson secretly, asking for permission to submit a "brief" outlining evidence against Norman; a copy of the letter can be found in the SISS files. Also see *Ottawa Journal*, 18 April 1957, and *Ottawa Citizen* of the same day. Predictably, clippings from the two papers identifying Walsh were sent to Hoover, along with the Agency's liaison officer's evaluation (Norman FBI file, 19 April 1957).

49 SISS files.

50 RCMP files.

51 RCMP files.

52 RCMP files, 18 October 1950; and Taylor, *Six Journeys*, p. 136; Taylor substitutes *friend* for *brother;* correspondence, Howard Norman, 18 October 1982.

53 RCMP files, Heeney to Wrong, 14 October 1950.

54 Ibid.

55 Ibid.

56 RCMP files.

57 RCMP files, Glazebrook to Pearson, "Top Secret and Personal," 18 October 1950.

Chapter 7—"A Man Who Might Have Existed"

1 RCMP files, Glazebrook to Pearson, "Top Secret and Personal," 18 October 1950.

2 Interview with Dr. Halim Doss, Cairo, 14 November 1984; Doss's recollection seems precise, despite the passage of time; Herbert uttered similar words to King Gordon in early April 1957 (see Ch. 11), and similarly to his sister Grace in August 1951 (Correspondence, Howard Norman, 20 October 1977). In Sidney Katz's "What Kind of Man *Was* Herbert Norman?" *(Maclean's,* 28 September 1957 p. 88), Herbert is quoted as saying to his childhood friend, Charles Holmes, "You can't wash off the poison of a smear from your emotions. How can you fight back against this sort of thing?"

3 Boston: Little, Brown and Co., 1950, p. 28.

4 RCMP files.

5 SISS files, National Archives, 73-A–1375, Washington, D.C., undated committee report.

6 Ibid.

7 Ibid.

8 Norman FBI file, 12 April 1957.

9 SISS files, National Archives, 73-A–1375, undated memorandum. Importantly, the FBI also has a file on Holmes; its number is 105–18139 and it is classified "Internal Security-Canada."

10 Interview, Mrs. E.H. Norman, Ottawa, 5 July 1983.

11 Regarding Park, see Harry Ferns, *Reading from Left to Right* (Toronto: University of Toronto Press, 1983), pp. 187–88.

12 This is only a deduction since the reference is to the Gouzenko papers, yet the same memorandum also refers to the Halperin Notebook material being given to the FBI; Public Archives, Ottawa, MG26N, ([Pearson papers], Vol. 33, file # D1–35A, Vol. 2); further, Bethel's 7 December 1950 message to Hoover refers to Bethel's access to RCMP Inspector Guernsey regarding the Norman investigation: FBI Norman file.

13 Interview, Ottawa, 5 July 1983.

14 RCMP files, 24 October 1950.

15 Correspondence to author, 24 October 1978. Kiernan recorded in his diary on 23 September 1947; "He [Norman] evidently felt that the business of earning a living obliges one to come to terms with one's conscience." Harry Ferns also recounts "Herbert's cold objectivity and detachment" toward him at the time of Ferns's departure from External Affairs. Norman later construed this departure as a forced resignation due to indiscretions; see *Reading from Left to Right,* pp. 211, 213–14.

16 Relevant here is a memo to Hoover from the Office of Naval Intelligence, dated 15 May 1957. The last sentence reads: "In 1943 Norman visited Jaffe only once [*sic:* Jaffe visited Norman] and thereafter stayed away and believes that the reason for that might possibly be due to the fact that when Elizabeth Bentley testified, she said that all her people were warned to stay away from Jaffe as he was too open with his Communist expressions." Department of Navy, Office of the Chief of Naval Operations.

17 RCMP files, 24 October 1950.

18 RCMP files.

19 Ibid.

20 Norman FBI file.

21 Ibid.

22 RCMP files.

23 Ferns, *Reading from Left to Right,* pp. 218–20.

24 Ibid., p. 214.

25 RCMP files.

26 Correspondence to author, 10 October 1978.

27 RCMP files, "Re: Egerton Herbert Norman," Top Secret, 1 December 1950.

28 Ibid.

29 RCMP files, Heeney to Wood, 1 December 1950.

30 RCMP files, Wood to Glazebrook, 23 January 1951.

31 Interview, Ottawa, 5 July 1983.

32 Ibid.

33 Telephone interview, 18 July 1986.

34 Witnessed by Arthur Menzies and told to Howard Norman; interview with Howard Norman, Toronto, 10 November 1977; and correspondence from Howard Norman, 10 October 1979.

35 Interview with Arthur Kilgour, Fraserville, Ontario, 10 November 1977. His sister Grace, with whom Herbert and Irene were living at the time of the questioning, described his ordeal in much the same way; correspondence, 18 October 1980.

36 Pearson papers, Public Archives, Ottawa, R. G. 32 C2 Vol. 338, file 1261, part two.

37 SISS files, Memoranda for File, 24 April 1957; and 30 April 1957; the latter memo also claims that Jaffe "has confidentially [been] assisting the Internal Security Subcommittee since approximately 1951."

Chapter 8—"Communist"

1 United States Senate Subcommittee to Investigate the Administration of the Internal Security Act and other Internal Security Laws, of the Committee on the Judiciary [SISS], "Institute of Pacific Relations," 7 August 1951, pp. 318–19; the subject of the "study group" is first introduced on p. 312. A typescript copy of Wittfogel's testimony appears in the RCMP files.

2 External Affairs Press Release, 9 August 1951, State Department file #310.342/ 8–1051; actual release came on 10 August, according to the American Embassy in Ottawa.

3 Greer, by no means unsympathetic to Norman's "smearing," nonetheless points out that a number of questions were "left unanswered," e.g., "Had he ever been a Communist or member of a Communist organization?" *The Toronto Star*, 10 August 1951.

4 External Affairs Personnel, Vol. 32, part two (January 1949 to September 1955), Public Archives, Ottawa. Holland's message, transmitted through the Canadian UN delegation, appears in the Pearson papers, Public Archives, MG26N, and is dated 9 August 1951. In the same file are copies of Canadian newspaper editorials, e.g., *Ottawa Citizen's* "The Contemptible Attack on Mr. Norman" and the *Globe and Mail's* "The Smear Comes North" both 11 August 1951).

5 Public Archives, Ottawa, Vol. 44 ("Norman Case — Parts I and II"), 13 August 1951.

6 State Department memorandum, concerning conversation between W. D. Matthews, Minister, Canadian Embassy, and State Department official H. Freeman Matthews, 14 August 1951, file #742.001/8–1451 ("Confidential"); copy of Ottawa's protest note appears in same file.

7 Annual SISS report to Committee on Judiciary, 27 December 1957, p. 102.

8 From Security Division to Commanding Officer, 441st Counter-Intelligence Corps, "Secret," Army Intelligence, 1 July 1957.

9 U.S. Army Intelligence and Security Command (hereafter Army Intelligence), "Subject: Egerton Herbert Norman," no date.

10 Army Intelligence, 1 July 1957.

11 Army Intelligence, G-2, GHQ, Inter-office memorandum, Roundtree to Willoughby, 30 November 1950. A communiqué of the same date, from G-2 Tokyo to G-2 Washington, refers to getting additional information "from Canadian sources."

12 Norman FBI file, "Summary of Information."

13 SISS files, National Archives, memorandum dated 30 April 1957. In defending her deceased husband, Mrs. Jaffe quotes from his unpublished autobiography: "After acquitted of the charge of contempt of Congress in 1950, . . . for the following three or four years I had carried on endless 'conversations' with several FBI agents, with Robert Morris of [SISS], as well as with Ray Cohn." Mrs. Jaffe writes: "I know that he saw Morris occasionally. My own guess is that they were being friendly, hoping to soften him into giving them information, and that he was trying foolishly, I think, to affect them in some way." Correspondence from Agnes Jaffe, 14 November 1983. In an earlier letter (25 October 1983), Mrs. Jaffe writes, "Having seen them [Herbert and Irene] together, we could never have used the word 'homosexual' in any way." In a letter to me written a few years before his death, Jaffe sent a portion of his unpublished ms. which discusses Norman's "unexpected coldness" toward Mrs. Jaffe in 1940 and reports that in 1943, when the Jaffes visited the Normans in Ottawa, "It became obvious very quickly that he was not too happy with our visit." Correspondence, 12 April 1978.

14 SISS files, Canning to Morris, 20 August 1951.

15 SISS hearings, "Institute of Pacific Relations," 28 March 1952, pp. 4153–54.

16 See n. 4 above.

17 SISS files, 73-A–1375, National Archives, Washington, D.C., 17 August 1951.

18 Public Archives, Ottawa, RG 32, C2, Vol. 339, file 1261, part five. External Affairs file #50069–1–40, Vol. 32, dealing with the period when Norman headed the American and Far East Division, indicates his work then for Under-Secretary Escott Reid was largely unconcerned with Korean War and security issues.

19 SISS, "IPR Hearings," p. 373.

20 RCMP files, esp. 8 September 1951, top-secret cable from Canada's High Commissioner in London to Glazebrook.

21 RCMP files, esp. 28 August 1951, secret airmail/special delivery letter from the RCMP's Washington Liaison Officer (C. H. Bayfield) to RCMP Commissioner regarding Elizabeth Bentley's naming of two Canadian officials, "one of whom was Mr. Norman." Obviously, according to Elizabeth Bently's testimony, the RCMP's information was wrong on this latter score; see Ch. 12.

22 New York Times, 15 August 1951.

23 See Ch. 12; and Sise FBI file, # 100–364301.

24 A 10 March 1952 Glazebrook to Heeney memorandum notes, interestingly, that "The United Kingdom have their own evidence on the Cambridge period, but [deleted] do not regard Communism in a Cambridge undergraduate as necessarily a continuing risk." RCMP files.

25 See n. 20 above.

26 RCMP file, 30 August 1951, Heeney to Glazebrook, reporting on conversation with Fleury.

27 RCMP files; a later secret memorandum from Glazebrook to Heeney refers to these letters and identifies the anonymous informant as "in a business of his own in Montreal." 28 February 1952.

28 Foreign Office file #371 B/31/40, Public Records Office, London, reveals

the existence of a file on Norman, but little of it is open to public inspection.

29 In this same top-secret note, Guernsey reports that the informant recommended Norman for a teaching position in Classics in 1935, when Herbert returned from Cambridge to teach at Upper Canada College, but not without warning the Headmaster "of Norman's ideology." RCMP files, 4 January 1952.

30 RCMP files ("Secret").

31 Ibid.

32 Ibid.

33 RCMP files, 18 January 1952, Glazebrook to Heeney.

34 RCMP files.

35 RCMP files.

36 Norman FBI file.

37 RCMP files, interrogation of 26 January 1952; emphasis mine.

38 Correspondence from Margaret Norman, 28 January 1985.

39 See n. 37 above.

40 Ibid.

41 Ibid.

42 Ibid.

43 Ibid., ellipses in original.

44 RCMP files, 31 March 1952, Glazebrook in "Memorandum for file."

Chapter 9—Diplomat

1 Herbert wrote to Howard (then in Japan) about their mother's death and the funeral. He provided considerable detail about the funeral itself and emphasized the "very great strain" on their sister Grace. About his own reaction he recalled that "one of the pleasantest memories" was her visit with him and Irene in Ottawa the summer before, although he said "the house in Kerrwood was painfully empty and different without her." He closed with the admission, "I have given you a rather bare account of her passing, but I do not trust myself to write in any other mode or fashion . . ." 30 December 1952.

2 Lester B. Pearson, *Mike: The Memoirs of the Rt. Hon. Lester B. Pearson, 1957–1968*, Vol. 3, Edited by John A. Munro and Alex I. Inglis (Toronto: Univ. of Toronto Press, 1975), p. 181. Public Archives, Ottawa, RG 32 C2, Vol. 339, file 1261, part five.

3 Interview with Ralph Collins, Ottawa, 13 August 1979.

4 State Department file #601.4244/2–2453, 24 February 1953.

5 Public Archives, Ottawa, 9 March 1953.

6 Public Archives, Ottawa, Vol. 32, part two (January 1949 - September 1955).

7 Ibid., 20 January 1954.

8 Correspondence to author, 10 August 1978.

9 The same article further cites Norman's hard-line anti-communist stand on the Korean War (". . . until the job is done we will stay there,") and on China (Canada "has not recognized Communist China and would not do so until that country ceased to be an aggressor."), 22 July 1953.

10 Correspondence to author, 10 August 1978.

11 External Affairs file #425–40, Vol. 4 (16 March 1955 - 30 October 1959), "Political Situation in New Zealand," 8 May 1956.

12 Public Archives,, Vol. 32, part two.

13 External Affairs file #10301-F–46, 30 September 1954.

14 Public Archives, Vol. 32, part two.

15 Public Archives,, RG 32 C2, Vol. 339, file 1261, part five, 15 March 1955.

16 Ibid., 7 April 1955.

17 Ibid., 5 January 1956.

18 See Taylor, *Six Journeys*, p. 144, quoting a British diplomat; and Sidney Katz, "What Kind of Man *Was* Herbert Norman?" *Maclean's*, 28 September 1957, p. 83.

19 Gamal Abdul Nasser, *Egypt's Revolution* (Washington, D.C.: Public Affairs Press, 1955), p. 103.

20 "Europe's Achilles' Heel," *The Economist* (4 August 1956): pp. 381–83.

21 Selwyn Lloyd, *Suez 1956: A Personal Account* (London: Trinity Press, 1978), p. 28.

22 Anthony Nutting, *No End of a Lesson: the Story of Suez* (New York: Clarkson N. Potter, Inc., 1967), p. 45.

23 External Affairs file #50153–40, Vol. 4 (1 May 1955 - 31 December 1956), Norman to External Affairs, 8 September 1956; 16 October 1956.

24 Ibid., Norman to External Affairs, 6 September 1956.

25 Nutting, *No End*, pp. 91–94.

26 Ibid., p. 93; and Lloyd, *Suez*, p. 164.

27 External Affairs file #50153–40, Vol. 4, cable, 21 November, 1956 (origin of cable not stated).

28 Pearson, *Mike*, II, 262.

29 External Affairs file #50153–40, Vol. 4, on Norman's presentation of his credentials. On 11 September Herbert wrote his brother Howard a two-page detailed description of the ceremony of presenting credentials, adding that following the ceremony he talked politics with Nasser and his foreign minister.

30 Pearson, *Mike*, II, 262, 271.

31 External Affairs file #50366–40, Vol. 3 (December 1956 - 10 December 1965), Norman to External Affairs, 9 December 1956. A letter to Howard, dated 20 December, mentions "a few days in Paris where Mr. Pearson had asked me to go for consultations with him" the previous week, or just shortly after the 9 December meeting with Nasser.

32 External Affairs file #50153–40, Vol. 4, no date.

33 External Affairs file #50153–40, Vol. 5 (1 January 1957 - 15 April 1958); Norman to External Affairs, 14 January 1957; 18 January 1957.

34 Ibid., 19 January 1957.

35 Ibid., 18 March 1957; the full text of Nasser's interview is found in the same External Affairs file.

36 External Affairs file #50153–40, Vol. 5, Norman to External Affairs, 29 March 1957.

37 Correspondence to author, 1 August 1978; Herbert wrote to Howard on 3 January 1957: "We spent a rather quiet Christmas here. One evening we had all the staff in, both Canadian and locally-employed, and on Christmas night we had the Canadians in town, which were, with the exception of two officers, all our staff, about 18 in all."

38 In Bowen, p. 74.

39 Interview, Cairo, 18 November 1984; and interview with Mr. Mounir Abdel Malik, Cairo, 13 November 1984; Norman's secretary in Tokyo between 1946 and 1949, Lorne Berlet, similarly has commented on his "eye for the beauty of nature and women" (interview, Ottawa, 13 August 1979), as has J. J. McCardle (interview, Ottawa, 16 August 1979), Norman's language officer in Tokyo between 1947 and 1948.

40 In Bowen, p. 75.

41 External Affairs file #50366–40, Norman to Ottawa, 15 March 1957.

42 In Bowen, p. 75.

Chapter 10—Victim

1 Norman FBI file, Belmont to Boardman, 24 April 1957.

2 Norman FBI file, Hoover to Scott McLeod, Department of State, 26 April 1957.

3 SISS file, National Archives, 73-A–1375, Washington, D.C. "Notes of meeting with State Department Officers," 20 March 1957.

4 RCMP files, Kilgour to Léger, 10 April 1957.

5 "Scope of Soviet Activity in the United States," Subcommittee to Investigate the Administration of the Internal Security Act and other Internal Security Laws of the Committee on the Judiciary, United States Senate, 85th Congress, First Session, Part 56, 12 March 1957, p. 3646.

6 Ibid., pp. 3660–61.

7 External Affairs 12174–1–40, 15 March 1957.

8 RCMP files, Kilgour to Léger, 10 April 1957.

9 Correspondence, 4 March 1957. This was Herbert's last letter to his brother.

10 Public Archives, Ottawa, External Affairs, "Middle East," Vol. 39, part 3 (1 January 1956 - 30 April 1957); and External Affairs file #11336–90–40, Vol. 2, 23 February 1957; and External Affairs file #50366–40, Vol. 5 (21 December 1956 - 31 January 1957).

11 RCMP files.

12 Ibid.

13 See n. 3.

14 Emmerson, *Japanese Thread*, p. 335.

15 SISS (see n.6 above for full citation), 21 March 1957, p. 3669.

16 Ibid., pp. 3672–73.

17 "Scope of Soviet Activity in the United States," Subcommittee to Investigate the Administration of the Internal Security Act and other Internal Security Laws," 26–27 March 1957, pp. 3695, 3696, 3699, 3702, 3710, 3711.

18 Ibid., p. 3756; he qualified his "yes" only with "As far as I can recall."

19 Ibid., pp. 3740–45.

20 Norman FBI file #100–346993–73, "Summary of Bureau Files, E. Herbert Norman," 17 April 1957.

21 RCMP files, 29 March 1957.

22 RCMP files, Kilgour to Léger, 10 April 1957.

23 Ibid.

24 Ibid.

25 Ibid.

26 Ibid.

27 Ibid.

28 See n.17, p. 3718.

29 Grant Goodman, *The Committee* (New York: Farrar, Straus and Giroux, 1968), p. 494.

30 RCMP files, Kilgour to Léger, 10 April 1957,

Chapter 11—Suicide

1 The account of Norman's suicide is drawn from a number of sources: interviews with Dr. and Mrs. Halim Doss, in Cairo, 13, 14 November 1984; letter from King Gordon to Lester Pearson, 7 April 1957, quoted with permission; Arthur Kilgour's letter to Lester Pearson of 10 April 1957 (RCMP files); Ambassador Raymond Hare's comprehensive account, relying on the testimony of Doss, Ashman, Roberts, and other American Embassy personnel, 26 April 1957, to State Department, Washington, file #601.4274/5–2657; interview with Omar Foda, Cairo, 12 November 1984; interview with M. A. Malik, Cairo, 14 November 1984; private correspondence from Norma Nadeau, 1 August 1978; RCMP files, containing handwritten and typed copies of the suicide notes; articles from the *Egyptian Gazette*, 5 April 1957; interviews with Mrs. E. H. Norman, the Rev. Howard Norman, and Arthur Kilgour.

2 Albert Camus, *The Myth of Sisyphus and Other Essays* (New York: Vintage Books, 1955).

3 In Bowen, pp. 160–61.

4 Ivan Morris, *The Nobility of Failure: Tragic Heroes in the History of Japan* (New York: New American Library, 1975).

5 A. Alvarez, *The Savage God* (New York: Random House, 1972), pp. 102, 104

6 Typed transcript of sermon, 6 April 1957. Also see *New York Times*, 7 April 1957.

7 Both quoted in *The Toronto Star*, 5 April 1957.

8 Interview with Irene Norman, Ottawa, 22 February 1985.

9 Public Archives, Ottawa, Pearson papers, Vol. 83, Robertson to Pearson, 9 April 1957.

10 Ottawa to Secretary of State, 9 April 1957.

11 "News and Information from the Episcopal Church, Diocese, New York," 8 April 1957 (4 pp.), about 7 April "Passion Sunday" sermon.

12 Okubo Genji has translated the speeches given by ten prominent Japanese scholars, workers, clerics, and businessmen, delivered on 4 May 1957 in Tokyo, and has entitled the twenty-four-page collection "To the Memory of Herbert Norman." Regarding the New Zealand memorial, see *Globe and Mail*, 24 April 1957 and *Ottawa Citizen*, 23 April 1957.

13 *The Toronto Star*, 6 April 1957. *The Telegram*, 5 April 1957. *Globe and Mail*, 5 and 6 April 1957.

14 *The Toronto Star*, 4 April 1957.

15 Public Archives, Ottawa, RG 32 C2, Vol. 339, file 1261, part two, Pearson

to Helen M. Dodds, 18 April 1957.

16 See Chapter 12. As regards the FBI, Pearson confirmed its worst fears in a *Maclean's* interview published on 7 June 1957; in the interview Pearson says that *no* External Officer had ever been dismissed because of "Communist affiliations" so long as "we're satisfied that you are a loyal officer. . . ." The remark is found in the Norman FBI file, and is also reported in the Montreal *Gazette,* 28 June 1957.

17 As noted, Pearson's rebuttal appeared in the 18 April Montreal *Gazette.* State Department file #601.4274/4–1857; the U.S. ambassador to Canada reported at length on Blakely's attack and Pearson's defense, 18 April 1957.

18 RCMP file.

19 Ibid.; Brynolf Eng writes that he and Norman "were friends but not specially close friends, perhaps more colleagues than friends. . . . Only once Norman phoned me, the tragic morning when he jumped from the roof of the building where I lived and worked." Eng writes: "In Norman's pocket the police found a letter addressed to me. It only asked me to forgive him that he used our house for his suicide; it was the only place he could jump omitting to hurt bypassers, he said." Correspondence to author, 22 November 1982.

20 Pearson, *Mike*, III, 185.

21 American Embassy, Cairo to Department of State, Washington, 26 April 1957, file #601.4274/4–2657. The memorandum is eleven typed pages in length.

22 Taylor, *Six Journeys*, p. 149.

23 Correspondence to author, 28 November 1984.

24 Pearson papers, Public Archives, Ottawa, Vol. 10 (included in Vol. 83 as Norman correspondence); released with permission of Geoffrey Pearson; W. H. H. Norman to Lester Pearson, 22 April 1957. Howard had written Pearson earlier, in April 1957 to express his "gratitude . . . for the way you stood behind Herbert and defended him"; and to apologize "for the trouble Herbert caused you."

25 Taylor, *Six Journeys*, pp. 150, 151.

26 Interview with Irene Norman, Ottawa, 5 July 1983.

27 See n. 21.

28 Pearson papers, Public Archives, Ottawa, Vol. 10 (included in Vol. 83), Gordon to Pearson, 7 April 1957. Quoted with permission of King Gordon.

29 External Affairs file #12174–1–40, Vol. 1. Both Pearson to Norman, quoted with permission of Mrs. E. H. Norman. As a 20 March 1957 telegram from Washington to Ottawa makes clear, "Cairo and certain other posts not served by teletype," resulting in "unfortunate delay(s)" of transmission of message.

30 Pearson papers, Public Archives, Canada, Vol. 10 (included in Vol. 83), Howard Norman to Lester Pearson, 22 April 1957.

Chapter 12—"Spy"

1 John Sawatsky, *Men in the Shadows: The* RCMP *Security Service* (Toronto: Doubleday, 1980), p. 145.

2 Telephone interview with James Jesus Angleton, 24 May 1983.

3 Telephone interview, Rolfe Kingsley, 27 June 1983.

4 RCMP file; House of Commons Debate, 24th Parliament, 1st session, Vol. 102, no.4, p. 92, 15 May 1958; and no.5, 16 May 1958, pp. 137–38.

5 Pincher, *Too Secret*, p. 418.

6 Correspondence with author, 30 May 1983.

7 Interview with confidential CIA informant, 26 June 1983.

8 Ibid., 26 and 27 June 1983.

9 Peter Worthington, *Financial Post*, 12 January 1985.

10 Pearson FBI file, Hoover to Kennedy, 30 April 1963.

11 Pearson FBI file, Heinrich to Belmont, 8 September 1951.

12 Ibid.

13 Pearson FBI file, Moynihan to Laughlin, 16 August 1951.

14 Sise FBI file, Special Agent in Charge (SAC), New York, to Hoover, 28 September 1951.

15 *New York Times*, 22 November 1953; *Washington Star*, 23 November 1953; see also Montreal *Gazette*, 24 November 1953.

16 Pearson FBI file, Hoover to Tolson, Ladd, Nichols, 29 November 1953; and see the *New York Times*, 18 November 1953.

17 Pearson's comments appear in the *New York Times*, 25 November 1953.

18 Quoted in the *New York Times*, 24 November 1953.

19 RCMP files, statement by the Honorable L. B. Pearson, Secretary of State for External Affairs, in the House of Commons, 10 April 1957;

20 Norman FBI file, 10 April 1957; and Cartwright to Hoover, attached to State Department note of 27 May 1957.

21 Diefenbaker's words are quoted in State Department dispatch, Ottawa to Washington, 10 April 1957. *Hansard*, p. 3462, has Pearson's 12 April House of Commons address, which can also be found in the RCMP file.

22 *Hansard*, p. 3462.

23 Department of State, Ottawa to Washington, "Confidential," 15 April 1957. Also see *The Canadian Tribune*, 22 April 1957, whose editorial attacks Pearson: "How can we give credence to his protestations of abhorrence to witchhunting when his own government provides information upon which these Senatorial

inquisitors feed?"

24 State Department "Norman" file, # 601.4274/5–1057, Ottawa to Washington, 10 May 1957.

25 SISS internal memorandum, 17 August 1951.

26 Pearson, *Mike*, II, 145, 147.

27 Quoted in 31 December 1957 *Report of the Subcommittee to Investigate the Administration of the Internal Security Act and Other Internal Security Laws*, Committee on the Judiciary, U.S. Senate, 85th Congress, First Session, Section VII (Washington, D.C., 1958), p. 101, n.1.

28 SISS files, National Archives, Washington, D.C., "E. Herbert Norman," 73-A–1375, undated memorandum.

29 SISS files, McManus to Morris, 29 April 1957.

30 Correspondence to author, 22 February 1985.

31 Interview with confidential CIA informant, 27 June 1983.

32 Norman FBI file, 14 May 1958.

33 State Department "Norman" file, 15 May 1958.

34 Los Angeles: St. George Press, pp. 251–58.

35 New Rochelle, New York: Arlington House, pp. 214, 233–34.

36 Norman FBI file, 27 September 1966.

37 Pincher, *Too Secret,* pp. 417–18.

38 Ibid., p. 418.

39 Ibid.

40 RCMP file; and interview, Ottawa, 5 July 1983.

41 *Too Secret,* p. 415.

42 *Ibid.,* pp. 416–17.

43 Watkins FBI file, 29 August 1951; SAC, New York, to Hoover, 15 October 1963; and see David Martin, *Wilderness of Mirrors* (New York: Harper and Row, 1980), pp. 166–67.

44 Ibid., p. 212; Petty correspondence to author, 31 July 1984.

45 Telephone interview with Petty, 27 June 1984.

46 Confidential CIA informant.

47 Boyle's book was published by Dial Press (New York); Straight's by Norton (New York).

48 Correspondence to author, 5 November 1984.

49 Ibid.

50 See London *Sunday Times,* 1 November 1981.

51 Correspondence to author, 5 November 1984. Through a Washington-based writer, I obtained the 6 June 1966 testimony of Michael Straight regarding "Harold [Kim] Philby, Espionage-Russia." The FBI report, dated 14 June 1966, concerned "his recollections of Americans who attended Cambridge University and were involved in Communist activities or recruited by Soviet Intelligence." Straight was shown a list "of eighty-five Americans who are known to have attended Cambridge University between the years 1930–34." Though pockmarked with heavy excisions, the following paragraph clearly refers to Norman: "xxxx further recollected there was a xxxx by the name of xxxxxxx who attended Cambridge University when he was there and who for a year or two, about 1935–36 [*sic*], was a member of one of the communist cells. This man was a graduate student [*sic*] and was preparing for a career in diplomacy at the time [*sic*]. xxxxxxxxxxxx xxxxx xxxx. . . . xxxx advised *he did not know* xxxx [Norman] well and knew nothing of his background. He stated xxxx had committed suicide eight or ten years ago by jumping out of a window in Montreal [*sic*] or perhaps Ottawa, Canada. xxxx advised he had related the information just above to a member of the British Intelligence Service [M.I.5] about four or five years ago during interview in Washington, D.C."

52 Pincher, *Too Secret,* p. 388.

53 Correspondence to author, 30 November 1984 and 13 December 1984. But equally important is the issue of Pincher's credibility in light of the 5 November 1981 article by Craig Seton in *The Times,* entitled "All the Spies Uncovered, Blunt Says." The opening paragraph reads, "Professor Anthony Blunt, who was publicly exposed two years ago as having worked as a Soviet spy, insisted that he had recruited only *two* men as undercover agents for Russia." (Emphasis mine.) Blunt identified the two men as Leo Long and Michael Straight. Also, telephone interview with Chapman Pincher, 6 November 1984.

54 Pincher, *Too Secret,* p. 387.

INDEX